MUSIC AND MODERNITY IN
ENLIGHTENMENT SPAIN

Music in Society and Culture

ISSN 2047-2773

Series Editors

VANESSA AGNEW, KATHARINE ELLIS
AND JONATHAN GLIXON

Consulting Editor

TIM BLANNING

This series brings history and musicology together in ways that will embed social and cultural questions into the very fabric of music-history writing. Music in *Society and Culture* approaches music not as a discipline, but as a subject that can be discussed in myriad ways. Those ways are cross-disciplinary, requiring a mastery of more than one mode of enquiry. This series therefore invites research on art and popular music in the Western tradition and in cross-cultural encounters involving Western music, from the early modern period to the twenty-first century. Books in the series will demonstrate how music operates within a particular historical, social, political or institutional context; how and why society and its constituent groups choose their music; how historical, cultural and musical change interrelate; and how, for whom and why music's value undergoes critical reassessment.

Proposals or queries should be sent in the first instance to the series editors or Boydell & Brewer at the addresses shown below.

Professor Vanessa Agnew, Technische Universität Dortmund,
Faculty of Cultural Studies, Room 3.211,
Emil-Figge-Straße 50, 44227 Dortmund, Germany
email: vanessa.agnew@tu-dortmund.de

Professor Katharine Ellis, Faculty of Music, University of Cambridge,
11 West Road, Cambridge, CB3 9DP, UK
email: kje32@cam.ac.uk

Professor Jonathan Glixon, University of Kentucky (emeritus),
email: jonathan.glixon@uky.edu

Boydell & Brewer, PO Box 9, Woodbridge, Suffolk, ip12 3df, UK
email: editorial@boydell.co.uk

Previously published titles in the series are listed at the back of this volume

MUSIC AND MODERNITY IN ENLIGHTENMENT SPAIN

Ana P. Sánchez-Rojo

THE BOYDELL PRESS

© Ana P. Sánchez-Rojo 2024

All Rights Reserved. Except as permitted under current legislation
no part of this work may be photocopied, stored in a retrieval system,
published, performed in public, adapted, broadcast,
transmitted, recorded or reproduced in any form or by any means,
without the prior permission of the copyright owner

The right of Ana P. Sánchez-Rojo to be identified as the author of this work
has been asserted in accordance with sections 77 and 78 of the
Copyright, Designs and Patents Act 1988

First published 2024
The Boydell Press, Woodbridge

ISBN 978-1-83765-115-3

The Boydell Press is an imprint of Boydell & Brewer Ltd
PO Box 9, Woodbridge, Suffolk IP12 3DF, UK
and of Boydell & Brewer Inc.
668 Mt. Hope Avenue, Rochester NY 14620-2731, USA
website: www.boydellandbrewer.com

The publisher has no responsibility for the continued existence or accuracy of
URLs for external or third-party internet websites referred to in this book, and
does not guarantee that any content on such websites is, or will remain, accurate
or appropriate

A CIP record for this title is available
from the British Library

Contents

List of Illustrations	vi
List of Musical Examples	viii
Introduction: With Apologies to Modernity	1
The Historiographical Trouble with Spanish Modernity	7
The Musicological Trouble with Spanish Modernity	13
The Trouble with Spanish Modernity in the Late Eighteenth Century	19
Chapter Summaries	24
1 Critics versus Musicians	29
The Standing of Professional Musicians	31
Critics versus Musicians: *El Censor* versus *El músico censor*	33
Critics versus Musical Theater: Pablo Esteve's *El teatro y los actores agraviados*	53
2 Music, Medicine, and Tarantism in Madrid, 1787	73
The Tarantism Craze in Madrid	74
Musical Medicine	94
From Theory to Practice to Satire	109
Tarantism and the Modern Lifestyle	115
3 Cosmopolitan Opera	133
The Italian Opera Comeback	135
Opera in the Civilizational Aspirations of Madrid's Aristocracy and the Bourbon Agenda	139
Educating the Audience	146
A Space for *Policía* and Civilization	157
Opera, Nationalism, and the Emergent Public Sphere	166
Rejection of Opera and Mercantilist Mentality	174
4 Bourbon Sentimentalities on the Musical Stage	179
Genre and Policy in *La Cecilia*	181
Those Treacherous Seguidillas	212
The Sentimental Musical Tableau	222
Conclusion	253
Final Thoughts	262
Bibliography	265
Index	285

Illustrations

Figures

1.1 "Música y poesía, en una misma lira tocaremos." Manuel Salvador Carmona, ca. 1779. Source: Tomás de Iriarte, *La música: Poema* (Madrid, 1779). 45

2.1 Tarantellas for the violin appended to Cid's *Tarantismo observado en España*. Source: Google Books. Original from the British Library. 104

2.2 Tarantellas for the guitar appended to Cid's *Tarantismo observado en España*. Source: Google Books. Original from the British Library. 105

4.1 "Atabalillos en las seguidillas boleras." Atabalillos were one of the diferencias. Marcos Téllez Villar, ca. 1790. Source: Memoria de Madrid. Original from the Museo de Historia de Madrid. 214

4.2 "Un pasar en las seguidillas boleras." Dancers walk past each other. Marcos Téllez Villar, ca. 1790. Source: Biblioteca Digital Hispánica. Source: Memoria de Madrid. Original from the Museo de Historia de Madrid. 215

4.3 "Paya/Paissane." Juan de la Cruz Cano y Olmedilla, 1777–1778. Source: Biblioteca Nacional de España. 225

4.4 "Jommelli before the very solemn assembly [of composers and musicians] / thus expounded the character / and progress of musical theater." Source: Tomás de Iriarte, *La música: Poema* (Madrid, 1779). Digital image from the British Museum. 239

4.5 Engraving opposite of title page of *Cecilia viuda* libretto, 1787. Source: Biblioteca Nacional de España. 241

4.6 *Parnassus* detail. Anton Raphael Mengs, after 1761. Source: Alamy (Image ID: 2A84M9R). 242

4.7 *El pastor enamorado a los pies de Gelasia*, José Antonio Ximeno y Carrera, ca. 1784. Source: Biblioteca Nacional de España. 244

4.8	"Perdonando y a las llamas entregando este testigo." Engraving opposite the first page of act 1, *Cecilia viuda* libretto, 1787. Source: Biblioteca Nacional de España	247

The author and publisher are grateful to all the institutions and individuals listed for permission to reproduce the materials in which they hold copyright. Every effort has been made to trace the copyright holders; apologies are offered for any omission, and the publisher will be pleased to add any necessary acknowledgement in subsequent editions.

Tables

2.1	Structure of *El atarantulado*	78
2.2	Characters in *El atarantulado*, in order of appearance	83
3.1	January 1787 events prior to Los Caños del Peral opening	148
4.1	Characters in *La Cecilia*	186
4.2	Musical numbers in *La Cecilia*	186
4.3	Characters in *Cecilia viuda*	187
4.4	Musical numbers in *Cecilia viuda*	188
4.5	Peasant musical numbers in *La Cecilia* and *Cecilia viuda*	204
4.6	Narrative thread of seguidillas in *Cecilia viuda*	221

Musical Examples

1.1	Introduction, second musical number, *El teatro y los actores agraviados*, bars 89–133	56
1.2	Introduction, mock march, *El teatro y los actores agraviados*, bars 151–57	66
2.1	Chorus 1, *El atarantulado*, bars 379–401	80
2.2	Coplas, ritornello/codetta, *El atarantulado*, bars 423–42	84
2.3	Coplas, choral refrain, *El atarantulado*, bars 459–75	87
2.4	Opening vocal phrase of the Marchioness's Andantino in *El atarantulado*, bars 138–49	119
2.5	Marchioness's Andantino, *El atarantulado*, bars 165–80	120
2.6	Count's reply, Andantino, *El atarantulado*, bars 181–85	121
2.7	End of Andantino duet, *El atarantulado*, bars 239–57	122
2.8	Motivic responses, Andantino, *El atarantulado*, bars 157–70	124
2.9	Opening phrase of Allegro moderado, *El atarantulado*, bars 270–82	125
4.1	"Bailete," *La Cecilia*, bars 1–14	194
4.2	"Canzoneta de payas," *La Cecilia*, bars 1–7	211
4.3	"Overtura," *Cecilia viuda*, bars 1–20	228
4.4	"Overtura," *Cecilia viuda*, bars 26–34	230
4.5	"Overtura," *Cecilia viuda*, bars 43–76	232
4.6	"Overtura," *Cecilia viuda*, bars 82–86	234
4.7	"Overtura," *Cecilia viuda*, measures 86–109	236

Introduction: With Apologies to Modernity

In his 1782 article about Spain for the *Encyclopédie Méthodique*, French geographer and poet Nicolas Masson de Morvilliers infamously asked, "Mais que doit l'Europe à l'Espagne?"—What does Europe owe to Spain?[1] Masson de Morvilliers's question unleashed a wave of indignation that rocked Spanish public life. Rebukes came via multiple books, pamphlets, and articles. The question distilled in a few words the long-lingering notion that Spain was dead weight for modern Europe. Answers to this question generated a national fission into two camps. In one were those who thought that Spain did not need Europe; on the contrary, Spain surpassed it. In the other were those who thought Spain was indeed lagging behind and needed to modernize in order to catch up. At the center of the contested question about the relationship between Spain and Europe, then, lay the question about Spain's modernity.

In this book I take seriously the controversy over modernization by showing how cultural production and reception—specifically, the production and reception of music—became a vector for heated debates over notions of progress and nationhood amid foreign pressure to modernize. I reveal forgotten arguments about the costs of the Enlightenment—arguments that help us better understand just what modernity was, what it challenged, and on what basis people promoted it or objected to it. I propose that, through discussion of the social function of music, late eighteenth-century Spaniards helped define their collective identity at a time when new ideas and mores challenged older senses of the nation. I examine four cultural debates concerning music and modernity. These include the challenge of music criticism—a new format—to received understandings of music; musical healing techniques; the "civilizing" qualities of cosmopolitan opera; and the advocacy of Bourbon political reforms through musical theater. Much of the discourse I'm concerned with played out in the popular press, which newly flourished in Madrid at the end of the eighteenth century. The archival records, eighteenth-century periodicals, and manuscript scores that form the basis of the book collectively challenge current dominant discourses in music history.

In the archival materials I surveyed, modernity and Enlightenment overlapped. Both terms were widely utilized in their adjectival forms (*moderno, ilustrado*), themselves converted into plural nouns (*los modernos, los ilustra-*

---

[1] Nicolas Masson de Morvilliers (1740–1789) edited the three *Géographie moderne* volumes of the *Encyclopédie Méthodique* with François Robert. He was also governor of Normandy.

2   *Introduction*

dos), but not as abstract nouns (*modernidad, ilustración*). *Los modernos* and *los ilustrados* were often used interchangeably to refer to the people and ideas that adhered to the new social order described in the previous paragraph. Whereas "modern" could refer to any recent practice in contrast to ancient ones, "enlightened" (*ilustrado*) referred to the current century. The term *el siglo ilustrado* meant the eighteenth century. "Enlightened" more restrictively denoted knowledge, ideas, and writing styles, whereas "modern" applied also to social mores. As this book looks precisely at the intersection between ideas and social mores, I have preferred the broader word "modernity."

I understand modernity as the collective experience of a major epistemological change. The change happened in the form of a series of transitions in modes of thinking about reality. The transitions moved from a fixed, monolithic reality to a relational, unstable one mediated by human experience. A good example of such an epistemological transition in music is observable in the eighteenth-century preference for a linguistic rather than a mathematical paradigm. Specifically, whereas in the mathematical paradigm music is an objective reality to be discovered and mastered, in the linguistic paradigm music is inextricable from human experience. Knowledge, including musical knowledge, became more malleable during this period. What Jonathan Sterne says about sound ("modernity marks a new level of plasticity in the social organization, formation, and movement of sound") can also be said about knowledge generally and musical knowledge specifically in the time and place I study in this book.[2] Hispanist Elena Delgado and art historians Jordana Mendelson and Oscar Vázquez wrote about "the protean nature of modernity." Malleability, multiplicity, mutability, and ephemerality in knowledge all stirred up the status quo.

As I pored over manuscript scores and printed periodicals, I found that new modes of thinking about reality correlated with a new social order. The latter was broadly characterized by new spaces for socialization and forms of communication, including the periodical press and musical theater; intergender mingling in public spaces such as cafes, promenades, parks, and *tertulias*; adoption of French fashions in attire, literature, and language; interest in philosophy as a discipline separate from theology; interest in technological artifacts accessible to the general public, such as hot air balloons or magic lanterns; budding interest in the choice of marriage partner and the nuclear family; and the emergence of an urban-public lifestyle as opposed to rural-domestic one, marked by urban planning in the cities and physiocratic (postmercantilist) reforms in the rural economy. Madrid's musical theater composers quickly picked up the signals of the changing social order and recreated them onstage for weekly display. Thus emerged the stock characters of frilly urban *petimetres* (petit-maître) and *petimetras* and their counterparts, the *majas(os)* and *payos(as)* of the working-class barrios and rural areas. These dichotomous caricatures of "the

---

[2] Jonathan Sterne, *The Audible Past: Cultural Origins of Sound Reproduction* (Durham, NC: Duke University Press, 2003), 182.

modern" and "the traditional" Spain were ways for the greater public to deal with the instability of modernization. For these reasons, scores and librettos, together with books and newspapers, are the sites for my research.

While the epistemological changes and the new social order of modern Western societies sometimes produced secularization or a democratic regime, this was not always the case. Certainly, Enlightenment philosophy, Newtonian science, and their applications to everyday life did not solely rely on the presumed God-given authority of absolute monarchies and the church to interpret the world for the rest of the people. Instead, they relied on the human experience of the world, albeit to different degrees in different times and places. In Spain, for example, the power of humans to experience and understand reality was conducive to divine truth. The delicate balance between the reach of human cognizance and divine authority is parsed out in chapter 2, where controversy over the healing of tarantula bites through music and dance leads to deeper questions about music, the body, and the soul. A consideration of the nuances of modernizing transformations dismantles the one-size-fits-all archetype of Western modernity. Traditionally, scientific advances, Enlightenment philosophy, and the industrialization leading to the breakdown of the ancient European regimes have been understood as the pillars of modernity. However, in this book I contend that modernization happens in the breakdown of one single explanation of the world, in the multiplicity of voices and spaces where those voices can be heard, and in the impermanence of the modes of knowledge. Consequently, modernization can take place at the margin of secularization and democratization, two processes that have been historically deemed central to modernity.

The events analyzed in *Music and Modernity in Enlightenment Spain* take place mostly in the 1780s. After surveying multiple primary sources, I realized that debates concerning music reached a peak in and around the transition between the reigns of Charles III (r. 1759–1788) and Charles IVs (r. 1789–1808). The 1780s were the third and last decade of Charles III's rule, during which the public sphere expanded thanks to a boom in the periodical press. By 1787, when the long-disused Teatro de los Caños del Peral reopened its doors to host Italian opera in Madrid, Spain had undergone almost thirty years of reforms spearheaded by the king and his powerful ministers. Even though some reforms were more successful than others, the regime had at least reached stability after the turbulence that marked the early years of Charles III's rule.[3] This stability, along with the rapid development of the peri-

---

[3] Charles III became king in the middle of the Seven Years' war (1756–1763). Spain joined the war in 1761 as an ally of France against Great Britain. In 1766, discontent with the rising cost of food staples led to the popular revolt known as the Esquilache Riots. People blamed the Italian Marquis of Esquilache, Charles III's right-hand man, for unpopular reforms. The following year (1767), the high-ranking government minister Pedro Rodríguez de Campomanes convinced Charles III that the Jesuits had instigated the Esquilache Riots, and the Jesuits were exiled from Spain.

4   *Introduction*

odical press and the renovation of the Italian opera theater in Madrid, allowed for an unprecedented flow of written and performed viewpoints about what the Spanish nation should be. However, the confluence of factors favorable to musical debate was short-lived. As one king died and the next took the throne, the French Revolution shook the European political landscape, rekindling fear of foreign and new ideas that threatened the Spanish absolutist regime. Fear of a growing public opinion led to severe curtailments of the periodical press. Still, the transformations associated with the umbrella idea of modernity did not come to a halt; they just lost momentum as the 1790s turned into the 1800s and Napoleonic France occupied Spain.

Each case study in the book, from furious back-and-forths in the newspapers to an unlikely sentimental heroine, attests to the confidence in a distinctively Spanish variety of European modernity. A good example of enlightened belief that Spain belonged in modern Europe is found in Tomás de Iriarte's didactic poem *La música* (1779). *La música* was perhaps one of the most authoritative texts regarding music aesthetics in the 1780s and 1790s, embraced by both pro- and antimodern authors. In the footnotes to the poem, Iriarte wrote that he "dispassionately believed that Spanish, Italians, French, and Germans deserve different praise because they have stood out in different branches of the musical science."[4] Optimism that Spain could be simultaneously cosmopolitan and true to itself permeated the cultural atmosphere of the intellectual circles. However, Iriarte's sense of national achievement collided head-on with some outside perception, most infamously (but not only) Masson de Morvilliers's "Spain" article for the *Encyclopédie méthodique*.

I believe that the terms of the intellectual and political climate precipitated by Masson de Morvilliers's rehash of the Black Legend in the *Encyclopédie méthodique* entry provide the most relevant frame for understanding the Spanish musical debates of the 1780s and 1790s.[5] Even though other authors and texts belittled Spain and its culture, Masson de Morvilliers's article is of particular interest for two reasons. Firstly, it articulates an encompassing notion of Spain common during the late Enlightenment, rather than focusing on one single aspect. Secondly, it triggered numerous responses from Spanish authors, from those who redoubled efforts to modernize Spain to those who fixated on glorifying the current status quo to prove him wrong. The latter came to be known as the *apologistas* of Spain, the defenders of the nation.

---

[4]   Tomás de Iriarte, *La música: Poema* (Madrid: Imprenta Real de La Gaceta, 1779), xxi.

[5]   The Black Legend refers to a series of historically developed prejudices against Spain, whereby Spain is an obscurantist, fanatic, and quasi-barbarian backward nation, especially compared with other European powers. The term was coined by writer Julián Juderías (1877–1918). Historian Ricardo García Cárcel has expressed skepticism that there is such a thing as an overarching "black legend:" *La leyenda negra: Historia y opinión* (Madrid: Alianza Editorial, 1992).

Introduction 5

The clash between Masson de Morvilliers and the apologistas was key to debates about music and modernity. In the absence of one dominant theoretical system devoted to music in late eighteenth-century Spain, the template of the apologista controversies provided a frame for examining and questioning musical practices. Even though the *apologías* of the 1780s concentrated on literature, the contention around them was so intense that any subject open to public discussion followed the ready-made template of Masson de Morvilliers versus the apologistas and the anti-apologistas. Confrontations between critics and musicians (chapter 1), for instance, put Spanish critics in the attackers' role and performers in the apologetic one. In chapter 3, the offending outsider was not a group of people but a genre, Italian opera, against which local audiences and performers felt they must defend themselves. In sum, each music-related debate in the book deals with the cost and benefits of modernity for the Spanish nation.

This book has limits, geographical and chronological. I have outlined why the book concentrates on the 1780s, the chronological limit. Before proceeding, I would like to address the geographical one. The book's case studies all take place in peninsular Spain, more specifically, in Madrid. One of my objectives is to highlight the thought process and ideological priorities explicitly manifested by the musicians and writers participating in the cultural debates about music and modernization. This methodological decision leads me to focus on the concerns of the authors I study in the book, most of them members of the intellectual, political, or social elites who were absorbed in the quandary of "whether defending their national history could go with the acknowledgement of some aspects of the European criticism."[6] The Spanish elites loudly opposed foreign attempts to push their nation beyond the bounds of Enlightenment modernization. Their intense response tells a story of "Eurocentrism within Europe's own borders," where authors like Masson de Morvilliers actively consigned Spain to "the dark side of Europe," fashioning the Iberian nation into a counterexample of Enlightenment.[7]

With respect to Spain's historical global moment, nuances in the empire's trajectory must be contemplated. On the one hand, the anxiety elites felt over Spain losing economic and political ground in relation to Europe resulted, all throughout the eighteenth century, in efforts to prove that Spain belonged in Europe. In their roles as intellectuals and cultural policymakers, they contributed to bolstering the empire by creating a narrative of Spain's Europeanness.

---

[6] Roberto Rodríguez-Millán, "Noah's Grandson and St. James: Rewriting the Past in Eighteenth-Century Spain," *European Legacy* 25, no. 7–8 (2020): 737.

[7] Yolanda Rodríguez Perez, "Being Eurocentric within Europe: Nineteenth-Century English and Dutch Literary Historiography and Oriental Spain," in *Eurocentrism in European History and Memory*, edited by Marjet Brolsma, Robin de Bruin, and Matthijs Lok (Amsterdam: Amsterdam University Press, 2019), 157; Jesús Astigarraga, ed., *The Spanish Enlightenment Revisited*, Oxford University Studies in the Enlightenment (Oxford: Voltaire Foundation, 2015), v, 3.

6   *Introduction*

On the other hand, the Spanish empire went through a period of prosperity in the late eighteenth century due to an expanding slave trade and burgeoning exports from the peninsula to the overseas territories.[8] Imperial growth generated administrative complexities resulting in discontent in the Spanish Americas, but the empire would not be in serious trouble until the nineteenth century. In the last years of Charles III, the morale was high because Spain had regained control of Florida with the 1783 Treaty of Versailles, a fact that surfaces in one of the songs discussed in chapter 4.

In what Gabriel Paquette has termed "the imperial turn," since the start of the twenty-first century, historians (art and music historians included) have emphasized the empire as part of the study of peninsular Spain.[9] While many present-day social studies and humanities, and to a lesser degree musicology, thoroughly acknowledge Spanish culture's transatlantic nature (at the time of the empire and now), eighteenth-century perceptions did not, particularly regarding nonmaterial culture like music. The French cared about the Spanish empire insofar as the peninsula extracted riches from the colonies and channeled them to the rest of Europe. Masson de Morvilliers and others lambasted the Spanish government for its neglectful management of overseas resources and wanted to get their own hands on such resources, boasting that they would exploit them more profitably. A different logic was applied to cultural products. Eighteenth-century Europeans, the Spanish comprised, did not consider a New World–born music such as the *chacona* a colonially sourced asset to covet and one Spaniards were wasting. Musical imports from the New World were perhaps cherished as novelties but not valued as riches affecting Spain's stature among European countries. Cultural and artistic foreign criticism chiefly targeted peninsular production, primarily literature. Spanish intellectuals and reformers reacted accordingly. I agree that Madrid does not stand for Spain, and the peninsula does not stand for intercontinental Spain. At the same time, I believe that modernization's contentions in Madrid illustrate those of greater Spain, especially if we understand modernity and Enlightenment as nonsystematic processes that exist only through their geographic variants instead of constituting a unidirectional social transformation.

The present book seeks both to bring the perspectives of Spanish cultural studies into musicology and to interpolate music into the cultural history of Spanish modernity. The implicit thesis against which research on Spanish eighteenth-century music is measured is that of "Spain's supposed resistance or tardy entrance intro 'modernity.'"[10] It was clear to me that the presumed back-

---

[8]   Gabriel Paquette, "The Reform of the Spanish Empire in the Age of Enlightenment," in Astigarraga, *Spanish Enlightenment Revisited*, 150.

[9]   Paquette, "The Reform," 163.

[10]   Margaret R. Ewalt, "How Eighteenth-Century Spain and Spanish America Challenge Scholarly Models of Modernity and Postmodern Enlightenment Paradigms," *Eighteenth-Century Studies* 43, no. 2 (2010): 268.

Introduction 7

wardness of Spain prevails in musicology when a colleague approached me at a conference after I presented one of the case studies in this book. They appreciated the new information, they said, because thus far all they had heard about eighteenth-century Spain was that they (composers, performers, theorists) had no clue what they were doing. I welcomed this comment, as it confirmed the need to put Enlightenment Spain on the musicological map.

The Historiographical Trouble with Spanish Modernity

Over time, the Spanish eighteenth century turned out to be as much trouble for the history of European (and Western modernity) as it had been for those who lived through it. Until relatively recently, Spanish historiography saw the eighteenth century as one of decline. The decline was attributed to the contamination of Spanish inventiveness by foreign ideas and artistic forms. In this narrative, the Habsburg period (1516–1700) represents the authentic, robust, Catholic Spain. In contrast, the Bourbon period is construed as decaying and succumbing to the French "false philosophy" of encyclopedism. The fact that the dynastic change from the Habsburgs to the Bourbons happened right in 1700 contributes to the watershed narrative contrasting one century and the next.

Roughly speaking, Spanish scholars have traditionally defined the eighteenth century as a period of decadence after the Golden Age, from which the nineteenth century had to recover. Writing in the late nineteenth century, prominent historian and literary critic Marcelino Menéndez y Pelayo sponsored this view in his *Historia de las ideas estéticas in España* (1883–1889). Menéndez y Pelayo's stance was shared by his contemporary, musicologist Felipe Pedrell. Pedrell embarked on a life-long endeavor to collect sources and create a historical discourse concerning Spanish music, wherein nineteenth-century zarzuela (different from baroque zarzuela) was the redeeming genre after eighteenth-century musicians had forgotten their roots. Pedrell's quest for national music derived partly from the heroic nationalism that characterized contemporary historical thinking, and partly from outside perceptions, not unlike those of Masson de Morvilliers a century earlier. Famously, Pedrell published in 1891 an open letter to Eduard Hanslick upon the latter's affirmation that "hardly any other civilized nation in music history has erected so few milestones [and] left behind so few traces, as has the Spanish nation."[11] A few decades before Pedrell,

---

[11] Hanslick wrote this in his review of Tomás Bretón's 1889 opera *Los amantes de Teruel*, printed in the *Neue Freie Presse*, October 6, 1991. Pedrell's open letter is titled "Carta Abierta al insigne crítico musical e ilustrado profesor de Estética Eduardo Hanslick." Judith Etzion, "Spanish Music as Perceived in Western Music Historiography: A Case of the Black Legend?" *International Review of the Aesthetics and Sociology of Music* 29, no. 2 (1998): 93.

8   *Introduction*

Mariano Soriano Fuertes had already seen in zarzuela the path to rescue Spanish music from decline and blamed Italian opera for triggering that decline starting around the same time the Bourbons came to power.[12]

The eighteenth century came thus to be Spain's lost century in many cultural and musical histories. At the same time, the eighteenth century was a crucial time for the consolidation of industrialization and the advent of the first democratic regimes and secular states, phenomena that have come to be considered the hallmark of European modernity. It follows that lacunae in the historiography of the Spanish eighteenth century result in lacunae in the narrative of modernity in Spain. On par with the general historiographical trend, Pedrell's formula of eighteenth-century decay and nineteenth-century recovery persisted relatively unchallenged for a good part of the twentieth century.[13]

Historians began to challenge the narrative of eighteenth-century decline starting around the mid-twentieth century, when Jean Sarrailh and Richard Herr substantially revised the history of Enlightenment Spain.[14] Sarrailh was partly reacting to philosopher José Ortega y Gasset's 1947 thesis that Counterreformation had "tibetanized" Spain in the 1600s, meaning that the Catholic Church's efforts to battle Protestant reformation had made the Spanish nation hermetic to outside influence and thus separated from early modern European, Cartesian modernity.[15] According to Ortega y Gasset, Spain never recovered from that isolation. However, historians have since then demonstrated that, by the eighteenth century, Spanish society basically thought and operated in terms on par with the rest of Europe.

Recent scholarship on Catholic Enlightenment has opened the possibility of alternative paths to modernity in the eighteenth century but has not yet made a deep enough dent in historiography. Writing in 1999, Spanish historian Francisco Sánchez Blanco resists altogether the idea of enlightened Christianity. In his view, this idea does not place equal weight on Enlightenment and Christianity. Rather, it is a way of maintaining Spain as fundamentally religious, and this

---

[12]   Juan José Carreras, "Hijos de Pedrell: La historiografía musical española y sus orígenes nacionalistas (1780–1980)," *Il saggiatore musicale: Rivista semestrale di musicologia* 8, no. 1 (2001): 137. Soriano Fuertes insisted on Italian opera as the reason for the decadence of Spanish music in *Historia de la música española desde la venida de los Fenicios hasta el ano de 1850* (Madrid: D. Bernabé Carrafa, 1855). Carreras underscores the major influence Francisco Asenjo Barbieri had on the historiography of Spanish music together with Soriano Fuertes and Pedrell.

[13]   Carreras, "Hijos de Pedrell," 167.

[14]   Jean Sarrailh, *L'Espagne éclairée de la seconde moitié du XVIIIe siècle* (Paris: Impr. nationale, 1954); Richard Herr, *The Eighteenth-Century Revolution in Spain* (Princeton, NJ: Princeton University Press, 1958).

[15]   David Soto Carrasco, "Contra la *tibetanización* de España. Una mirada sobre las lecturas del s. XVIII de Marías, Maravall y Díez del Corral," *Res Publica* 22 (2009): 399–400.

religiousness was only superficially eroded by changes of mentality in Europe.[16] Fast-forward eighteen years, and we can read Germanic studies scholar Ritchie Robertson suggesting that the phrase "Catholic Enlightenment" is no longer an oxymoron.[17] Furthermore, one of the central books in this emerging area of study is titled *A Companion to the Catholic Enlightenment in Europe*, acknowledging that Catholicism was not an exotic practice exclusive to the Iberian or Italian peninsulas.[18]

Indeed, Spanish intellectuals and policymakers stood firmly rooted in Catholicism while simultaneously advocating for sociocultural and even religious reform. Charles III's government famously combatted popular religious devotions that he and his ministers deemed superstitious, including *autos sacramentales*, the medieval liturgical dramas populated with supernatural characters and special effects. Rather than disappearing or surrendering, Spanish Catholicism underwent scrutiny and reforms following the need to modernize the nation according to rational principles. Regalist policies, destined to curb the Catholic Church's power so that it could not compete with the monarchy, indirectly opened a window to criticize certain religious practices. Even though Enlightenment and modernity are different, they are closely related in the European eighteenth century, as evidenced by the different case studies portrayed in this book.

The archival documents I encountered while conducting research for this book bring to light a dynamic musical and intellectual life far from isolated from current events and ideas. The letters, petitions, scores, and librettos written by composers and audiences highlight their self-perception as active agents who get to decide who they are and how they collectively manage the changes modernity generated. The image of the musical culture of the late eighteenth century that emerged from my archival findings found echo in the works of Spanish cultural historians and literary critics from the 1990s to the present.

My research on the 1780s has led me to agree with other scholars that to change our historical understanding of the relation between Spain and European modernity, we must think of modernization as a reflexive process. By reflexive process I mean a shared awareness among individuals of being Spaniards living in *the enlightened century* (el siglo ilustrado). As scholarly works in different disciplines have proved and the sources consulted for this book confirm, Spain had as many debates about modernity as other European countries, only in different versions. Page after page and song after song, I kept encountering references to "the modern" and "the enlightened century" as tangible realities altering the social life of Spanish urban centers. It struck me that

---

[16]   Francisco Sánchez-Blanco, *La mentalidad ilustrada* (Madrid: Taurus, 1999).

[17]   Ritchie Robertson, "The Catholic Enlightenment: Some Reflections on Recent Research," *German History* 34, no. 4 (2016): 630–45.

[18]   Ulrich L. Lehner and Michael O'Neill Printy, *A Companion to the Catholic Enlightenment in Europe* (Leiden: Brill 2010).

Introduction

such omnipresent awareness of modernization countered, in itself, the alleged anachronism of Spanish musical and cultural life.

Indeed, researchers inquiring into the Western eighteenth century have foregrounded collective self-reflexivity as a key component of both modernity and Enlightenment throughout Europe. Devin J. Vartija thinks it "indisputable" "that there was [during the Enlightenment] a consciousness of the dawning of a new era," which "would only later be labelled modernity."[19] He further suggests that a productive definition of modernity is "a reflection on processes of state formation, population growth, urbanization, and increasing literacy and access to news media." All the processes Vartija lists figured high on the Spanish Bourbon governments' list of priorities in the second half of the eighteenth century and trickled down into everyday public concerns. Dipesh Chakrabarty makes an analytical distinction between *modernization* as "processes of building the institutions (from parliamentary and legal institutions to roads, capitalist businesses, and factories) that are invoked when we speak of modernization" and *modernity* as "the development of a degree of reflective, judgmental thinking about these processes."[20] For his part, Stuart Hall understands the cultural vector of European modernity to be "the construction of a sense of belonging which draws people together into an 'imagined community' and the construction of symbolic boundaries which define who does *not* belong."[21] I would like to further emphasize the crucial role that this collective self-reflexivity that came to life in the interpersonal, intergroup, and international relations played in modernization processes in Spain.

Certain musical forms created the channels through which individuals and groups of people could communicate to arrive at collective self-reflexivity. These forms included musical theater, songs for domestic consumption, and dance music insofar as it organized social spaces. Musical theater in Madrid reached the widest variety of audiences, compared to private concerts and academias or even to popular music played during festivities. Many of the songs advertised for sale in the newspapers are now lost, although the advertisements let us know they were in high demand and some pieces seems to have been widely known, much like pop hits today. Musical theater scores for the Madrid theaters, on the contrary, were collected and preserved as part of the theaters' libraries and are now available in copious numbers. Most of the manuscript scores and librettos are currently hosted in the music collection of the Biblioteca Histórica Municipal, as of 2022 located in the former Conde-Duque palace in Madrid. Because these manuscripts were used for rehearsals and

---

[19] Devin J. Vartija, "Introduction to the Special Issue 'Enlightenment and Modernity,'" *International Journal for History, Culture and Modernity* 8, no. 3–4 (2020): 236.

[20] Dipesh Chakrabarty, "The Muddle of Modernity," *American Historical Review* 116, no. 3 (2011): 669.

[21] Stuart Hall, "Introduction to Formations of Modernity," in *Modernity: An Introduction to Modern Societies* (Cambridge, UK: Polity Press, 1995), 8.

Introduction 11

performances, we can see the annotations and edits made through the years, together with the censorship approvals in some of them. There are further (but fewer) scores at the Biblioteca Nacional de España (BNE), along with a few nineteenth-century transcriptions by musicologist Francisco Asenjo Barbieri, as well as at the Real Conservatorio Superior de Música. The BNE also hosts the documents relative to the Teatro de los Caños del Peral and the Barbieri Papers, loose notes about musical theater collected by Barbieri. The majority of eighteenth-century Spanish newspapers and journals are digitized and offered through open access at the Hemeroteca Digital. Treatises and aesthetic writings can be found through the digital repositories of several libraries throughout Spain, but some documents still required in-person consultation. To this end, I visited libraries and archives in Madrid, Toledo, Barcelona, and Valencia over the span of seven years. Reflexivity about modernization and its implications for the national identity reappears from one source to the next across different formats, suggesting that the controversies studied in this book circulated extensively, quite possibly in oral exchanges as much as in written ones.

Primary sources strongly suggest that for the Spanish urban population of the late eighteenth century, the question of nationhood was as pressing and loaded as that of what it meant to be modern. General histories of eighteenth-century Spain since at least the 1960s have located modernization in Spain's awareness of itself as a nation and the networks it developed to transmit ideas and values, rather than in discrete thinkers or cultural artifacts. Philosopher Julián Marías points to the eighteenth century as the moment where "Spain becomes its own project for the first time in its history," which we could paraphrase as a nation-focused version of Alexander Pope's "the proper study of Mankind is Man": "the proper study of Spaniards is Spain."[22] Indeed, Marías believes that "self-interpretation [as a nation]" was "the intellectual theme" of the century.[23] Marías more specifically underscores a specific form of eighteenth-century patriotism detectable in Enlightenment thinkers such as Cadalso and Jovellanos, who identify as men of their century as much as Spaniards. This enlightened patriotism confirms that both for those who the future of Spanishness saw in cosmopolitan modernization and those who put nation and the modern at odds, the terms of the equation were the same. Even Forner's antimodern arguments attest to the collective self-reflexivity Marías describes.[24] The modern could be welcomed or rejected but not ignored.

---

[22] Julián Marías, *España inteligible. Razón histórica de las Españas* (Madrid: Alianza, 1985), 254. Quoted in Alejandro Diz, *Idea de Europa en la España del siglo XVIII* (Madrid: Centro de Estudios Políticos y Constitucionales, 2000), 25.

[23] Julián Marías, "La España posible en tiempos de Carlos III," in *Obras* (Madrid: Revista de Occidente, 1966), 316 ff. Quoted in Soto Carrasco, "Contra la *tibetanización*," 404.

[24] Both Julián Marías and José Antonio Maravall have read the symptoms of modernity in Forner's *oración apologética*. See "Contra la *tibetanización*," 407, 11. Juan Pablo Forner, *Oración apologética por la España y su mérito literario* (Madrid: Imprenta Real, 1786.)

12   *Introduction*

The same ambiguity around the modern, cultural, and national formation I detect in the musical debates of the late eighteenth century persisted over the nineteenth, twentieth, and into the twenty-first centuries, ever adapting to new historical circumstances. Juan José Carreras estimates that, in Spanish historiography, what he calls "the national myth" that Spanish music is "purely and substantially different from the foreign, has covered, without breaks, the temporal arch covering approximately the two centuries in between 1780 and 1980." The two-century continuity Carreras observes in musical historiography seems to extend to other disciplines as well, since cultural histories of Spain keep returning to the issue of modernity and nation. For example, the foundational anthology *Spanish Cultural Studies* (1995, edited by Helen Graham and Jo Labanyi), centered around the twentieth century, is subtitled "The Struggle for Modernity," pointing to the persistent, unresolved historiographical trouble surrounding this subject matter. Even though the volume studies a later period, the way Graham and Labanyi conceptualize the acceptance of and resistance to modernity bears a striking similarity to my own inferences in *Music and Modernity in Enlightenment Spain*.

The relatively new field of Spanish cultural studies has convincingly argued that while the dominant Anglo-Saxon narrative of modernity explains the modernization processes in England, Germany, and France, it obscures those in Spain and other enclaves of Western culture. More than a decade after Graham and Labanyi's *Spanish Cultural Studies* appeared, the issue of modernity resurfaced in "Recalcitrant Modernities: Spain, Cultural Difference and the Location of Modernism," a special issue of the *Journal of Iberian and Latin American Studies* (2007). The issue's editors chose the word "recalcitrant" to describe modernization paths that resist the standard Anglo-Saxon paradigm. In one of the articles in "Recalcitrant Modernities," Hispanist Andrew Ginger returns to modernization's reflexivity and relational nature, calling for a rhizomatic model (my term). He suggests we consider modernity "part of a series of worldwide interactions and interrelationships," prioritizing networks over discrete nations.[25] Again, many of Ginger's observations on nineteenth-century Spain apply to the previous century. For example, he notes that lack of interest in Spanish modernization derives from the assumption that "Spain was backward or overwhelmingly conservative," a skewed perception that applies just as well to the Enlightenment period.

---

[25]   Like eighteenth-century scholars, he too concludes that "the story of Spanish modernity is more complex, and consistent with that of other nations, that has been acknowledged. Questioning the critical commonplace of a Spanish elite entrenched in their opposition to modernity, Ginger reframes the question to show that the Spanish elite was adaptable, open to change, and part of urban and international networks that make untenable longstanding assumptions about Spain's difference." Elena L. Delgado, Jordana Mendelson, and Oscar Vázquez, "Introduction to *Recalcitrant Modernities– Spain, Cultural Difference and the Location of Modernism*," *Journal of Iberian and Latin American Studies* 13, no. 2–3 (2007): 106.

The Musicological Trouble with Spanish Modernity

Spanish Cultural Studies' scholarship on modernity has barely touched Anglo-American musicological narratives. Musical histories of the Western eighteenth century still deal with Spain in terms of similarity with and difference from hegemonic European paradigms and not in its own terms. The hegemonic versions of the Enlightenment and eighteenth-century modernity histories center around northwestern Europe (France, England, Germany).[26] In musicology, the dominant discourse also includes Italy and Austria, especially toward the end of the century as the homeland of canonical composers.[27] This is the tacit core of eighteenth-century Western music, and the rest is supposedly marginal. The alleged marginality of Spanish (or Polish, Irish, Portuguese, Swedish, etc.) music has very real consequences, starting with the paucity of sources sanctioned by authoritative Anglo-American institutions. The near absence of books and articles leads to a weak intertextual web, so that the few scholarly contributions that look carefully at Spanish music have little resonance in musicology. In other words, the lack of basic knowledge about countries that are not canonical in eighteenth-century music history impedes readings and hearings from within the noncanonical tradition, literature, or practice.

As a result, if and when taken into account, Spanish musical practices and cultural debates risk being read primarily in light of their coincidences and con-

---

[26] These hegemonic historical versions are often present in textbooks. See, for example, Dorinda Outram, *The Enlightenment*, New Approaches to European History (Cambridge: Cambridge University Press, 2019). The opening chronology of the European eighteenth century lists forty-five relevant events from England, thirty-five from France, fifteen from Germany, eight from the United States, eight from Austria, five from Italy, three each from Russia and Spain, and two each from Portugal and Poland. This is not Outram's choice entirely, but a reflection of the predominant views on the eighteenth century.

[27] The prominence of these four countries in Anglo-American music histories of the eighteenth century is again visible in textbooks. For example, Grout, Burkholder, and Palisca's tenth edition of *A History of Western Music* includes two subsections on Spain for the sixteenth century, one for the seventeenth, none for the eighteenth, and one for the nineteenth. Taruskin and Gibbs's *The Oxford History of Western Music* has a chapter titled "Music in Italy, Germany, France, and England: 1600–1740," and no subsections at all devoted to Spain from the Middle Ages to present time. The Cambridge Press journal *Eighteenth-Century Music* has published, from 2004 to March 2023, forty-one articles focused on Austria, thirty-eight on Germany, thirty on England, twenty-one on Italy, seventeen on France, six on Spain, two each on the United States and Scotland, and one each in Malta, Ireland, Portugal, Indonesia, the Spanish Americas, Haiti, and Poland. See Donald Jay Grout, J. Peter Burkholder, and Claude V. Palisca, *A History of Western Music*, 10th ed. (New York: W. W. Norton, 2019); Richard Taruskin and Christopher Howard Gibbs, *The Oxford History of Western music*, college edition, 2nd ed. (New York: Oxford University Press, 2019).

14   *Introduction*

nections with France, England, Germany, Austria, or Italy. Since Spanish musical praxis is so little known, the methodological approaches are comparative. For example, when discussing the stage tonadilla, connections must be made to the Italian intermezzo in order to present the otherwise unknown genre. The questions that follow usually fall into two categories, to proceed with the fictional example: how is the stage tonadilla similar to the intermezzo? And how is it different? Other questions I have heard are: What instruments comprise the Spanish orchestra of this period? Is there a guitar? And if there is not, how is this Spanish music? Other times, scholars look for anchoring points in the traditional research paths applied to dominant countries, for example, the copious books and articles still being published on J. S. Bach, Handel, Haydn, or Mozart. Familiarity with these works prompts questions such as: Who were the main composers of stage tonadillas? What were their influences? Were they educated in the Italian school? Did they know Mozart's music? To some extent inevitably, due again to the scarce sources in English the comparative perspective on eighteenth-century Spanish music depends on similarities and differences. The similarity approach expects to find non-Spanish antecedents or referents for almost every musical production or debate generated in Enlightenment Spain. For example, reading about intents to reform musical theater in this book may lead to the question of whether such debates were based on those around Gluck's operas in France. Spanish music and musical thought are measured against their European counterparts in terms of either aping or remaining indifferent to current stylistic "developments." Alternatively, in this canonical European musicological narrative and mainstream discussion, Spanish music is valued based on its difference, a satellite phenomenon that brings local color to the core corpus of eighteenth-century European music. This approach prizes unique and hybrid cultural manifestations and has been part of Anglo-American music history at least ever since the travel literature of the eighteenth century.

We could, indeed, ask Masson de Morvilliers's question on behalf of Anglo-American musicology: What does late eighteenth-century music owe to Spain? Answers will be sparse, especially regarding peninsular Spain. Music studies parallel the ebbs and flows of literary ones, where the attention has concentrated for decades on the so-called Spanish Golden Age, which spans the sixteenth and most of the seventeenth century. Any American university with a prestigious program in Spanish will have at least one "Golden Age" scholar in its roster, but not necessarily an eighteenth-century specialist. Writing in 1998, Judith Etzion perceived that Western music historiography had

> virtually [paralyzed] the history of Spanish music after its so-called "Golden Age" of the sixteenth century. The subsequent centuries have generally been described as a prolonged, static period of musical "decline," during which the Spaniards essentially clung to church music, preferably in the stile antico. Although it was often noted that Spain did embrace Italian and French musical fashions, its national ingenuity lay,

Introduction   15

supposedly, in the cultivation of "low" musical idioms, such as popular songs and dances, local dramatic genres (e.g., the tonadilla escénica and the zarzuela), and folk instruments (e.g., the guitar and castanets). Only toward the end of the nineteenth century does Spain re-enter the European scene—with the "trilogy" of Granados-Albéniz-Falla—following resurgent interest in the peripheral national schools.[28]

Thus, Renaissance musico-literary *cancioneros* and the polyphony of Guerrero, Victoria, and Morales have attracted their share of attention in Anglo scholarship, as have the poetry of Garcilaso de la Vega or Saint John of the Cross in literature. The seventeenth is the century of Miguel de Cervantes, Lope de Vega, Francisco Quevedo, and Pedro Calderón de la Barca, author to many of the zarzuelas studied by Louise Stein in *Songs of Mortals, Dialogues of the Gods* (1993). In music, it is the century when villancicos flourished. This devotional repertory has globally earned a place in music history, performance, and recording repertory.[29]

The study of villancicos and related genres in the Spanish Americas also responds to a musicological interest in postcolonial and de-colonial approaches. For the most part, critical considerations of colonialism focus on the transatlantic exchange, abiding by the model where peninsular Spain is the "center" and the colonies are the "margins." As a result of the growing effort to acknowledge the global dimensions of Western music history, the baroque Spanish Americas have been more researched than the peninsula, a trend that continues when it comes to the eighteenth century. What to make, then, of a set of musical practices and debates obsessed with the hierarchies of Enlightenment modernity, whereby peninsular Spain is at the margin and Europe at the center? Such is the circumstance of the case studies in this book.

Enter the eighteenth century, and the cultural narrative of peninsular Spain becomes blurred. Naming literary authors, composers, or musical genres from eighteenth-century Spain can be challenging even for Spanish speakers, especially in the post-Farinelli decades (1759–1800). There is Farinelli's tenure in Madrid during the second quarter of the century, together with the instrumental music of Domenico Scarlatti and Luigi Boccherini. All three Italians

---

[28] Etzion, "Spanish Music as Perceived," 94–5.

[29] The editions by Robert Stevenson and Samuel Rubio provided some of the earliest sources for the performance and study of villancicos. Stevenson was also the first Anglo scholar to focus the study of villancicos on Latin America rather than Spain (*Renaissance and Baroque Musical Sources in the Americas* [Washington, DC: Organization of the American States, 1970). See also Robert Stevenson, *Christmas Music from Baroque Mexico* (Berkeley: University of California Press, 1974); idem., *Latin American Colonial Music Anthology* (Washington, DC: Organization of American States, 1975); Samuel Rubio, *Forma del villancico polifónico desde el siglo XV hasta el XVIII* (Cuenca: Instituto de Música Religiosa de la Ecxma. Diputación Provincial, 1979); Antonio Soler and Samuel Rubio, *Siete villancicos de navidad* (Cuenca: Instituto de Música Religiosa de la Excma. Diputación Provincial, 1979).

16   *Introduction*

worked mainly at the Bourbon court, for one or another royal family member. Perhaps only the painter Francisco de Goya escapes anonymity. His portraits and engravings reveal a changing, defiant, at times tormented Spain very much in tune with the debates in this book.

Publications in English dealing with the Spanish eighteenth-century are rare. In this context, Elisabeth Le Guin's books on Luigi Boccherini (2005) and stage tonadilla (2014) give precious insight into this period's mostly unknown musical history. The same is true of several chapters in Malcolm Boyd and Juan José Carreras's edited volume *Music in Spain during the Eighteenth Century*, which is of value because it was simultaneously published in English and Spanish (2000). Of these, Michael F. Robinson's chapter on the finances of the Theater of Los Caños del Peral is especially relevant to this book. Miguel Ángel Marín is responsible for significant contributions regarding instrumental music, with more recent contributions by violinist and musicologist Ana Lombardía. Susan Boynton's first chapter in her study about the recuperation of Toledo Mozarabic chant as a nationalistic project in the mid-eighteenth century directly addresses the convergence between music and Enlightenment in Spain, as does Le Guin's *The Tonadilla in Performance* (albeit for the latter part of the century). Spanish musicologist Aurèlia Pessarrodona has recently published scholarship in English as well.[30]

The list of resources considerably grows if we look at the scholarship in Spanish.[31] The works of Aurèlia Pessarrodona regarding stage tonadillas consti-

---

[30]   Malcolm Boyd and Juan José Carreras López, *Music in Spain during the Eighteenth Century* (Cambridge: Cambridge University Press, 1998); idem., *La música en España en el siglo XVIII* (Madrid: Cambridge University Press, 2000); Miguel Angel Marín and Màrius Bernadó, *Instrumental Music in Late Eighteenth-Century Spain* (Kassel: Edition Reichenberger, 2014); Ana Lombardía, "From Lavapiés to Stockholm: Eighteenth-Century Violin Fandangos and the Shaping of Musical 'Spanishness,'" *Eighteenth-Century Music* 17, no. 2 (2020): 177–99; Susan Boynton, *Silent Music: Medieval Song and the Construction of History in Eighteenth-Century Spain* (New York: Oxford University Press, 2011); Elisabeth Le Guin, *Boccherini's Body: An Essay in Carnal Musicology* (Berkeley: University of California Press, 2006); idem., *The Tonadilla in Performance: Lyric Comedy in Enlightenment Spain* (Berkeley: University of California Press, 2014); Aurèlia Pessarrodona, "Viva, viva la Tirana: Clarifying an Elusive Spanish Dance Song," *Journal of Musicology* 39, no. 4 (2022): 469–539.

[31]   Aurèlia Pessarrodona, *Jacinto Valledor y la tonadilla: Un músico de teatro en la España ilustrada (1744–1809)* (Sant Cugat, Barcelona: Editorial Arpegio, 2018); Aurèlia Pessarrodona i Pérez, "El estilo musical de la tonadilla escénica dieciochesca y su relación con la ópera italiana a través de la obra de Jacinto Valledor (1744–1809)," *Revista de musicología* 30, no. 1 (2007): 9–48; "La tonadilla a la Barcelona del darrer terç del Set-cents més enllà de la Casa de Comèdies," *Scripta: Revista internacional de literatura i cultura medieval i moderna* 3 (2014): 122–42; Germán Labrador López de Azcona, Begoña Lolo, and Albert Recasens Barberà, *La música en los teatros de Madrid* (Madrid: Editorial Alpuerto, 2009); José Subirá, *La tonadilla escénica* (Madrid: Tipografía de Archivos, 1928); idem., *El compositor Iriarte (1750–1791) y el cultivo español del melólogo*

tute prime examples of the new musicological research. Pessarrodona's prolific output, Le Guin's books, and the works of several literary scholars recuperate and revise the encyclopedic writings on tonadilla produced by José Subirá Puig in the early twentieth century.[32] Subirá's publications on tonadillas and melólogos, Emilio Cotarelo y Mori's on theater, and Luis Carmena y Millán's *Crónica de la ópera italiana en Madrid* remain essential references to be complemented with more updated approaches. Germán Labrador López de Azcona has focused on the connections between Spanish musical theater and Enlightenment, in addition to cataloguing the works of Gaetano Brunetti. For his part, José Máximo Leza has written extensively about musical theater in Spain, including zarzuela and opera all along the eighteenth century. In 2014 Leza, Miguel Ángel Marín, Álvaro Torrente, Juan José Carreras, and Leonardo Waisman published the fourth volume (*La música del siglo dieciocho*) of the series *Historia de la Música en España e Hispanoamérica*. Leza's proficiency on the matter is evident in the first chapter of the volume, which provides an overview of the century's secular and sacred music, including theory and historiography—the chapter could stand alone as a book. Judith Ortega has studied music produced under royal and aristocratic patronage. To end this summary and selective list of eighteenth-century music scholarship in Spanish, I refer the reader to Alberto Hernández Mateos's thorough doctoral dissertation about the musical thought of Antonio Eximeno. Yet, despite this valuable body of new research, especially in Spanish, no consistent image of eighteenth-century Spain has permeated into mainstream, international academia.

(melodrama) (Barcelona: Instituto Español de Musicología, 1949); Emilio Cotarelo y Mori, *Orígenes y establecimiento de la opera en España hasta 1800* (Madrid: Tipografía de la "Revista de archivos, bibliotecas, y museos," 1917); idem., *María del Rosario Fernández, La Tirana, primera dama de los teatros de la corte* (Madrid: Sucesores de Rivadeneyra, 1897); Luis Carmena y Millán, *Crónica de la ópera italiana en Madrid desde el año 1738 hasta nuestros dias* (Madrid: Impr. de M. Minuesa de los Rios, 1878); José Máximo Leza, *El teatro musical* ([Madrid]: Gredos, 2003); idem., "Ispirazioni per la riforma: trasformazioni operistiche nella Spagna di fine Settecento," in *D'une scène à l'autre, l'opéra italien en Europe: Les pérégrinations d'un genre* (Brussels: Mardaga, 2009); idem., "Metastasio on the Spanish Stage: Operatic Adaptations in the Public Theatres of Madrid in the 1730s," *Early Music* 26, no. 4 (1998): 623–31; idem., *Historia de la música en España e Hispanoamérica: La música en el siglo XVIII* (Madrid: FCE, 2014); Judith Ortega, "El mecenazgo musical de la casa de Osuna durante la segunda mitad dell siglo XVIII: El entorno musical de Luigi Boccherini en Madrid," *Revista de Musicología* 27, no. 2 (2004): 643–97; idem., "La música en la Corte de Carlos III y Carlos IV (1759–1808): De la Real Capilla a la Real Cámara" (PhD diss., Universidad Complutense de Madrid, 2010); Alberto Hernández Mateos, *El pensamiento musical de Antonio Eximeno* (Salamanca: Ediciones Universidad de Salamanca, 2013); Germán Labrador López de Azcona, *Gaetano Brunetti (1744–1798): Catálogo crítico, temático y cronológico* (Madrid: AEDOM, 2005).

[32] Several literary scholars have researched tonadillas, including Alberto González Troyano, Alberto Romero Ferrer, Begoña Lolo Herrans, and Albert Recasens Barberà.

18   *Introduction*

Given that intersections and controversies have proved a fruitful site to understand late eighteenth-century Spain in other cultural studies areas, I propose cultural debates around music as a musicological point of inquiry. An interdisciplinary view of the cultural life of the time seems unavoidable to me. As Spanish musicologist José Máximo Leza points out, the most significant changes to the musical discourse of the eighteenth century came not from the pen of composers or musicians but of writers and thinkers who discussed music connected to Enlightenment ideas, social policy, and the other arts, literature and drama in particular.[33] This "nonmusical," interdisciplinary corpus, ran parallel to the production of counterpoint, composition, plain and figured chant treatises written by professional musicians, telling two different stories that are sometimes at odds. *Music and Modernity in Enlightenment Spain* is concerned with the first set of writings, those that touch on music as an ingredient of other cultural affairs that preoccupied the educated elite and policymakers but also trickled down to more popular sectors of Madrid's population through the press and the theater. Foremost among those affairs was national competency in the face of modernity. Therefore, I rely on cultural and literary historians of the Spanish Enlightenment.[34]

Music and Modernity in Enlightenment Spain seeks to reverse Masson de Morvilliers's notorious question (what does Europe owe to Spain?) to ask in its stead, "What does Spain owe to Europe?" This is not because the answer lies in any measurable degree of influence that allows us to determine whether Spain owed little (isolation) or a great deal (lack or original contribution) to its neighbors. Rather, because reversing Masson de Morvilliers's question turns the tables on the historiographical agency. Histories of modern Europe have fixated on Spanish backwardness, questioning now (as then) whether Spain kept the pace of modernity or remained in a premodern limbo haunted by the Inquisition. Less often do we get to hear the questionings of Spanish authors and artists about the validity of modern ideas as a suitable paradigm for their nation. In the debates I analyze, Spain is the center of its own musical activity and thought, not the periphery of England, France, Germany, or Italy. The book presupposes audiences and authors in Spain as the primary agents of these

---

[33] Leza, *La música en el siglo XVIII*, 98.

[34] Here, scholarly contributions in different languages are too vast to enumerate even in abridged form. Several researchers have looked for the Spanish Enlightenment in sites of contention present in the public sphere of the time. Along these lines we can mention Alejandro Diz's *Idea de Europa en España del siglo XVIII* (Madrid: Centro de Estudios Políticos y Constitucionales, 2000), the inquiries into the contentious term "civilization" by José Antonio Maravall and Joaquín Álvarez Barrientos, and Ana Hontanilla's studies on fashion and cultural stereotypes: José Antonio Maravall, "La palabra 'civilización' y su sentido en el siglo XVIII" (paper presented at the Actas del Quinto Congreso Internacional de Hispanistas, Bordeaux, 1977); Ana Hontanilla, *El gusto de la razón: Debates de arte y moral en el siglo XVIII español* (Madrid: Iberoamericana, 2010).

practices. Even when the genres or the debates adopted and adapted texts from other countries, these texts were used and arranged in ways corresponding to Spanish needs and concerns. The chapters that follow let eighteenth-century Spanish authors interrogate Europe, the Enlightenment, and modernity.

The Trouble with Spanish Modernity in the Late Eighteenth Century

The Spanish experienced late eighteenth-century modernization as a tide to either be immersed in or survive. However, what constituted modernity and its consequences was far from set. Composers and authors used the concept malleably, according to their own views, because "modern" per se did not refer to a specific time period or set of ideas. Like in the rest of Europe, "modern" was a synonym of contemporary, of the time, very similar to "recent." The fact that modernity was (is) polysemic made it fertile ground for uncertainty and debate. A 1788 Madrid journal stated that "it is evident that this generic voice *modern, modernism,* under which several schools of varying gradation and merit are comprehended, and even diametrically opposed in many points, cannot be applied to this one or that one to resolve any kind of philosophical issue." In this sense, modernity was a wild card. Only consensus separated the modern from the ancient and ascribed them positive or negative value. Consensus about modernity fluctuated from one debate to the next, but eventually some notions prevailed over others. As a constant, it was harder to evaluate the modern than the ancient because modern time is ongoing. Was the path to national growth to get on board with modern ideas and adapt them to "the national character," or to laugh them off and rely on the nation's own way of doing things, whatever that meant? History had not yet issued a verdict.

Spain dealt with the two faces of modernity during the last third of the century. On the one hand, the Bourbon administration of Charles III pushed for economic and cultural modernization to make Spain competitive with its European neighbors. On the other hand, Enlightenment ideas, especially those of the French Encyclopedists, seemed to threaten Spanish mores. To further complicate the matter, French and Italian authors questioned the Spanish contribution to European modernity, even asking whether they were contributing to it at all. In response, Spanish intellectuals, artists, and politicians looked for unique ways to become part of that larger, fast-moving European modernity while at the same time filtering modern ideas to fit the needs of a Catholic nation ruled by an absolute monarch.

Thanks to the press boom of the 1780s, discussions of modernity reached the reading public, comprising merchants, bankers, militaries, government officers, and the nobility. These controversies reached an even wider audience through musical theater, where people of all classes could see and hear different takes on "the modern" and participate in the exchange of ideas. Together with

20   *Introduction*

writers and intellectuals, the general public was aware that life was becoming caught in the whirlwind of modernity.

While many Spanish thinkers and policymakers of the 1780s felt confident that their country belonged in modern Europe, others decried the corruption and irreligiousness of new social mores and modes of knowledge coming from "los modernos" (the modern ones) and "los ilustrados" (the enlightened ones). This last group, which included the apologistas, saw modernity as a ridiculous novelty devoid of substance, doomed to eventually crumble down upon its own superficiality, like a house made of straw. The fashion (*moda*) of modernity would expire, and then all those Anglophiles and Francophiles would come running to seek shelter in the brick house of cumulative and authoritative (Aristotelian) knowledge. New trends, from Theism to coffee shops, from criticism to décolletage and elaborate coiffures, would be exposed for what they were: hollow pretenses at superiority. Behind the idea of modernity lurked that of power imbalance, the suspicion that European aspirations to progress rested on using one foot to step forward and the other to push Spain back into feudal times and outside of Europe. The division into two camps, one embracing and the other rejecting modernity, is an oversimplification. The in-betweens were manifold.

Masson de Morvilliers's "what does Europe owe to Spain?" aggravated the differences between pro- and antimodernity stances. His article was supposed to represent Spain in the *Géographie moderne* volume of the *Encyclopédie méthodique* but instead reads like a compilation of evidence to support his thesis that Spain has not one single thing to contribute to modern Europe. According to Masson de Morvilliers, the Spanish grandeur was but a large corpse without substance in the time of Philip III (quote, 555). This beautiful kingdom, which in the olden days impressed Europe with terror, had gradually fallen in a decadence from which it would have trouble rising (555). The heat is unbearable in the summer. The Spanish diet is too spicy (559). Spain is a paralyzed nation, a people of pygmies thanks to a lethargic, despotic administration, religious ceremonies, priests, and friars. The Inquisition! (The exclamation point is Morvilliers's), that odious tribunal, restricts liberty, suffocates any useful perspective, and cultivates a slave and hypocrite population (559). Spaniards are resilient and have a deep spirit, but they are lazy. Europeans should look at Spain with compassion, for having the richest of natures, it disdains the sciences and the arts (556), which makes it the most ignorant nation in Europe (565). Spain could be, but it is not; was, but is not anymore. Historian François López sees the article "Espagne" as "an actual pamphlet against the Spanish government" that happened to be included in a prestigious encyclopedia.[35] In fact, the *Encyclopédie Méthodique* was sold by subscription in Madrid even after Masson de Morvilliers's contribu-

---

[35]   Quoted in Isabel Román Gutiérrez, "De polémicas y apologías: El debate sobre el progreso de la España en las respuestas a Masson de Morvilliers y la historiografía ilustrada," *Dieciocho: Hispanic Enlightenment* (2021): 133.

Introduction   21

tion, enjoying the admiration and approval of the reading public. For the most part, the outrage was against the "Espagne" article, not against the monumental encyclopedia edited by Charles-Joseph Panckoucke.

Masson de Morvilliers's unidimensional perception of Spain was strategic to the project of European modernity in the eighteenth century. Like other civilizational projects, enlightened modernity is defined by its boundaries. These boundaries were often mapped onto the civilized metropoles versus the barbaric colonies. Masson de Morvilliers and many others chose to place Spain on the other side of, or better outside, of modernity:

> Today Denmark, Sweden, Russia, even Poland, Germany, England, and France, all these nations, [whether] enemies, friends, rivals, all blaze with a generous competition for the progress of the sciences and the arts! Each one ponders over the achievements they should share with the other nations; each of them has so far made some useful discovery which has turned out to be for humanity's benefit! But what do we owe to Spain? And after two, four, ten centuries, what has she done for Europe? Today, she is like those weak and unhappy colonies, which incessantly need the protective arm of the metropolis: We need to help her with our arts, our discoveries; and yet she is like those people who, hopelessly ill but completely unaware of their illness, reject the arm that brings them life! (565)

Thus reads the core paragraph of the "Spain" entry for the 1782 "Modern Geography" volume of the *Encyclopédie méthodique*. Masson de Morvilliers was not the first and certainly not the last to trope the "black legend." Six decades earlier, Montesquieu had derided Spanish character, literature, climate, and economy in the *Lettres persanes* from 1721. Montesquieu's sneer lingered, and in 1768 the writer José Cadalso published a *Defensa de la nación española contra la carta persiana LXXVIII*. Montesquieu's and Masson de Morvilliers's texts were perhaps the two most impactful instances (if not the only ones) of foreign criticism in the eighteenth century. The fact that both texts came from pens associated with the Enlightenment gave old prejudices a modern lining. Both informed the Spanish reactions to modernity and Enlightenment beyond the literary realm.

Replies to Masson de Morvilliers proliferated in the so-called apologista discourses, "apologetic" in the sense of defending the nation. The apologista movement reached a peak with authors like Antonio José Cavanilles (*Observations de Mr. L'Abbé Cavanilles sur l'article Espagne de la nouvelle Encyclopédie*, 1784), Juan Pablo Forner (*Oración apologética por la España y su mérito literario*, 1786), and Carlo Denina (*Réponse à la question: Que doit-on à l'Espagne?* 1786).[36] Valencian botanist and clergyman Antonio José de (L'Abbé) Cavanilles

---

[36]   Nevertheless, such discourses circulated since before the *Éncyclopedie Méthodique*. We have, for example, exiled Jesuit Francisco Javier (Saverio) Lampillas'd *Saggio storico-apologetico della Letteratura Spagnola*, where he rebuked Pietro Signorelli's evaluation of Spanish theater, as well as his contemporaries Girolamo Tiraboschi and Saverio Bettinelli, who both accused Spanish literature of corrupting Italian one. Fellow

22   *Introduction*

makes it clear that the French author's article constituted a national offense for many Spaniards. For Cavanilles, defending Spain was a matter of patriotic, public duty: even if what Masson de Morvilliers said were true, "national pride would be justly wounded" by his brashness, "but when deceit is joined by the most insulting tone, it is then that the love for the patria must demand satisfaction from the public."[37] The public took this duty at heart. Few followed Cavanilles's methodical approach (he was a specialist in scientific plant classification), but many joined him in the sentiment of injured pride. This sentiment and the corresponding urgency to defend the patria pervaded the cultural atmosphere of cities, newspapers, satires, and musical theater.

Among the apologías of the 1780s, Forner's *Oración apologética* is most emblematic of the nationalist mistrust of modernity.[38] He conflated "modern" and "anti-Spanish" in a way that echoed and was echoed in popular discourse from newspapers and pamphlets to sainetes and stage tonadillas. Forner's tenet in the *Oración apologética* is that modern philosophy and science are scams designed to trick people, akin to the convoluted arguments of the ancient sophists. Modern ideas give the appearance of knowledge, but they lack a consistent reality and exist only in the realm of speculation. Forner's conviction that all incriminations coming from "foreign pens" "proceed not from our ignorance, but from theirs" nullified the possibility of conciliation between Spanishness and modernity. Modernity for Forner was a smoke screen.

Forner's extreme nationalism contributed to polarizing the tension between pro- and antimoderns. His *Oración apologética* exasperated his moderate contemporaries who, like Iriarte, believed international collaboration and emulation were the pathways to progress. More liberal thinkers such as the authors of the enlightened journal *El Censor* laughed at Forner's provincialism and denial of modern philosophy and science. Iriarte, to a lesser degree *El Censor*, and many others also considered sixteenth-century humanism the pinnacle of Spanish literature and invoked it as the remedy for the decadence of the seventeenth century. However, unlike Forner, they embraced European modernity and Enlightenment thought as part of the corrective. Even though Forner's

---

exiled Jesuits Juan Andrés (Forner's uncle) and Juan Francisco Masdeu also wrote defenses of Spanish literature, and Josefa Amar y Borbón promptly translated Lampillas's apologetics into Spanish in 1782–1789: Saverio Lampillas, *Saggio storico-apologetico della letteratura spagnuola* (Genova: Felice Repetto, 1778); idem., *Ensayo historico-apologético de la literatura española contra los opiniones preocupadas de algunos escritores modernos italianos*, trans. Josefa Amar y Borbón (Zaragoza, 1783); Juan Francisco Masdeu, *Historia critica de España, y de la cultura española: Obra compuesta y publicada en italiano* (Madrid: Antonio de Sancha, 1783); Juan Andrés, *Origen, progresos y estado actual de toda la literatura*, trans. Carlos Andrés (Madrid: Antonio de Sancha, 1784).

[37]   Antonio José de Cavanilles, *Observations de M. l'abbé Cavanilles sur l'article "Espagne" de la Nouvelle Encyclopédie* (Paris: chez Alex. Jombert jeune, 1784).

[38]   Forner was also a lawyer of the Reales Consejos.

Introduction   23

stance was not typical among intellectuals or writers, he articulated an academic version of antimodern and antiforeign ideas circulated informally. In the eyes of Enlightenment supporters, it was bad enough to have ordinary people mock modernity, but for educated writers to publish such ignorant prejudices was disastrous national publicity.

Faith in modernity crystallized in the Italian opera project at Los Caños del Peral, while discreditation of modernity took root in stage tonadillas, the main attraction at the daily theater shows in Madrid and often presented as the antipodes of Italian opera. Madrid was different from other European court cities because the king only minimally intervened in direct decisions about the theaters and did not attend any of them. Court opera had dwindled to a halt in 1777. As a result, music spectacle revolved around the city theaters: the Coliseos of La Cruz and El Príncipe. Popular since the 1750s, tonadillas performed during the intermissions of a play possessed many tools fit for the satire and criticism widespread at the time of the apologista polemics. The genre was comic, short, and based on popular styles. Humorousness lent itself to parody and satire; the short length contributed to a fast rate of production that could keep up with current events; and the musical style delivered an unmistakably national feeling. Tonadillas othered modernity to better deal with it. They conveyed the boiled-down, common-currency version of intellectual and official debates about modernity found in the apologías. Simply put, most tonadillas laughed in the face of modernity, voicing the public's vexation with the enlightened elite's insistence on civilizing (Europeanizing) culture. For their part, elites pushed Italian opera as a civilizational tool, but the literary apologetics had built a climate of vulnerability and defensiveness such that the first instinct was to question foreign cultural forms. The skepticism about opera marked Los Caños del Peral from the start: Should the Spanish people embrace or reject Europe's most fashionable musical genre for public consumption?

Whether in casual conversations or the pages of newspapers and treatises, music discussions defined the collective self. The debates about music and its social uses communicate the preoccupations and hopes for keeping the integrity of the Spanish nation in the context of impending European modernity. At the same time that music serves as a medium for social communication, it operates as branding, in this case, a branding of the Spanish nation geared to other Europeans but also geared to the Spanish themselves. Thus, music represented the Spanish people and their power to interact with the paradigms of modernity as Enlightenment scientific and philosophical ideas progressively became the European common currency. As the apologista and anti-apologista reactions to Masson de Morvilliers show, both proponents and detractors of modern times shared an acute sensitivity to foreign perceptions that led them to rethink and reformulate their own nation. The public beyond the enlightened elite also participated in the exercise of national self-recognition in historical time. As they interacted with ideas and artifacts coming from abroad, they publicly communicated their responses through the press, the theater, or in other media such as conversation, where they clashed with other responses.

24   *Introduction*

The quick pace and inflamed tone of the reactions created a collective state of alert that raised the stakes on debates on modernity.

The printed debates and works of musical theater I investigate all have in common what Graham and Labanyi call "the anxiety over the role of culture in nation formation." Graham and Labanyi suggest that cultural studies as a discipline "grew out of the nineteenth-century concern with the role of culture in nation formation."[39] In the case of Spain, I would add that this concern predates the nineteenth century. During the eighteenth century, hundreds (if not thousands) of pages were written on the constructive or destructive social repercussions of theater, perhaps because of its popularity in Madrid. Several journals in the 1780s–1790s had sections dedicated to the theaters, attesting to their relevance for everyday life. Because the issue of theatrical representations had such a strong presence in legislation, in theoretical discussions, in journalism, and other public forums in Madrid, concerns regarding the cultural consequences of musical practice for the Spanish nation were often subsumed in discussions of theater. At the same time, musical theater performances enacted the twofold anxiety facing the modern. The elite, enlightened face of this cultural anxiety had to do with fear that national musical theater was uncivilized and would push the masses away from the transformations needed to modernize Spain up to European standards. The other face of the anxiety revealed fear of identity loss if foreign genres and modes of performance were to be adopted. For the Spanish public to feel uneasy about the implications of musical practices for the nation, they first had to acknowledge that the times were changing and that the shape the nation would take was in question. Furthermore, they had to acknowledge that their musical choices mattered at the level of the nation, hence the urgency of the matter.

Chapter Summaries

I have identified three printed debates and one musical theater production born of the negotiations between modernity and Spanishness, taking place between 1785 and 1788, with some repercussions into the 1790s. These were the critical years of the apologistas and their print battle with *El Censor* and related periodicals. These were also the years when the project for Italian opera at Los Caños del Peral was conceived, approved, and executed. *El Censor* was interdicted in 1787, Charles III died in 1788. The French Revolution occurred in 1789, and in 1791 the count of Floridablanca, the most powerful minister of the new king, Charles IV, banned all periodical publications except three.[40] The apologistas' and their

---

[39]   Graham and Labanyi continue: "... and out of subsequent worries—from the 1930s to the 1950s–about the growth of mass culture." Helen Graham and Jo Labanyi, *Spanish Cultural Studies: An Introduction. The Struggle for Modernity* (Oxford: Oxford University Press, 1995), 2.

[40]   The official publications *Gaceta de Madrid*, *Mercurio Histórico y Político*, and the *Diario de Madrid*.

detractors' competing ideas of nation emerge through the controversies in each chapter. For the most part, I focus on the efforts to conciliate Spanishness and modernity. These efforts range from the rare tabula rasa approach to traditional ideas and practices to lightly updated versions of the systems already in place.

Side by side with the apologista controversies, the specific examples each chapter examines reveal the sway that the eighteenth-century Spanish brand of literary neoclassicism held on all artistic manifestations, including music. Iriarte's didactic poem *La música* functioned as the ambassador of neoclassicist aesthetics in music. While a thorough reading of the poem far exceeds the purpose of this book, *La música* appears recurrently in support of arguments of all kinds, even opposing ones. Iriarte's poem's ubiquity suggests it functioned as the primary theoretical-aesthetic reference for Spanish music in the late eighteenth century, even though that had not been the author's primary intention. Next to it stand the works of the exiled Jesuits Esteban de Arteaga and Antonio Eximeno, but Eximeno's works were not translated into Spanish until 1796. Conservative authors received Eximeno's theses as an attack, so they did not hold the same universalist appeal Iriarte's poem did.

Chapter 1 contends that criticism destabilized musical knowledge in late eighteenth-century Spain. Printed criticism was a distinctly modern form of knowledge, which upset the status quo of knowledge forms based on authority or technical proficiency. When critics started assessing Spanish musical practices and calling for modernizing reforms, performers felt personally and professionally assailed. Spanish authorities and intellectuals had been vigilant regarding the criticism works of Enlightenment, keeping control of the influx of ideas through press censorship. Caution, even suspicion against critics pervaded public perception. The reading public and practical musicians alike questioned the epistemological value of musical criticism, often perceiving it as calumny. For their part, critics strove to update the artistic models inherited from the baroque, which contravened the natural simplicity that characterized Enlightenment aesthetics. The first of the chapter's two case studies involves a 1786 polemic between the Enlightenment journal *El Censor*'s author and a senior member of Madrid's Royal Chapel. *El Censor*'s author castigated Spanish musical pedagogy and practice, notably that of musical chapels. Inspired by the writings of Charles Batteux, Jean-Jacques Rousseau, Antonio de Eximeno, and the literary neoclassicists, he proposed a return to the lyricism of ancient Greek melody. Since such a reform would upend the music chapel system, founded on traditional music theory and counterpoint practices, Royal Chapel musician Manuel Cavaza replied at length in an essay titled "The Musician [who censors] the Non-Musician Censor." In his essay, Cavaza denounced critics as mere "sayers" extraneous to the musical craft, ignorant of music theory, and incapable of producing legitimate knowledge.

In the second case study of chapter 1, critics and performers quarrel over who has the last word on musical theater matters. The push for modernization in late eighteenth-century Spain took place not only in print but also in the performative, interactive space between audiences and the stage at the city *coli-*

26   *Introduction*

seos. Journalistic criticism jeopardized the careers of the Madrid city theaters actor- and actress-singers because it created a permanent trace of otherwise oral genres such as stage tonadillas. Therefore, printed criticism judging performers, composers, and playwrights opened musical theater to public scrutiny. Poor reviews of tonadillas or performers could lead to audience rejection, resulting in lower ticket sales and lesser or terminated contracts for authors and performers. And so in this chapter I focus on the exchange of recriminations surrounding composer Pablo Esteve's stage tonadilla *El teatro y los actores agraviados* (1787) to confirm that practical musicians resisted modern criticism.

Chapter 2, "Music, Medicine, and Tarantism in Madrid, 1787," turns to cases of tarantism, the compulsion to dance in reaction to a tarantula bite. These cases invigorated debates over the effects of music on the body—debates that also expressed competing visions of modern versus traditional scientific knowledge. Tarantism cases circulated in the periodical press and even in musical theater, feeding a tarantism craze in Madrid during the summer of 1787. The tarantism fad reveals that modern public opinion was beginning to form in late eighteenth-century Spain. I discuss two medical treatises on tarantism. The first, published by Toledo physician Francisco Díaz Cid in 1786, committed to sensism and empiricism while endorsing belief in the invisible—in this case, the unseen mechanism whereby music acted on the body. The second treatise is a 1787 medical report wherein Bartolomé Piñera y Siles details his treatment of and observations about a local case at the Madrid city hospital. Like Cid, Piñera experimented with different remedies, settling on the tarantella music to prompt the patient's dancing and subsequent healing. Cid and Piñera are representative of late Spanish Enlightenment authors who strove to reconcile new scientific ideas with received traditions. Both physicians expected their research on musical healing to advance Spanish science to attain international recognition and contribute to modernized medical practices in Europe.

New views on music, sensation, disease, and the body intrigued the Spanish public beyond medical treatises, percolating into popular media such as the press and musical theater. Tarantism was so in demand in 1787 that composer Pablo Esteve wrote a stage tonadilla titled *El atarantulado* (The Tarantula-Bitten Man) to replicate the case at the Madrid city hospital. Chapter 2 analyses sections of *El atarantulado* to elucidate the role musical theater played in the formation of public opinion. In the tonadilla, Esteve uses tarantism as an excuse to comment on certain nervous diseases, such as the vapors, which some contemporary authors, like the Swiss Samuel Tissot, attributed to the modern lifestyle of European cities. *El atarantulado* bridged a regional affair (tarantism cases) to the broader effects of modernization on the human body and spirit.

Chapter 3, "Cosmopolitan Opera," discusses press quarrels following the reopening of Madrid's Italian opera theater in 1787 in the context of broader debates about cosmopolitanism and civilization as the gateways to modernity. The new theater represented a sector of the Madrid population's aspirations to cultured entertainment, and with it, the possibility of catching up with the pace of modern Europe. Comparisons between national and foreign musical genres in turn led to controversies over discursive authority and the role of public opinion in the theatrical life of the city. Many elites in late eighteenth-century Madrid saw Italian opera as a civilized and civilizing enterprise. Opera was therefore briefly supported by the Bourbon administration, which placed great emphasis on the decorum of public entertainment, especially theater. Sponsored by the city through a board comprising nobles and rich merchants, the Los Caños project was intended to put Madrid on par with other European cities by offering both nationals and visitors first-class cosmopolitan entertainment.

But not everyone in positions of influence felt that Los Caños was good for Spain. Some critics reacted skeptically. At the core of the ongoing discussions lay the discomfort with the imported genre of opera together with its equally imported, very costly Italian performers. Whereas cosmopolitan-oriented patrons called for an open-armed welcome, their opponents saw in Los Caños either a subpar imitation of European opera houses or a threat to national musical theater. As in the other cases I explore, music was not simply a vector for modernization or its rejection but rather provided a forum for debate over modernity's promise and peril.

Chapter 4, "Bourbon Sensibilities on the Musical Stage," turns to pastoral and sentimental topics adopted in Spanish musical theater to promote Bourbon ideals of progress. Spanish playwrights and composers during the reigns of Charles III and Charles IV recast the pastoral and the sentimental in didactic terms, using them to communicate Bourbon policies to audiences while entertaining them. The Bourbon vision of progress included happy and dynamic rural communities, which, according to physiocratic ideas promoted in France, would strengthen agricultural production and bolster the national economy. Achieving this sort of well-functioning agricultural sector necessitated improved relations between landlords and laborers, which playwrights and composers aimed to depict. Showing their support of the monarchy and its reforms, these playwrights and composers wrote musical plays portraying exemplary landowners and peasants working in harmony for the benefit of the crown.

The chapter centers on two plays that reflect the compromises between popular and official approaches to modernity: Luciano Francisco Comella's *La Cecilia* (1786) and its sequel *Cecilia viuda* (1787), both with music by Blas de Laserna. Comella and Laserna were attuned to the Bourbon concern with agricultural reform, but their connections to the city theaters also gave them a clear sense of audience demands. In the two *Cecilias*, they satisfied Bourbon interests while serving popular tastes with expressions of Spanishness and sentimental scenes. Comella followed the models of French comédies larmoyantes and Goldonian librettos, combined with Golden Age Spanish dramatic standards of the sixteenth and seventeenth centuries. Laserna infused Spanish regional styles into Italianate music, to add local color. Through the merging of

28   *Introduction*

European and traditional styles, the *Cecilia* plays struggle with the benefits and disadvantages of modernization.

In any case, even the most modernizing stances did not attempt to overthrow the Old Regime or secularize the nation. In general, Spanish intellectuals favored strands of Enlightenment that coexisted with belief in God and approval of the monarchy. Sensism, the understandings of nature and humanity of Bacon, Locke, and Condillac, left a deep imprint. The changes generated by Enlightenment and modernity in Spain needed to follow a pace and a course different from the "radical Enlightenment" (cf. Jonathan Israel) of some of the philosophes, or from the revolutionary enterprise of the Jacobines in France. Modernity did not upturn Spain during the 1780s–1790s; instead, the new paradigms permeated identities and mentalities until they progressively became integrated into a new understanding of Spanishness.

1

Critics versus Musicians

Críticos satíricos
Que sin compasión
A todos alcanza
Su murmuración

Satirical critics
Who, without compassion
Reach everybody
With their rumors

Thus sang the trio of performers in Pablo Esteve's 1787 tonadilla *El teatro y los actores agraviados* ("The Slighted Theater and Actors"). But who were these merciless critics threatening to ruin Madrid's theater? When the periodical press took off in the 1780s, the critic became a consolidated figure in Spanish discourse, with his new and unauthorized public voice.[1] Emerging from the deluge of printed pages, this newly minted character disregarded traditional social structures and modes of communication. Embracing modernization, the critic demanded swift changes to centuries-old ways of doing things. Music, speech, writing, knowledge, authority, self-reflection, and worldly speculation—all were vulnerable to the scrutiny of the critic's pen and his penchant for modernization. In Madrid, the print boom opened a new platform from which to discuss music and its public meaning. In the 1780s and early 1790s publications, such discussions featured quarrels over the social utility of local musical theater in early attempts at music criticism.

A distinctly modern form of knowledge, printed criticism disrupted the presumed unilateral authority of the king and the Catholic Church to prescribe social rules. Even when critics did not question the crown's or the church's official postures, their very multiplicity contradicted a single, unchanging interpre-

---

[1] Even in the 1760s Madrileños complained about too many publications: "En los periódicos publicados entre 1761 y 1765 leemos, como si fuera un tópico de género, continuas alusiones a la gran cantidad de papeles públicos que se publican y a los muchos que se dedican a escribir en ese medio, sin tener la preparación necesaria para llevar a cabo los objetivos culturales y de trabajo por la felicidad pública que se proponen." Joaquín Álvarez Barrientos, "El periodista en la España del siglo XVIII y la profesionalización del escritor," *Estudios de Historia Social* 52/53 (1990): 29–39.

30   *Music and Modernity in Enlightenment Spain*

tation of events.[2] As periodicals increased avenues for public communication, more people started experimenting with voicing an opinion. Each new critical voice—printed, spoken, or sung—prescribed a different formula for social well-being depending on the particular critic's vision for Spain as progressive, conservative, or in between. In the words of a contemporary author, "it seems that now anyone with a hint of enlightenment has attained despotic power to meddle in criticism and publish their leaflets."[3] Critics thus encountered resistance from members of the public who believed that only top-down, unilateral interpretations of reality secured the permanence and cohesiveness of a core social ethos that was the source of Spanish identity. Paradoxically, such critics of the modern fashion printed or sang their own critiques, spurring the criticism cycle. Criticism, or opinion, was independent of practical proficiency and tradition. As such, it was of unclear epistemological value: Did it merely attack personal reputations, or did it express ideas? While critics saw their craft as contributing to currents of European aesthetic thought, artists steeped in tradition saw criticism as an assault on their professional standing.

This chapter studies the wake of instability that criticism introduced in the field of musical knowledge during the late 1780s and early 1790s. Through two case studies from 1786–1787 (a journalistic essay and its response, a stage tonadilla and its review), I argue that while critics saw their craft as a contribution to national improvement, music practitioners saw criticism as an assault on their professional standing. The first concerns musical knowledge at the theoretical level. In the absence of a definitive musico-theoretical system, music practitioners clung to counterpoint and seventeenth-century music treatises—such as those of Pietro Cerone—while critics and audiences supported or attacked them. Thus, in 1786 controversy raged over a discourse published in *El Censor*, the most innovative periodical of the time. Channeling ideas from beyond Spanish borders, *El Censor* advocated simplicity as the best path to imitate nature. The paper hailed ancient Greek music as the antidote to baroque counterpoint's artificiality. The riposte from Manuel Cavaza, a musician member of Madrid's Royal Chapel, titled "El músico censor del Censor no músico" (The Musician [who censors] the Non-Musician Censor), scolded

---

[2]   "Criticism and journalism played a decisive role in the formation of public opinion [in the transition from the eighteenth to the nineteenth century] and as a medium for expression that opened the ideological and aesthetic debate to new voices theretofore often silenced:" "Prólogo," in *La crítica dramática en España (1789–1833)*, edited by María José Rodríguez Sánchez de León (Madrid: Instituto de la Lengua Española, 2000), 17.

[3]   "Parece que ya todos los que tienen alguna tintura de ilustracion, han logrado un despotico dominio para meterse á criticos y publicar sus papelillos:" Mademiselle de Bouville, *Criticas reflexiones que hace Mademiselle de Bouville ... sobre el estado presente de la Literatura Española, en vista de los inumerables papeles que se dán a la luz pública* (Madrid: Hilario Santos Alonso, 1786), 9. The author may have been Elisabeth de Drouin, third daughter of French nobleman Charles François de Drouin.

critics as purveyors of fake knowledge, as merely those who *said* but could not *do*. The confrontation between the author of *El Censor*'s "Discourse 97" and Cavaza exposes the frictions resulting from opposing conceptions of music, one verbal, one mathematic; one anchored in natural expression, the other in technical skill.

The second case study concerns a confrontation between critics and performers over musical theater, specifically stage tonadillas. Printed criticism extended the shelf life of a singular performance through discussions lasting days, even months, resulting in authors' and artists' increased exposure to public scrutiny. From this position of extended vulnerability, theater makers rebuked critics before the authorities. Focusing on the volley of accusations among performers, composers, and critics concerning Pablo Esteve's stage tonadilla *El teatro y los actores agraviados* (1787), I argue that the discourse surrounding this particular work exposes composers' and performers' anxieties around coping with modern knowledge practices.

In both cases, critics adopt the role of "sayers" who challenge musicians as "doers," in response to which musicians defend their professional authority and the value of their craft. The sayer/doer dynamic made visible new configurations in the Western system of the arts, whereby music was no longer a craft but a fine art. Spanish critics expressed Western European aesthetic concerns with naturalness and mimesis in the fine arts using the Bourbon rhetoric of progress and civilization mixed with formal rules taken from literary neoclassicism. To better understand these debates between critics and musicians, consider the Spanish chapel system, where most professional musicians received their education.

The Standing of Professional Musicians

Critics clashed with professional musicians in late-eighteenth century Spain because each group stood on opposite sides of a twofold epistemological change: from the mathematical to the verbal paradigm of music and from understanding musicians as skilled craftsmen to viewing them as artists akin to poets or painters. Epistemological change does not occur in the void. On the contrary, it alters the beliefs and lives of real people, in this case, professional musicians' careers. This chapter's first case study, a printed debate between the anonymous author (probably a lawyer) of *El Censor*'s "Discourse 97" and Madrid Royal Chapel oboist Manuel Cavaza, one a critic, the other a professional musician, is a concrete manifestation of how epistemological modernization processes operate. As new knowledge systems move in, they displace older ones, provoking collective resistance. In late eighteenth-century Spain, making room for music criticism meant giving up the chapel system's monopoly over musical discourse, exposing musicians to public scrutiny.

32   *Music and Modernity in Enlightenment Spain*

The chapel system had a virtual monopoly on Spain's professional musician-ship. Since neither opera nor national theater required a steady supply of musicians in Madrid, only the church provided professional musicians with formal musical education and employment. Court opera became less frequent after Ferdinand VI's death and Farinelli's subsequent departure from Madrid in 1759, practically disappearing between 1776 and 1787.[4] Dwindling opera performances meant fewer Italian singers residing in Madrid. For their part, Spanish musical theater singers did not receive any formal training, as stated by Le Guin and corroborated by the fact that, as late as 1790, Blas de Laserna proposed the creation of a Spanish music school for actors.[5] Spain did not have conservatories like Naples or Venice. Instrumentalists who played at the theater or private events were often members of one Madrid's many chapels, including the three royal chapels, those affiliated with convents and monasteries, and a few private ones.[6]

Chapel musicians had a guild mentality inherited from previous centuries when music was considered a craft. The guild mentality extended to the ownership of musical knowledge. For practitioners like the oboist Cavaza, if music remained a trade or craft, even a standalone art, musicians could preserve guild-like organization. On the contrary, changing the status of music from technical art to fine art would also move the loci of musical practice to an institution akin to the Real Academia de San Fernando, out of the church's dominion and more importantly out of the control of chapels, organists, and chapel masters.

The concept of the guild is key to understanding the professional system of musicians operating in Spain during the second half of the eighteenth century. As long as music chapels remained anchored in the medieval and Renaissance system of guilds, new theoretical systems had little chance of adoption. Other than polymath Benito Feijóo in the first half of the eighteenth century, authors of music texts were all professional musicians serving in chapels, usually as organists and then as chapel masters. The list includes Pablo Nassarre (organist) and José de Torres (Royal Chapel master) in the early part of the century, and Antonio Soler, Antonio Rodríguez de Hita, and his rival theorist Antonio Roel del Río (chapel masters) in the mid-century. Cavaza, among others, continued the tradition of the musician-theorist in the late part of the cen-

---

[4] In contrast, Italian opera was performed continuously in Barcelona throughout the eighteenth century.

[5] Elisabeth Le Guin, *The Tonadilla in Performance: Lyric Comedy in Enlightenment Spain* (Berkeley: University of California Press, 2014). When Laserna proposed creating a music school for actors, he was inspired by Cristóbal's (Cristoforo) Andreozzi's school of Italian music. Andreozzi was the first violin at the Teatro de los Caños del Peral orchestra: Francisco Asenjo Barbieri, *Papeles Barbieri* (Las Rozas de Madrid: Discantus, 2020), vol. 14, 100–2.

[6] Three chapels bore royal status in eighteenth-century Madrid: the Royal Chapel and the chapels of the royal monasteries of the Descalzas Reales and of La Encarnación, property of the Poor Clares and the Augustinians Recollects respectively.

tury, when more nonmusicians such as Tomás de Iriarte, Esteban de Arteaga, and Antonio Eximeno published their ideas on music. Theoretical treatises and manuals that defended counterpoint and perpetuated singing with hexachordal mutations had an institutional, syndical counterpart vying to dominate musical production, education, and musical discourse.

The changes in musical knowledge that late eighteenth-century Spanish critics advanced rattled the institution of music chapels. *El Censor*'s "Discourse 97" gives us insight into these changes and their connections to the Enlightenment.

Critics versus Musicians: *El Censor* versus *El músico censor*

"Discourse 97" was published in the Enlightenment journal *El Censor*, which ran from 1781–1787. During its run, *El Censor* published a total of 167 weekly discourses satirizing Spanish citizens, their mores, religious practices, the clergy, and the government. Of the 167, "Discourse 97" is the only one devoted to music. Its author signed with the pseudonym Simplicio Greco y Lira. He is likely the journal's main editor, Luis María García Cañuelo Heredia, although precise attribution remains unproven.[7] Due to its editors' independent thinking and run-ins with censorship, *El Censor* became a metonymy for critical publication, such that newspapers and journals were called "censores." According to the bibliographer and jurist Juan Sempere y Guarinos, *El Censor* had "more taxing and riskier aims" than other journals because it did not merely ridicule but offered serious analysis.[8] By 1786, *El Censor* routinely inflamed anger and prompted the publication of pamphlets and edicts rebuking its most recent discourse. In the case of "Discourse 97," the offended party was Cavaza, who replied in a 246-page "pamphlet" under the pseudonym Lucio Vero Hispano.[9] In the context of the pamphlet war surrounding *El Censor*'s last years, Cavaza's extensive reply constitutes an apology for both the national musical apparatus and the mathematical paradigm of music, newly besieged by language-based compositional approaches.

Reformist in spirit, *El Censor*'s "Discourse 97" adapts widespread Enlightenment ideas about music and the arts to the circumstances of Spanish musical practice and aesthetic theory. Such widespread Enlightenment ideas are organized around two axes. The first axis is the mimesis of nature as the

---

[7] Despite the absence of conclusive evidence, there is some consensus that other enlightened men of letters such as Gaspar Melchor de Jovellanos collaborated anonymously in some of *El Censor*'s discourses: Isabel Román Gutiérrez, "De polémicas y apologías: El debate sobre el progreso de la España en las respuestas a Masson de Morvilliers y la historiografía ilustrada," *Dieciocho: Hispanic Enlightenment* (2021), 141.

[8] Juan Sempere y Guarinos, *Ensayo de una biblioteca española de los mejores escritores del reinado de Carlos III*, vol. 4 (Madrid: Imprenta Real, 1787), 191–94.

[9] Manuel Cavaza, *El músico censor del Censor no músico, ó Sentimientos de Lucio Vero Hispano, contra los de Simplicio Greco, y Lira: Discurso unico* (Madrid: Alfonso López, 1786), 30.

common principle for the fine arts, including music, represented in the writings of Charles Batteux. This includes responding to questions such as: How does music relate to the other arts, especially poetry? Does our music move the affections beyond pleasing the ear? Is our music natural, that is, does it imitate nature? The second axis concerns the shared origins of music and language and the consequent primacy of melody over harmony as formulated by Étienne Bonnot de Condillac, Jean Jacques Rousseau, and Antonio Eximeno. This premise contested the mathematical paradigm of music that structured Spanish musical pedagogy and counterpoint. Forming a patchwork of these Enlightenment trends, "Discourse 97" calls for a modernization of music theory and practice in Spain. For music theory, this meant abandoning counterpoint rules based on the hexachordal system and church modes. For musical practice, such modernization meant forsaking castrati and rejecting polyphony altogether in favor of highlighting the human voice over instruments.

The following sections examine the sources and references found in *El Censor*'s "Discourse 97" to understand why its author's modern views on music subverted the status quo of authority-based musical knowledge in Spain, prompting Cavaza's inflamed response. These sections will be useful to grasp the epistemological roots of the controversy at hand and to illustrate how Spanish authors, in this case the anonymous author of "Discourse 97," adapted and adopted Enlightenment ideas to their local and national realities. At twenty-four octavo pages (4052 words), "Discourse 97" had a sharpness that belied its brevity.

Music in the System of the Arts

"Discourse 97" opens and closes with a call to reframe musical theory and practice as philosophical endeavors, not technical ones. This epistemological shift required national musical practices to focus on the nature of music over its usage rules. Consequently, the author of "Discourse 97" proposes that the direction of Spanish music be entrusted to philosophers and not to music practitioners. By philosophers, he means men of letters (Cañuelo, editor of *El Censor* was himself a lawyer) versed in modern understandings of human perception and emotion and up-to-date in aesthetic standards of natural simplicity.

To achieve the natural simplicity required to move the passions, "Discourse 97" proposes that Spanish music emulate that of Greek antiquity, which the author considered the most natural and therefore most efficacious music. While most European authors advancing musical reforms connected ancient Greek music to opera, the author of "Discourse 97" has music chapels in mind. He imagines an ideal sound that is monodic, perhaps accompanied by the lyre, and that closely follows the words of respected poetry written by only the best Spanish authors. He fittingly signs with the pseudonym Simplicio Greco y Lira (Simplicius Graecus et Lyra). According to Simplicio Greco y Lira's standards, music must derive from nature and effortlessly move the human heart. He reasons that if Greek poetry, oratory, architecture, painting, and sculpture were the very best, how could their music not be the perfect model?[10] The premises of "Discourse 97" are rooted in a reconsideration of music as a fine art separate from the sciences and technical arts. Since the late seventeenth century, European intellectuals were preoccupied with this reclassification project, culminating in Batteux's *Les beaux arts réduits à un même principe* (1746).[11] For Batteux, if music were to move the passions like the other arts, it had to imitate nature.

The reform of the arts directed toward imitation of nature adhering to the Greek model had practical consequences. Neoclassicist reforms across Europe held that society would progress if current dramatic and musical practices were rectified. "Discourse 97" advocated musical reform in order to modernize the Spanish arts and "divest them from the roughness and extravagance they acquired during the barbarian centuries."[12] Simplicio Greco y Lira believed that Spanish music fell to its nadir with the baroque mix of complex counterpoint and florid melodic ornamentation, and the return to Greek simplicity was the cure. Many eighteenth-century literary and musical reformers who endeavored to modernize European nations shared this conviction and sought to replicate Greek tragedy's "marvelous effects." Translated into the civilizational projects of the European Enlightenment, Greek tragedy and music offered the possibility to steer human behavior at the civic level.

Like other reformers, Spanish neoclassicists working under Charles III's rule believed that improvements in the arts would start a chain reaction, eventually spurring agricultural and manufacturing growth. This notion was hardly unique to Spain. The reverberating effect of artistic reform in national improvement depended on Enlightenment-era changes in the classification of knowledge, whereby the fine arts as articulated by Batteux moved between practical and scientific knowledge. This logic operates in the preface to Antonio Planelli's *Dell'opera in musica* (1770), where he presents the fine arts as the link between the mechanical arts and "the most sublime sciences." Planelli writes:

> The state of the fine arts is an article of the greatest importance for the happiness and luster of nations. Since these pleasant faculties occupy the middle of that golden chain that connects the mechanical arts with the most sublime sciences. From this connection proceeds that where one understands painting, sculpture, architecture, etc., where a Palladio, a Michelagnolo [*sic*], a Raphael flourishes, agriculture is once again understood, there are excellent blacksmiths, and weavers.[13]

---

[10] Simplicio Greco y Lira [Luis María García Cañuelo y Heredia], "Discurso XCVII," *El Censor* 97 (1786): 531.

[11] Charles Batteux, *Les beaux arts [réduits a un même principe]* (Paris: Durand, 1747).

[12] Simplicio Greco y Lira, "Discurso XCVII," 526.

[13] "E lo stato delle Belle Arti un articolo della maggiore importanza per la felicità e'l lustro delle nazioni. Conciossiachè queste piacevoli facultà occupano il mezzo di quell'aurea

36   *Music and Modernity in Enlightenment Spain*

Different nations focused on reforming different artistic practices for the national betterment. For example, Italian scholars like Francesco Algarotti, Padre Martini, Esteban de Arteaga, Saverio Mattei, Antonio Eximeno, and Planelli focused on opera, while Spanish scholars foregrounded spoken theater and ecclesiastical music.

Batteux's theory that all fine arts are reducible to the principle of imitation proliferated during the Enlightenment. For example, Jean le Rond d'Alembert, in his "Discours préliminaire" (1751) to the *Encyclopédie méthodique*, refers to the division of human knowledge into practical (mechanical), speculative, and a mix of the two. For d'Alembert, the fine arts form a mixture of speculative and practical knowledge since they imitate nature following the same set of principles. In this regard, Batteux's influence on d'Alembert is undeniable. D'Alembert admits that the boundaries between different types of knowledge are far from clear, especially in fields like music that blend theory and practice.[14] Musical knowledge was particularly hard to classify. On the one hand, music has had a long speculative tradition as a numerical science dating back to the Pythagoreans, which had granted it a place in the medieval quadrivium alongside arithmetic, astronomy, and geometry. On the other hand, eighteenth-century Western European musicians underwent much technical training, which was often hard to integrate with speculative treatises. Finally, it was hard for both Batteux and d'Alembert to determine how exactly music imitated nature to fulfill the eighteenth-century ideal of mimesis. Ultimately, Batteux determined that because music could imitate nature it therefore belonged in the modern system of the arts.

From the first paragraph of "Discourse 97," it is clear that its author had in mind this recently minted system of the arts. The author lists music as one of the fine arts together with poetry, rhetoric, architecture, painting, and sculpture.[15] This new canon represents a significant change in the taxonomy of the arts, given that only painting, sculpture, and architecture were officially considered "noble arts" in Spain. As noble arts, painting, sculpture, and architecture enjoyed institutional protection and crown affiliation through the Royal Acad-

---

catena, che connette le arti meccaniche colle più sublimi scienze; dalla qual connessione procede, che dove ben s'intenda la pittura, la scultura, l'architettura etc., dove fiorisca un Palladio, un Michelagnolo [sic], un Raffaello, là s'intenda ancora l'agricoltura, là si trovino eccellenti fabbri, e tessitori. ..." Antonio Planelli, *Dell'opera in musica* (Naples: Nella stamperia di Donato Campo, 1772), 6.

[14] "Il faut cependant avoüer que nos idées ne sont pas encore bien fixées sur ce sujet. On ne sait souvent quel nom donner à la plûpart des connoissances où la spéculation se réunit à la pratique." Jean le Rond d'Alembert, "Discours préliminaire des éditeurs," edited by Robert Morrissey and Glenn Roe, *ARTFL Encyclopédie* (1751), vol. 1, xii, https://encyclopedie.uchicago.edu/node/88.

[15] The canon of the arts in Spain included six disciplines, adding rhetoric to the usual five. Helmut C. Jacobs, "La función de la música en la discusión estética de la Ilustración española," *Dieciocho: Hispanic Enlightenment* 32, no. 1 (2009): 49–73.

emy of San Fernando, whose professors were even conferred hidalgo status.[16] For its part, music fell somewhere in the Spanish legal category of "arts and trades," leaving it subject to regulation by ecclesiastical chapters and chapels. For music to attain the status of a fine art it had to cut its scientific ties with medieval astronomy and geometry and abandon its Pythagorean notions of number and harmonic proportion. Music also had to divorce itself from the mechanical arts. In the new system, the mechanical arts operated far below the fine arts and sciences because they did not require any degree of intellectual activity and catered only to basic human needs.[17] Therefore, musicians had to justify their practice as a fine art if they wanted to obtain artist status.

Batteux was well received in Spain, both because his mimesis principle matched the aesthetic normative of Spanish literary neoclassicism and because Batteux defended Christian religion as part of the natural order.[18] Highly respected literary theorist Ignacio de Luzán had in 1737 already identified imitation as the ultimate artistic goal. The contents of "Discourse 97" suggest that its author knew Batteux's writings on both mimesis and music, but the text sticks to Luzán's hierarchy when it comes to poetry's supremacy. Lacking a corpus of Spanish music criticism to draw from, the author of "Discourse 97" appealed to Luzán to justify discontinuing Spanish musical practices inherited from the baroque. Simplicio Greco y Lira believed music needed a neoclassicist reform like the literary reform Luzán had launched fifty years earlier. Subjecting music to the same high standards to which neoclassicists held poetry would elevate music to the level of the other arts within Batteux's system or within "the modern system of the arts."[19] Like Luzán and Nicolas Boileau-Despreaux, "Discourse 97" upholds poetry's supremacy over all other arts, a supremacy Batteux abated. In fact, Batteux demonstrated that poetry imitates "la belle nature" just like all other fine arts, including music. Batteux's revaluation of music as one of the fine arts encouraged authors such as Simplicio Greco y Lira to demand the same standards for poetry and music, nudging music away from the mathematical-Pythagorean approach and toward the verbal paradigm.

16 Ferdinand VI of Spain, "Título XXII, Ley I. D. Fernando VI, en Aranjuez por céd. De 30 de Mayo de 1757. Establecimiento en Madrid de la Real Academia de las tres Nobles Artes con el título de San Fernando; y privilegios de sus individuos y profesores," in *Novísima Recopilación de las leyes de España* (Madrid: Galván Librero, 1805 [1766]), 174.

17 Batteux classifies the arts into three groups: mechanical, fine, and mixed. Mechanical arts use nature to satisfy basic human needs of shelter, nourishment, or transportation. The fine arts—poetry, painting, sculpture, music, and dance or pantomime—imitate nature, create pleasure, and satisfy spiritual needs. The mixed arts (rhetoric and architecture) are intended both to be useful and pleasurable.

18 Sections of Batteux's *Les beaux arts réduites à un même principe* were translated by Francisco Mariano Nipho in his 1760s periodical *Caxón de sastre* and reprinted in the 1780s. Marcelino Menéndez y Pelayo, *Historia de las ideas estéticas en España por el doctor D. Marcelino Menéndez y Pelayo* (Madrid: Impr. de A. Pérez Dubrull, 1890), 1262.

19 Paul Oskar Kristeller, "The Modern System of the Arts: A Study in the History of Aesthetics (I)," *Journal of the History of Ideas* 12, no. 4 (1951): 496–527.

38   *Music and Modernity in Enlightenment Spain*

Batteux elaborates with the caveat that not all arts imitate nature equally. For Batteux, while painting and sculpture imitate visible things, music and dance represent human passions. Batteux warns that music and dance are prone to straying from mimesis at the risk of being merely noises and jolts. Hence, music's relation to nature and means of expression required unique strategies. For Batteux, music only becomes a true art when it moves the human heart. To achieve this, the musician must stimulate his own imagination such that he "exits himself" and inhabits the situation he is trying to represent. Once the musician is transported to the represented realm—be it a battle or an episode of joy or mourning—he will experience the corresponding feelings and communicate them to the listener. Otherwise, cautions Batteux, music fails to convey anything, remaining mere sound.[20] Similarly, "Discourse 97" emphasizes sensation and emotion in aesthetic experience. Simplicio Greco y Lira moves away from the rational taste characteristic of Luzán or Lodovico Antonio Muratori and toward the sensist theories of John Locke and Étienne Bonnot de Condillac, while also drawing on Rousseau's nature-oriented aesthetics. Simplicio Greco y Lira's approach to mimesis is affective, even mystical, unmediated by taste.

Heeding Batteux's principles, "Discourse 97" denounces practices that prevented Spanish chapel musicians from inhabiting their music's emotional content. Simplicio Greco y Lira says musicians should be "transported with the same spirit" of the poet and describes his experience listening to a choir of monks in terms of "motions," a word connoting both mood changes and divine inspiration. The main shortcoming of chapel musicians, Simplicio Greco y Lira writes, is that they don't understand the texts they sing. If the lyrics are in Latin, they don't know the language. If the lyrics are in Spanish, performers and composers still lack the education to understand learned poetry "and everything turns into Latin."[21] This lack of poetic literacy results in composers setting lyrics to inadequate music. Singers' poor pronunciation and focus on technical skill exacerbates the problem:

> Who will be able to tell apart prose from verse in an opera, with the repetition and disruption of the verses, of the words, and even of the syllables, [...] with too much lingering in some vowel to display the flexibility of the singer's throat, and finally, without scruple when it comes to accentuation?[22]

When singers or listeners do not understand the words, passions will not arise, and music will be pointless.

---

[20]   Batteux, *Les beaux arts*, 15, 35.

[21]   "Discurso XCVII," 535.

[22]   "¿Quién podrá distinguir en un aria el verso de la prosa, con la repetición y el trastorno de los versos, de las palabras, y aun de las sílabas [...] con la demasiada detención en alguna vocal para hacer lucir la flexibilidad de garganta del cantor, y finalmente con ningún escrúpulo en los acentos?" "Discurso XCVII," 536–37.

El Censor versus El Músico Censor: Two Different Conceptions of Music

A modernized understanding music as a fine art akin to painting or even poetry demanded forsaking the older versions of the mathematical paradigm that ruled Spain's musical chapel system in favor of an imitation of nature inspired by ancient Greek practices. This demand did not sit well with Cavaza, since it discredited all his and his peers' years of education and experience. Furthermore, the epistemological change to the verbal paradigm pierced into the core belief in an immovable truth. "Discourse 97" pokes holes at the tenet that music exists independently of human beings. The suggestion that music's essence changed over time threatened the lineage of Western music theorists' epistemological authority and questioned music chapels' monopoly over music pedagogy, which in turn destabilized the notion of one Spanish nation under one hereditary authority.

The author of "Discourse 97" defends Rousseau's notion that music and language share their origin in the primordial cry of men. The "verbal paradigm" claims that the more music *imitates* spoken prosody, the closer it will be to nature and to perfection.[23] Conversely, the further music strays from prosody toward harmonic proportions, the more artificial it becomes, and the less it moves human passions. Music can enhance discourse in two ways: it may highlight or supplement textual meaning. The first stance suggests that music, grammar, and rhetoric operate in similar ways to bring meaning to life. The second stance relies on music to amplify the emotional effect of the lyrics. For example, Esteban de Arteaga believes that melody makes it possible for music to be an imitative art since melody can imitate the different accents of the passions through prosody inflections.[24] Arteaga accepts the use of harmony with the caveat that music built solely on harmonic principles is "without life or spirit" because harmony comes from abstract proportions and numerical ratios that will never account for the infinite language inflections.[25] For Arteaga, a simple melody guarantees that music will remain true to nature, whereas textual repetitions, polyphony, and melismas all disconnect music from its linguistic origins. "Discourse 97" took Arteaga's propositions even further.

---

[23] Downing A. Thomas, *Music and the Origins of Language: Theories from the French Enlightenment*, New Perspectives in Music History and Criticism (Cambridge: Cambridge University Press, 1995); Jean Jacques Rousseau defines song as "a modification of the voice … which must naturally arise and be formed." Music, however, "is not so much the simple accent of speech as this same accent imitated." Jean-Jacques Rousseau and John T. Scott, "On the Principle of Melody," in *Essay on the Origins of Languages and Writings Related to Music*, The Collected Writings of Rousseau (Hanover, NH: University Press of New England, 1998), 260–62.

[24] Esteban de Arteaga, *Le rivoluzioni del teatro musicale italiano dalla sua origine fino al presente* (Bologna: Stamperìa di C. Trenti, 1783), vol. 2, 2.

[25] Arteaga, *Le rivoluzioni*, vol. 2, 8–9.

Simplicio Greco y Lira takes the verbal paradigm to the extreme, proposing to strip music down to pure melody without rhythm, perhaps to the accompaniment of a lyre. His description of Greek chant as "simple melody," a "pronunciation and chant of sorts" that "knew how to augment the melody of language," recalls Étienne Bonnot de Condillac, another beloved author of the Spanish Enlightenment next to Locke. In his *Essai sur l'origins des connassainces humaines* (1746), Condillac devoted a chapter to Greco-Roman prosody and song. In it, he affirms that Greek and Roman declamation was notated and accompanied with an instrument and was therefore "a true chant (song)." Harmony in song "augments" the text's expressivity. Condillac argued that the separation between modern speech and song did not exist in Latin and Greek because ancient peoples spoke with much more inflection.[26] Condillac also wrote a separate chapter of the *Essay sur l'origins des connaissances humaines* on music without words, where he judges ancient music inferior to modern music. What Condillac differentiated into "declamation-song" and "music," Simplicio Greco y Lira conflated into a single definition: music is declamation-song and the rest (rhythm, instruments, polyphony) is decadence. He finds that, among the repertory then in practice in Spain, only plainchant, while inferior to Greek chant, suits the reformation, "or better, the restoration of true music," that he sought.[27] To restore music to its linguistic origins was to maximize its mimetic potential and therefore justify its inclusion as a fine art.

The verbal paradigm ultimately pursues what "Discourse 97" calls "philosophical music": music that touches all aspects of human life, from individual sensation to politics, from imitation of nature to fulfillment of the natural law. For Simplicio Greco y Lira, musicians should be enhancers of society, visionaries joining poets' and painters' sublime labor of translating nature. From his point of view, pedagogical emphasis on counterpoint's meticulous rules and complex techniques hinders philosophical music, rendering music a mechanical skill. The more a musical piece reveals its undergirding technical work, the less it achieves its affective goal. On the contrary, the musician-philosopher knows how to guide listeners to an understanding of nature and "agreeably move[s] our heart towards the object presented, and not to the hand that presents it."[28] For Simplicio Greco y Lira, Spain is full of musicians capable of techné, but never of poiesis. He believes that Spanish music remains outdated because these same technical musicians oversee writing treatises and teaching.

Like Arteaga and his contemporary Saverio Mattei, *El Censor* found the mechanical or mathematical model of music both artificial and dated. Arteaga, Mattei, and Simplicio Greco y Lira thought that chapel musicians who pub-

---

[26]   Etienne Bonnot de Condillac, *Essai sur l'origine des connoissances humaines: Ouvrage où l'on réduit à un seul principe tout ce qui concerne l'entendement humain*, 2 vols. (Amsterdam: Chez Pierre Mortier, 1746), 25–28.

[27]   "Discurso XCVII," 547.

[28]   "Discurso XCVII," 528.

lished music treatises were like authors of spelling and grammar manuals. In other words, knowing the rules of counterpoint amounts to knowing grammar and nothing more. Arteaga and Simplicio Greco y Lira see the rules of counterpoint and harmony as nonmusic, mere techné. Mastery of these rules will never make a true musician, Arteaga writes, "in the same way that the sole rules of grammar will rather make a pure and regulated discourse, but will never be enough to make an eloquent writer."[29] Mattei laments that musicians are trained only in "grammar," but not in rhetoric or poetry. In a critique of the traditional music education system, he equates counterpoint to grammatical concordances: following counterpoint's rules will prevent basic mistakes, but it will not make anyone a musician. Simplicio Greco y Lira equates José de Torres's 1700 edition of Pablo Nassarre's *Fragmentos músicos* to baroque author Juan Díaz Rengifo's *Arte Poetica* (1592, full of technical rules). Both Torres and Rengifo adhere to baroque aesthetics grounded in precepts and formulae, hence their works encapsulate for Simplicio Greco y Lira the mechanical way of making music At the same time, Luzán's *Poetics* (1737) and Iriarte's *La música* (1779) stand for the natural, modern way of making music, which coincides with the verbal paradigm. Luzán and Iriarte epitomize the modern philosopher-artist Simplicio Greco y Lira envisioned, one who derives his knowledge from a profound imitation of nature.

Polemics pitching the verbal against the mathematical paradigm of music intertwined with ancient-modern debates concerning Greek music. Quarrels over the relative superiority of ancient or modern music led scholars to the more profound question of music's dependence on human agency. Scholars who declared that either ancient or modern music was superior implicitly accepted that the ancients' music was qualitatively different from the moderns' music. This highlighted human agency, so that concrete location and time changed music. It followed that music was contingent upon human activity, as was language. The mathematical paradigm, on the contrary, tends to see music as abstract and non-spatiotemporal. The abstract view of music underlies harmonic theory in Giuseppe Tartini's or Jean Philippe Rameau's style and hints at the existence of a truth-out-there, independent from human activity. For example, for Tartini, "the source of every truth is nature, to be understood as all the phenomena which fall under our senses and are exempt from any intervention of man throughout history."[30] Authors who favor the mathematical music paradigm often discard the debate over Greek and modern music because they believe they are both one and the same. For such authors, music exists as such in nature, and no artistic practice can alter that. For the author of "Discourse 97," however, there is no music-out-there without humans since music depends

---

[29]   Arteaga, *Le rivoluzioni*, vol. 2, 7.

[30]   Pierluigi Petrobelli, "Tartini, Giuseppe," *Grove Music Online* (2001), https://www. oxfordmusiconline.com/grovemusic/view/10.1093/gmo/9781561592630.001.0001/ omo-9781561592630-e-0000027529.

Music and Modernity in Enlightenment Spain

on language. The ancient versus modern music debate becomes complicated because even though both those who argue for either the verbal and mathematical paradigms claim that the purpose of music is to imitate nature, they deploy incompatible understandings of nature.

Consider these different understandings of nature in the exchange between "Discourse 97" and Manuel Cavaza's *El músico censor del Censor no músico*. The author of "Discourse 97" believes in an intrinsic connection between nature and humanity, demonstrated by his preference for the human voice over musical instruments. This intrinsic connection is the source for mimesis. Hence, in "Discourse 97" mimesis emerges from within people, as human experience unfolds in the natural world. Such is the reasoning behind the verbal paradigm: music, like language, emerges from humans. Antonio Eximeno states that "it is indispensable ... that man have within himself the origin of music."[31] Master oboist Cavaza, loyal to the mathematical paradigm of his training, would never agree with Eximeno's assertion. In fact, in *El músico censor* he writes that "music's essence remains immovable and what changes are ideas about music."[32] In other words, for Cavaza, music exists independently of humans. The deeper disagreement between the author of "Discourse 97" author and Cavaza is thus whether music is an art emanating from human-mediated imitation of nature or the result of formulae mirroring natural proportions.

The European clash over music's verbal and mathematical models overlapped in Spain with late Enlightenment efforts to debunk the remnants of scholasticism in educational institutions: seminaries, schools, music chapels and, most notably, the University of Salamanca. By the eighteenth century, supporters of the Enlightenment understood university scholasticism as an obstacle to Spain's national modernization.[33] For pro-modern authors like *El Censor*'s editors, Salamanca and its convoluted philosophical methods stood for antiprogress, especially when it came to economic applications of science. The scholarship produced at Salamanca was largely speculative, disconnected from the Newtonian physics and experimental methods at the root of European scientific modernization. Scholasticism also rejected Cartesian skepticism and relied on authoritative discourse. In scholasticism, one cannot rely solely on oneself to know reality but must verify even one's most rational conclusions with the ideas of others who know better.[34] Furthermore, authoritative consensus has been compiled in

---

[31] Antonio Eximeno, *Del origen y reglas de la música, con la historia de su progreso, decadencia y restauración*, 3 vols. (Madrid: Imprenta real, 1796), 165.

[32] Cavaza, *El músico censor*, 43.

[33] The whole press quarrel unleashed by Juan Pablo Forner's *Oración apologética por la España y su mérito literario* (Madrid: Imprenta Real, 1786) was focused on scholasticism and traditional theology, both of which Forner upheld against modern science and criticism.

[34] "Thomas [Aquinas] understands philosophizing to depend upon antecedent knowledge, to proceed from it, and to be unintelligible unless, in its sophisticated modes,

a corpus of books from which anyone can learn the truth about any matter without needing to search for answers in the self. By contrast, for example, Eximeno's belief that music originates in man has no place in scholasticism. Hewing closely to Eximeno's principles, "Discourse 97" represents the antithesis of Salamanca's scholasticism, wherein Thomist realism played a major role.

Cavaza's text reveals philosophical affinities with scholasticism, specifically Thomism, without openly defending it. Cavaza's use of "essence" and "immovable" to describe music reminded readers of debates around essence and existence central to the sixteenth-century Thomist revival at the University of Salamanca. Cavaza's "immovable essence" of music aligns with the Thomist realist belief that the world can and should be known as it is. Further traces of Thomist realism appear later in *El músico censor* as Cavaza says harmony is "hidden in melody by the Supreme Creator since Creation." Following Tartini, Cavaza explains that each sound is either principle or part of a triad determined by the Sovereign Author: man only discovers triads through nature's indicators and reduces such discovery to theoretical principles. Music, according to Cavaza, comes not from within men but from natural harmonic proportions that men translate into a well-organized art that made natural harmony pleasant to the ear.[35] Cavaza justified counterpoint as the codification of natural sounds according to the logic of natural law. The philosophical School of Salamanca, or simply Salamanca, revived the Thomist version of natural law. In Thomas Aquinas's philosophical system, God regulates the universe through an eternal law, which can be partly known through natural law, accessible to reason.[36] Applying the logic of Thomist realism to music, counterpoint and music theory based on harmonic relations are limited models created by human reason to try and understand the universe's eternal, God-given harmony.

Another point of contention between Scholasticism and Enlightenment philosophies concerned the limits of human intervention in the world: To what extent is it the prerogative of humans to change reality? Under Thomist realism, knowledge of truth is the goal, wherein the mind "seeks not to change the world but to understand it."[37] Applying this principle to music means that the music scholar's task is to learn and follow its immutable laws. This is Cavaza's position when he maintains that four-part harmony is God-given.[38] For him, it is not only futile but also arrogant to try and change music. As an epistemo-

---

it can be traced back to the common truths known to all." Ralph McInerny and John O'Callaghan, "Saint Thomas Aquinas," ed. Edward N. Zalta, *Stanford Encyclopedia of Philosophy* (2018), https://plato.stanford.edu/archives/sum2018/entries/aquinas/.

[35] Cavaza, *El músico censor*, 133.

[36] Thomas Izbicki and Matthias Kaufmann, "School of Salamanca," edited by Edward N. Zalta, *The Stanford Encyclopedia of Philosophy* (2019), https://plato.stanford.edu/archives/sum2019/entries/school-salamanca/.

[37] Izbicki and Kaufmann, "School of Salamanca."

[38] Cavaza, *El músico censor*, 132–33.

44   *Music and Modernity in Enlightenment Spain*

logical code of conduct with roots in Thomist realism, this "to understand but not to change" attitude made many Spanish scholars and laymen alike uncomfortable with all forms of criticism. Since criticism involves proposing changes of social mores, including musical practices, criticism appeared in general perception as an act of arrogance, for who are men to try and change the world?

For those invested in preserving the mathematical, immovable paradigm of music "out there in nature" and shielding it from critics, it was crucial to separate speculative (theoretical) and practical music. Someone like Cavaza granted that practices could change, but the theoretical apparatus remained valid and timeless. In *El músico censor*, Cavaza separates composers from performers and thinks that performers have no obligation to know how the music relates to the text.[39] He attributes any possible malpractice in the Spanish chapels to performers' individual limitations rather than to the theoretical system or the chapel system's structural practice. From Cavaza's perspective, counterpoint is a compositional technique that can properly move the affections; the problem is idle musicians who do not take its study seriously, or singers who do not work in their technique enough to properly enunciate syllables. In other words, for Cavaza and like-minded authors, traditional music theory is the right way to understand music and to imitate nature. Perfection is only a matter of achieving proficiency in the system currently in place. Since, for Cavaza, the problem lies in individual shortcomings, critics' objections to current musical practices amounted to personal attacks trampling on charity, prudence, and wisdom.[40] By contrast, there is no evidence of any separation between speculation and practice in "Discourse 97." Quite the opposite, Simplicio Greco y Lira advocates the fusion of the two in what he calls "philosophical music." Under the model of "Discourse 97," all musicians are responsible for the highest aesthetic standard.

When it comes to vocal music, Simplicio Greco y Lira and Cavaza disagree over singers and the connection between oratory and music. While European musical reforms had claimed that poetry was supreme for centuries, *El Censor*'s author added a distinctly Spanish flavor to the argument when he foregrounded rhetoric alongside poetry. "Discourse 97" deploys a taxonomy that considers rhetoric among the six fine arts, which explains why the author is attuned to prosody, accentuation, punctuation, and even grammar in singing. In fact, he calls vocal music "musical oratory," a reference to Iriarte's didactic poem *La música*, and even extends Iriarte's famous engraving of music and poetry "playing on the same lyre" (see figure 1.1) to include oratory: "music,

---

[39]   Theorist and chapel master Antonio Rodríguez de Hita, writing thirty years before Cavaza, maintained the same division between composers and performers. He thought only "maestros" have an obligation to know the theoretical music treatises: *Diapasón instructivo consonancias musicas y morales, documentos a los profesores de música, carta a sus discípulos, de don Antonio Rodríguez de Hita ... sobre un breve y facil methodo de estudiar la composición, y nuevo modo de contrapunto para el nuevo estilo* (Madrid: Imprenta de la viuda de Juan Muñoz 1757).

[40]   Cavaza, *El músico censor*, 92.

Figure 1.1 "Música y poesía, en una misma lira tocaremos."
Manuel Salvador Carmona, ca. 1779. Source: Tomás de Iriarte,
La música: Poema (Madrid, 1779).

46   *Music and Modernity in Enlightenment Spain*

which has such close kinship to poetry and eloquence; who seem inflamed by the same numen," Simplicio Greco y Lira writes. The neoclassicist concept of "musical oratory" captures Rousseau's parallel between speech—the art of transmitting ideas—and melody—the art of transmitting feelings.[41] For Spanish neoclassicism, just as a good sermon persuades the listener, a good song moves the heart via the threefold appeal of words (*logos*), emotion (*pathos*), and accurate representation of human essence (*ethos*). However, "*Discourse 97*"'s musical oratory must not be understood as the compartmentalized arrangement of musico-rhetorical figures aimed at triggering discrete emotions.[42] In fact, Simplicio Greco y Lira derides composers who, in midst of a plaintive song, insert an upbeat motif to highlight the word "laughter" in lyrics—an idea he may have taken from Francesco Algarotti.[43] Instead, in "Discourse 97" rhetoric is subsumed into the beautiful imitation of nature, in this case, imitation of affective language. In other words, "Discourse 97"'s author thinks music should mimic not emotions themselves but rather how emotions surface in speech.[44] Similar concerns with affective speech characterize not only Iriarte's *La música* but also sentimental novels and opera where interrupted sentences or altered patterns of speech aim at rousing audiences' feelings.

Simplicio Greco y Lira complains that professional singers stray from the natural voice. He contends that when singers surrender to virtuosic skill, the voice becomes mechanistic and ceases to be human. He starts on the well-trodden path of music's failure to serve the text when melismas and repetitions obscure the poetry of arias "to flaunt the flexibility of the singer's throat." He then returns to Iriarte's concept of musical oratory to insist that accentuation and punctuation of the text be preserved when setting and performing an aria. In the end, Simplicio Greco y Lira reckons, listeners should feel an affective reaction to an aria's text, not to the singer's skill. He exalts the natural quality of the human voice to a level unattainable by musical instruments, which are reduced to mechanical sound. For his part, Cavaza strives to separate music and oratory as two distinct disciplines. While Cavaza concedes that instruments should only prepare, accompany, and highlight the vocal part, he complains that *El Censor* supports the higher status of the voice not with proper musical arguments but with words that "smell of Cicero."[45]

---

[41]   Rousseau and Scott, "On the Principle of Melody."

[42]   Discrete musico-rhetorical figures are found in the treatises of Joachim Burmeister and Christoph Bernhard at the dawn of the seventeenth century.

[43]   To better understand Algarotti's possible influence on the author of "Discourse 97," compare the paragraph found in "Discourse 97," 535, with Francesco Algarotti, *Saggio sopra l'opera in musica* (Bologna: F.A.R.A.P. S. Giovanni in Persiceto, 1763 [1755]), 35–36.

[44]   According to José Máximo Leza, Iriarte adopted a similar posture in *La música:* Leza, *La música en el siglo XVIII*, 109.

[45]   Cavaza, *El músico censor*, 89.

Critics versus Musicians   47

"Discourse 97" denounces two practices in the hiring of church singers that, in Simplicio Greco y Lira's opinion, made the singers sound mechanical: *capones* (castrati) and chant leaders (*sochantres*). For Simplicio Greco y Lira, singers fixated on vocal display were not unlike stage machines. "Is the quite extraordinary by any means natural?" he asks, and his answer is a resounding no.[46] He thinks capones and sochantres are "weird men" who, once hired in the music chapels, "will not be useful for a thing, except singing mechanically." For him, capones are the ultimate example of the dehumanization of the voice: "Amongst us, those voices considered exquisite are not so according to nature: the voice of a *capón* is not the human voice, it is only a trivial instrument that utters words."[47] Spain had its own tradition of capones or castrated ecclesiastical singers since the sixteenth century.[48] By the late eighteenth century, capones were active in Spanish churches even though castrati were no longer performing on the stage.[49] Repudiation of castrati was all the rage in Enlightenment writings of the 1780s, with authors writing variously about effeminacy, mutilation, immorality, or artificiality.[50] Among this variety of accusations against castrati, "Discourse 97" is only concerned with artificiality. Because the discourse's author believed capones to be word-uttering machines, their voices rank low in his epistemological hierarchy, where the fine arts are closer to nature than the mechanical ones.[51] We must remember that many of the awe-inspiring androids of the late eighteenth century played music, confirming the suspicions of authors such as Simplicio Greco y Lira that music performance could

---

[46] The mechanical and the marvelous were two enemies of naturalist neoclassicism. Eighteenth-century neoclassicist reforms of theater in Spain abhorred baroque spectacle as much as Charles III's government chastised superstition. Neoclassicists bashed all unrealistic theater components, including the saints, devils, and angels in the older, traditional autos sacramentales, not to mention the newer, popular *comedias de magia* full of special effects and stage machinery. (After José Clavijo y Fajardo campaigned to end public performance of autos sacramentales, Charles III in 1765 ratified Ferdinand VI's ban).

[47] "Entre nosotros pasan por voces exquisitas las que no lo son según la naturaleza: la voz de un capón no es voz humana, es sólo un instrumento que pronuncia palabras." "Discurso XCVII," 538.

[48] Some Spanish capones obtained positions at the papal chapel in Rome, as is the case of Francisco Soto de Langa (ca. 1534–1619). Boys were still being castrated by the end of the eighteenth century, although the practice was more infrequent than in the seventeenth century: Ángel Medina, *Los atributos del capón: Imagen histórica de los cantores castrados en España*, Música Hispana Textos. Estudios. (Madrid: ICCMU, 2001), 50ff.

[49] Through Cavaza's *El músico censor*, we know that the Catholic Church allowed capones to become priests, possibly because most church singers were ordained or took at least minor orders anyway.

[50] Martha Feldman, "Denaturing the Castrato," *Opera Quarterly* 24, no. 3–4 (2008): 179.

[51] "Discurso XCVII," 538.

48 *Music and Modernity in Enlightenment Spain*

be quite literally mechanized.[52] Simplicio Greco y Lira proposes using young boys' voices instead of castrati to sing treble lines, a solution to that makes no sense in opera but befits music chapels.[53]

In addition to opposing hiring of capones, "Discourse 97"'s author denounces cathedrals that seek out "brawny" chant leaders (sochantres) and choir singers who "make the vaults shudder with their tremendous gushes [of voice]." Phrases such as "large voice" and "bulky voice" were used in contemporary cathedral records to describe desirable candidates to the choir, so this type of singer was not a figment of Simplicio Greco y Lira's imagination. Church choirs were conducted by the sochantre, who intoned all plainchant, led polyphony, and could also teach choirboys. Hence, cathedral chapters often voted in favor of a loud voice that could be heard throughout the temple building over an otherwise pleasant but smaller voice.[54] For Simplicio Greco y Lira, voices that impressed for their volume sounded as mechanical as those that impressed for their skill. They may be extraordinary, but they are not natural. In fact, they are unnatural precisely because they are extraordinary. Greco y Lira further recommends that churches invest the money spent on the salaries of castrati and chant leaders elsewhere. A choir of monks, he suggests, could be heard just as well as one loud singer, with the added benefit that in a choir, distinct vocal timbres are blended such that no soloist commands attention to their skill. His concerns over capones mirror those of another antiestablishment writer of the Spanish Enlightenment, poet and satirist León de Arroyal (1755–1813). Arroyal rejects capones as one of many luxury items in the personal and social lives of the many clergymen who held positions in cathedral choirs. Like "Discourse 97"'s author, Arroyal complains that loud voices render cathedrals sites to "exercise the lung" rather than places of divine worship.[55]

In "Discourse 97"'s perspectives on music, European concerns regarding musical aesthetics overlap with national practices.[56] Most Italian and French authors debating over ancient and modern music focused on the issue of opera, since the genre weighed heavily in the collective identity of both nations. In

---

[52] Among the various music-playing androids were La musicienne (harpsichord) by Pierre and Henri-Louis Jaquet-Droz, 1772–1774, and La joueuse de timpanon (dulcimer) by David Roentgen and Peter Kinzing, 1785. See Adelheid Voskuhl, *Androids in the Enlightenment: Mechanics, Artisans, and Cultures of the Self* (Chicago: University of Chicago Press, 2013).

[53] "Discurso XCVII," 538–39.

[54] Leza, *La música en el siglo XVIII*, 47. See also Medina, *Los atributos del capón*, 118–20. The loudness and resonance of the singing voice was crucial in the admission of some chapel positions, such as the sochantre.

[55] Medina, *Los atributos del capón*, 56.

[56] As Alberto Hernández Mateos has observed, "the context in which debates on music theory happen in Spain rarely exceeds the limits of music chapels, so that ideas do not usually refer to secular music or transcend into the civic society sphere." Alberto Hernández Mateos, *El pensamiento musical de Antonio Eximeno* (Salamanca: Ediciones Universidad de Salamanca, 2013), 178.

Spain, however, ecclesiastical music chapels held a monopoly over music education and theory, that is to say, over musical knowledge. Chapel masters and organists selected older pieces for performance, composed new ones, managed boys' musical education, and judged musicians' skills for admission exams and promotions. They also wrote theoretical and pedagogical treatises and justified musical decisions for the approval of church or civil authorities. Traditional music theory's intellectual apparatus, tied to music's mathematical paradigm, had its operating counterpart in music chapels.

In terms of texts and treatises available for musicians to study, the many "Artes de canto llano y figurado" published throughout the century recycled the same principles found in Pablo Nassarre's *Fragmentos músicos* (1683) in its 1700 expanded edition by the Royal Chapel master José de Torres. These *artes de canto* of various lengths constituted the core of textbooks for singers and instrumentalists, and they typically included a section on plainchant and one or more sections on *canto de órgano* or counterpoint, with notated examples for musicians to practice.[57] Manuel Cavaza himself handwrote one such singing manual in 1754, with the breathless title "The Instructed Singer or Thus Relieved Teacher in This Noblest Profession's Difficult Principles. With All That a Singer Must Know according to the Modern and Latest Style Laid Out with Practical Examples That Explain It for the Student's Greater Understanding."[58] When Cavaza wrote "The Instructed Singer" in the mid-eighteenth century, the modern style was Italian recitative and aria da capo with basso continuo, as opposed to the ancient style of polyphonic counterpoint. The manual was intended for chapel singers. As was customary, each chapter of "The Instructed Singer" introduces one topic, for example, hexachordal mutation. The chapter presents an explanation illustrated with musical examples or tables followed by a series of questions and answers between a disciple and his master to review the topic. While this structure is common to other singing manuals, Cavaza already shows in his early work an acute awareness of the differences between Spanish and foreign musical practices. This awareness would resurface more than thirty years later in *El músico censor* and in a second manuscript manual titled "Rudiments and Elements of Practical Music" (1786), both written amid the heat of the apologista movement.[59] In "Rudiments and Elements" Cavaza

---

[57] Francisco León Tello lists over thirty treatises on plainchant and figured chant produced during the eighteenth century: Francisco José León Tello, *La teoría española de la música en los siglos XVII Y XVIII* (Madrid: Consejo Superior de Investigaciones Científicas, Instituto Español de Musicología, 1974).

[58] Manuel Cavaza, "El cantor instruido o Maestro aliviado assi en los difíciles principios de esta nobilísima professión como en todo lo que un cantor debe saber según el moderno y último estilo, dispuesto con exemplos prácticos, que lo declaran para mayor inteligencia del que estudia," ca. 1754, Biblioteca Histórica de la Universidad Complutense.

[59] "Rudimentos y elementos de la música práctica escrita," 1786, Biblioteca Nacional de España.

relied on the same principles of his 1754 "The Instructed Singer," reasserting the Guidonian hexachordal solmization, or Spanish method, as the right way to teach music to choirboys.

Most Spanish music theory authors recognized a professional division between maestros (*profesores*) and practitioners, corresponding respectively to the knowledge branches of speculative and practical music. While all maestros needed to demonstrate their technical skills, not all practitioners were expected to be fluent in theoretical knowledge. Even a conservative musician like Manuel Cavaza recognized the difference between theory and practice and admitted that the challenges of counterpoint and polychoral compositions belonged in the category of "artificious music," which was appropriate for training and examination purposes "but not for public use."[60] To be credentialed as a *profesor de música* in eighteenth-century Spain required mastery of the canon of past centuries' music theorists.[61] In his *Diapasón instructivo* from 1757, Antonio Rodríguez de Hita lists the theorists profesores de música should know: Pietro Cerone (*El melopeo y maestro*, 1613), Francisco de Montanos (*Arte de música teórica y práctica*, 1592; edited and expanded in 1648 and again in 1734), Andrés Llorente (*El porqué de la música*, 1672), and Pablo Nassarre (*Fragmentos músicos*, 1683, ed. José de Torres 1700; *Escuela música según la práctica moderna*, 1723–1724). Rodríguez de Hita admits that few maestros have studied the treatises he recommends and wishes they would read d'Alembert's *Élemens de la musique*, which he erroneously attributes to Rameau. Rodríguez de Hita bemoans that profesores de música "do not read the first [the traditional authors], and since Rameau is in French, the musicians are left without any books to study."[62]

When *El Censor*'s "Discourse 97" was published in 1786, the gap between modern demands and the centuries-old apparatus of ecclesiastical chapels had widened to a point where practice and theory struggled to coexist. On the one hand, the chapels' music pedagogy ecosystem revolved around plainchant, counterpoint study, and the hexachordal system. On the other hand, musicians had to be fluent in the galant style to play newer church repertory and also to take part in the multiple gigs that supplemented their salary. The gap between the education provided by chapels and the everyday professional demands was especially pronounced for composers and instrumentalists making a living in cities like Madrid or Cádiz, with active theaters and noble houses that regularly called for freelance musicians. Each civic or private event could require several musical performances such as a Mass, matins, or vespers, a procession, serenades, chamber music, orchestral pieces, cantatas, oratorios, and musical theater, thus requiring that musicians master a gamut of techniques.

---

[60]   Cavaza, *El músico censor*, 131–32.

[61]   In addition to mastery of technical skills such as points of imitation (*pasos*) and polychorality, required in chapel exams.

[62]   Rodríguez de Hita, *Diapasón instructivo*, 4–5.

In the 1770s and 1780s, new writings penned by critics offered an alternative approach to musical knowledge, one that blurred the division between *profesores* and practitioners by suggesting that musicians were artists and thinkers. The author of *El Censor*'s "Discourse 97" proposes a "musician-philosopher," expecting all musicians to approach their art not from the mathematical paradigm but from the verbal one. If music was an art closely tied to poetry, Simplicio Greco y Lira reasoned, then the musician must rise to poet-philosopher's status. This musician-philosopher would elevate music from techné to an art "reduced to the same principle" as all the other fine arts. "Discourse 97" (1786) of the journal *El Censor* is exceptional because music criticism in the Spanish press of the 1780s–1790s is mostly subsumed under theater criticism. Compared to theater criticism, aesthetic or "philosophical" debates about music were scant. For example, "Discourse 97" was published a decade before the exiled Jesuit Antonio Eximeno's aesthetic treatise *Delle origine e regole della musica* (1774) came to public attention via its 1796 Spanish translation. Likewise, Esteban de Arteaga's 1783 *Le rivoluzioni del teatro musicale italiano* (Bologna) only reached Spanish journals six years later in 1789. The only Spain-produced text about music to circulate widely in the 1780s was Iriarte's poem *La música* (1779). Still, Iriarte's poem is more didactic reflection than criticism. "Discourse 97," on the contrary, questions general practices and theories of music, focusing on those of music chapels, which pervaded Spanish musicianship.

Eximeno and Arteaga also advocated for an epistemological change in how music was taught and practiced in society. Eximeno sneered at the music chapels' *profesores* in his didactic novel *Don Lazarillo Vizcardi*, written during the very early 1800s and published posthumously in 1872. In the novel, elderly maestro Agapito Quitóles loses his mind while reading Nassarre and Cerone, the two emblems of Spanish music theory. Eximeno's disdain for old-school professional musicians had already surfaced in his *Dell'origine* (1774), where he toys with writing the adventures of a quixotic maestro named Pandolfo "who from being a weaver and local organist, came to be chapel master." Eximeno seems to have conceived the fictional character Pandolfo to parody traditional musicians who received *Dell'origine* with suspicion because it debunked music's mathematical paradigm.[63]

Arteaga further clarifies the role of the musician-philosopher in society and the traps of techné. Like Simplicio Greco y Lira and others, he argues that musi-

---

[63] The characters in *Don Lazarillo Vizcardi* personify the clash between the old mathematical paradigm and the new verbal paradigm of musical knowledge that played out in the earlier controversy between "Discourse 97"'s author and Cavaza. The novel's plot narrates a competition for a chapel master position in an imaginary Spanish city. The character Cándido Raponso represents the school of intricate counterpoint competing against Narciso Ribelles, who represents Eximeno's stance that music has nothing to do with numbers and everything to do with language. Hernández Mateos, *El pensamiento musical de Antonio Eximeno*, 40.

cians were also poets, singers, legislators, and philosophers in ancient Greece. Arteaga thinks that in modern times these functions have separated, so each of them is less capable of shaping society. Poets and musicians who are fettered by their craft's technical aspects no longer have political or civic influence. Consequently, Arteaga concludes, social musical practices such as theater are licentious and superficial, lacking the pathos that "should be the great end of all representational arts." Because it is capable of more complex sounds, modern music is less moving than ancient music. Modern music's complexity comes from counterpoint, the extended instrumental ranges, smaller rhythmic subdivisions, and the "weakening [of] the voice from making it subtle (*subtilize*)" in order to sing the many ornaments of operatic arias. The more complex music becomes, Arteaga warns, the more it abandons its imitative purpose and the less emotional impact it has.[64] Therefore, he concludes, simplicity is the only way to return to the kind of philosophical music that improves society and guides the nation, which is the same premise behind "Discourse 97."

Polemics surrounding the nature of musical knowledge and musicians' professional status arose in other parts of Europe, such as Italy. Since these reforms had real-life consequences on the status of musicians, counterarguments frequently ensued. A little-known work from 1785 by Neapolitan Saverio Mattei titled *Se i maestri di cappella son compresi fra gli artesani* debates the issue of musicians' professional status. Mattei was hired as the defense lawyer for a chapel master named Cordella, who went to court demanding payment for a late-delivered commission. The judge ruled in his favor based on a legal clause applicable to lawyers, spice merchants, artisans, and servants. Given that Cordella was not a lawyer, spice merchant, or servant, Mattei deduced that the judge considered the chapel master an artisan, thus demoting Cordella from philosopher to artisan. According to Mattei, this demotion affected the Neapolitan nation because it denigrated musicians' contributions to civil society. Mattei thought chapel musicians were useful to society at large in fulfilling the role of the musician-philosopher: "The serenity of the spirit and the nowadays so-praised sensitivity of the human heart depend on the chapel master."[65] *Se i maestri di cappella* exemplifies an effort to recast existing musical institutions and practices.

In all fairness, by the end of the century, oboist Cavaza represented the old guard, but he was neither an isolated case nor the last author to cling to traditional music theory. The polemics unleashed by the Spanish translation of Eximeno's *Dell'origine delle regole della musica* in 1796 resurrected points

---

[64] Arteaga, *Le rivoluzioni*, 179–85.

[65] Saverio Mattei, *Se i maestri di cappella son compresi fra gli artigiani, probole di Saverio Mattei, in occasione d'una tassa di fatiche domandata dal maestro Cordella* (Naples: G. M. Porcelli, 1785). Mattei's justification for philosophical music is based on the scriptural description of ancient Hebrew prophets and kings (Saul, David, Solomon) as musicians.

of contention between "Discourse 97"'s author and Cavaza. As late as 1802, Agustín Iranzo y Herrero printed his *Defense of the Art of Music, Its True Rules, and Chapel Masters* to refute the nonmusician Eximeno. As Cavaza did with "Discourse 97"'s author, Iranzo y Herrero accuses Eximeno of knowing less music "than those artists [who are] well instructed in their craft," shifting once more the emphasis to the skill in the craft of music and the protection of chapel musicians from outsiders' criticism.

Professional musicians like Cavaza feared for their reputations, salaries, and careers if the Spanish newspapers started publishing music criticism. They worried that the public would side with the critics. Therefore, they needed to concretely distinguish musical knowledge from criticism. Over dozens of pages, Cavaza is at pains to disqualify "Discourse 97"'s author as an outsider inferior to music professors. Becoming a profesor de música took years of training and climbing up the chapels' hierarchy, years that professional musicians were not willing to have jeopardized by the pen of self-appointed critics. Cavaza had been a member of Madrid's Royal Chapel for nearly fifty years, which put him in the upper ranks of the hierarchy, next to chapel masters and organists, even though he was an oboist. He had thorough insider knowledge of the chapel system and of the music theory behind it. Cavaza may have been an old-style chapel maestro, but he was no fool. Abandoning counterpoint like "Discourse 97"'s author and others demanded required altering the entire formative process of choirboys as well as the examination system and, therefore, the hierarchy of position in the chapels. Musicians protested the critics' indifference toward the profession's practical matters. For their part, critics opposed the musicians' resistance to modern European musical theories and practices.

Even though modern music (Italianate or otherwise) was practiced throughout Spain both in secular and sacred contexts, it lacked theoretical justification and institutional support. Chamber music remained a private affair. Musical theater was incorporated into the public discourse about national theater that the intellectual class and the government had been developing for decades. Due to the public nature of the city theaters, everybody had something to say about the theater, in the form of edicts, books, and street jokes. Yet theater music was somehow not considered music proper. Besides the meager formal training and music literacy of theater singers, the fact that women were the public face of the musical stage left little room for them to be taken seriously as musicians.

Critics versus Musical Theater:
Pablo Esteve's *El teatro y los actores agraviados*

Composers for the theater and actor-singers endured the same woes of criticism that afflicted chapel musicians. Composers could be trained in the chapel system when young but made a livelihood as theater contractors by the year

Music and Modernity in Enlightenment Spain

and fulfilling private commissions. Lacking formal training, actor-singers often learned their craft through familial ties to cities' theaters, be it Madrid, Barcelona, Cádiz, Seville, or any other major urban enclave. Their yearly contracts depended on their reputations and their success with audiences. Their livelihood hinged on public acceptance much more than that of chapel musicians. Consequently, like Cavaza, they felt alarmed when criticism of musical theater escalated in the 1780s, thanks to a boom in the press. A 1787 trio tonadilla by theater-employed composer Pablo Esteve, titled the *El teatro y los actores agraviados*, illustrates well the feud between theater performers and critics. The tonadilla attests to the material ways in which modernization disrupted social life, more specifically, how changes in the balance of oral and written media subverted the communication channels that structured society.

Critics discussed theater performers much more frequently than they discussed chapel musicians. While the polemic between "Discourse 97"'s author and Cavaza's *El músico censor* took place entirely in print, theater artists more often replied to printed criticism viva voce from the stage. Critics routinely rejected the repertory programmed in Madrid's theaters, pushing instead for more decorous shows that adhered to neoclassical aesthetic ideals. These ideals can be summarized into observing the unity of time, place, and action, and showcasing edifying, civilized behavior on stage, stripped from the impropriety or barbarism of Spanish traditional genres such as the autos sacramentales or the *comedia de figurón*. Confrontations between critics and theater staff began in the 1760s with exchanges between journalist Francisco Mariano Nipho and *costumbrista* playwright Ramón de la Cruz. While all aspects of theater performance were subject to scrutiny, short genres such as sainetes and tonadillas especially attracted the ire of neoclassicists because such forms consistently strayed from the classical unities and contravened decorum. These forms' comedic tone, underclass characters, colloquialisms, music, and dancing all offended intellectual elites wishing to modernize public entertainment according to the cosmopolitan standards of opera houses or the Comédie-Française. Dissatisfied playwrights, composers, and performers used sainetes and stage tonadillas to express their disagreements with critics.

The following excerpt from *El teatro y los actores agraviados*'s introduction shows to what extent theater managers, playwrights, composers, and performers resented the critics' obtrusive discourse:[66]

(Josefa:) Tal turba de censores	(Josefa:) Such a mob of censors
se han levantado,	has arisen
que a sátiras destruyen	who throwing satires
nuestros teatros	destroy our theaters

---

[66] Pablo Esteve, "El teatro y los actores agraviados," tonadilla, 1787, Parte de apuntar, BHM Mus 146-3.

(Garrido:) Pues diles, si murmuran	(All three:) Well, if they spread rumors
de mis bobadas,	about my goofiness,
si sus apologías	ask them if their apologies
tienen más gracia	are any funnier

Musically, the quick, ornamented seguidilla style Esteve chose to set "the mob of censors" in this passage (example 1.1) conveys the indignation and flustering of the actors.

The short passage indexes a few issues pitching performers against critics. First, criticism is on the rise, so that performers perceive a "mob of censors" surrounding them, censors meaning journal critics in this case. Second, journalistic criticism is destroying Madrid's theaters by satirizing productions and theater staff. Third, critics are "sayers" who spread rumors about "doers," the theater composers, playwrights, and performers but cannot produce plays to entertain audiences.

The Rising Presence of Press Criticism

Confrontations between performers and critics intensified in the late 1780s because the Spanish periodical press was booming. It was only in the eighteenth century's last two decades that Spain was rocked by the "journalistic wave" sweeping across Europe.[67] Earlier journalistic undertakings such as Francisco Mariano Nipho's *Diario Noticioso* (starting in 1758, later *Diario de Madrid*) and *Cajón de Sastre* (1762), and José Clavijo y Fajardo's weekly *El Pensador* (1763–1767) waned because civil and ecclesiastical authorities had effectively monopolized the press, leaving private journals little room to prosper.[68] Spanish editors and readers were not ready to consolidate press activ-

---

[67] Elisabel Larriba, *Le public de la presse en Espagne à la fin du XVIIIe siècle (1781–1808)*, Bibliothèque de littérature générale et comparée (Paris: Honoré Champion, 1998); Paul-J. Guinard, *La presse espagnole de 1737 à 1791, formation et signification d'un genre*, Thèses, mémoires et travaux, 22 (Paris: Centre de recherches hispaniques, Institut d'études hispaniques, 1973), 219–20. Larriba's study of the Spanish press from 1781 to 1808 continues the inquiries of Paul Guinard about the period from 1737 to 1791. Joaquín Álvarez Barrientos supports this perspective: "Periodicals as literary vehicles appeared in Spain on the second half of the eighteenth century, when they had been around in the rest of Europe for several decades" ("El periodista," 30).

[68] *El Pensador* was published in 1762–1763 and 1767 by the press of Joaquín Ibarra. *Cajón de sastre, o montón de muchas cosas* was published weekly in 1760–1791 by the press of Gabriel Ramírez. Also from the 1760s are *El Belianis Literario*, edited by Juan López Sedano in 1765, and *Semanario Económico*, created by Pedro Araus in 1765. Madrid had two official periodicals: the *Gaceta de Madrid* and the *Mercurio Histórico y Político*. Unofficial newspapers "practically disappeared" after the Esquilache Riots in 1766: Francisco Sánchez-Blanco, *El absolutismo y las Luces en el reinado de Carlos III* (Madrid: M. Pons, 2002), 303.

Example 1.1. Introduction, second musical number, *El teatro y los actores agraviados*, bars 89–133.

—(continued)

Example 1.1—concluded

ity until 1781 when production shifted from state or church patronage to a subscription-based market. This shift in funding, along with reduced postal rates, left newspapers and journals with enough resources to generate their own reading public and influence collective opinions.[69] At least ten new periodicals launched publication in the 1780s, including *El Censor*.[70] By the end of the 1780s, enough journals and newspapers circulated in Madrid to foster a multidirectional conversation among editors, the reading public, and theater audiences and performers.[71] Even though the first journal devoted to music would be published in Madrid only in the mid-nineteenth century, the flourishing of the press toward the end of the eighteenth century fostered early attempts at music criticism, out of which emerged music critics' voices as distinct from those of performers and composers.[72]

---

[69] Guinard thinks that subscriptions increased in the 1780s because postal rates decreased, and he interprets the lower prices as a short-lived state effort to encourage printed press. Guinard, *La presse espagnole*, 66–68.

[70] Modeled after Addison and Steele's *The Spectator*, El Censor was published between 1781–1787. The *Correo Literario de la Europa* was likely edited by Francisco Antonio Escartín y Carrera and published weekly by the office of Hilario Santos Alonso between 1781 and 1787. Joaquín Ezquerra and Pedro Pablo Trullenc initiated the *Memorial Literario, Instructivo y Curioso de la Corte de Madrid*, issued mostly between 1784 and 1787, and biweekly between 1787 and 1790, published by the Imprenta Real. Antonio de Manegat edited the *Correo de los Ciegos de Madrid*, biweekly between 1786 and 1790, and weekly from 1790 until February 1791. The *Diario Curioso, Erudito, Económico y Comercial* was edited by French book merchant Jacques (Santiago) Thevin as a continuation of the one launched by Nipho in 1758. It was published daily during 1786–1787 by the press of Manuel González, changing titles to *Diario de Madrid* starting on 1788 (the *Diario* had suspended publication between 1781 and 1786). Closest in spirit to *El Censor* and nemesis to apologista Juan Pablo Forner, Pedro Centeno and Joaquín Ezquerra published only a few articles in the sixteen issues of *El Apologista Universal* between 1786 and 1788 (a single issue of *El Corresponsal del Apologista* responded to *El Apologista* in 1786). Cristóbal Cladera oversaw the *Espíritu de los Mejores Diarios Literarios que se Publican en Europa*, initially published three times per week and later weekly between 1787 and 1791 by the José Herrera press. Antonio Valladares de Sotomayor edited *Semanario Erudito* between 1787 and 1791, printed by Blas Román. *El Corresponsal del Censor* was edited by Manuel Rubín de Celis y Noriega and published between 1786 and 1788. *El Observador* was also printed for the first time in 1787.

[71] For a detailed breakdown of subscribers to periodicals see Larriba, *Le public de la presse*.

[72] Jacinto Torres Mulas disagrees with previous consensus that the first Spanish periodical devoted to music was *La Iberia Musical*, founded by Mariano Soriano Fuertes in Madrid in 1842. Torres Mulas thinks other musical journals were in circulation since at least 1830 (*El Nuevo Anfión*) or 1834 (*La* [nueva] *Lira de Apolo, El Eco de la Opera*): "Music Periodicals in Spain: Beginnings and Historical Development," *Fontes Artis Musicae* 44, no. 4 (1997): 336.

60   *Music and Modernity in Enlightenment Spain*

Theater and the press were natural rivals. Theater shows in major Spanish cities like Madrid and Cádiz fulfilled a similar role to newspapers: they succinctly presented information in ways that the public could easily relate to.[73] Unlike books, journals improved public accessibility to cultural conversations thanks to their relative brevity and their topical treatment of events. Even those unaccustomed to reading could handle an eight-page *Correo de los Ciegos* issue. Newspapers such as the *Correo de los Ciegos* explicitly sought to digest information for a general readership. The *Correo*'s main goal was "the vulgarization of educational information," or the translation of European scientific and literary knowledge into a format legible to its readers. The newspaper's educational thrust thus equipped publishers with the capacity to start conversations within the middle- and upper-class populace. Wealthy Madrileños purchased subscriptions to one or more journals, but anybody could buy single issues at bookstores and bookstands in very public spots, like the Plaza del Sol. Newspapers could be performed when read aloud for family, friends, or passersby on the street. In sum, the public that periodical publications reached traversed multiple urban social sectors.[74] The proliferation of periodicals increased public exposure to literature and ideas from beyond national borders and generated a sufficiently large reading public that these ideas permeated into everyday life. As public access to diverse ideas increased exponentially, knowledge became more fluid and fragmentary, if not fully democratized. Periodicals began to compete with other communication media such as theater, edicts, sermons, books, and conversations.

Newspapers' power to popularize ideas was paralleled in musical theater, which also sought to engage the public by influencing opinion. Oral communication, especially the theater, extended and expanded the written word. In fact, theater reached a broader and more diverse audience than newspapers did. In 1795, the editors of the *Correo de Cádiz* compared the relative impacts of the press and the theater:

> Out of one hundred people, we can establish that ninety-five form the public; readers do not account for three percent. According to these numbers, the public would be tiny; but it is not, for in those three readers out of a hundred are included those who form their own opinion and make those who do not read do the same; and hence they bring publicity up to the number of ninety-five [percent]. *Every one man that reads speaks his mind before a family, and a man or a woman in a theater can*

---

[73]   For a succinct summary of periodical press publications in and beyond Madrid, and their connection to theater criticism, see Francisco Aguilar Piñal, *Introducción al siglo XVIII*, ed. Ricardo de la Fuente, Historia de la Literatura Española (Madrid: Júcar, 1991), 152–57.

[74]   Peter B. Goldman, "Dramatic Works and Their Readership in 18th-Century Spain—Social Stratification and the Middle Classes," *Bulletin of Hispanic Studies* 66, no. 2 (1989): 130.

shape the opinion of a couple of thousand people in a few minutes. In this public are found all professions, all interests, all views, and all needs for progress.[75]

Theater and press complemented each other and vied for public attention, while members of the theater and press also feared exposure to the same public's uninformed judgments.

The analogy between criticism and theater as two media channels for the formation of public opinion is particularly noticeable in stage tonadillas. Theater composers were expected to write up to sixty-two new tonadillas per year because the genre had recently shifted from comic musical miscellanea to satire, functioning like criticism of mores. Since tonadillas from the 1780s and 1790s were mainly intended to criticize social mores, they needed to stay current, like newspapers.[76] Hence, tonadillas were less permanent than long-format plays, comparable to newspapers and journals' ephemerality when juxtaposed to books. Whereas the city theaters regularly staged century-old comedias from the Spanish Golden Age due to their popularity, tonadillas had a shorter shelf life.[77] Furthermore, because authors of tonadilla lyrics were largely anonymous, the views they expressed could more readily belong to the community rather than to a specific individual.[78] Parallels notwithstanding, tonadilla transmission was almost exclusively oral, while newspapers relied on print for their existence—keeping in mind that press "readership" also included those who listened to news being read aloud.

---

[75]   *Correo de Cádiz*, February 3, 1795, issues no. 1, 2. Quoted by Elisabel Larriba, *El público de la prensa en España a finales del siglo XVIII (1781–1808)*, trans. Daniel Gascón, Ciencias sociales (Zaragoza: Prensas de la Universidad de Zaragoza, 2013), 4. Emphasis mine.

[76]   Begoña Lolo sees in the tonadilla "an element to disseminate the frenzy of new events, a journalistic newscast of sorts to bear witness to the demands of the actor-singers and the world of theater itself, to the setbacks or successes of businesses, to romantic customs and the convenience of courtships ... and endless topics that settled naturally in the music and verses of this kind of lyrical theater, with great popular acceptance." "Itinerarios musicales en la tonadilla escénica," in *Paisajes sonoros en el Madrid del S. XVIII: La tonadilla escénica*, edited by Museo de San Isidro (Madrid: Museo de San Isidro, 2003), 16–20.

[77]   For an analysis of the reception of Spanish Golden Age theater in the eighteenth century, see René Andioc, *Teatro y sociedad en el Madrid del siglo XVIII* (Madrid: Fundación Juan March, 1976), chap. 1.

[78]   Nonetheless, some of the best-known writers of the second half of the eighteenth century authored tonadillas. Begoña Lolo names Luciano and Joaquina Comella, Ramón de la Cruz, Tomás de iriarte, Luis Moncín, Sebastián Vázquez, Gaspar de Zavala y Zamora, Vicente Rodríguez de Arellano, and Manuel Fermín Laviano, among others. In the 1780s–1790s, coliseo head composers wrote many of the lyrics of tonadillas as part of their annual contracts, given that otherwise they had to pay librettists out of pocket. Lolo, "Itinerarios," 17.

62   *Music and Modernity in Enlightenment Spain*

Whether to print tonadilla lyrics for public access remained undecided. Both critics and composers knew that printing lyrics would make tonadillas more indelible. In the end, the vast majority of tonadillas existed only as manuscripts possessed by theater libraries and as libretti submitted to censors for authorization. Therefore, the tonadilla critics relied solely on memory or third-person accounts of the performance. This lack of printed libretti may explain the scarcity of tonadilla reviews. Tonadillas' impermanence frustrated newspaper authors and composers who feared that critics and audiences would misinterpret their lyrics. Laserna and his collaborators noted this frustration in a 1795 prospectus for the never-realized *Espíritu del teatro*, a journal he planned to devote to theater and music criticism:

> If the drama were set to music, the lyrics of those arias, rondos, etc. with precepts or singularities worthy of attention, will be offered in advance, as will be the lyrics of tonadillas, which most of the time fail to generate in the audience the intended feelings because their intelligence is robbed, slipping past the composer's endeavors, by imprecise notes, or the obscure pronunciation of actors.[79]

Conversely, access to tonadilla texts could also give critics the upper hand over composers and performers. In 1787 the editors of the *Correo de los Ciegos* asked the mayor of Madrid, José de Armona, to provide the texts of the tonadillas and sainetes performed at La Cruz and El Príncipe "with the purpose of expanding moral satire, which will result in the benefit of the audience, and will be useful to [theater] companies." The managers of the city's two coliseos protested that the *Correo* editors intended to profit from selling the texts of tonadillas. Managers Eusebio Ribera and Manuel Martínez further argued that once audiences could read the lyrics, they would stop attending the theater, or worse, they would count on too many arguments to criticize the performers. Ribera and Martínez claimed to act in the performers' best interests. The performers, their bosses said, would suffer at the expense of an excessively informed audience. The printed texts would stifle the novelty of theater, and "any blind man singing on a corner would claim to be better than the actors."[80] The Madrid theater companies have done well, the managers said, without the

---

[79] "Cuando el drama fuere en música se anticipará la letra de aquellas arias, rondoes, etc. que contengan sentencia o particularidad digna de atención, y asimismo la de las tonadillas que las más veces no producen en el público la sensación que debieran a causa de robarles su inteligencia, burlando el esmero del compositor, la precisión de los tonos, o la oscura pronunciación de los actores." Excerpt from the 1795 petition, published in María José Rodríguez Sánchez de León, "Tres intentos fracasados de publicar una revista de teatros (1795, 1802 y 1804)," in *El siglo que llaman ilustrado: Homenaje a Francisco Aguilar Piñal*, edited by José Checa Beltrán (Madrid: Consejo Superior de Investigaciones Científicas, 1996).

[80] Francisco Asenjo Barbieri, "Carta de Martínez y Rivera a Don Juan Laví y Zavala," 1787, Biblioteca Nacional de España.

new enlightened editors (*ilustrados editores*). The managers sensed that the press critics interfered with the success of theater employees and defended them accordingly.

Press Criticism and Defamation

Tonadillas were vital to the rapport between theater artists and the public in late eighteenth-century Madrid because many tonadillas directly addressed the public and the constant rotation of tonadillas kept patrons coming back to the theater.[81] There are testimonies that audiences came to the theater to hear tonadillas rather than the main play. But what happened when newspapers started printing theater reviews? Whereas before the theater staff interacted directly with the public, now a third party, the critic, wanted to set the rules of the game. Tonadilla writers and performers strongly reacted against the critics' interference in their relationship with the Madrid audiences.

The materiality of the printed word made modernization palpable in late eighteenth-century Spain. *El teatro y los actores agraviados* begins with acclaimed comic actor and singer Miguel Garrido pacing the stage; holding "newspapers, censors, and papers"; and singing a two-section solo.[82] What Garrido sang when the awaited tonadilla started shows that he, like Cavaza in his response to "Discourse 97," felt pilloried by critics.

De quantos papelotes	Of the many papers
hoy los críticos sacan	that critics issue today
todos sobre los teatros	all of them on the theaters
todos descargan	all of them unload [their weapons]
Actores y comedias	Actors and plays
los muerden y los rajan	they bite and tear
y todo se critica	and everything is criticized
con furia y rabia	with fury and rage
Paciencia, Garrido, mas paciencia no	Patience, Garrido … but no patience!
que callar no quiero	For I do not want to remain silent
a tanto baldón	before such ignominy
Teman mi venganza,	Fear my revenge,

---

[81] Theater staff included actor-singers, composers, one musician (to support or cover for the composer), prompters, ticket clerks, coat-check attendants, and company managers. While playwrights were not part of the payroll, they also formed part of the public face of theater.

[82] Miguel Garrido started working on the Madrid stages in 1773, and by 1800 he was still active. He tried to retire in 1791 because he was sick and lacked most of his teeth, but the Junta denied him retirement. Barbieri, *Papeles Barbieri*, vol. 12, 345; vol. 14, 135.

teman mi furor	fear my frenzy
esos escritores	Those newly-appeared
que han salido hoy	writers
Críticos satíricos	Satirical critics
que sin compasión	(that) without compassion
a todos ultraja	Everybody is insulted
su murmuración	with their murmuration

The stage direction about Garrido holding newspapers confirms printed paper's symbolic value as a metonym for criticism. Abstract philosophical knowledge suddenly took the concrete form of a newspaper that jeopardized the profession of the theater singer.

Garrido's opening verses foreground the common perception that critics slandered (*ultrajar*) theater makers. Ubiquitous in cultural debates found in the press, the blurred line between philosophical criticism and mere bad-mouthing can be understood through Spain's legal history of reputation. Consider the value of honor and reputation in Spanish culture since the Middle Ages. Because hearsay carried judicial weight, rumors criticizing a person were serious matters. This legal tradition dates to at least the thirteenth-century statutory code *Las Siete Partidas*, the seventh of which acknowledges hidalgos' right to duel upon being accused a liar. By the sixteenth century, accusations of infamy required formal legal evidence, but they still began with mere words.[83] The stakes of oral testimony about others' reputation were life-and-death. For example, if the Inquisition accused someone of heresy, their neighbors and family were called to testify to the individual's character. If one of them reported to have heard rumors of the accused's dubious reputation, imprisonment or even a death sentence could follow. This historical lineage of the vital stakes of reputation informs composers' and performers' experience of journalistic criticism as a grave insult to their persons and their profession.

El teatro y los actores agraviados gives evidence that critics were easily regarded as agents of defamation in late eighteenth-century Spain. In the passage above, Garrido indistinctly refers to criticism as murmuration because he (and Esteve, together with possibly all the performers) perceived journalistic criticism as gossip aiming at destroying others' reputations. Shared by many Spaniards at the time, this conception of criticism stemmed from medieval and Renaissance ideas of *fama*. Reputation bore legal weight in medieval Spain, and even after the legal consequences of a bad reputation disappeared, criticism continued to be understood as harmful defamation. Cavaza, too, saw *El Censor's* "Discourse 97" as defamation of professional musicians. Even legislation subscribed to the defamatory view of criticism. For example, in 1785, Charles III approved the right to sue "any kind of printed work" attacking a person's reputation and

---

[83] Marta Madero, "El duellum entre la honra y la prueba según las Siete partidas de Alfonso X y el comentario de Gregorio López," *Cahiers d'Études Hispaniques Médiévales* 24 (2001): 343–52.

Right header: *Critics versus Musicians* 65

to demand a public retraction.[84] According to the edict, complainants should present their grievances to the *juez de imprentas* (print judge), who regulated printing presses and settled conflicts among booksellers, printers, and authors. The boom of the periodical press in the 1780s prompted regulations of this kind, bringing a modern twist to the centuries-old affair of defamation.

Esteve wanted *El teatro y los actores agraviados* to communicate to audiences how much theater makers felt defamed by critics. In the tonadilla's introduction, Esteve turns to the battle trope to set up the strife between performers and critics. After Garrido's initial solo, a short *parola* (spoken interlude) calls for a drum roll as the performers prepare to fire back with their "ammunition:" songs on stage.

Garrido:	Pero decid, ¿qué hay de nuevo?	Pray tell, what is new?
Josefa:	Escucha	Listen
Alfonso:	Dame atención	Pay heed
Both:	Y arma contra los Herodes del teatro	and arms against the Herods Of theater
Garrido:	Toca, tambor, Y pues su cañón nos tira sufra nuestra munición	Drum, roll, And since their cannon fires let them suffer our ammunition

The introduction wraps up with an overt war declaration "by fire and sword" (*a sangre y fuego*). The battle trope was ubiquitous in Spanish Golden Age cloak-and-sword drama. In *El teatro y los actores agraviados* the critics take the role of the enemy troops, and newspapers replace swords as the weapon of choice. Knowing that the audience was familiar with the battle musical topic, Esteve set the *cómicos'* "war declaration" passage to a marchlike, homophonic, syllabic music where all three actors sing together in preparation for the coplas. Keeping up the topic, the words "fiery critics" are sung with dotted notes over a bass playing only tonic and dominant notes (C3-G3-G2-C3) imitating military bugles (example 1.2).

Críticos fieros	Fiery critics,
pues nos tiráis, paciencia,	so you shoot at us, patience,
e id recibiendo,	and prepare to receive our charge
que guerra declaramos	for we declare
a sangre y fuego	truceless war

Right after declaring war in the short chorus (example 1.2), Garrido asks his peers what their reaction is to critics: "I shall listen, in what state do they put us?" (*He de escuchar, ¿cómo nos ponen?*), to which the performers reply: We are desperate.

---

[84] Charles III (Spain), "Ley XXXIV. D. Carlos III, por real resolución de 19 de noviembre de 1785, comunicada al Consejo y Juez de Imprentas, 'El Juez de Imprentas oiga y administre justicia al que se queje del autor de cualquier impreso,'" in *Novísima recopilación de las leyes de España* (Madrid: Galván Librero, 1805 [1766]), 142.

Example 1.2. Introduction, mock march,
El teatro y los actores agraviados, bars 151–57.

In case there was any doubt they were referring specifically to journalistic criticism, the coplas went into further detail. While the introduction sets up the battle, the coplas are the ammunition proper, the denunciation of the critics. The coplas are the core section of stage tonadillas both because they happen around the middle of the piece and because their lyrics give the specifics of the issue at hand. Coplas are strophic, syllabic, and their melodies are simple compared to the rest of the musical numbers, thus highlighting lyrical content over singing prowess. Here is the first of the coplas of *El teatro y los actores agraviados*:

Los periódicos papeles	The periodical papers
nos desacreditan tanto	discredit us so much
que al fin vendremos a ser	that we will end up being
de las gentes el escarnio	the scorn of people

The three performers on stage are speaking (singing) for all their guild in public defense of their craft. Let us talk about the performers and their roles in this piece. *El teatro y los actores agraviados* is a trio tonadilla deploying three characters: Miguel Garrido, Josefa Torres, and Alfonso Navarro, all performing themselves. The words, however, were not necessarily their own but those of either an anonymous lyricist working for Esteve or Esteve himself. Ensemble tonadillas (duet, trio, quartet, etc.) most often followed a narrative plot that included some spoken dialogue, as opposed to the mostly through-sung solo tonadillas. Because there was usually a story, the performers in ensemble tonadillas acted representationally; they played fictional characters in the scripted story as if the audience were not there, upholding the fourth wall. In contrast, actress-singers in solo tonadillas regularly acted presentationally, that is, they performed themselves and acknowledged the audience. *El teatro y actores agraviados* breaks the fourth-wall convention of ensemble tonadillas since the three performers represent both themselves and generic actor categories (the comic, the lady, and the handsome young man) who sing to audiences directly about their problems. Audiences at the Madrid theaters were familiar with presentational acting and liked to engage in it. Numerous written accounts attest to the spirited ventures of *chorizos* and *polacos*, the "fan clubs" of the city theaters of El Príncipe and La Cruz during the second half of the eighteenth century. In acting as ambassadors of their fellow actor-singers, the performers in *El teatro y los actores agraviados* reinforce a guild identity akin to the one Cavaza advanced in *El músico censor*.

Critics Are "Sayers," Not "Doers"

El teatro y los actores agraviados complained of critics' pretentiousness and lack of authority to cast judgment over theater. The critic personified philosophy, the greatest epistemological intruder of el siglo ilustrado in Spain. Criticism was associated with *ilustración* (Enlightenment, but also eruditeness or

68   *Music and Modernity in Enlightenment Spain*

learnedness) and with *filosofía*. Until the early nineteenth century, *crítica* and filosofía (less often *ciencia*) remained largely synonymous and indistinct.[85] Hence, criticism had not yet become an intellectual activity separate from philosophy and science. The *Diccionario de autoridades* (1780) defines "filosofía" as "the science that deals with the essence, properties, causes, and effects of natural thing." However, it was the second dictionary entry that prevailed in daily use: "By extension [of the first definition], it is said of the *personal opinion*, or *manner of apprehending*, or thinking about any particular issue or point of this science." The emphasis was on the opinion rather than on the science. The foreword to a 1789 pamphlet by the then–royal librarian thus summarized how most Spanish people understood philosophy in the late-eighteenth century: "In the present [century], called *the philosophers' century*, boldness and superficiality rule, and quackery and the art of keeping the appearances prevail over true merit."[86] Filosofía was eminently discursive, as the secondary dictionary entry for "filosofar" (to philosophize) highlights: "also said of the one who starts talking, wanting to seem learned in matters that he does not understand or teach."[87] The discourse of filosofía was related to beliefs and practices perceived to be "enlightened" and "modern." What "enlightened" and "modern" denoted differed from one European nation to the next and among authors within the same nation. Amid such multiplicity of meaning, some constants remained—namely, that criticism is discursive, emits value judgments, and finds justification in an intellectual system considered superior to common beliefs.[88]

The philosophical endeavor appeared to many Spanish eyes as futile at best and arrogant at worst. The perfect metaphor for a philosopher trying to change the world was Don Quijote, Miguel de Cervantes's seventeenth-century wandering knight who fought windmills because he believed them giants. Popular perception that critics were disconnected from reality, preferring to build castles in the air, led people to believe that, contrary to what "the moderns" proposed, written criticism actually detracted from progress. *El teatro y los actores agraviados* accuses newspaper critics of *quijotismo*, the delusional endeavor to right the world's wrongs.[89]

De corregir el mundo	Of rectifying the world
Hablan los tales,	such [critics] speak
Y es necio que presuman	and it is foolish of them to presume
Podrá enmendarle	that they will be able to emend it

---

[85]   María José Rodríguez Sánchez de León, *La crítica dramática en España (1789–1833)* (Madrid: Instituto de la Lengua Española, 2000), 25.

[86]   Tomás Antonio Sánchez, *Carta de Paracuellos* (Madrid: Vda. de Ibarra, 1789), vi–viii.

[87]   *Diccionario de la lengua castellana*, 1780, s.v. "filosofar," "filosofía," my emphases.

[88]   Rodríguez Sánchez de León, *La crítica dramática*, 25.

[89]   "De corregir al mundo / hablan los tales / y es necio que presuman / podrá enmendarle:" Esteve, "El teatro y los actores agraviados."

Critics versus Musicians   69

...	...
Quijotes nuevos	New quixotes,
que han tomado a su cargo	who have taken it upon them
deshacer [en]tuertos	to right wrongs

As much as Esteve and the performers in *El teatro y los actores agraviados* dismissed Enlightenment press critics, they could not stop such criticism affecting their professional activity, which was such a problem that they produced an entire tonadilla to address the issue. Although contemporary tonadillas repeatedly complained about "the fashionable savants" (*eruditos de moda*) and "the enlightened century," Esteve and his colleague Laserna showed awareness of their inevitable role in the criticism loop.

El teatro y los actores agraviados presents criticism as an assault launched by a privileged group of "enlightened authors" against Madrid's ordinary people— namely, the theater crew and the public. In summary, the tonadilla accuses critics of thinking that they are better than their fellow Madrileños, writing for profit "to squeeze the cash out of the readers." Like true "Herods of theater," critics behead actors, playwrights, and composers, leaving their reputations bloodied.

Mas chito chitito que pueden oir	But hush, hush, for they may hear,
los sabios sujetos critica-defectos	The wise subjects, criticizers of faults,
que sus malos picos	Whose evil beaks
tratan de borricos	Call the people of Madrid
a los de Madrid	asses
Con capas de sabios	Wearing the wise-man's cape,
agravan a varios	they aggravate the many,
Y cuánto en sus obras	And, how much in their satirical,
satíricas, tontas,	dumb works
hay que corregir [!]	has to be fixed [!]

Actors, playwrights, and composers further resented critics feeling superior because these critics did not write any plays suitable to the Madrid's theaters and only attacked the ones already in the repertory.

Both in its introduction and the coplas, the tonadilla highlights the conflict between press critics and theater crews: critics are sayers, not doers. They belong in the neoclassicist contingent of reformists and apologistas but do not produce any theater pieces. According to the tonadilla, critics find fault with the "old authors" (Golden Age playwrights such as Lope de Vega and Calderón de la Barca, whom neoclassicists despised but the public enjoyed) but have nothing to offer in exchange. The performers challenge critics to write successful plays instead of reviews:[90]

---

[90] On how modern critics defame ancient poets: "If the ancient poets / saw themselves being so slandered / they would eat them [the critics] and their criticisms / by the mouthful." *El teatro y los actores agraviados*, fourth copla.

70 *Music and Modernity in Enlightenment Spain*

Second copla

Josefa:	Los eruditos intrusos	The intruding erudites
	de discretos blasonando	boasting their discretion
	se ríen de las comedias	laugh at the plays
	que al pueblo representamos	we perform for the people
Garrido's reply:	Pues que escriban ellos unas	Well, let them write some [plays]
	y veremos en el teatro	and we shall see at the theater
	si sus obras son mejores	if their works are better
	que las que están censurando	than those they censor

On the one hand, the challenge to produce marketable plays neoclassicist rehashes the sayers-versus-doers formula found in the controversy between "Discourse 97"'s author and Cavaza. The basic argument is that there is no place for you in the musical or dramatic circles if you cannot compose music or write a play. But, on the other hand, the tonadilla raises the uncomfortable but very real absence of a neoclassicist repertory that satisfied both audiences and critics. Most of the dramatic works by theater reformers and literary critics fared poorly in Madrid. Theater spectators considered them dull, a reaction that did not escape Esteve or Garrido, who were much more in tune with the daily response of audiences.

Critics spoke up when required to excel as "doers." In his satirical *Los literatos en cuaresma* (1773), Tomás de Iriarte contended that critics served the nation by publicly sharing their informed judgment; therefore, they were exempt from producing artistic works. Showing the elitism characteristic of Enlightenment authors, Iriarte disagreed with the common perception that critics were mere sayers while authors and artists were doers. He validated the role of the critic-sayer, insisting that critics "need not, as the uneducated masses expect, demonstrate ingenuity and inventiveness when all they need to do their job is to give proof of learnedness and discernment."[91] However, the public continued to cast doubt on the critic's social role.

Critics' stance that popular taste was unreliable surfaced in a one-page anonymous letter published in the *Correo de los Ciegos* on February 20, 1787, complaining about *El teatro y los actores agraviados*, denouncing composer Pablo Esteve and the three tonadilla performers for publicly disparaging critics. For this critic, composer Pablo Esteve was the primary culprit because he abused his salaried position as a theater composer for the City of Madrid. In the letter writer's logic, Esteve lacked moral direction for refusing to comply with theater reform guidelines proposed by Enlightenment elite. The letter's author considered *El teatro y los actores agraviados* a "foolish, amoral, and harmful" form of public entertainment written to please actor-singers. For him, the tonadilla was

---

[91] Iriarte's ideas about criticism are based on Alexander Pope's *An Essay on Criticism* (1711). Tomás de Iriarte, "Los literatos en cuaresma," in *Colección de obras en verso y prosa de D. Tomás de Yriarte* (Madrid: Imprenta Real, 1805), 14–18.

about "the actors [*cómicos*] wanting to defend their extravagances against the fair criticisms made [of them] in some public papers, or to better put it, they profess to linger in their nonsense in spite of all that the writers say."[92] The anonymous letter writer demanded that censors reclaim control over theater programming from "mercenary composers." This letter's author reaffirmed the Enlightenment idea that only a privileged elite could lead the masses to progress. He saw himself and other critics as spokespersons for official policy on social reform. Hence, he responded with perplexity when theater workers refused to correct their vices and heed critics' voices. The letter writer shirked the obligation to write dramatic pieces complying with neoclassicist standards, separating the role of the critic from that of the playwright or composer: "They [the performers] say that the critics should come up with better comedias; but to say that a thing is bad, or has such and such shortcomings, is not to offer to make it better." In other words, the *Correo* letter writer vindicated the "sayers" of society, reaffirming that they neither need to become "doers" nor rely on their approval.

The *Correo* author further revealed his loyalty to European, modern standards when he expressed his wish for "corrupted" city coliseos to adhere to recently published regulations for the Italian opera theater. The idea was to revamp national theater to conform to European standards at the scale of its performances, buildings, and audiences. The seemingly petty dispute between performers and critics showcased in *El teatro y los actores agraviados* was in fact a matter of national importance requiring qualified leadership, at least in the eyes of the elite. In *Los literatos en cuaresma*, Iriarte made the point that while defamation "may harm the credit of any given person, of a specific family," antimodern criticism "directly damages an entire nation" because "it opposes everything that is useful, everything that is new, and discourages authors [*ingenios*], dispirits creators [*artífices*]." Iriarte urged his contemporaries to distinguish criticism from satire, new ideas coming from "learned subjects" from the reactions of "the uneducated masses [*vulgo*]."[93] The author of the *Correo de los Ciegos* letter believes that legislators and writers, "the intelligent ones," must correct composers, playwrights, performers, and audiences who "persist in their barbarism." "Discourse 97"'s author took a similar path when he distinguished practical musicians from philosopher-artists. In both approaches, the Enlightenment elite demands that the uneducated, unenlightened practitioners submit to their modern views.

Both critics and theater-makers claimed to care about Spain's national interest, but what exactly constituted that national interest remained contested. *El teatro y los actores agraviados* and its corresponding review in the *Correo de los Ciegos* each professed to defend public instruction and foster civilized behavior. Both sides maintained the importance of satisfying the public, but their definitions of public satisfaction diverged. For composers and performers,

---

92   "Otra [carta]," *Correo de los Ciegos*, February 20, 1787, 156.

93   Iriarte, "Los literatos en cuaresma," 2–9.

"pleasing" meant soliciting the audience's cheers and applause. For his part, the author of the *Correo de los Ciegos* review held critics and the press, not performers, responsible for ensuring that the public is pleased, and by pleased, he means edified. To this effect, according to the *Correo* letter writer, critics ought to have the right to dictate the practices and repertoires of musical theater. What critics understood as their right to provide authoritative guidelines for the national betterment within a modern societal order, theater workers saw as self-serving arrogance to the detriment of the common good.

The periodical press and the critics were unwelcome agents of the modern for many Spanish musicians. Criticism essays such as *El Censor's* "Discourse 97" and press reviews such as the open letter published in response to *El teatro y los actores agraviados* erupted in Spain as a new medium that caught Madrid composers, performers, and playwrights off guard. Chapel and theater musicians alike were used to a guild-like model where they learned their musical skills from their peers, either formally, in the case of chapel musicians, or informally, in the case of theater actress- and actor-singers. The skills they learned through the years and the connections they formed with their colleagues provided them with job security and opportunities to obtain better paid positions. For theater performers, audience support was crucial because it ensured their permanency in the Madrid theater companies, managed by city authorities.

When the periodical press flourished in 1780s Spain, critics' voices threatened the stability of musicians' careers. Seasoned critics such as *El Censor's* authors as well as occasional letter writers in newspapers complained that Spanish musical practices were not up to date with those of modern Europe. Critics' views were influenced by Enlightenment ideas such as connecting music to language instead of numbers and proportions, and Batteux's inclusion of music in the fine arts. Critics also relied heavily on the parameters set by eighteenth-century Spanish literary neoclassicists, who insisted that national arts should edify and entertain, abiding by the classical unities. The intellectual and political elites supported neoclassicist aesthetics because they saw in them a path to cultural modernization.

However, neoclassicist principles resulted in few successful theater pieces in the 1780s, and there were no fruitful attempts to apply them to musical pieces. This gap manifested in musical debates of the late 1780s and early 1790s as an opposition between sayers (the critics) and doers (the musicians). Confrontations between critics and musicians in late Enlightenment Spain, amplified by the boom of the periodical press at the time, attest to the instability that criticism brought to musical knowledge and practice.

2

Music, Medicine, and Tarantism in Madrid, 1787

A prominent case of tarantism gripped Madrid in the summer of 1787. On June 25, a fourteen-year-old boy was brought to the Madrid General Hospital. Ambrosio Silván presented with facial paralysis, body spasms, sweats, fever, nausea, and an accelerated pulse. He could not walk. Twenty-five-year-old doctor and medical translator Bartolomé Piñera y Siles (1762–1831) was initially stumped by the case but after a few days of observation concluded that the patient had been bitten by a tarantula. With some hesitation, he decided to treat the patient with music. Ambrosio's music-and-dance treatment lasted about forty days; during this time, Madrid's elite visited the hospital to see him frantically dance to the beat of a tarantella played by two medical interns. The boy, the music, and the spider captivated Madrid's attention for a good part of 1787. Soon, Madrid was divided between the *incrédulos*, who rejected tarantism, and those who had accepted it.

Tarantism in the eighteenth century was much more than a quaint disorder: it raised the issue of the nature of the soul and its connection to the body. Such conversations stirred up competing visions of modern and traditional scientific knowledge, testing Spanish scientists' reputations amid Enlightenment trends toward encyclopedism and taxonomy. Tarantism blurred the borders between the organic and the psychological or spiritual, allowing the public to vicariously experience the tarantula's bite either through their own fear or as spectators of healing dance sessions. In this chapter I discuss medical treatises on tarantism that merged theories of sensation, the human body, disease, and music. The first treatise, published by Toledo physician Francisco Xavier Cid, drew some attention from the international press. The second, by Bartolomé Piñera y Siles, fueled a tarantula craze in Madrid in the summer of 1787. Piñera allowed prominent Madrid characters to attend the healing sessions and meet Ambrosio Silván at the General Hospital. The general public read about the fantastic case in the papers or learned of it secondhand. So enraptured was the public that composer Pablo Esteve memorialized the story in his stage tonadilla *El atarantulado* (The Tarantula-Bitten Man).

Tarantism debates confirm that Spanish physicians and the reading public were aware of recent discussions of nervous disease and the effects of music on the body and the soul/mind. One window into modernization in late eighteenth-century Spain is to investigate how scientists reconciled Enlightenment and tradition. Cid and Piñera are representative of late Spanish Enlightenment authors who reconciled new scientific ideas with received traditions and gen-

74   *Music and Modernity in Enlightenment Spain*

eral theories with specific local conditions. Their treatises extended work by the Croatian-Italian Giorgio Baglivi, who had studied tarantism in Apulia, Italy, toward the end of the seventeenth century. In embracing Baglivi, they distanced themselves from contemporary French and Italian medical authors who had dismissed Baglivi's musical treatment of tarantism as a fantastic story for the gullible and uneducated or as a psychosomatic disorder. The dismissal of Baglivi's theories epitomized two challenges that certain strands of Enlightenment such as Cartesianism and materialism posed for Spanish intellectuals: first, the rejection of received knowledge; second, the refutation of belief in the invisible, in this case, the belief that music could heal. Taken to its extreme, this course of Enlightenment thought threatened Catholicism, since it could lead people to reject Church tradition, miracles, and even God's existence. But while Cid and Piñera vindicated earlier seventeenth-century medical authors like Baglivi and Athanasius Kircher, they also hewed to more contemporary scientific premises of sensism and mechanicism.

Tarantism was also a social phenomenon in 1787 Madrid, demonstrating that modern public opinion was already in formation in late eighteenth-century Spain. Another window into modernization processes lies in tarantism's circulation among medical treatises, the press, and the musical stage. Despite their primarily rural existence, tarantulas crawled into urban Madrid's imagination as residents feared their impending spread, whether real or imagined. Media responses in journals, printed music, and the theater soon followed. Capitalizing on public interest in tarantism, periodical press authors and composers like Esteve addressed the issue of "fashionable diseases." These were nervous afflictions that contemporary authors had connected to the modern lifestyle of European urban centers. Careful attention to the information dissemination processes shows a public opinion in the making, an essential component of modern Western societies. In these tarantism cases, Spaniards across social strata contested ideas about music and its capacities as Spain negotiated whether and how to be modern.

The Tarantism Craze in Madrid

The Tarantula-Bitten Man and the Spectators

On an evening in the late summer of 1787, regulars at the Madrid theaters anticipated a new stage tonadilla to spice up the night's show. The tonadilla, composed by Pablo Esteve, featured a new actress-singer, Francisca Rodrigo, or "La Rodrigo," and tenor Alfonso Navarro, one of the Manuel Martínez company's *galanes* or semi-serious male actors. The actor who played the main character, Doctor Don Celedonio, was the famous Miguel Garrido, who for many years held the position of "gracioso" or "comic actor" in the Madrid theaters. The tonadilla started like so many others, with a critique of Madrid's upper-class urbanites' modern mores. A Marchioness complains about a headache, her platonic lover takes her suffering too seriously and calls Doctor Don Celedonio pointlessly, while two young girls pay them a social visit and chat about superfluous issues. However, toward the end of the first act, the tonadilla turns to a far more specific matter by then omnipresent in Madrid's collective imagination: tarantism. Esteve titled the tonadilla *El atarantulado*, The Tarantula-Bitten Man.

El atarantulado's plot combines social critique with commentary on the current issue of tarantism. In act 1, the Marchioness has a migraine, so her special male friend (*cortejo*), the Count, calls for the doctor. In the meantime, the Duchess's young daughters stop by to call on the Marchioness and the Count. When Doctor Don Celedonio arrives to tend to the Marchioness, she already feels better thanks to the Count's gallantries. Upset that he was called for in vain, the doctor grumbles that he has more important things to do, like curing a man bitten by a venomous animal. He then invites the party to join him and witness the patient's healing through music. In act 2, Doctor Don Celedonio directs the tarantula-bitten man's dancing therapy while a musical intern plays the guitar, and the rest of the characters observe. While the doctors and noble characters of *El atarantulado* personify Madrid's allegedly corrupted mores, they also occasionally represent real people involved in the tarantism case, as reported by Piñera. Such is the case of the doctor, the medical intern, and the patient in the tonadilla. As there were no other officially acknowledged cases of tarantism in Madrid, Esteve's Doctor Don Celedonio was evidently modeled after Piñera and the bitten boy after Ambrosio.

El atarantulado is the only theater piece so far known that is devoted entirely to tarantism in Madrid. The score and libretto are available at Madrid's Biblioteca Histórica Municipal. The tonadilla comprises one solo number by Garrido (the doctor), three ensembles, three choirs and several parolas. The orchestral accompaniment calls for first and second violins, two oboes alternating with two flutes, two horns alternating with two trumpets, and contrabass. In table 2.1, white cells indicate musical numbers heard for the first time, light gray cells indicate repeating numbers, and dark gray cells mark the spoken sections (parolas). The total duration of the music is roughly eighteen minutes without parolas and closer to twenty-five minutes with spoken dialogue, action, and set change. As the table shows, the tonadilla's tarantism plot develops mostly during its second half when the characters leave the Marchioness's house to go to the hospital. By contrast, the first half is devoted to musical entertainment.

Tarantism was a scary yet exciting scientific and social phenomenon. Shared fear made tarantism real for the average Spanish citizen. Hence, Esteve put equal effort into depicting tarantism and its public reaction. After a few musical numbers unrelated to tarantism (1–4 in table 2.1), Doctor Don Celedonio reveals that "a poisonous bug" lurks in Madrid, much to the dismay of his aristocratic interlocutors. A short, spoken dialogue (*parola*) ensues:

| Marchioness: | Decid pues el nombre de este animalito y qué efectos causa | Pray, say the name of this little bug and the effects it causes |
| Doctor: | Voy a referirlo; es un avichucho a manera de una araña, y se llama … se llama … la tarántula. | I will now tell; it is a bug in the manner of a spider, and it is called … it is called … the tarantula. |

Garrido's mention of the tarantula prompts the first of the tonadilla choruses, performed by a choir of three women and three men together with the aristocratic characters (table 2.2). Esteve wrote *El atarantulado* while working for the Manuel Martínez theater company, one of three companies operating in the City of Madrid in 1787. *El atarantulado* was a *tonadilla general*, that is, it called for much of the company's participation, which made such ensemble tonadillas more spectacular than regular ones.[1] Ensemble tonadillas, sometimes adorned with choruses, often marked special events such as the beginning and end of the comedic year, the yearly theater cycle starting on Easter and ending before Lent. Like most choruses in Spanish musical theater of the time, *El atarantulado*'s first chorus comprises one stanza and represents a group reaction to the situation at hand:

¡Qué susto, qué pasmo!	How frightening, how shocking!
¡Qué cosa tan rara!	What a strange thing!
No quieran los cielos	Heavens forbid
me de una picada	it takes a bite off me

The chorus further builds up the mystery surrounding this new phenomenon with homorhythmic vocals singing crotchets over relentless quaver arpeggios in the violins.

The chorus singers in *El atarantulado* stood for Madrid's public. That summer, Madrileños had come across tarantism either visiting the General Hospital to see one of Ambrosio's therapeutic sessions, hearing case accounts, or reading one of the "tarantula pamphlets" illustrated with the spider's engraving.

In act 2 of *El atarantulado*, Esteve reproduced the details of Ambrosio's case at the Madrid's General Hospital and Piñera's treatment. The set design (*mutación*) described in the libretto confirms that Esteve intended to reenact Piñera'a tarantism case. The set simulates "the room of the patient; he is in his bed *mimicking the real tarantula victim*, and several *citizen spectators* watching him. An intern arrives and pushes them away [from the patient]."[2]

---

[1] According to José Subirá, any tonadilla featuring more than six actor-singers could be considered *general*. José Subirá, *La tonadilla escénica* (Madrid: Tipografía de Archivos, 1928), 117.

[2] Pablo Esteve, "El Atarantulado," 1787 (Ms 187–4, Biblioteca Histórica de Madrid), emphasis mine. All quotes of lyrics are taken from the manuscript cited here. The manuscript's folios are not numbered.

Music, Medicine, and Tarantism in Madrid, 1787   77

No further indications are provided as to how "mimicking the real tarantula victim" should be staged. Therefore, even before Piñera published his medical report, the stage notes presume the actors' familiarity with Ambrosio's case to the extent that they could reenact his dance sessions. This was possible because when Piñera started treating Ambrosio, he allowed spectators in.

The mythos of Spanish tarantism Esteve reenacted in *El atarantulado* took shape through publications and by word of mouth as the public poured into Madrid's General Hospital to witness Ambrosio's dancing. In fact, soon after Piñera's diagnosis of tarantism and prescription of daily dance sessions for Ambrosio, Madrileños crowded the hospital doors demanding to witness the healing process. On July 5, 1787, Piñera wrote:

> Once the news of this unique phenomenon spread, men and women of all classes and conditions, some out of curiosity, and some out of disbelief, came to the hospital and requested to see Ambrosio's dance. Neither locks nor guards were enough, for the people's bustle and horde broke the former and knocked down the latter more than once. In spite of the judicious measures implemented by Your Excellency [the director of the hospital's board], from that day on, the hospital room was nearly always full of people at the time of the dance.[3]

As he testifies, Ambrosio's disease and treatment had become half-scientific, half-miraculous summer entertainment for Madrid's residents. Public entertainment slowed in Madrid during the summer because the theaters offered fewer weekly shows compared to the fall, winter, and spring seasons. All kinds of performers, including the actor-singers working for the theaters, arranged productions of acrobats (*volatines*) and puppets to compensate.[4] People were avid for novelty shows and oddities, and Ambrosio's case fit the bill. With laypeople flowing through the hospital, tarantism had moved from academic pages of Cid's *Tarantismo observado en España* to the realm of informal knowledge and public opinion.

While many Madrileños read the press, even more had access to music and theater. Stage tonadillas at the city coliseos and songs sold to play at home afforded the public compact, witty formats to formulate easily shareable opinions. In the summer of 1787, people wanted to hear about tarantism and talk about it, as Piñera's account of crowds gathering at the General Hospital's gates and the popularity of the *Retrato de la tarántula* pamphlet demonstrate. Like pamphlets, short-format musical products fulfilled the demand for a token of the tarantula bite dance. As studies on gossip have revealed, informal codifica-

---

3   Bartolomé Piñera y Siles, *Descripcion histórica de una nueva especie de corea, ó baile de San Vito, originada de la picadura de un insecto, que por los fenómenos seguidos á ella se ha creido ser la tarántula. Enfermedad de la que ha adolecido y curado á beneficio de la música Ambrosio Silvan: narracion de los síntomas con que se ha presentado, y exposicion fiel y circunstanciada del plan curativo que se ha practicado. Informe dado á la Real Junta de Hospitales.* (Madrid: Benito Cano, 1787), 21.

4   The same happened during Lent, when comedias were banned.

Table 2.1 Structure of *El atarantulado*

	Musical number	Ensemble	Characters	Key, meter	Approx. duration	Th	Form	Winds
1	Allegretto	Solo	Doctor	B♭, $\frac{2}{4}$	2'20"	3	D.S.	ob, E♭ hn
2	Andantino	Duet	Marchioness Count	G, $\frac{2}{4}$, C, $\frac{6}{8}$	3'14" 1'45"	3 3	D.S.	---
3	Allegretto moderado	Quartet	Marchioness Count 2 Duchess's Daughters	A, $\frac{3}{8}$	2'06"	3	D.S.	---
	P A R O L A (bolero dance?)							
4	Andante vivo	Quintet	Doctor Marchioness Count 2 Duchess's Daughters	G, $\frac{3}{4}$	2'08	3	D.S.	G hn
	P A R O L A: mentions tarantula							
5	Chorus 1 (Allegretto)	Choir	All	C, $\frac{6}{8}$	0'42"	1	---	ob, G hn
	P A R O L A: explains tarantism in two lines							
5	Chorus 1 (Allegretto)	Choir	All	C, $\frac{6}{8}$	0'42"	1	---	ob, G hn
	P A R O L A: all head to the hospital in a carriage							
6	Chorus 2 (Allegro)	Choir	All	C, $\frac{6}{8}$	0'32"	1	---	ob, C tpt
	SET CHANGE: HOSPITAL ROOM							
7	Coplas + Coleta (Andante)	Solo + Choir	Intern Choir	C minor, $\frac{3}{8}$	2'33"	2	D.S.	Fl

P A R O L A: doctor prepares dance session and shows tarantula to observers

#								
8	Chorus 1	Choir	All	C, $\frac{6}{8}$	0'42"	1	---	ob, G hn

ACTION/P A R O L A:
Interns play guitars. Bitten man dances. They change the tune.
Doctor: Come on, dance. Victim: I can't.

| 9 | Coleta | Choir | Choir | C minor, $\frac{3}{8}$ | 0'25" | 1 | --- | Fl |

ACTION/P A R O L A:
Interns play again. Doctor: He sweats now.
The four officers who brought the victim on stage wrap him on bed sheets and put him in bed.

| 10 | Final Chorus (chorus 2') | Choir | All | C, $\frac{6}{8}$ | 0'44" | 1 | --- | Ob, C tpt |

Example 2.1. Chorus 1, *El atarantulado*, bars 379–401. All musical examples in this chapter transcribed from Pablo Esteve, *El atarantulado*, tonadilla general, 1787, Parte de apuntar, 2 vln, 2 fl/ob, 2 hn/tpt, cb. BHM Mus 187-4.

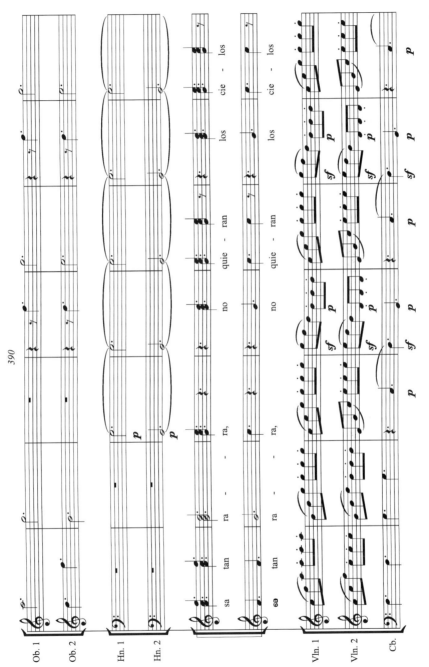
—(continued)

Example 2.1—concluded

Music, Medicine, and Tarantism in Madrid, 1787

Table 2.2 Characters in *El atarantulado*, in order of appearance.

Character	Actor-Singer	Position	Seniority[a]
The Doctor, Don Celedonio	Miguel Garrido	1st gracioso	15
The Marchioness	Francisca Rodrigo	4th dama	New
The Count	Alfonso Navarro	7th galán	8
Duchess's Daughter 1	Rosa García	6th dama	7
Duchess's Daughter 2	Josepha Torres	7th dama	3
The Medical Intern	Fermín Rojo	supernumerary	New

[a] Seniority in years hired by the Madrid theaters. Francisca Rodrigo was hired in 1787 for the Eusebio Ribera company but soon moved to the Manuel Martínez one. Fermín Rojo came from Cádiz: Emilio Cotarelo y Mori, *Don Ramón de la Cruz y sus obras* (Madrid: J. Perales y Martinez, 1899).

tions of knowledge and experience, while perhaps less impressive than scientific treatises and journals, also shaped and continue to shape modern public opinion.[5] Short, current musical theater pieces such as Esteve's *El atarantulado* functioned as communication media linking Madrid performers and audiences through social criticism and current events commentary.

El atarantulado's coplas give us a snapshot of Ambrosio's treatment by Piñera at the Madrid General Hospital. The set change between the tonadilla's first and second acts indicates to audiences that the register of reality has shifted from long-extant conditions—nervous diseases, cortejos, a vacuous aristocracy in the first act—to the contemporary craze over tarantism. At this turning point, when the set has changed, the audience is presented with the tonadilla coplas. The coplas constitute the musical core of tonadillas, where social criticism is voiced. In this case, the coplas coincide with the plot's climax, when both the fictive and the real audience gaze upon the tarantula-bitten man. Act 2 of the tonadilla begins with the actor "mimicking the real patient," presumably having a seizure while a group of people watches him. The coplas' ritornello sounds as background music. Esteve wrote the coplas to stand out and grip the audience's attention. For example, this is the tonadilla's only number that starts in a minor mode (C minor). It also contains the only instance of flutes replacing oboes to play a short "solo" duet in bars 11 through 20. The pizzicato bass and the muted violins of the ritornello create a tense quietness in expectation of the scientific miracle soon to take place (example 2.2).

---

[5] For studies on gossip see Heather Kerr and Claire Walker, *Fama and Her Sisters: Gossip and Rumour in Early Modern Europe* (Beligum: Brepols, 2015); Nicola Parsons, *Reading Gossip in Early Eighteenth-Century England* (London: Palgrave Macmillan, 2009).

Example 2.2. Coplas, ritornello/codetta, *El atarantulado*, bars 423–42.

Esteve's musical design for the coplas underscores that, in Ambrosio's case, there were three main characters: Ambrosio, Piñera, and the Madrid public. The Medical Intern appears on stage to sing the first copla as he pushes onlookers away from the patient. The accompaniment plays pizzicato and muted: "Silent, gentlemen, move over there, for you shall see him heal shortly." Typically, coplas were sung by soloists, but Esteve transforms the usual copla form of a body plus a refrain into a body plus a short chorus or "coleta" (codetta). Each copla concludes with a short plaintive chorus-codetta reacting to the medical professionals' information on the patient: "Poor wretched thing, what a pity we feel for him!" the observers sing. Two secondary dominants (bars 467 and 472) highlight this section's intense pathos (example 2.3), especially considering that tonadillas' tonal language usually comprises simple chord progressions. Chromatic alterations are typically sparse and seldom do composers write in keys with more than three sharps or flats. (example 2.3, bars 464–75).

The chorus repeats thrice with the same lyrics, once at the end of each copla. With this persistent choral refrain, Esteve lent voice to his audience, ensuring their participation in Ambrosio's tarantism case was heard.

With a now attentive audience, Doctor Don Celedonio solemnly requests a guitar for his assistant to play the tarantella. While the medical intern prepares the hospital room for the dance healing, Doctor Don Celedonio shows a tarantula to the on-stage actors: "Look! Behold the tarantula!" he says, frightening the "citizen spectators." At this point, the tarantism dance begins with the backing of diegetic guitar. According to the parola, the doctor and his assistants experiment with changing the tarantella to a different tune, just as actual spectators had requested at the General Hospital when visiting Ambrosio.

Ponen los practicantes al enfermo en medio del tablado, y tocan para que baile el enfermo: después mudan a otro toque y para de bailar el enfermo.	The interns place the patient in the middle of the stage and play for him to dance: then they change the style and the patient stops dancing.
PAROLA/ Doctor: "Vaya, baile usted"	PAROLA/ Doctor: "Well, dance"
Patient: "No puedo"	Patient: "I cannot"

The on-stage observers reiterate their compassion for the patient with a reprise of the codetta (example 2.2). As the diegetic guitar music resumes, the *atarantulado* sweats, indicating the treatment's efficacy. The lack of orchestra parts for the tarantella suggests that it was played on-stage with only guitar.

Vuelve a tocar el practicante, y baila el enfermo, llega el médico estando bailando, y después de tentarle la frente dice/ Doctor: "Ya suda;"	The intern plays again, and the patient dances. The doctor arrives while he is dancing, and after touching his forehead he says/ Doctor: "He sweats;"

A esta voz los cuatro que le pusieron en medio, salen con cuatro sábanas, le arropan, y le llevan a la cama, y canta el coro: [coro final] "¡Que viva Don Celedonio..."	To this cue the four [officers] who put the patient in the middle [of the stage] come out with four bed sheets, wrap him, and put him in bed, and the choir sings: [final chorus] "Long live Don Celedonio..."

Regarding what exactly the *El atarantulado*'s medical intern played for the healing scene taking place after the coplas, the tonadilla's context suggests a basso ostinato melody and variations. Like in the real case at the Madrid General Hospital, the medical intern plays a tarantella they learned from a blind musician called Bernardo Merlo with a guitar, as opposed to the violin Cid cites in some of his accounts. Though brief and lacking any musical transcriptions, Piñera report describes the music that the two medical interns played for Ambrosio. Like Cid, Piñera insists that the tarantella is the only effective musical remedy for tarantula poison. For Piñera, the tarantella's healing power resides in its melody rather than on discrete musical parameters. According to him, although the first notes of the tarantella are the same as those of the then popular fandango, the fandango did not incite Ambrosio to dance.[6] While it is unclear what Piñera means by comparing the tarantella with the fandango, it seems as if Merlo's tarantella at the hospital reminded Piñera of the fandango, which the average person in Madrid would have recognized before the foreign tarantella. Fandangos, like tarantellas, are variations on a basso ostinato.

Both the fandango and tarantella are lively dance pieces, usually in the minor mode and in triple meter. The older fandango was performed as variations over a descending tetrachord basso ostinato harmonized i-VII-vi-V in the minor mode, or VI-V-IV-III in the major mode. By the late eighteenth century, when it was a staple of Spanish ballrooms and musical theater, the fandango could include a sung section after the variations and was often harmonized using tonic and dominant chords, with an emphasis on the dominant. The opening melody of fandangos follows a descending tetrachord with a Phrygian melodic cadence (approaching the tonic by a semitone above), which we can see in some of Cid's tarantella transcriptions (see fig. 2.1, ex. 1 section b, ex. V section b). It is possible that the musicians Cid and Piñera heard playing the tarantella harmonized the tarantella like a fandango, especially given their similarities. It is also possible that Spanish musicians from La Mancha, such as Recuero and Merlo, combined tarantella melodies with regional fandangos.

Piñera devotes only a short paragraph to the tarantella's musical traits in his *Descripción de und nueva corea*, reproducing information he allegedly obtained

---

[6]   Piñera y Siles, *Descripción histórica*, 30–31.

Example 2.3. Coplas, choral refrain, *El atarantulado*, bars 459–75.

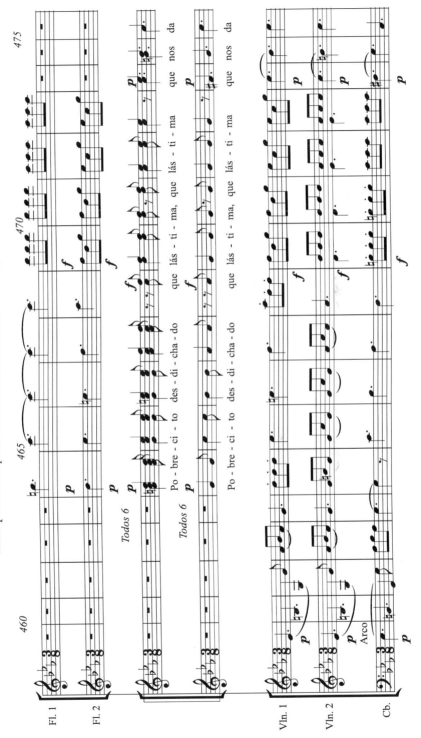

88   *Music and Modernity in Enlightenment Spain*

from a professional musician. He describes the music in terms of modal theory, using Gioseffo Zarlino's second system nomenclature:[7]

> The music or sonata that has been played for and has cured Ambrosio is the tarantella, which, as a music professor has informed me, is a little song very similar to a contradance, formed in the Greek mode called Mixo-Lydian, corresponding to the one called sixth tone, which is vigorous, because its mode is major. That is, the sensation that it introduces into the spirit through the ear is more active if it is major, and more opaque and despondent if it is minor. From the said sixth tone it quickly and artlessly passes to the Phrygian mode, to conclude. This Greek mode corresponds to the one called first tone diapason, which is a semiditone (or degree) and a half lower than the said sixth tone, the sensation of which is that of a minor mode. The fundamental note of the Mixo-Lydian is F. Faut, and that of the Phrygian mode is D. Lasolre.[8]

In tonal terms, Piñera's paragraph describes a binary dance form with the first section in F major and the second section in D minor, the key in which fandangos were often played. According to Piñera, Ambrosio reacted to Merlo's particular tarantella but did not react to Recuero's tarantella, which Cid transcribed and later played at the General Hospital with the intention of experimenting on the patient.[9] In reality, it is hard to know how similar the two versions were, since Cid only provides the melody and Piñera only discusses the harmony. What seems clear is that the pieces were lively, followed an ostinato progression, and had at least two sections, one of them in minor mode.

Besides descriptions of the music played at the Madrid General hospital that could have inspired Esteve, *El atarantulado*'s final chorus confirms that the tarantella played during the tonadilla coplas consisted of variations over a basso ostinato. After the patient sweats and is healed, the tonadilla concludes with a chorus applauding the Doctor's wisdom: "Long live Don Celedonio, medicinal Orpheus, who heals the deadly tarantula to the tune of the folias." The chorus suggests once

---

[7] See Harold S. Powers et al., "Mode," *Grove Music Online. Oxford Music Online.* (Oxford University Press), http://www.oxfordmusiconline.com/subscriber/article/grove/music/43718.

[8] "La música ó sonata que se le ha tocado, y curado al Ambrosio, es la tarantela, y esta, según me ha informado un Profesor de música, es un juguetillo muy semejante a una contradanza, y está formado en el modo Griego llamado Mixô-Lidio, correspondiente al que se dice sexto tono, que es vigoroso, por ser su modo mayor; esto es, la sensación que introduce por el oído al ánimo, más activa si es mayor, y más opaca y avatida si es menor. Desde dicho sexto tono pasa prontamente y sin arte al modo Frigio, para concluir. Este modo griego corresponde al que en España se llama diapason de primer tono, que dista del diapason del sexto referido, un semiditono ó grado, y medio más abajo, cuya sensacion es de modo menor. El punto fundamental del Mixô-Lidio es F. Faut, y el del modo frigio es D. Lasolre." Piñera y Siles, *Descripción histórica*, 40.

[9] Piñera y Siles, *Descripción histórica*, 20.

Music, Medicine, and Tarantism in Madrid, 1787   89

more that Spanish people heard the tarantella as an ostinato-variations genre similar to the fandango, according to Piñera's report, or the folias, according to Esteve.

Tonadillas in the 1780s often functioned as news commentary parallel to the periodical press and the city's gossip, as *El atarantulado* exemplifies. With Ambrosio's case, tarantism became mediatized through newspapers, pamphlets, and theater. Previous to Piñera's treatment of Ambrosio, tarantism had come to the attention of a few via Francisco Xavier Cid's *Tarantismo observado en España*, a lengthy medical treatise on tarantism, complete with dozens of case reports Cid compiled in the region of La Mancha, in the arid plains southeast of Madrid. Turning disease into a spectacle in the summer of 1787, Piñera brought the musico-medical phenomenon of tarantism from La Mancha's arid countryside into the Spanish Empire's metropolis. Esteve took note and brought the citywide sensation to the musical stage. *El atarantulado* capitalizes on the publicity and the believers versus skeptics controversy surrounding Ambrosio, Piñera, and even Cid's treatise, staging tarantism details for the public's observation, judgement, and reaction.

Tarantism in the Press

Interest in tarantulas and tarantism spiked in Madrid in the late 1780s following publication of Cid's treatise, a number of related pamphlets, Ambrosio's case, and Piñera's report. Controversy ensued between those who believed tarantism was a legitimate disease attributable to bodily fluid mechanics and curable through music, as Cid and Piñera affirmed, and those who associated tarantism with exalted imaginations and social panic.

While curious phenomena and crowds were nothing new to Madrid, the periodical press's rise in popularity made tarantism a public issue. Ambrosio's case and Cid's treatise raised printed debates in several journals at a time when the press was flourishing in Spain and a reading public was emerging as the proto-subject of public opinion. Controversies over tarantism continued for at least five years after Piñera dismissed Ambrosio from Madrid's General Hospital. Through at least twenty-eight tarantism-related articles in Madrid periodicals between 1787 and 1790 and two more in 1793, newspapers put tarantism squarely in the center of public debate. The printed exchange of ideas on tarantism could not have occurred in Spain just one decade earlier, because the reading public had not consolidated before the 1780s. The publicity of the tarantism debate is evident in: (1) a range of contrasting opinions that refused to settle into one authoritative answer regarding tarantism's existence, and (2) the quasi-democratic access the people of Madrid had to the debates.

Everybody wanted to see the tarantula and the condition it caused. Cid had included an engraving of tarantulas and their eggs in his *Tarantismo observado en España*. Since then, medical arguments about tarantism were almost invariably printed along with tarantula descriptions or images. For instance, an eight-page pamphlet by an unknown author titled *Retrato de la tarántula* (Portrait of

90 *Music and Modernity in Enlightenment Spain*

the Tarantula) was printed in July 1787 while Ambrosio was still hospitalized.[10] This pamphlet circulated more widely than either Cid's or Piñera's books: it was sold at three bookstores in Madrid and was even reprinted in Barcelona.[11] This pamphlet excerpted Cid's *Tarantismo observado en España* and summarized Ambrosio's case. Significantly, *Retrato de la tarántula* reprinted Cid's drawings of the spider from his own treatise, which has led some authors to attribute the pamphlet to Cid.[12] Those who sought a more hands-on experience could come to the Calle de las Carretas in downtown Madrid to see a live tarantula for only four quarters per person and "with the authorization of the General Superintendent of the Police."[13] In *El atarantulado*'s second act, Esteve reproduced the Calle de Las Carretas tarantula display on stage by having Doctor Don Celedonio show a fake spider to the other characters, who gasped in horror.

Like Garrido fueling the tonadilla characters' curiosity, real-life doctors also participated in the tarantula craze, swaying the public with their professional opinions. On August 8, 1787, physician Miguel Bea de Navarra sent his own observations on tarantism in a letter to the *Diario de Madrid*. Bea de Navarra went to visit some of his patients at the porcelain factory, located next to the windmill by the Manzanares River where Ambrosio had been bitten. While at the china factory, one of the workers showed him a curious "bug" (*animalillo*) that would crawl up his clothes with rhythmic movements when he played the guitar. This factory worker had seen a drawing of a tarantula, probably the one in *Retrato de la tarántula*, and connected the incident to tarantism. Bea de Navarra took the spider with him to Madrid and conducted further musical tests in the presence of colleagues who played tarantellas and watched the spider first freeze, as if entering a trance, then move to the beat.[14] Some supporters of tarantism believed that tarantulas danced to the tarantella because their bodily fluids reacted to the tune; when they bit a person, these same fluids were transferred into the person's body, causing them to dance.[15] Articles like the *Diario* one about Bea de Navarra's dancing spider drove tarantism one step closer to Madrileños.

---

[10] Anonymous, *Retrato de la tarántula macho y hembra, de los ovarios y nido que fabrican: su historia natural, y efectos de su veneno, y la relación del tarantado del Hospital General* (Madrid: Imprenta de González, 1787).

[11] For the bookstores where this pamphlet was sold see *Correo de los Ciegos*, August 15, 1787, 379.

[12] Íñigo Corral and C. Corral, "Neurological Considerations in the History of Tarantism in Spain," *Neurosciences and History* 4, no. 3 (2016): 108.

[13] *Diario curioso, erudito, económico y comercial*, July 30, 1787, 122.

[14] "Tarantismo," *Diario curioso, erudito, económico y comercial*, August 8 1787, 158–59.

[15] This was a modernized explanation for what German ethnomusicologist Marius Schneider considers to be a mystical identification between animal and human. Schneider interprets tarantism as an animal dance, in which the bite victim must imitate the tarantula's movements to counteract the venom. His interpretation derives from a broader theory that encompasses a correspondence between humanity and the cosmos, articulated through music and a "common rhythm." See Marius Schneider, *La*

Music, Medicine, and Tarantism in Madrid, 1787

By late summer in 1787, tarantism had become widely popular. Neither medical professionals nor commentators could control the flow of information, much less separate truth from fiction. The *Diario de Madrid* played an important role in the tarantism controversy, presenting the more rationalist perspective that prevailed in France and Italy, albeit without animosity. In an editorial note following the article about the china factory, the *Diario* expressed suspicion about the sequence of events from Cid's *Tarantismo observado en España*, to Ambrosio's diagnosis at the General Hospital thereafter, to the rapid increase in publications about and cases of tarantism in Madrid. The editors cautioned Madrid's residents not to overreact since tarantulas were seldom found within the city. Furthermore, the editors continued, scholars had not unanimously accepted tarantism. As an example, they mentioned French physicist Jean Antoine Nollet (1700–1770), who after visiting Apulia started to doubt tarantism, and naturalist Jacques-Christophe Valmont de Bonare (1731–1807). As tarantulas crept closer to city dwellers' imagination, music that could invoke the spider acquired an aura of danger.

Tarantism's physical or psychosomatic nature remained in question. According to the same *Diario* article that published Bea de Navarra's experiments, rumors spread of people playing the harpsichord and inadvertently conjuring dancing spiders. The *Diario* tried to dispel such rumors:

Para aquietar los ánimos de algunas personas sobradamente crédulas, diremos que este insecto es poco común en todas partes; y en Madrid siempre se ha tenido por rarísimo ...	To calm down some excessively credulous people's spirits, we shall say that this insect [the tarantula] is uncommon most everywhere, and in Madrid it has always been considered extremely rare ...
Desearíamos desterrar todo temor en esta parte; y especialmente persuadir a las señoritas aficionadas a la música sigan ejercitando su habilidad al clave o guitarra con todo sosiego, sin recelar que a esta o a la otra semana se aparezca alguno de estos animalejos, de que tanto se habla en el día; no debiendo dudar que la música contribuirá por sí misma a sosegar una imaginación sobresaltada por dar demasiado crédito a cuentos inventados con poca reflexión.[16]	We would like to dismiss all fear in this regard, and especially to persuade young ladies who are music enthusiasts to continue practicing their guitar or harpsichord skills calmly, without wariness that one of these strange creatures, about which everybody speaks today, will show up either this week or the next. Undoubtedly, the music itself will continue to quiet an imagination startled by giving too much credit to made-up stories lacking judgment.

---

danza de las espadas y la tarantela: Ensayo musicológico, etnográfico y arqueológico sobre los ritos medicinales (Madrid: Institución Fernando el Católico, 2016).

[16] "Tarantismo," *Diario curioso, erudito, económico y comercial*, 159.

92   *Music and Modernity in Enlightenment Spain*

The *Diario* hinted that tarantism may, after all, not be a poisonous disease affecting La Mancha peasants but a nervous disease seizing the imaginations of city girls. Cid's cases are male patients (except for two) who worked in the fields and slept outdoors or in barnyards, effectively exposed to the bite of black widows. Ambrosio, treated at the General Hospital, fits the same profile. Eighteenth-century Spanish tarantism differs considerably from the ritual, psychogenic phenomenon studied by anthropologist Ernesto De Martino in the mid-twentieth century, where most *tarantati* are women.[17] Cid accepted psychogenic versions of tarantism such as Giorgio Baglivi's *Carnevaletto delle donne* and French physician François Boissier de Sauvages's "tarantism musomania," or the immoderate impulse to dance.[18] He even suggested the possibility of a female *tarantismus nimphomania* equivalent to *furore uterino*, but at the same time made it clear that he was not dealing with any of those subtypes of the malady.[19] The *Diario* editors, by contrast, steered public attention to psychosomatic symptoms in women and even suggested music as a cure.

An intense tarantism *querelle* ensued between believers, otherwise characterized as irrational, and disbelievers, otherwise characterized as enlightened.[20] The latter were unhappy with the blurred boundaries between scientific and popular knowledge. The *Diario* referred to the famous tarantula engravings as "images that circulate completely unsubstantiated" since Cid's and Piñera's works were published.[21] A week after Bea de Navarra's article about the china factory, an open letter to the *Correo de los Ciegos* (the other Madrid daily) derided the *Diario* and the triweekly *Espíritu de los Mejores Diarios* for vulgarizing their content like the *Retrato de la tarantula* pamphlet had vulgarized tarantism.[22] The letter was signed "Lucas Alemán y Aguado," the pen name of the medical author, journalist, and playwright Manuel Casal y Aguado (1751–1837). The brouhaha surrounding Ambrosio's case did not escape Casal, who balked at newspapers' involvement. As a physician and writer, he may have read the books by Cid and Piñera, and he surely knew the *Retrato de la tarantula* pamphlet because he refers to it in his letter. Casal fabricated an anecdote to

---

[17]   Ernesto De Martino and Dorothy Louise Zinn, *The Land of Remorse: A Study of Southern Italian Tarantism* (London: Free Association, 2005).

[18]   Giorgio Baglivi, "Intorno all'anatomia, morso ed effetti della tarantella," in *Opere complete medico-pratiche ed anatomiche di Giorgio Baglivi* (Florence: Sansone Coen, 1841), 698–700.

[19]   Francisco Xavier Cid, *Tarantismo observado en España ... y memorias para escribir la historia del insecto llamado Tarántula, efectos de su veneno en el cuerpo humano, y curación por la música ...* (Madrid: Manuel Gonzalez, 1787), 12–14.

[20]   The *Diario* called believers in tarantism "excessively credulous:" "Tarantismo," *Diario curioso, erudito, económico y comercial*, 159.

[21]   "Tarantismo," *Diario curioso, erudito, económico y comercial*, 159.

[22]   Lucas Alemán y Aguado [Manuel Casal y Aguado], "Otra [carta]," *Correo de los Ciegos*, August 15, 1787, 375–76.

convey his mockery of Madrid's periodical press. At the end of his letter to the *Correo de los Ciegos*, he transcribed several satirical verses railing against the newspapers, which he claimed he saw printed on a paper cone that the grocer used to hand him his legumes—of course, the verses were his own. The fictional story of the paper cone helped Casal express indignation that the *Espíritu de los mejores Diarios* "[was] going around the public deposits of ointments, oil, and similar cheap products," just like "the Gaiferos verses, the *Tarantula Account* [*Retrato de la tarántula* pamphlet], and the portrait of La Caramba."[23] By this, Casal meant that Madrid's newspapers existed merely as objects of popular consumption bereft of true literary or scientific interest, much like the *Retrato de la tarántula* pamphlet and Esteve's tonadilla.[24] In his perception, the *Diario de Madrid*, the *Espíritu*, and the Madrid theaters (La Caramba was a prominent actress-singer) possessed only a cheap entertainment value unfit for commanding public opinion within the Republic of Letters.

Whereas the *Diario* editors and perhaps even Casal had reservations about tarantism, other press letter-writers expressed sincere belief and accused skeptics of stubbornness. A week after Casal published his verses, the *Correo de los Ciegos* printed a letter and a sonnet defending Cid and Piñera from "many stubborn [people], *especially two physicians.*"[25] This letter finds "the stubborn" guilty of incredulity despite the evidence provided by Cid and by Piñera. The following September of 1787, however, objections against Piñera prevailed again in a long letter spread over issues 95, 96, and 97 of the *Correo*. The letter's anonymous author considers tarantism an antiquated belief, "an illusion or deceit" already declining in Apulia but gaining traction in Spain. While he does not completely deny tarantism's existence, he maintains that Ambrosio most definitely did not suffer from it.[26]

El atarantulado's scene where the Doctor reveals the tarantula before the rest of the cast captured a dilemma that the Enlightenment posed for Spanish scientists, writers, and readers: to believe or not to believe in modern ideas. In the tonadilla, the characters believed in tarantism because Doctor Don Celedonio delivered the knowledge and invited them to see the phenomenon for themselves. After the Doctor mentions the tarantula and the other characters

---

[23] "Gaiferos verses" probably refers to the sung poem *Romance de Don Gaiferos*. "Otra [carta]," *Correo de los Ciegos*, 375.

[24] Casal also listed the portrait of La Caramba, then Madrid's most famous actress-singer, as another worn-out, hand-to-hand item. "Otra [carta]," *Correo de los Ciegos*, 375. The portrait of La Caramba was an engraving created by Juan de la Cruz Cano y Olmedilla as part of his *Colección de trajes de España*, published in 1777 to 1778. See Elisabeth Le Guin, *The Tonadilla in Performance: Lyric Comedy in Enlightenment Spain* (Berkeley: University of California Press, 2014), 83.

[25] The two alleged critics were likely Irañeta and Casal. [R.J.S.D.S.M.], "Otra [carta]," *Correo de los Ciegos*, August 22, 1787, 388.

[26] "Madrid. Carta," *Correo de los Ciegos*, August 15, 17, and 19, 1787, 436.

94 *Music and Modernity in Enlightenment Spain*

respond by singing the "How frightening, how shocking!" chorus, he concisely explains tarantism's symptoms and cure in one sentence.

Doctor:	Al que pica le sobreviene un letargo, y se cura ... y se cura ... bailoteando	Those who are bitten suddenly feel lethargic, and it is cured by ... it is cured by ... dancing

Upon learning about the strange disease, the characters sing the chorus again, then recite in unison: "You are deceiving us." The Doctor reassures them he is telling the truth, "and to prove it, if you want to see a patient I am treating, you shall be convinced." The characters accept the Doctor's invitation, hop in a carriage, and witness the therapeutic session like Madrid elites had done, encouraged by Piñera. The fictional and the actual doctors wanted the public to come, see, and give their verdict on the science applied to cure this disease.

Esteve's tonadilla provided tarantism basics to entertain Madrid's literate and illiterate audiences, while Francisco Xavier Cid's treatise addressed the European scientific community. Despite their differences, they both approach tarantism as a liminal reality between the visible and the invisible, offering palpable and audible cues to persuade the skeptics that musical healing was possible. Since Cid's work stirred up the tarantula craze in 1780s Madrid, examining its premises will elucidate why firsthand observation was central to tarantism debates.

Musical Medicine

Empiricism in Francisco Xavier Cid's Tarantismo observado en España

Cid's long book, *Tarantismo observado en España*, was printed in 1787 to vindicate tarantism as a legitimate disease that could be healed through music. Upon finding current writings by skeptical physicians who had discredited this idea, Cid decided to prove them wrong, relying on mechanistic and neo-Hippocratic medical paradigms. Cid's approach responded to encyclopedist and taxonomic Enlightenment endeavors, which tended toward universal systems instead of considering local particularities.

Cid became enthralled with tarantism after reading the work of Giorgio Baglivi (1668–1707) along with other sixteenth- and seventeenth-century sources.[27] In 1695, Baglivi wrote a short treatise titled *De anatome, morsu, et effectibus tarantulae* (*Of the Tarantula's Anatomy, Bite, and Its Effects*), later reprinted several times as part of his *Opera omnia*. Cid also referred to the German Jesuit Athanasius Kircher (1602–1680) and the French natural historian Noël-Antoine Pluche (1688–1761), who both discussed tarantism in their

---

[27] Cid lists the authors he had read regarding tarantism, in addition to Baglivi and Kircher: Pietro Andrea Mattioli, Epifanio Fernando, Andrés Piquer, Thomas Sydenham, Gerard Van Swieten.

studies of nature. In a section on insects under the "tarantula" entry, Pluche had described tarantism as recently as 1733 in his popular *Le spectacle de la nature*. Skepticism about the disease and its musical treatment increased during the eighteenth century. Examples of those discrediting tarantism include French physicians Charles-Augustin Vandermonde (1727–1762) and François Boissier de Sauvages (1706–1767)—who in turn quoted the Italian Francesco Serao (1702–1783) and the pope's own doctor—invalidated beliefs that tarantula bites compelled people to dance or induced lethargy curable through music and dance.

By his own account, a few years after he had read Baglivi and Kircher, Cid encountered the entry "Tarantisme" in Vandermonde's *Dictionnaire portatif de santé dans lequel tout le monde peut prendre une connaissance suffisante de toutes les maladies*, originally published in Paris in 1759 but only known to Spanish authors in its third edition from 1761.[28] Vandermonde acknowledged the symptoms of the tarantula bite but dismissed musical healing as "fabulous" and specifically targeted Baglivi. Vandermonde's Italian sources assured him that dancing did not prevent tarantism patients from dying. Vandermonde did not distinguish tarantula bites from snake bites, which should be treated with an antidote and not with music. The only plausible connection he found between tarantism and music was psychological, since victims reportedly became melancholic upon being bitten.[29] After the *Dictionnaire portatif*, Cid encountered the medical writings of François Boissier de Sauvages de la Croix. In the seventh volume of his *Nosologia Medica*, Boissier de Sauvages defined tarantism as an "immoderate desire of dancing" and classified it under "diseases that affect reason" and "depraved desires and aversions," together with nymphomania, bulimia, and homesickness.[30] In his description of tarantism, Boissier de Sauvages opposed Baglivi's view that tarantula bites cause the disease by citing Neapolitan physician Francesco Serao, who had observed cases of tarantula bites in Rome. Serao had never seen bite victims healed through

---

[28]   Cid, *Tarantismo*, 2.

[29]   Charles-Augustin Vandermonde, *Dictionnaire portatif de santé, dans lequel tout le monde peut prendre une connoissance suffisante de toutes les maladies, des différents signes qui les caractérisent chacune en particulier, des moyens les plus sûrs pour s'en préserver, ou des remedes les plus efficaces pour se guérir, & enfin de toutes les instructions nécessaires pour être soi-même son propre médecin. Le tout recueilli des ouvrages, tant anciens que modernes, des médecins les plus fameux, & augmenté d'une infinité de recettes particulieres, & de spécifiques pour toutes sortes de maladies. Par Mr. L***, ancien médecin des armées du Roi, & Mr. de B***, médecin des hôpitaux. Nouvelle édition*, 3rd ed., 2 vols. (Paris: Philippe Vincent, 1761), 504–5.

[30]   François Boissier de Sauvages, *Nosologie méthodique ou distribution des maladies en classes, en genres et en especes suivant l'esprit de Sydenham, & la méthode des botaniste par François Boissier de Sauvages, … traduite sur la dernière édition latine, par M. Gouvion, docteur en médecine. On a joint à cet ouvrage celui du chev. von Linné, intitulé Genera morborum, avec la traduction française à côté*, 10 vols., vol. 7 (1772), 695–700.

96 *Music and Modernity in Enlightenment Spain*

dance, only through diaphoretics or sweat inducers. The observation that sweating could rid the body of tarantula poison differed from Baglivi's and Cid's belief in the healing power of music and dance. Boissier de Sauvages then concluded that only prejudice attributed Apulian tarantism to the tarantula bite.[31]

Cid considered Baglivi a fellow scientist and Vandermonde, Boissier de Sauvages, and Serao as critics (nonscientists). For Cid, disbelief characterized modern criticism: "This is the character of the century's *bels esprits*: to deny everything without examination, and to believe or fake, at their discretion, whatever may serve to support their ideas."[32] Cid saw in criticism the same flaws that empiricists saw in Cartesianism and other forms of rationalism—namely, that they relied on speculation and opinion rather than on experimental data. Empiricist anti-Cartesianism had shaped Spain's medical tradition since the times of the pre-Enlightenment physician and philosopher Martín Martínez (1684–1734). In his treatise, Cid aimed to prove his theories about tarantism through experimentation and observation while rebuking Vandermonde's and Boissier de Sauvages's rationalist approaches.[33] The French physicians attributed music's effects on tarantism to the mind rather than the body. Vandermonde said music was perhaps used as a cure because patients were often melancholic after the spider bite and not because it had any physiological benefits.[34] Boissier de Sauvages classified tarantism as a *folie* (insanity). Moreover, neither of them substantiated their new interpretations of tarantism with experimental data, possibly because Vandermonde and Boissier de Sauvages only considered tarantism tangentially within their larger nosological projects. But there were deeper implications to these eighteenth-century French classifications and descriptions of illness.

While one might understand Cid's *Tarantismo observado en España* merely as an anachronistic text clinging to Baglivi's and Kircher's seventeenth-century theories, debates about the classification of nature and illnesses exemplified the eighteenth-century fixation on taxonomy. Boissier de Sauvages's systematic *Nosologie méthodique* approximated the biological cataloguing efforts of Carl Linnaeus, who was friends with Sauvages. In his *Systema naturae* (1735), Linnaeus classified plants according to a sexual system based on the number of male and female organs they presented. However, this classificatory scheme was Linnaeus's arbitrary decision, insofar as nothing in nature determines that sexual organs are the criterion by which plants are grouped into genera

---

[31] Boissier de Sauvages, *Nosologie*, 695.

[32] "Este es el carácter de los bellos espíritus del siglo: Negarlo todo sin examen, y creer o fingir a su arbitrio lo que pueda servir a sostener sus ideas." Cid, *Tarantismo*, 50.

[33] Empiricism also dominated medical activity at Madrid's hospitals, where Piñera y Siles worked. Physicians and surgeons mistrusted systematic approaches informed by rationalism. Juan Manuel Núñez Olarte, *El hospital general de Madrid en el Siglo 18: Actividad médico-quirúrgica* (Madrid: Editorial CSIC, 1999), 156–57.

[34] Vandermonde, *Dictionnaire portatif de santé*, 505.

and species. Hence, other scientists such as Georges-Louis Leclerc (Comte de Buffon) called Linnaeus's classification an artificial system. Artificial systems based on useful if arbitrary criteria became very popular in modern Western science.[35] According to historian of science Janet Browne, "this [Linnaeus's] system, often called the numerical or sexual system, was understood as a method of classifying plants *purely for human convenience*, for it grouped plants together on the basis of numbers alone. Buffon, who favoured a naturalistic scheme, critiqued it harshly."[36] The confrontations between Linnaeus and Buffon were known and debated in Spain precisely around the time Cid published his tarantism treatise. For example, Madrid's head botanist defended Linnaeus's system in a December 1786 *Diario de Madrid* article.[37] It was also widely known in the European scientific community that Boissier the Sauvages had used Linnaeus as a model. Cid seemed to have only partial knowledge of the debates around Linnaeus's classificatory system, since he did not mention key figures of the antisystematic critique, such as Condillac and Buffon. Hence, while Cid took the conservative side in a current controversy over artificial systems, he was not necessarily operating under seventeenth-century parameters. Should scientists limit their activity to observing and recording, or should they organize knowledge into human-designed systems? It is in this question's context that Cid interpreted Vandermonde's and Boissier de Sauvages's takes on tarantism to be unfounded, insofar as they privileged deductive reason over empirical observation.[38]

Like many contemporary Spanish writers, Cid was suspicious of the rationalist strain of French Enlightenment associated with Voltaire and Jean-Jacques Rousseau and often linked to secularism. An aversion to mind-centered diagnoses ran deep in the Spanish medical tradition. Like Baglivi and most physicians in Spain, Cid favored empiricism over Cartesianism, insisting on the value of observation.[39] He lamented that Vandermonde, Boissier de Sauvages,

[35] John E. Lesch, "Systematics and the Geometrical Spirit," in *The Quantifying Spirit in the 18th Century*, edited by Tore Frängsmyr, H. L. Heilborn, and Robin E. Rider (Berkeley: University of California Press, 1990), 76–78.

[36] Emphasis mine. "The popularity of the artificial system percolated through other disciplines. Boissier de Sauvages classified diseases in this manner and Antoine-Laurent Lavoisier did the same for chemistry. In 1869, Dmitrii Mendeleev became known as the Linnaeus of chemistry for ordering chemical elements in a structured series of relationships, the periodic table." Janet Browne, "Classification in science," *The Oxford Companion to the History of Modern Science* (2003), https://www.oxfordreference.com/view/10.1093/acref/9780195112290.001.0001/acref-9780195112290-e-0136.

[37] Relación de los Ejercicios públicos de Botánica, tenidos en la Sala de esta enseñanza en el presente mes de diciembre," *Diario de Madrid*, December 20, 1786. For another endorsement of Linnaeus by Spanish botanists, see Real Jardín Botánico," *Memorial Literario*, July 1787, 306–8.

[38] Cid, *Tarantismo*, 3.

[39] Cid, *Tarantismo*, 2, 7, 10, 24, 46, 51, 59, 61, 106, 16, 92, 264–5, 305.

98 *Music and Modernity in Enlightenment Spain*

and Serao did not back up their new tarantism theories with observations.[40] He cited sixteenth- and seventeenth-century authors and then confirmed their theories with tarantism cases' observations.[41] In the introduction to his *Intorno all'anatomia, morso ed effetti della tarantella*, Baglivi explicitly adhered to an antirationalist methodology and asked the reader to "attribute [my inconsistencies] to my natural fear of cutting the straight thread of nature with my either unlearned or inelegant reasoning," should his tales of tarantism sound irrational.[42] He argued that because human reason was inferior to nature's mechanisms, deductive reasoning should not interfere with observation.

Cid's anti-Cartesianism was compounded by his antiskepticism. He profoundly mistrusted thinkers for whom received knowledge carried no more authority than their own deductions. Cid regarded medical knowledge as the result of accumulation rather than of discovery. Because the novelty or obsolescence of tarantism theories did not concern him as much as the amount of observational evidence provided to support those theories did, all the sources he cited in support of tarantism date from the fifteenth to the seventeenth centuries.[43] From an antiskeptical perspective, it would take a similar volume of new evidence compiled "over a long series of years" to overturn the old evidence.[44] From Cid's cumulative perspective, the scientist must aggregate firsthand observations and secondhand accounts of tarantism, since a lifetime may not be enough to gather enough data. Such reasoning explains the fact that all cases in Cid's treatise are third-person accounts relayed to him by the people of his hometown, Toledo, or by medical colleagues working in the area who sent him letters.[45] Cid considered third-person knowledge as empirical data,

[40] Cid, *Tarantismo*, 2–3.

[41] Cid, *Tarantismo*, 51.

[42] "Tu vedrai che secondo il mio costume in nulla mi diparto dalla osservazione et dalla pratica, alle quali do sempre il primo luogo in ogni cosa." Baglivi, "Intorno," 683.

[43] In his introduction, Cid refers the authors he consulted to verify Baglivi's theories: Juan Eusebio Nieremberg, *Oculta filosofía* (Madrid, 1645, 1649); Oliva del Sabuco (*Nueva filosofía de la naturaleza del hombre*, La Mancha, 1587); Pedro Mexía, *Silva de varia lección* (Sevilla, 1540); Matiolo [Petrus Andreas Mattioli, *Commentarii secundo aucti, in libros sex pedacii*, 1560], John Johnston, *Thaumatrographia Naturalis* (Amsterdam, 1632, Scottish); Athanasius Kircher, *Magnes, De arte magnetica* (1641); Noël-Antoine Pluche, *Spectacle de la nature* (1739); Étienne-François Geoffroy, *Tractatus de materia medica, Tomus tertius: De regno animali* (1741). Later in the treatise he cited Epifanius Ferdinandus, Piquer Sydenham, and the Baron of Vanswieten.

[44] "Las observaciones requieren una larga serie de años si en ellas hemos de apoyar nuestros discursos, y tal vez en muchas vidas no hay oportunidad para ellas: en cuyo caso la correspondencia epistolar de los curiosos y verdaderamente sabios nos pueden poner en estado de juzgar los hechos." Cid, *Tarantismo*, 7–8.

[45] Cid was the physician for Toledo's archbishop and priests of the cathedral chapter. Written correspondence was a recognized medical practice in the eighteenth century, especially in small cities and rural areas. Patrick Singy, "The Popularization of Medi-

Music, Medicine, and Tarantism in Madrid, 1787　　99

provided that sources supported their findings with observations. While Vandermonde (1759) and Boissier de Sauvages (1774) cite other authors in their rejection of tarantism, they do not report any specific cases. This lack of case studies sufficed for Cid to categorize them as "sayers" contradicting "doers." Cid's and Baglivi's treatises have different purposes than Vandermonde's and Boissier de Sauvages's, the former collecting evidence to support tarantism and the latter creating an encyclopedic classification of diseases and their causes. Cid's concern with defending the authority of received knowledge through empirical evidence aligned with the premises of absolute monarchic power and one true Catholic faith.

By highlighting the particulars of tarantism, Cid further distanced his views from the universalist efforts of encyclopedism. While encyclopedist authors try to subsume tarantism under broader pathological categories, Cid emphasizes the role of regional geographical conditions. Consider that, for Vandermonde, tarantula venom resembled that of snakes and therefore bites from these animals should be treated similarly.[46] Boissier de Sauvages classifies tarantism as a nervous disease akin to nymphomania and hypochondria. Such views overlook tarantism's culturospatial specificities, which Cid (and before him Baglivi) underlined.[47] Cid considers his own region of La Mancha, however, "the Spanish Apulia," thus linking two particular geographic locations with similar climates (dry, hot) wherein tarantism *was* real, if not transposable to other locations.[48] Vandermonde, Boissier de Sauvages, and Serao were maybe writing about different animal species than Cid, since Apulian and La Mancha tarantulas were likely black widow spiders of the species *Latrodectus tredecimguttatus*, common in the Mediterranean basin but not found elsewhere in Europe.[49] "Tarantula" in the eighteenth century denoted any large spider, corresponding to what we now call tarantulas (*Theraposidae*), wolf spiders (*Lycosidae*), and black widows (*Latrodectus*). Of the three, only black widow bites inject enough venom to cause the symptoms identified by Spanish authors. Hence, Cid was

---

　　cine in the Eighteenth Century: Writing, Reading, and Rewriting Samuel Auguste Tissot's Avis au peuple sur sa sante," *Journal of Modern History* 82, no. 4 (2010): 773.

[46]　Vandermonde, *Dictionnaire portatif de santé*, 504–5.

[47]　Cid called Vandermonde a "contradictory spirit" who attempted to change minds with only words and without any observational foundation to support criticism of received theories. *Tarantismo*, 3.

[48]　About the climate similarities between Apulia and La Mancha, see Cid, *Tarantismo*, 8, 64. While Cid, like Boissier de Sauvages and Baglivi, acknowledges a psycho-hormonal variant of tarantism called *carnevaletto delle donne*, unrelated to tarantula bites, he focuses on tarantism caused by poison. Since tarantulas abound in rural, dry climates, those susceptible to their bite are mostly field workers and in this case men. Therefore, most case studies in Cid's treatise are of male patients.

[49]　Corral and Corral, "Neurological considerations," 100. Anna Gruszczynska Ziolkowska, "La danza de la araña: En torno a los problemas del tarantismo español (1)," *Revista de Folklore* 317 (2007): 147–65.

100   *Music and Modernity in Enlightenment Spain*

right in his insistence that his and Baglivi's cases were different from those reported in other places.[50]

Cid sought to verify the information he had received from authors like Baglivi and Kircher through his own observation and data collection, rather than simply trust them. To this end, Cid observed tarantulas and their nests under the microscope and corresponded with fellow physicians in different towns of La Mancha. In addition to Baglivi's and Kircher's works, Cid acknowledged other eighteenth-century authors who wrote about tarantism, such as John Johnston, Noël Pluche, and Francesco Serao.[51] However, he complained that none of these authors conducted their own experiments but simply accepted or denied musical healing based on their own preexisting beliefs and on others' writings. While some (Johnston and Plüche) repeated previously recorded accounts of tarantism, others (Serao, Vandermonde, and Boissier de Sauvages) denied tarantism for the sole reason that healing through music was "too prodigious."[52] Cid protested modern authors who refuted previous theories of tarantism without their own firsthand or secondhand observation of the phenomenon. For Cid, such refutation is acceptable when supported by new, contradicting data.

Music, the Body, and the Soul

Rejection of tarantism and of musical healing were, for Cid, signs of a bigger problem—namely, the rejection of faith in the invisible and the miraculous. In vindicating tarantism's existence, Cid intended to support belief in an invisible, divine power. Many contemporary authors saw accounts of tarantism as fabulous lore, so Cid built his arguments methodically in accordance with the principles of empirical science. In this respect, Cid and Baglivi differ from Kircher, whose understanding of the connections between tarantula venom, music, and dancing can be traced to Renaissance natural magic.[53] Instead, Cid and Baglivi explained tarantism through

---

[50]   Both authors undoubtedly believe music to be the most effective treatment for tarantism, and both recommend the use of music to treat other ailments as well. For example, "Del resto rimangono affatto inutili tanto questi, quanto gli altri remedii que possono proporsi, se non si adopri prontamente la música ... Di fatto la musica è il principale per coloro che sono morsi dalla tarantella" (Baglivi, "Intorno," 702–3); "De lo dicho hasta aquí se infiere que las sangrías, alkáli volátil y alexifarmacos no son tan poderosos remedios en la curación del tarantismo como quiere persuadir el Dr. Irañeta, y que únicamente le es la música Tarantela ó alguna otra sonata análoga al veneno" (Cid, *Tarantismo*, 203–4).

[51]   Francesco Serao, *Della Tarantola, o sia Falangio di Puglia, lezioni accademiche* (1742).

[52]   Cid, *Tarantismo*, 50.

[53]   Kircher had written about tarantism in his *Magnes, De arte magnetica* from 1641. According to Ernesto De Martino, Kircher's mid-seventeenth century work epitomizes the humanistic interest in tarantism as a phenomenon that gave insight into the effects of music on the mind and body. Ultimately, De Martino continues, Kircher's ideas harken back to the natural magic of classical antiquity. Ernesto De Martino, *La*

Music, Medicine, and Tarantism in Madrid, 1787   101

mechanistic physiology. Cid compared music's medicinal effects to those of other invisible natural phenomena such as electricity, magnetism, and tidal ebb and flow, in which the acting force is invisible but has visible effects. In the case of tarantism, the invisible force is music and the effect is the patient's dancing.

The way in which music affects the human body in Cid's treatise (and in Baglivi's) combines humoral theory with a fibro-centric model espoused in Spanish medicine throughout the eighteenth century.[54] Fibro-centrism stems from iatro-mechanism (*iatros*: healer, doctor), that is, the application of physics to medicine, "a system based on a view of the blood as a congeries of particles in corpuscular agitation and of the body as a set of mechanical tubes, engines, and implements"[55] Iatro-mechanism was the paradigm that prevailed in English and French medicine until vitalism, which held that life cannot be reduced to mechanics, gained ascendancy in the late eighteenth and then the nineteenth centuries.[56] Iatro-mechanism adopted modern scientific premises while maintaining humoral theory. The widely read Swiss doctor Samuel-Auguste Tissot (*Avis au people sur sa santé*, 1761) adhered to fibro-centric iatro-mechanism. According to the fibro-centric model, movement and vibration stimulate or irritate the nerve fibers, which in turn transmit mechanical signals to the brain.[57] Cid directed his attention more specifically to iatro-phonics, the application of sound to medicine, which Spanish friar Antonio Rodríguez had studied in his little-known 1744 treatise "Yatro-Phonia, o medicina musica."[58] Rodríguez's work was published more than a decade before a better-known work on iatro-phonics by French physician Joseph-Louis Roger, *Tentamen de vi soni et musices in corpus human* (1758). Cid knew the Latin version of Roger's work before its 1803 translation into French as *Traité des effects de la musique sur le corps humaine.*[59] The iatro-mechanics and iatro-phonics of Rodríguez,

---

   terra del rimorso (Milan: EST, 1996), 242–43.

[54]   Pilar León-Sanz, "Music Therapy in Eighteenth-Century Spain: Perspectives and Critiques," in *Music and the Nerves, 1700–1900*, edited by James Kennaway (New York: Palgrave MacMillan, 2014), 104.

[55]   Theodore M. Brown, "The College of Physicians and the Acceptance of Iatromechanism in England," *Bulletin of the History of Medicine* 44, no. 1 (1970): 12.

[56]   "From Mechanism to Vitalism in Eighteenth-Century Physiology," *Journal of the History of Biology* 7, no. 2 (1974): 184.

[57]   See León-Sanz, "Music Therapy," 103. Irritability of the nerves had been studied by English anatomist Francis Glisson in the 1670s and experimentally corroborated by Swiss physiologist Albrecht von Haller in the 1760s: Brown, "From Mechanism to Vitalism."

[58]   In *Tarantismo*, Cid refers several times to Rodríguez's treatise as "*Jatrophonia*." Antonio José Rodríguez (O.Cist), "Yatro-Phonia, o Medicina Musica," in *Palestra critico-medica en que se trata introducir la verdadera Medicina, y desalojar la tirana intrusa de el Reyno de la Naturaleza* (Madrid: Imprenta Real de la Gaceta, 1744).

[59]   Paolo Gozza, "Number to Sound. Introduction," in *Music and the Renaissance: Renaissance, Reformation, and Counter-Reformation*, edited by Philippe Vendrix (London:

102   *Music and Modernity in Enlightenment Spain*

Tissot, and Roger allowed Cid to provide a scientific explanation of invisible phenomena, including the soul.

Cid details music's effects on humans in a chapter entitled "Philosophy of Music." Parts of this chapter resemble Menuret de Chambaud's *Encyclopédie* article "Effets de la musique" insofar as they deal with the general influence of music on human beings, while other sections specifically concern tarantism.[60] Both Cid and Menuret de Chambaud agree that sound has a mechanical impact on bodily fibers and fluids via vibrational transmission through the air. This principle of sound transmission through an elastic medium (air) had been demonstrated by Robert Boyle in the seventeenth century.[61] Since Boyle was both an experimental philosopher and a theologian who accepted the existence of God and the soul, his ideas were well received in Spain.[62] In the case of tarantism, Cid notes, the rhythm, tempo, meter, and melody of the tarantella target the venom fluids that have entered the body. Sound moves venomous fluids through air vibration, causing the victim to dance involuntarily. Cid provides his readers with specific instructions to produce the correct sound. He believed the tarantella had to be played with a *vihuela* or a violin to achieve optimal results. Triple meter and a lively rhythm were for Cid the most important musical elements for healing to be effective.[63] For his part, while Menuret de Chambaud in the *Encyclopédie* accepts that music can prompt involuntary dancing in poisoned patients, he does not distinguish between the bites of scorpions, snakes, and tarantulas. He also cautiously notes that it is hard to know exactly how music acts upon venom because "we are still limited to a blind empiricism on this point," an empiricism wherein Cid finds an open door for miracle.[64] Convinced of music's healing power and of the tarantella's unique iatro-mechanic effects on the patient's body, Cid warned that any delay in musical treatment could be fatal.[65]

Taylor and Francis, 2001), 243.

[60] Jean-Joseph Menuret de Chambaud, "Effets de la musique," vol. 10, *Encyclopédie* (1765), https://artflsrv03.uchicago.edu/philologic4/encyclopedie0521/navigate/10/3795/?byte=9449483&byte=9449490&byte=9449493&byte=9449513.

[61] Cid rejects Spanish *novator* Benito Feijóo's idea that sound moves only the lightest of air particles capable of traversing solid matter: "Campana, y crucifijo de Lugo / Benito Jerónimo Feijoo / Cartas eruditas y curiosas / tomo 2" (Madrid: Imprenta Real de la Gazeta, 1773). Georges-Louis LeClerc suggested a similar theory of "sonorous particles" in his *Histoire Naturelle*.

[62] For example, a biographical sketch on the *Correo de Madrid* (formerly *Correo de los Ciegos*) from February 20, 1790, calls Boyle "one of the restorers of the good Physics," whose "heart was adorned with such qualities, that made him endearing to all." The sketch also notes that Boyle was "zealous when it came to religion." "Boyle," *Correo de Madrid*, February 20, 1790, 2713.

[63] Cid, *Tarantismo*, 15–17.

[64] Menuret de Chambaud, "Effets de la musique," 909.

[65] Cid, *Tarantismo*, 288.

Just like Cid attributed La Mancha and Apulia tarantism to these locations' distinct hot, dry weather, he attributed healing power to the tarantella's unique sonic properties. According to Cid, the tarantella is the only "sonata" that cures those bitten by a tarantula. Cid wrote about a blind man from La Mancha named José Recuero who specialized in playing the tarantella. La Mancha doctors and families often called Recuero to play for tarantism patients, and the rumor was that he had learned the tarantella from a Milanese musician in 1760.[66] Another story reported that in 1787 La Mancha peasants had learned to dance the tarantella from the bitten patients themselves and had incorporated the dance into their *saraos*, or music and dance parties.[67]

To help his readers avoid medical errors, Cid provided in his book transcriptions of five simple tarantella tunes for violin and guitar. All the melodies use the A harmonic minor scale, with an augmented second from E to F sharp. The tarantellas feature compound triple meter and follow binary dance forms (fig. 2.1, I, II, III; figure 2.2, I, II), have more than two repeating sections in continuous movement (fig. 2.1, V; fig. 2.2, III), or a single repeated melody (fig. 2.1, IV; fig. 2.2, IV, V). Cid emphasizes the music's repetitive nature by comparing the tarantella tunes to fandangos, folías, canarios, "or a mixture of all three" basso-ostinato patterns native to Spain and the Spanish Americas but popular throughout Europe since the seventeenth century.[68] The healing process Cid prescribed demanded significant physical exertion from both the musician and the patient. The short pieces needed to be played in a loop for an hour or more, and if the musician were to change the melody to something other than a tarantella, the bitten man would immediately stop dancing and fall back into a spasmodic state.[69] Similarly, if the musician lost his pace or went out of tune, the patient was said to feel sorrow or sadness.[70]

Although Cid conceives of the human body as a machine responding to external stimuli, he also maintains that "nothing happens in the body without the intervention of the soul as a sentient principle."[71] Cid affirms that music acts not only on the senses but also on the soul and affections. Thus, we see in Cid's iatro-mechanical approach a continuity between the soul, the mind, the body, and the external world that does not exist in the thinking of tarantism's detractors. Following the baroque doctrine of the affections, Cid believed that "passions reside in certain parts of the body" and respond mechanically to

---

[66] Pedro Martínez de Anguiano, *Tratado completo de higiene comparada*, vol. 2 (Madrid: José María Magallón, 1871), 194.

[67] Vicente Aguilera, "Descripción de la tarántula, su picadura y efectos que causa, con las observaciones hechas hasta ahora por D. Vicente Aguilera, Cirujano titular de la Villa de Manzanares," *Memorial literario, instructivo y curioso* 51 (1787): 575.

[68] Cid, *Tarantismo*, 15.

[69] Cid, *Tarantismo*, 99.

[70] Cid took the idea that a poorly played tarantella made the patient suffer directly from Baglivi. Compare *Tarantismo*, 174, and Baglivi, "Intorno," 703.

[71] Cid, *Tarantismo*, 259.

Figure 2.1. Tarantellas for the violin appended to Cid's *Tarantismo observado en España*. Source: Google Books. Original from the Bavarian State Library.

the appropriate stimuli.[72] In his model of musical perception, the intermediary between the senses and the soul that animates the body is the common sensorium. In terms of the mechanistic physiology Cid shared with European physicians of the mid-eighteenth century, Aristotle's common sensorium (*koinē aísthēsis*) consists of a series of "small organs" and "tiny machines" spread throughout the body that operate the soul's movements.[73] In Cid's writings, it is precisely these small organs and tiny machines that music vibrates, causing them to alter the soul and body of the person. The common sensorium allowed Cid to describe detailed perceptual processes while maintaining the soul's existence—a crucial point for most Spanish Enlightenment thinkers.[74]

---

[72] Cid, *Tarantismo*, 97.

[73] Cid, *Tarantismo*, 236.

[74] In this respect, there is a connection between Cid's mechanistic stance and that of Scottish Enlightenment physician Robert Whytt (1714–1766). According to literature and science historian Nima Bassiri, "for Whytt, a theory of the nerves could not avoid a certain amount of philosophical reflection into the relationship between the body and

Figure 2.2. Tarantellas for the guitar appended to Cid's *Tarantismo observado en España*. Source: Google Books. Original from the Bavarian State Library.

Cid was not the only European physician to support iatro-mechanist or Neo-Hippocratic principles to add a "beyond" or mystical dimension to their medical theories. Medical theories that foregrounded a continuity between the soul, the mind, and the body often supported universal remedies targeting the whole of a person without any undesirable side effects. For Cid, music was one such universal remedy. Universal remedies characterized diverse eighteenth-century neo-Hippocratic practices unified by a holistic approach to medicine that sought to balance the body's humors. Neo-Hippocratism was compatible with empiricism and proposed simple remedies accessible to the public, some of which—bloodletting and purgatives—had been popular since antiquity. Cid's methodology of compiling case studies to arrive at the description of a disease is also Hippocratic, following the traces of Herman Boerhaave and Thomas Sydenham (1676). Enlightenment revivals of Hippocrates ranged from the radical materialism of Julien Offray de La

---

the soul." Whytt elaborated a theory of the nervous system that involved "an immaterial sentient principle" very similar to Cid's. Nima Bassiri, "The Brain and the Unconscious Soul in Eighteenth-Century Nervous Physiology: Robert Whytt's 'Sensorium Commune'," *Journal of the History of the Ideas* 74, no. 3 (2013): 426.

Mettrie, a hedonist exiled from France due to his quasi-atheist ideas in *The History of the Soul* (1745), to the animistic mechanism of Scottish physician Robert Whytt who promoted the "sentient principle," to the vegetarianism of proto-psychiatrist George Cheyne. Where Cheyne recommended the universal remedy of a vegetarian diet and exercise to promote well-being, Cid prescribed music as "the noble, useful, and innocent remedy" for numerous diseases.[75]

In considering the soul a part of the mechanistic body, Cid differs from vitalist approaches that had gained ascendancy in the scientific and medical community since the 1750s. For the new vitalists, the principle of life was usually one fluid or another. Menuret de Chambaud, straddling iatro-mechanism and vitalism, concedes in "Effets de la musique" that music operates on a purely mechanical level and on a level defined by "the pleasure that modified sound ... incites in us." However, Menuret de Chambaud carefully avoids the term "soul," explaining this second effect of music in terms of "pleasure" (*plaisir*) or "taste" (*gôut*). For Menuret de Chambaud, pleasure or taste is activated through the movement of a "nervous fluid" that runs through the body.[76] Thus, we see two differences between Menuret de Chambaud and Cid's theoretical approaches: (1) Menuret de Chambaud mixes mechanism and vitalism, while Cid sticks to the older paradigm of fibro-centric mechanism; and (2) Menuret de Chambaud locates the principle of life in a nervous fluid, while Cid connects the principle of life to the soul as a "sentient principle," a mechanistic version of the Christian soul.

Believing-upon-Seeing

His mechanistic principles notwithstanding, Cid considers music "divine medicine" because music's ultimate effects, he claims, remain scientifically unverifiable:

... el *divino* medicamento de la música ¿Divino? Sí. Pues además del modo con que concebimos que obra hay otra influencia secreta e inteligible, y como que envuelve o dice cosa divina. Hipócrates llamaba *quid divinum* lo que producía las enfermedades oculto en el aire, y lo que estas tenían de particular; no por otra razón, sino porque era inescrutable. Lo mismo sucede con la música.[77]

... the *divine* medicine of music. Divine? Yes. For in addition to the way we understand it works, there is another secret, inteligible influence, such that it envelopes or says a divine thing. Hyppocrate called *quid divinum* what, occult in the air, produced diseases, and the particulars of these diseases, not for any other reason, but because it was inscrutable. The same happens with music.

[75] Cid, *Tarantismo*, 272.

[76] Menuret de Chambaud, "Effets de la musique," 907.

[77] Cid, *Tarantismo*, 315.

Cid traces a parallel between music's intangibility and divine mysteries.

In Cid's view, music triggers mechanistic reactions in the body that ultimately reach the soul, where science cannot reach. His position does not deny science but subordinates it to metaphysical knowledge of presumably divine origin. Most importantly, he does not see rigorous science and religion as being at odds but rather as existing within an epistemological continuum. He presents mechanicism as a complex chain of progressively intangible phenomena, wherein the human body effortlessly leads to the supernatural. Within this framework, music operates "almost miraculously," and its effectiveness can be verified through empirical observation, if not inferred through reason Cid's anti-Cartesianism strongly emerges in the following passage:

¿Pues quién había de creer, guiado únicamente por la razón, que la sonata tarantela era el correctivo del veneno de la tarántula comunicado al cuerpo humano si así la experiencia no lo hubiera decidido? ¿Y quién por sola la razón o a priori sería el que rastrease que un vehemente dolor de cabeza se había de calmar con el estrépito y molesto ruido del tambor si el mismo hecho no lo hubiera acreditado? ¿Habrá alguno tan arrogante y presuntuoso que fiado en su ilustración y penetración asegura que cierta y determinada enfermedad es curable con la música de esta o la otra naturaleza, y con esta o aquella sonata? No.[78]

For, who would have believed, guided by reason alone, that the tarantella tune was the correction for the tarantula venom communicated to the human body, if experience had not determined so? And who, by reason alone, or a priori, would be the one to find that a pounding headache would be calmed through the drum's racket and obnoxious sound if fact itself had not confirmed this? Will there be anyone so arrogant and conceited as to, relying on their enlightenment and penetration, claim that any particular disease can be cured with music of certain characteristics, and with this or that tune? No.

Ultimately, Cid hoped his experimental observations would impress los ilustrados, or enlightened ones, so that they would "bow down their proud necks before the mysteries of musical healing and move from these to worship holier ones."[79]

For Cid, accepting tarantism when confronted with case studies based on empirical observation was the equivalent of the biblical believing-upon-seeing where the risen Jesus invited Thomas the Apostle to touch the wounds in his hands and side to see for himself that he is, indeed, Jesus.[80] The title page of Cid's *Tarantismo observado en España* foregrounds its ultimate mission: to counter disbelief with empirical observation. Consider the below translation:

[78] Cid, *Tarantismo*, 315, 21.

[79] Cid, *Tarantismo*, 92.

[80] John 20:27.

> TARANTISM
> OBSERVED IN SPAIN,
> TO PROVE THAT OF APULIA,
> DOUBTED BY SOME,
> AND DEEMED FABULOUS BY OTHERS
> And memoirs to write the history of the insect called tarantula, effects
> of its venom in the human body, and cure through music explaining
> how it works, and its application as a remedy for diverse maladies

On the verso of the title page, a Latin epithet taken from Apulian physician Epifanio Ferdinando (1569–1638) invites the incredulous to "come, see, and make experiments. For the truth is, what we write we shall discover."[81] Cid, like Jesus did with Thomas, encourages the modern ilustrados to stop doubting and believe in tarantism.

Many of the thirty-five tarantism stories collected by Cid in *Tarantismo observado en España* resemble resurrection narratives: the poisoned one lies inert until he hears the tarantella and begins moving. In Cid's collected stories, this reanimation occurs in the presence of the attending physician and other witnesses, who then give testimony of the healing.[82] Cid's twenty-ninth case study epitomizes the biblical Thomasian trope. In this case, the mayor of the small town of Almodóvar del Campo refused to believe tarantism stories, so his fellow townsmen took him to see a youth recently bitten by the spider. They found the lad "voiceless, completely motionless ... like a log," while some musicians played the tarantella. For a while, the patient did not move, prompting the incredulous mayor to laugh at the crowd of believers. Nonetheless, the locals maintained their trust in the musical remedy. Slowly, the human "log" began to move until he jumped up and danced "with flawless beat," leading the mayor to "turn his salacious comments toward those who had tried to persuade him of the veracity of the phenomenon into astonishment and admiration, declaring that it was hard to believe it despite seeing it." Through direct observation, this uppity disbeliever had no choice but to join the local believers.[83]

The fact that Cid adopts the myth of resurrection in some of his tarantism reports does not mean that he understood the disease as supernatural or the musical healing as miraculous. Rather, he draws the parallel to demonstrate that not everything that is real is apparent to the naked eye. Just as skeptics rebuke divine mysteries, so too do they dismiss tarantism because they cannot see it. For Cid, natural and mechanical phenomena are taking place when music heals, however fantastic the process seems.

---

[81] Epifanio Ferdinando reported one hundred different medical case studies in his *Centum historiae sev observationes et casus medici* (Venice: Apud Thomas Ballionum, 1621). Case number eighty-one, by far the book's longest, is about tarantism.

[82] Not all the patients in Cid's collected cases survived. Some relapsed, and some died of diseases apparently unrelated to tarantism.

[83] Cid, *Tarantismo*, 190–92.

Music, Medicine, and Tarantism in Madrid, 1787 109

Cid's mistrust of Vandermonde and Boissier de Sauvages is prototypical of two conflicts that the French Enlightenment often posed for Spanish intellectuals: one, that skepticism of received knowledge rubbed against adherence to authority, and two, that secular Enlightenment left little room for belief in the invisible—in this case, that music could heal. This strain of enlightened thought threatened Catholicism, since it could lead to rejection of church traditions, belief in miracles, and ultimately God. On the contrary, Cid's scientific enterprise of musical healing is meant to serve God's interests. Quoting Antonio Rodríguez's *Iatro-phonia*, Cid writes that "it is not in God's disservice to heal the sick using natural remedies."[84] In believing that music could heal, Cid left the door open for other kinds of invisible phenomena such as God's existence. While Cid might seem to be simply recalling seventeenth-century authors like Baglivi and Kircher, his treatise decidedly favors Enlightenment ideas rooted in sensism, mechanicism, and empiricism over those of the French philosophes.

From Theory to Practice to Satire

Cid's *Tarantismo observado en España* would have held specialists' interest if Ambrosio's case had not gripped Madrid shortly after its publication. Having considered Cid's efforts to reconcile mechanistic and fibro-centric paradigms with faith in the invisible, let us now move from La Mancha's fields to Madrid's hospitals and theaters.

A young and ambitious physician, Piñera, thought he had discovered in Ambrosio a new type of Saint Vitus's dance that would expand on recently published European nosologies. When Piñera saw Ambrosio's spasms and partial paralysis, he diagnosed him with Saint Vitus's dance (today called Sydenham's chorea), an infectious bacterial disease that affects the brain and produces jerking movements of the face, legs, and arms. The disease had first been described by Thomas Sydenham (1624–1689), a champion of medical observation whom Piñera sought to emulate by prizing empirical inspection over general hypotheses. However, Ambrosio did not react to treatment for Sydenham's chorea. Upon learning of an insect bite the boy had suffered when his symptoms appeared, Piñera declared him the first detected case of a subtype of Saint Vitus's dance that he called *tarantismus chorea Santi Viti*, combining both diseases' diagnoses.[85] Placing his own study alongside the observational work of Sydenham and the nosologies of Rudolph August Vogel (1754), Linnaeus (1759), William Cullen (1769), and François Boissier de Sauvages (1772), Piñera aspired to incorporate Spanish tarantism into the categories of modern medical science.

---

[84] Cid, *Tarantismo*, 281.

[85] Piñera y Siles, *Descripción histórica*, 35.

Piñera's taxonomic approach is characteristic of late Enlightenment encyclopedism in the natural sciences.[86] While Cid is preoccupied with empirical observation as a gateway from the visible to the invisible, Piñera avoids pointing to any kind of truth beyond direct observation and meticulous description. Whereas by amassing thirty-five cases of tarantism, Cid abides by the traditional authority of cumulative knowledge, Piñera focuses in detail on only one case. For example, in the introduction to his report, Piñera declares that impartial, individual inductive observation is the only way to advance medicine, never deduction.[87] Such observations, he stresses, ought to be devoid of *l'esprit de système*, the epistemological model that favors a priori hypotheses and which Condillac and d'Alembert rejected as obsolete. *L'esprit de système* associated with traditional metaphysics meant for d'Alembert "holding on to one's hypothetical and speculative opinions as dogma and simultaneously disregarding any criticism or contrary facts of principle."[88] D'Alembert thought that although *l'esprit de système* was previously valid "because the issue then was not so much to think well, but to learn to think for oneself," it had become obsolete by the mid-eighteenth century.[89] Thus, Piñera revealed his familiarity with encyclopedism and asserted his support of the scientific method against the dogmatic scholasticism lurking in Salamanca lecture halls.

As an individual, Ambrosio came to embody tarantism, the disease described in Cid's book and in Piñera's medical report. One day, during Ambrosio's lengthy stay at the Madrid General Hospital under Piñera's care, a pharmacist dressed in red accompanied Piñera to visit the boy. Ambrosio jumped up to hug the pharmacist, which reminded Piñera of Giorgio Baglivi's account of tarantula bite patients who developed a penchant for the color red.[90] Ambrosio then remem-

---

[86] Gunnar Broberg, "'The Broken Circle," in *The Quantifying Spirit in the 18th Century*, ed. Tore Frängsmyr, H. L. Heilborn, and Robin E. Rider (Berkeley: University of California Press, 1990).

[87] Piñera y Siles, *Descripción histórica*, 4.

[88] Denis Diderot and Jean le Rond d'Alembert, "Philosophy," trans. Julia Wallhager, in *The Encyclopedia of Diderot & d'Alembert Collaborative Translation Project* (Ann Arbor: University of Michigan Library), available at http://hdl.handle.net/2027/spo. did2222.0003.145.

[89] On *l'esprit de système*, see d'Alembert, "L'esprit d'hypothese & de conjecture pouvoit être autrefois fort utile, & avoit même été nécessaire pour la renaissance de la Philosophie; parce qu'alors il s'agissoit encore moins de bien penser, que d'apprendre à penser par soi-même. Mais les tems sont changés, & un Ecrivain qui feroit parmi nous l'éloge des Systèmes viendroit trop tard." d'Alembert, "Discourse préliminaire," *Encyclopédie, ou dictionnaire raisonné des sciences, des arts, et des métiers*, vol. 1, xxxi.

[90] Kircher also thought that tarantula victims loved some colors (red) and loathed others (black): "De tarantismo, siue Tarantula Apulo Phalangio eiusque Magnetismo, ac mira cum Musica sympathia," in *Magnes siue De arte magnetica opvs tripartitvm, quo praeterqvam qvod vniversa magnetis natvra, eivsqve in omnibvs artibus & scientijs vsus noua methodo explicetur, è viribus quoque & prodigiosis effectibus magneticarum, aliarum-*

bered that, about a month earlier, "an insect with many legs" had bitten him in a mill on the Manzanares river in Madrid's outskirts. With this new information, Piñera changed his diagnosis from St. Vitus's dance to tarantism and decided to treat Ambrosio with music.[91] It is unclear whether Piñera had learned about Baglivi and tarantism from Cid's book or from other sources.

It was one thing for Cid to try and persuade the medical community of tarantism and musical healing from his Toledo office; it was another for Piñera to implement these musical methods in Madrid's main hospital. Hospital authorities would not tolerate any musical treatment in their establishment. They said music and dance were highly inappropriate inside the hospital and feared the whole city would jeer at the hospital and write satires if the treatment failed.[92] At this time, an acquaintance of Ambrosio's mother named Bernardo Merlo told her that he knew how to play the tarantella and would cure her son.[93] At Ambrosio's mother's insistence, Piñera convinced the hospital board's director to permit the tarantella as treatment. Merlo came to play in one of the hospital's private chambers. Moments after Merlo started playing his vihuela, the patient smiled blissfully and, "propelled by the tune's vibrations," moved his head and one arm, but when the doctor asked the musician to play faster, Ambrosio began to dance, even though he had not been able to walk since falling ill.[94] Piñera's report insists that Ambrosio danced well, despite reportedly lacking the talent when he was healthy. From this experiment with Merlo playing the tarantella, Piñera concluded that the dance was helping his patient and arranged for daily music therapy sessions. Merlo taught two medical interns how to play the tune. In the rest of his report, Piñera describes his patient's daily progress from July 1 to August 11, 1787.

Media competed and borrowed from each other seeking to publicize tarantism. Cid's *Tarantismo observado en España* was published only a few days before Ambrosio's admission to the Madrid General Hospital. Piñera treated Ambrosio from July to September 1787. The particulars of Ambrosio's diagnosis and treatment must have leaked profusely early on, because an eight-page pamphlet titled *Fenómeno raro y singular del primero que se ha conocido entrar en el Hospital General de Madrid for haber sido picado del insecto llamado tarantula* was issued while Ambrosio was still under treatment.[95] The booklet's author may

---

q[ue] abditarum naturæ motionum in elementis, lapidibus, plantis & animalibus elucescentium, multa hucusque incognita naturæ arcana per physica, medica, chymica & mathematica omnis generis experimenta recluduntur (Coloniae Agrippinae: Kalcoven Iodocum, 1643), 758.

[91] Piñera y Siles, *Descripción histórica*, 10–12.

[92] Piñera y Siles, *Descripción histórica*, 14.

[93] Bernardo Merlo was a native of Valdepeñas, a town in the La Mancha region where Cid lived and had collected his cases.

[94] Piñera y Siles, *Descripción histórica*, 17.

[95] I consulted a digital copy of this booklet generously provided by Rupert Baker, library manager at the Royal Society of London. The booklet is bound preceding Cid's *Tarant-*

112   *Music and Modernity in Enlightenment Spain*

have been Cid himself, because *Fenómeno raro y singular* ends with the recommendation to read Cid's *Tarantismo observado en España*, providing information about where to purchase a copy. The Toledo physician probably saw an opportunity to advertise his publication to a wider audience. For his part, Piñera denies any knowledge of Cid's treatise and declares Baglivi to be his only source, thus claiming all the diagnostic credit for himself.[96] Piñera published his medical report, *Descripción histórica de una nueva especie de corea*, around early September 1787. Based on theater programs in the *Diario de Madrid*, I suggest *El atarantulado* was staged at some point between August 8 and August 19.[97] Additions and corrections to the score and libretto support a reading that the tonadilla was indeed performed.

The same critical narrative components of tarantism cases appear in Cid's *Tarantismo*, Piñera's *Descripción*, the anonymous *Fenómeno raro y singular*, and Esteve's *El atarantulado*. Despite its brevity, *Fenómeno raro y singular* retains the basics of the tarantism mythos we find in both Cid's and Piñera's accounts: (1) a tarantula bites a young man in a rural location south of Madrid, during the warm season; (2) the bite causes inflammation about the size of a grape; (3) the victim experiences physical pain and emotional affliction; (4) doctors attempt different remedies that yield no results; (5) optionally, the victim shows a penchant for or aversion toward certain colors or objects; (6) a doctor decides to try his luck with music, since music cannot harm the patient; (7) there are spectators to the musical sessions, as well as skeptics who ridicule musical treatment and try to prove it a hoax; (8) someone plays the tarantella with a violin or vihuela and the victim involuntarily and vigorously dances, sweating profusely and collapsing in bed after each dance; (9) if the tarantella stops or the tune changes, the victim stops dancing; and (10) the victim heals after a variable number of dance sessions.[98] *El atarantulado* preserves the last five items because those involve an audience.

Piñera's treatment made tarantism a public matter. As Madrileños followed the case's evolution through July and August 1787, professional and lay opin-

---

ismo observado en España. A handwritten note states that it was presented by Don Francisco Xavier Cid on March 6, 1788. Francisco Aguilar Piñal reports another copy of the booklet printed in Barcelona, Vda. de Piferrer, 1787, in the holdings of the Biblioteca de Catalunya, call number F. Bon. 9633.

[96] Piñera y Siles, *Descripción histórica*, 34–35.

[97] *El atarantulado* possibly premiered on August 8, 1787. On that day, the *Diario de Madrid* announced a new tonadilla by the Martínez Company at the Coliseo del Príncipe with characters played by Francisca Rodrigo, Miguel Garrido, and Alfonso Navarro. Ensuing *Diario* issues only mention "a good tonadilla" by the Martínez Company. Another tonadilla debuted on August 20, performed by Rodrigo and Garrido. Thus, the tarantula tonadilla may have been staged anytime from August 8 until August 19.

[98] As Priscilla Wald contends in her study of narratives of contagion, it is through "repetition of particular phrases, images, and story lines" that formulaic plots for diseases take shape. See her *Contagious: Cultures, Carriers, and the Outbreak Narrative* (Durham, NC: Duke University Press, 2008), 2.

Music, Medicine, and Tarantism in Madrid, 1787 113

ions contesting Piñera's medical decisions proliferated.[99] Piñera had anticipated criticism from colleagues. A notable opponent of musical healing was Madrid physician Manuel Irañeta y Jáuregui. Irañeta had published a 1785 treatise in which he accepted tarantism as a disease but denied the effectiveness of music therapy, instead recommending ammonia as a more effective remedy. Both Cid and Piñera rebuked Irañeta. Irañeta's book prompted partisanship between those who believed in musical healing and those who did not. To add insult to injury, Irañeta declined Piñera's invitation to witness one of Ambrosio's dance sessions at the General Hospital.[100] The dispute between the two Madrid physicians reproduced the believers versus skeptics feud Cid had set up in his *Tarantismo observado en España*. Esteve reproduced the same contention for the lay audience, having celebrated actor-singer Garrido play Piñera's mock version and convince Madrid's upper society (the Marchioness, the Count, and the Duchesses' Daughters) of music healing's powers.

The public also weighed in on Piñera's medical decisions. Following the holistic treatment typical of neo-Hippocratism, Piñera supplemented music therapy with other remedies such as baths and infusions as he saw fit based on his daily patient evaluation. For example, on July 16, 1787, he noted that Ambrosio had been losing weight and canceled the dance session, a decision that triggered "the invectives, satires, and taunts that envy and slander started firing at me."[101] This note suggests that the public followed the case daily. Rumor spread throughout the city that Ambrosio was dying due to Piñera's fanatical practices. Dodging criticism, Piñera then decided to resume musical treatment on July 31 without informing the greater Madrid society, but wealthy and noble visitors were still allowed to watch Ambrosio dance inside the hospital. These wealthy visitors were allowed to conduct their own tests at will. For example, some demanded that the interns trick Ambrosio by playing different tunes or wave objects in front of him to see his reaction—all in an effort to prove Piñera a liar.[102] Later in the summer, hospital authorities forbade all visitors. Ambrosio danced from August 2 to 11 and was discharged from the hospital on September 5, 1787.[103] The show in the hospital may have ended, but not in the city.

---

[99]   In addition to the general public, Madrid General Hospital's head nurse and on-duty board members frequently attended the dance sessions as onlookers.

[100] I do not discuss Irañeta's treatise here because it excludes musical healing. Manuel Irañeta y Jáuregui, *Tratado del tarantismo, ó enfermedad originada del veneno de la tarántula según las observaciones que hizo en los Reales Hospitales del Quartel General de San Roque ... Se trata de paso de los efectos de otros animales venenosos, y su curacion* (Madrid: Imprenta Real, 1785).

[101] Piñera y Siles, *Descripción histórica*, 25.

[102] Piñera y Siles, *Descripción histórica*, 29–31.

[103] "Extracto del informe dado a la Real Junta de los Hospitales General y Pasión de esta Corte por el Dr. D. Bartolomé Piñera y Siles, sobre la historia de una nueva especie de corea o baile de San Vito, originada de la picadura de un insecto que por los fenómenos

114   *Music and Modernity in Enlightenment Spain*

As a composer, Esteve shared with the much younger Piñera a high regard for his own abilities and demanded that authorities and patrons acknowledge his talent. *El Atarantulado* portrays Doctor Don Celedonio as a talented professional undervalued by his aristocratic employers, a circumstance that Esteve himself likely experienced in his years as chapel master and theater composer. In the tonadilla, both the Marchioness and the Count abuse their privileged positions by wasting the Doctor's time: when he arrives "tired and worn out" to tend to her migraine, the Marchioness responds that her headache is gone. Before Don Celedonio can protest, the Count disparagingly calls him in the first draft of the libretto "a paid physician" on the Marchioness's payroll. Esteve, like his colleague Blas de Laserna, was overworked and received little recognition for his work with the Madrid theaters. With sixty-two new tonadillas per year, plus all the music for comedias and sainetes, theater composers could not keep up. In fact, throughout the 1780s, several actor-singers accused Esteve of writing bad tonadillas and denying all company members the same opportunities to showcase their talent.[104] In 1783, several formal complaints were mounted against Esteve, claiming that he frequently missed rehearsals. In response, Esteve penned a letter to Madrid city officials airing his grievances with the theater company in the third person:

> Don Pablo Esteve ought to be a Madrid composer in the fashion of Paris and other courts, who have their assigned salaries, as do the actors; yet the music master and the author [of dramatic texts] *are not actors, but maestros*, established to serve audiences, whereas the [theater] company wrongly believes that the composer is a useless part of the company who has been included in the companies' rosters only out of kindness on the part of Madrid.[105]

In *El atarantulado*, Doctor Don Celedonio claims for himself the same recognition that Esteve never received. He vindicates his professional activity from the opening musical number ("Blessed be my science, which shall immortalize me!") to the final chorus. Esteve considered his music, like Don Celedonio's, to be necessary to Madrid's society.

In keeping an open-door policy for Ambrosio's treatment and later publishing *Descripción de una nueva especie de corea*, Piñera fostered publicity and even donned an air of showmanship. Piñera published *Descripción de una nueva espe-*

---

     seguidos a ella se ha creído ser la tarántula; curada a beneficio de la música," *Memorial literario instructivo y curioso de la Corte de Madrid*, April 1788, 643. Piñera y Siles dated his *Descripción histórica* September 7, 1787.

[104] Felipe Pedrell, *Diccionario biográfico y bibliográfico de músicos y escritores de música españoles* (Barcelona: Tipografía de V. Berdós y Feliu, 1894), 606–7.

[105] "Don Pablo Esteve debe de ser compositor de Madrid al modo de París y otras cortes, que están con sus sueldos señalados, e igualmente los cómicos; pero el maestro de música e ingenio no son cómicos, sí maestros establecidos para el servicio del público, y no que está la compañía en el error de que es el compositor igual a una inútil parte de la compañía que por pura benignidad de Madrid le ha incluido en la formación de las compañías." Subirá, *La tonadilla escénica*, vol. 1, 178. Emphasis mine.

cie de corea to counter criticism against his therapeutic practices. He dedicated this extensive report to "the most excellent sir, and sirs, of the Royal Hospital Board."[106] The most excellent sir, the *hermano mayor* (eldest brother) of the hospital board was at the time Pedro de Alcántara Fernández de Híjar y Abarca de Bolea, Ninth Duke of Híjar (1758–1808). This name is significant because the board of the hospital and the theater were one and the same; the duke of Híjar was head director in 1787. Piñera's performativity did not escape Cid. When the controversy over tarantism resurfaced three years later, Cid wrote in a letter to the *Correo de Madrid*, concerning Piñera's report that "there are those who say that his [Piñera y Siles's] document resembles a theater piece, wherein the actor [Piñera] plays several roles opposed to each other, consistent only in praising himself and despising others." If the rumors Cid alluded to were real, then Piñera managed the case such that it invited dramatic reproduction.

Tarantism and the Modern Lifestyle

A Modern Musical Form for a Modern Disease

El atarantulado is a meta-drama where the elite spectators at the General Hospital tarantella sessions become the object of scrutiny for coliseo audiences. This two-act tonadilla stages Ambrosio's case in the context of the everyday lives of Madrid's upper-class and performs tarantism alongside the fashionable disease known as the vapors. While the reenactment of tarantism was widely amusing, Esteve reserved *El atarantulado*'s harshest satire for the tonadilla's noble characters: the Marchioness, the Count, and the Duchess's young daughters, all portrayed as superficial and whimsical, in a word, modern. For instance, after hearing about the tarantula-bitten man from the doctor, the Duchess's daughters fear that a tarantula might bite them too, just as young ladies had feared for their own safety amid Madrid's craze of tarantism, a fear the *Diario de Madrid* had admonished. So afraid are they that they ask the doctor to change the conversation: "Stop it, gentlemen! We get upset! We get scared!" the girls sing. In the previous scene, the Marchioness feigns ailments while her *cortejo*, the Count, fusses over these minor ailments.[107] The tonadilla's first act, where most of the musical numbers occur, spotlights psychosomatic "fashionable diseases" among the Spanish urban upper classes, contrasting with the physical disease of tarantism showcased in the second act. Esteve brings to the stage psychosomatic diseases as fake ailments resulting from the nobility's

---

[106] Normally, the report would have been presented only to the hospital board: Aurelio Valladares Reguero, "El médico ubetense Bartolomé Piñera y Siles y la polémica sobre los efectos curativos de la música: El tarantismo en el siglo XVIII," *Códice* 12 (1997): 41.

[107] In Madrid, courtships (cortejos) such as the one between the Marchioness and the Count were widespread among the upper classes, yet seen as an unacceptable aspect of modern behavior, a corruption of decent Spanish mores borrowed from the French.

116   *Music and Modernity in Enlightenment Spain*

modern lifestyle. Let us next consider the initial duet between the Marchioness and the Count and see how it portrays the fashionable diseases of the eighteenth century in a Marchioness with a fickle headache and her lovesick *cortejo*.

For his social critique of the nobility, Esteve avails himself of galant musical conventions. Despite their substantial differences, *El atarantulado*'s musical style resembles that of the two-act Italian intermezzo. If an intermezzo characteristically employs a scaled-down version of opera buffa's language and resources, then a tonadilla is a further step from the intermezzo with respect to opera buffa. Of course, each form abides by its own conventions, but all three share melodic and harmonic traits from the galant vocabulary. In *The Tonadilla in Performance*, Elisabeth Le Guin views the galant as the unmarked style in eighteenth-century music, a translucent medium wherein diverse musical topoi can develop. In the case of tonadillas, such topoi included "regional dance types, social stereotypes, improvised *lazzi*, parodic 'scenes' from opera seria, comic dialogues, *buffo*-style finales, displays of vocal virtuosity, or some clever mixture of the above."[108] While regional dances do not feature prominently in *El atarantulado* and neither does vocal virtuosity, there are parodies from opera seria in the first act's love duet and mock buffo finales in the choruses.

The tonadilla's first act revolves around the Marchioness's headache and the Doctor's stress. In the opening solo, Garrido as Doctor Don Celedonio appears strained because he is overworked, yet he needs to call on the Marchioness of the Gran Castañar because she has a migraine. Esteve wrote the only solo number for Garrido/the Doctor, the cast's senior performer and celebrity.[109] Doctors had been a staple of Spanish theater since the seventeenth century and had ties to the *Dottore* of commedia dell'arte. They became one of the stock characters in sainetes and tonadillas of the 1760s. Several fictional Spanish quacks were modeled after Molière's Sganarelle, the protagonist of *L'Amour médecin* and *Le Médecin malgré lui*. In the plots of comedias, sainetes, and tonadillas, fake stage doctors were often called to treat fake or nervous illnesses related to amorous intrigues. Such is the case, for example, in Ramón de la Cruz's 1768 sainete *El mal de la niña*, a modified translation of Molière's *L'Amour médecin*. In *El mal de la niña*, a fake doctor who "heals without syrups, solely through words, and dance, and seguidillas" gets his girlfriend's father to agree to their marriage.[110] De la Cruz's sainete includes a chorus like the one in *El Atarantulado*: "Long live the great, wise doctors, inventors of prescribing!"

---

[108]   Le Guin, *Tonadilla in Performance*, 104.

[109]   The 1786 literary satire *Segunda carta del sacristán de Berlinches al organista de Móstoles* quotes a fictional gentleman who commented upon leaving the theater: "The comedia was good, but Garrido was not on the stage," confirming that Garrido was one of the main theater celebrities of Madrid. Antonio Bernal, *Segunda carta del sacristán de Berlinches al organista de Móstoles* ([Madrid]1786), 36.

[110]   Ramón de la Cruz and Emilio Cotarelo y Mori, *Sainetes de Don Ramón de la Cruz en su mayoría inéditos* (Madrid: Bailly Bailliere, 1915), 464.

("Vivan los grandes sabios doctores, inventadores de recetar!"), celebrating the wit of the suitor disguised as a physician.[111] In *El atarantulado*, the Doctor's solo introduces the entire work, securing the public's attention. Since neither the libretto nor the score mention any stage props or set, Garrido's song may have been performed as a preface on the proscenium. When he leaves, four chairs are brought on stage to serve as the minimal props needed to suggest the kind of social visit then so popular among Madrid's elite (*gente de estrado*). The Marchioness and the Count enter the stage for the next musical number.

Esteve addresses the issue of nervous ailments in the duet between the Marchioness (Josefa Rodrigo) and the Count (Alfonso Navarro). He portrays the two *cortejo* platonic lovers beset by modern diseases: she gets a migraine whenever left alone and he aches seeing his beloved suffer. The love duet is the longest and most elaborate number in the tonadilla, and the only one with two distinct sections in different meters and keys (table 2.2, row 2), each with its own thematic material. Esteve highlights the sentimental nature of the lovers' afflictions with a mock rondò aria form, in vogue during the late eighteenth and early nineteenth centuries. Rondòs were reserved for the prima donna or primo uomo to express intense emotions; Mary Hunter has called the rondò "the paradigmatic sentimental utterance," most often sung by "women from the upper strata of society."[112] Not to be confused with the instrumental rondo, the vocal rondò had two tempi, usually one slow and one fast, preceding the nineteenth-century double aria's cavatina and cabaletta. Two-tempi rondòs are best known through Mozart's operas, but composers like Baldassare Galuppi, Niccolò Piccinni, and Tomasso Traetta had introduced the form since the 1760s and 1770s, and by the 1780s it was generally used by Domenico Cimarosa, Giuseppe Sarti, and Giovanni Paisiello, among others.[113] Beginning in 1760, the form enjoyed growing popularity in Spain, perhaps more than any other aria type. Rondòs frequently functioned as showpiece placeholders: some Spanish comedias of the 1780s and 1790s indicate "rondò" where the featured singer could insert any fitting aria. Rondòs could be sung in Italian in the middle of a Spanish piece and strongly hinted at a more operatic style. Esteve had used the form and was familiar with it, so he likely would have labeled the piece "rondò" if he had so intended; he possibly did not do so because the form most often belonged in noncomic genres such as sentimental plays. One can conclude, nonetheless, that *El atarantulado's* duet parodies the sentimental rondò.[114]

---

[111]   de la Cruz and Cotarelo y Mori, *Sainetes de Don Ramón de la Cruz*, 462.

[112]   Mary Kathleen Hunter, *The Culture of Opera Buffa in Mozart's Vienna: A Poetics of Entertainment*, Princeton Studies in Opera (Princeton: Princeton University Press, 1999), 147.

[113]   Don Neville, "Rondò," *Grove Music Online* (2001), https://doi.org/10.1093/gmo/9781561592630.article.23788.

[114]   Hunter provides examples by male characters in Sarti's *L'amore artigiano* and *Fra i due litiganti il terzo gode* where a song that begins cantabile breaks down into other

118   *Music and Modernity in Enlightenment Spain*

The Marchioness opens the duet with an andantino stanza caricaturing the prototypical late eighteenth-century aria of the suffering heroine. Whereas the sentimental heroine traditionally endures life's great injustices, the Marchioness's woe resides in the headache she gets when the Count diverts his attention from her. The headache is so intense that it drives her crazy (*me trastorna la cabeza*), blurring the distinction between physical and psychological malady. Esteve was acquainted with sentimental opera since in 1765 he had written supplemental music for a Spanish translation of Niccolò Piccinni's *La buona figliuola o La Cecchina*. Based on this experience, Esteve knew sentimental arias such as "Una povera ragazza" firsthand. The Marchioness in *El atarantulado* begins singing her stanza, "As soon as I am left alone, headache overcomes me," in G major, $\frac{2}{4}$ meter. From *La buona figliuola* and other works, a Spanish listener from the period might recognize the aria's stylistic features: moderate tempo, duple meter, walking bass, midregister tessitura in the opening phrases, and a cantabile melody. Esteve further hints at sentimentality through onomatopoeia and gesture. The Marchioness seems to have shortness of breath in the descending quavers of bars 145 to 147 (example 2.4) and sighs with the downward leaps in bars 165 and 170 (example 2.5), leading to a sequence of painful "*ohimès*" ("ayes") in bars 175–180 (example 2.5). The work's intimate chamber setting also matches the style, for the chairs on stage suggest an *estrado*, the carpeted room where Spanish ladies traditionally received visitors.

The rondò's G major section contrasts two musical affections, the Marchioness's fragility and the Count's earnestness. After two stanzas of duple meter andantino sung by the Marchioness (examples 2.4, 2.5), the tempo speeds up to an allegro and the meter changes to $\frac{6}{8}$, as the Count interrupts the laments of the Marchioness, alarmed by her condition. Short, brisk phrases convey the Count's agitation (example 2.6).

Audiences liked the sudden change of affections and the linear progression of the rondò, which, combined with the intense dramatic content at peak moments of the opera and sung by the best performers, secured an aura of prestige for this selective aria form.[115] A real rondò would be a solo, not a duet, and would not return to the slow section. Esteve, however, combines this two-tempi structure with a dal segno form, switching roles for the repetition: the Count sings the andantino and the Marchioness the allegro. *El atarantulado*'s duet ends with the second, faster tempo, preserving the rondò's linear design in contrast with the da capo's cyclic one.

At the end of the dal segno, the mock rondò moves on to a second, shorter part in C where the Marchioness's migraine is cured and the two cortejos sing a conclusion together: "What a joy, what a pleasure two loving bosoms feel" (example 2.7). Before the happy ending, however, Esteve dramatizes the healing

---

emotions and faster tempi, to lighten up the sentimentality in a comic context. Hunter, *Culture of Opera Buffa*, 148–49.

[115]   Daniel Heartz and Thomas Bauman, *Mozart's Operas* (Berkeley: University of California Press, 1990), 306.

Example 2.4. Opening vocal phrase of the Marchioness's Andantino in *El atarantulado*, bars 138–49.

Example 2.5. Marchioness's Andantino, *El atarantulado*, bars 165–80.

Example 2.6. Count's reply, Andantino, *El atarantulado*, bars 181–85.

Example 2.7. End of Andantino duet, *El atarantulado*, bars 239–57.

Music, Medicine, and Tarantism in Madrid, 1787

of the headache with a switch to C minor and a one-bar recitative where all instruments stop at a half cadence. This micro-recitative reinforces the movement's operatic parody. Together with the opening cantabile, the romance topic, the upper-class characters, and the ceremonious language of the text, *El atarantulado*'s duet would be clearly recognized as operatic.

To further ridicule the scene's sentimentality, Esteve interjects one- or two-bar instrumental "responses," or motives that disrupt the flow of the vocal melody (examples 2.8 and 2.9). Such short motivic comments were among Esteve's favorite resources for creating comic effect in tonadillas. For example, in the $\frac{2}{4}$ andantino following the repetition of the opening vocal phrase, Esteve punctuates the otherwise sentimental song with comedy by interjecting a two-bar unison motive in the strings (example 2.8, bars 161–62). Just two bars later another motivic comment in the violins confirms the absurdity of the Marchioness's situation (example 2.9 bars 164–65).

Esteve reinforces the association between high status and nervous disease in the tonadilla's next musical number, a quartet involving the Marchioness, the Count, and the two Duchess's daughters (example 2.9). This ensemble emulates the polite conversation of a social visit, during which the girls inform their hostess that their mother "is quite bothered by the vapors" (*los flatos le causan molestia bastante*).

Esteve's social criticism of Madrid's nobility echoes eighteenth-century medical theories that correlated status with vague disease. In 1786, one year before Esteve wrote *El atarantulado*, a joint Spanish translation of Samuel Tissot's *De la santé des gens de lettres* (1768) and *Essai sur les maladies des gens du monde* (1770) appeared in Madrid under the title of *Aviso a los literatos, y poderosos acerca de su salud o tratado de las enfermedades más comunes* (1786). Tissot dedicated *Essay sur les maladies des gens du monde* to "the peoples of fashion," in particular to "the ladies of fashion" who suffered from hypersensibility due to their sedentary life, late bed time, and rich diet. He warns such women that all the care and attention of a physician will not improve their health without a modification in their lifestyle. Tissot's holistic approach blurs the line between physical and moral sensibility to the point where

> delicate persons soon become valetudinary, by a habit which prevents the faculties from operating regularly, so that without any apparent disease, they are often out of order without being able to assign the cause. Without doubt there is a cause, but so trifling as to be unperceivable. ... They are hardly ever well. ... They suffer a general depression without being able to point out their complaint.[116]

---

[116] Samuel Auguste Tissot, *An Essay on the Disorders of People of Fashion*, trans. Francis Bacon Lee (London: Richardson and Urquhart, 1771), 2–3.

Example 2.8. Motivic responses, Andantino, *El atarantulado*, bars 157–70.

Example 2.9. Opening phrase of Allegro moderado, *El atarantulado*, bars 270–82.

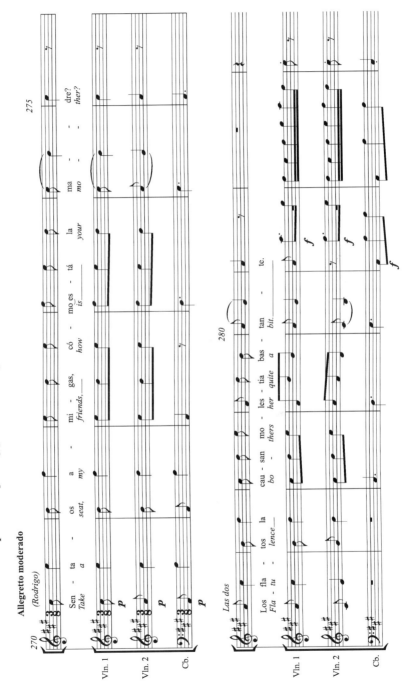

126   *Music and Modernity in Enlightenment Spain*

The essay goes on to list the vapors (*jaqueca, flatos*) as a disease "of excessive violence" "too common among people of fashion."[117] Esteve's tonadilla tells us that the Madrid were well acquainted with the vapors and other undetermined nervous diseases such as the ones Tissot described. He demonstrates his awareness of the high-status connotations of nervous disease by ascribing it to noble characters.

El atarantulado's love duet connects current medical theories with the in-vogue two-tempi sentimental rondò to musically parody Madrid's upperclass. Esteve had served time in prison in 1779 for mocking the Countess of Benavente (María Faustina Téllez Girón) and another noblewoman in a tonadilla about cortejos, and he served time again in 1785.[118] Perhaps because there were no direct allusions to any living person, no retaliation against this tonadilla was recorded in the press. Nevertheless, *El atarantulado* proves that the Catalan composer Esteve refused to stop portraying the Madrid upper classes on stage and continued to write biting critiques of Spanish nobility.

Tarantism, Enlightenment, and Nervous Diseases

Whether tarantism was a physical or psychosomatic "fashionable" disease continued to be debated intermittently until 1790 in the Madrid press. The study of tarantism delved into the mind's (or the soul's) connection to the body, raising questions concerning human nature. Cases of and literature on tarantism also stirred up arguments over who had the authority to sanction scientific knowledge for public consumption. Certainties about tarantism were scarce, complicating the notion that there was one definitive way for disease and music to affect the body. Disputes reached beyond Spain, engaging writers, readers, and the greater public in the national dilemma over reconciling modern European ideas with traditional ones.

Amid the 1787 tarantism press *querelle*, the *Diario de Madrid* and the *Espíritu de los mejores diarios* tried to broaden the discussion by referencing foreign publications, especially the works of well-known scientists such as Jean Antoine Nollet or Francesco Serao, the latter of whom Cid had discredited. These two periodicals had a strong presence in Madrid's public life a the time tarantism emerged as a public issue. The *Diario de Madrid* (titled *Diario curioso, erudito, económico y commercial* in 1786–1787) had resumed publication in 1786 after a five-year hiatus, under the new direction of Santiago (Jacques) Thevin.[119] A long-time Spanish resident, Thevin was a book merchant who in 1782 obtained a contract to introduce the *Éncyclopedie* to Madrid, both in the

---

[117] Tissot, *An Essay on the Disorders*, 50–51.

[118] Pedrell, *Diccionario biográfico y bibliográfico*, 606.

[119] Originally from France, Santiago Thevin was a former disciple of Francisco Mariano Nipho, founder of the *Diario* in 1758.

original French and in Spanish translation. He had partially succeeded but in 1788 the Inquisition confiscated all copies of the *Éncyclopedie*.[120] Nonetheless, and within the limits of censorship, Thevin's connections to French Enlightenment publications emerge intermittently in the *Diario*, such as in the tarantism disputes. For its part, the *Espíritu de los mejores diarios* devoted its short life (1787–1791) to circulating in Spain the latest scientific and humanistic ideas published across Europe. Its editor, Cristóbal Cladera, endorsed liberalism and was also a professional translator, most notably of the works of Joseph Addison. Since the *Diario* and the *Espíritu* had connections to European Enlightenment, these newspapers' editors strove to bring an international perspective to the local tarantism events.

In October through November of 1787, both the *Diario de Madrid* and the *Espíritu de los mejores diarios* announced a new foreign *Mémoire sur la tarentule* published in French by one Count of Borch, a Polish naturalist living in Naples.[121] The *Diario* editors hoped that Borch's report would "contribute to resolving the doubts, and the diversity of judgments, still enduring among the public, and among certain professors, about the truth of the poison and the cure for its rare effects."[122] Borch relegated tarantism to popular legend, "fable," and "fanaticism."[123] The so-called disease was for him misguided consensus unrelated to science: "the crowds, who always adopt the decisions of those they see as oracles, granted all the consensus and consistency due to the most authentic truth to a popular judgment, a fable." For Borch (and likely for the *Diario* editors, who published Borch's *Mémoire sur la tarentule* to "clarify … the history of this spider, which for a while has been exciting the imagination of some and the credibility of others"), gullibility was the real disease that needed to be eradicated. Borch lamented that the endeavors of the enlightened elite had not uprooted belief in tarantism: "Several enlightened individuals, among them the abbé Nollet, tried to *heal* these *wounded imaginations*, yet their efforts were fruitless."[124] After describing the tarantula, Borch assessed music's effects on alleged *tarantati* from Naples and Apulia. He thought that people living in warm climates such as that of southern Italy were lazy and prone to melancholy because their bodily humors thicken, an environmen-

---

[120] Robert Darnton, *The Business of Enlightenment: A Publishing History of the Encyclopédie, 1775–1800* (Cambridge, MA: Belknap Press, 1979), 465.

[121] Michael-Johann von der Borch (1751–1810) wrote *Mémoire sur la tarentule* and sent it to one of the editors of the *Journal d'Histoire Naturelle*. "Mémoire sur la tarentule," *Journal d'Histoire Naturelle* 10 (1787): 57.

[122] "Historia natural," *Diario curioso, erudito, económico y comercial*, October 12, 1787.

[123] "Memoria sobre la Tarántula. Por el Conde de B … Staroste de Polonia e individuo de varias academias," *Espíritu de los mejores diarios que se publican en la Europa*, November 15, 1787, 567.

[124] "Historia natural," *Diario curioso, erudito, económico y comercial*, 418.

128 *Music and Modernity in Enlightenment Spain*

tal determinism often associated with Montesquieu.[125] The explanation for tarantism is simple, Borch continues: Sweating thins the humors, "lightens the machine [the body] ... and cheers the spirits up," but people need motivation to exercise. Here is where music comes in. Music for Borch does not cause a direct mechanical reaction, as Cid would have it. Instead, it "flatters the ear" with the tunes that each regional population prefers.[126] In Borch's view, it just so happens that southern Italians prefer the tarantella.

Arguments against tarantism such as Borch's did not dampen Cid's influence. The last 1787 article about tarantism appeared in the December issue of the *Memorial literario*, published twice a month and compiling and translating excerpts from European and Spanish books along with articles more serious than those released in the *Diario de Madrid* or the *Correo de los Ciegos*. The tarantism piece in question was a brief dissertation and case study by La Mancha physician Vicente Aguilera (possibly an acquaintance of Cid's).[127] In seven pages, Aguilera mostly summarizes Cid's work but adds the curious detail that he shaved the hair off a cat's back and made a tarantula bite the animal. The next day, musicians played the tarantella for the cat, which started moving its tail and ears and then ran toward a pile of vine trunks never to be found again. Contrary to what Borch proposed, Aguilera's experiment suggested that tarantism had nothing to do with preferences or taste but remained a mystery deeply connected to the body.

After 1787 controversy over tarantism quieted without entirely disappearing. In medical research throughout Europe, there was a broader interest in the boundaries between the mind and the body in relation to disease. Thus, Cid's treatise caught international attention, especially from London, where Cid personally sent his work to the Royal Society of London, where it remains today. Spanish physicians, writers, and men of letters felt that Cid's book and Ambrosio's case connected them to this broader discussion. A few isolated articles from 1788 and 1789 steered the issue of tarantism toward more abstract ruminations on music. For example, in April of 1788, the *Memorial literario* published an extract of Piñera's report. Attesting to the questioning of the boundaries between the mind and the body, these isolated articles present a more psychological, even sentimental understanding of music's effects on the body, with emphasis on the listening preferences of the subject undergoing musical therapy.

[125] "Continuación de la memoria sobre la tarántula," *Diario curioso, erudito, económico y comercial*, October 13, 1787, 423. Parts of Montesquieu's *L'Esprit des lois* have frequently been read as environmental determinism, although some authors disagree. See Karl Marcus Kriesel, "Montesquieu: Possibilistic Political Geographer," *Annals of the Association of American Geographers* 58, no. 3 (1968): 557–74.

[126] "Continuación de la memoria," *Diario curioso, erudito, económico y comercial*, 423.

[127] Aguilera, "Descripción de la tarántula."

Music, Medicine, and Tarantism in Madrid, 1787 129

In November 1788, the *Memorial literario* printed an article, signed by "D.L.A.M.," that refuted Aguilera's 1787 dissertation and feline experiment. D.L.A.M. considered the types of music used in treating tarantism patients and rejected the idea that only one tune could heal the patient. Like Borch, this article's author believed that the music's healing effects derived not from musical genre (here the tarantella), but from sonic properties such as triple meter, *sesquialtera* proportion, incorporation of dance airs (like contradance, minuet, or fandango), or short rhythmic values of quavers and semiquavers. This author reasoned that once the tarantella's musical traits were abstracted, Spanish musicians could compose multiple songs for musical therapy. He recommended that doctors try different instruments, each according to the status of the victim: flutes or bagpipes for shepherds; guitars or violins for peasants and servants; and violas, psalteries, or keyboards for those of the upper-class ("*gentes de estrado*"). After such class-oriented reflection, the author then asks Vicente Aguilera to simply apply musical therapy and stop analyzing it, lest pride corrupt him as it had corrupted many philosophers.[128]

The *Diario de Madrid* in turn published two short articles about musical healing in France and England. The one article from April 21, 1789, reports two "new and impressive effects of music's influence"—namely, in one case of epilepsy in England, and in one of delirium in France. The English epileptic patient was reportedly cured through dance, but the French patient presented a subtler bodily reaction, his fever receding when music was played in his chamber.[129] In both cases, the only condition for effective treatment was that the music fit the patient's taste. In expanding the range of diseases that music was believed to cure to ailments beyond tarantism and extending the range of musical genres fit for therapy, these two cases served the article's author to point in the direction of music as the universal remedy Cid had suggested.[130]

The second *Diario de Madrid* article, from December 11, 1789, associates tarantism with the nervous ailments characteristic of modern urban populations, called "fashionable diseases" by eighteenth-century authors such as Samuel Auguste Tissot.[131] David E. Shuttleton, a historian of literature and medicine, has found that diseases such as hypochondria and vapors, among others, became fashionable among the middle and upper English classes of the late eighteenth century. According to Shuttleton, diseases became fash-

---

[128] D.L.A.M., "Advertencias sobre la descripción de la tarántula," *Memorial Literario, Instructivo y Curioso* 73 (1788): 400. The initials could refer to playwright (Don) Luis (Antonio) Moncín, although he customarily signed his name "L.A.J.M."

[129] "Efectos admirables, y nuevos de la influencia de la música," *Diario de Madrid*, April 21 1789.

[130] Cid, *Tarantismo*, 272.

[131] Miguel Bea de Navarra, "Carta erudita probando los buenos efectos de la música, tomada como medicina," *Diario de Madrid*, December 11, 1789; Tissot, *Essay on the Disorders*.

130   *Music and Modernity in Enlightenment Spain*

ionable as a consequence of "a more modern form of sentimentalized selfhood [originated in the eighteenth-century] in which character was judged less upon actions than individual feelings."[132] Suffering from hypochondria or the vapors was symptomatic of sensibility and creativity, two of the signs of a sophisticated modern self. The *Diario de Madrid* article from December 1789 is subtitled "Medicina Musical" and authored by Miguel Bea de Navarra, the same doctor who two years earlier caught a tarantula at the porcelain factory and allegedly saw it dancing when the tarantella was played. He was invested in the topics of tarantism and musical healing in general.

In his 1789 *Diario de Madrid* article, Bea de Navarra drew on Cid's tarantism treatise to comment on current controversies regarding public entertainment in Madrid, especially those surrounding opera. The newly rehabilitated Teatro de los Caños del Peral had brought opera to the forefront of discourse on theater's social function during the late 1780s and 1790s. Detractors of Italian opera argued that its productions were too expensive for the city budget and that Madrid's audiences disliked such lofty entertainment in a foreign language. In response, defenders of Italian opera contended that high-quality, learned entertainment would make society more civilized. Combining the pro-opera civilizational efforts with theories on fashionable diseases, Bea de Navarra reasoned that opera would benefit the health of Madrid's society. Opera could bring the healing effects of music en masse to an increasing number of cases of hypochondria in men and vapors (*flato histérico*) in women. In Bea de Navarra's opinion, hypochondria and vapors afflicted the Spanish capital because Madrid "comprises the most educated among the nation," people with "very intense souls" whose "subtle feelings" make them vulnerable to such ailments.[133] Because these diseases are chronic and difficult to treat as a physician, he suggests that perhaps music as public entertainment could mitigate them. The article implicitly suggests that the prevalence of nervous maladies proved that Madrileños were a cosmopolitan audience ready for opera.

Controversy rekindled shortly after the publication of Bea de Navarra's article. On December 23, 1789, a long letter signed by Doctor Patricio Sánchez and published in the *Correo de los Ciegos* challenged Cid to respond to criticism of his *Tarantismo observado en España*.[134] Sánchez rubbed salt in Cid's wound by recalling the *Diario* editors' comments to Bea de Navarra's 1787 article about the dancing porcelain factory tarantula. He reminded Cid that the shameless

---

[132]   David E. Shuttleton, "The Fashioning of Fashionable Diseases in the Eighteenth Century," *Literature and Medicine* 35, no. 2 (2017): 271.

[133]   Bea de Navarra, "Carta erudita probando los buenos efectos de la música, tomada como medicina," *Diario de Madrid*, 1380.

[134]   Patricio Sánchez was the physician at the Real Monasterio de San Millán de la Corolla in Ágreda, Province of Castilla-León. He posted his letter on April 26, 1789, but it was not published until December 23. Patricio Sánchez, "[Señor Editor del Correo ...]," *Correo de Madrid*, December 23, 1789.

Diario editors had doubted tarantism when they advised their readers not to panic and published Borch's "Report about the Tarantula," which further questioned Cid's account of the disease. Sánchez also cited Piñera's denial that his handling of Ambrosio's case owed anything to Cid. Sánchez thought the *Diario* editors and Piñera dishonored Cid when they doubted his word, emphasizing the divide between "insolent" criticism and Cid's authoritative "truth."[135] He interpreted the tarantism disputes as another instance of criticism ruining personal reputations. In this case, different medical opinions were but attacks intended to defame Cid in ways that resemble modern criticism's association with defamation in Spain (see chapter 1). The anticriticism prejudice that it was impossible to impart knowledge in a brief periodical article fit defenses of Cid well, because Cid's treatise surpasses all others in length and references to past authorities. Cid's *Tarantismo observado en España* stood for authentic knowledge, whereas the rest of the publications (including Piñera's eighty-page report) represented criticism's spurious knowledge.

Cid responded to Sánchez's challenge in six letters published in the *Correo de los Ciegos* in February 1790. In these letters, Cid asserts his observations' local validity: what holds true in Apulia and "the Spanish Apulia" (La Mancha) may not elsewhere. Hence, for Cid, unless someone has conducted experiments in these two places, their input does not count. This includes French scientists and writers from Naples like Serao and Borch. Cid compares Spanish newspaper editors' incredulity to the general disbelief displayed by "the French nation," and confirms that he mainly wrote his *Tarantismo* to rebuke French authors.[136] Cid specifically blamed the *Diario* editors who in 1787 had written that young ladies had nothing to fear because tarantulas did not inhabit Madrid, as well as castigating the international medical community for not accepting tarantism, accusing them of despotic capriciousness. He denied the newspaper editors the authority to speak for the nation:

> It seems as though these gentlemen [the *Diario* editors] *by their own authority* have sat on the chairs of the nation's literary court, and like those who are spared to account for their actions, they decide, resolve, and determine for no reason other than their whim. Indeed, any judicious man would oppose such despotism and verdicts so unfounded and affirmations so absolutely false, if only to avoid shaming those who, *lacking merit of any kind*, seem to carry the nation's voice in matters of criticism around the foreign kingdoms.[137]

---

[135] "[Señor Editor del Correo ...]," *Correo de Madrid*, 2583.

[136] Francisco Xavier Cid, "Carta primera, Carta segunda," *Correo de los ciegos*, February 3, 1790, 2678.

[137] "Parece que estos señores de propia autoridad se han sentado en las sillas del tribunal literario de la nación, y como á quienes no se ha de tomar residencia, deciden, resuelven y determinan sin más razón que su antojo. Efectivamente á semejante despotismo, á fallos tan infundados y afirmativas tan absolutamente falsas no hay hombre de juicio que no

132   *Music and Modernity in Enlightenment Spain*

Cid again draws the line between tarantism and nervous diseases, attributing the first exclusively to tarantula bites in specific regions, and the second to a weak disposition shaken by too active an imagination. There were no further responses to Cid in 1790 and press debates of tarantism faded away to return to medical treatises.

The journalistic debates around tarantism bring to life social reactions to a medical phenomenon and participate in discussions critics' authority over knowledge. Such debates also lead the present-day reader through a wandering path between older and newer beliefs still in the making, not only about tarantism but also about nervous disease and about the effects of music on the mind and the body, both issues discussed in the *Éncyclopedie*, in many eighteenth-century nosologies, and in treatises about nervous or "fashionable" diseases. Newspaper editors, at least those of the *Diario de Madrid* and the *Espíritu de los mejores diarios*, engaged with the latest international publications on these matters and offered their perspective to a reading public eager for novelty and information.

With this case study of tarantism in 1786–1787 Madrid, I have demonstrated that the late eighteenth-century Spanish medical authors, reading public, and theater audiences adopted new scientific paradigms through intense negotiation across diverse media, including music. Ambrosio's case of tarantism raised controversies around medical practices for the medical community, as well as for the general public who visited Ambrosio at the hospital or followed his case by reading newspapers and pamphlets. Cid's *Tarantismo observado en España* and Piñera's treatment of Ambrosio happened at a time when nosologies like that of Boissier de Sauvages and the works of authors like Samuel Auguste Tissot had kindled discussion of nervous diseases. Spanish physicians like Cid and Piñera, each from their own perspective, emphasized empirical observation over theories when it came to diagnostics, treatments, and results. This allowed them to support musical healing of tarantism. Older theories of affections and bodily humors commingled with modern ways of experiencing the self through sensation and emotion. Such theories were made fashionable through theater, music, and literature. Tarantism dramatized the rift in the late-eighteenth century Spanish population between those willing to accept cumulative knowledge, like Cid, and those who would rather give credit to recent discoveries, like the *Diario* editors. We can gain insight into the formation of modern public opinion in Spain through close attention to changing social modes of communication, such as printed periodicals, press controversies, and tonadillas triggered by cases of tarantism. In late Enlightenment Spain, tonadillas functioned as social commentary capable of disseminating knowledge and fostering critical attitudes among Madrid's theatergoers.

---

se oponga por no exponerse á sonrojar sujetos que prescindiendo del mérito, sea el que quiera, parece que llevan la voz de la nación en punto de crítica por los reinos extranjeros." "Carta primera, Carta segunda," *Correo de los ciegos*, 2067. Emphases mine.

3

Cosmopolitan Opera

On the evening of January 27, 1787, the middle and upper social tiers of Madrid's theater audience congregated at the Teatro de los Caños del Peral, across the plaza from where the current Teatro Real stands. This was the first time an Italian opera company performed in a public theater in nearly fifty years. A few patrons held bilingual librettos, but most were left to their own devices to interpret the plot of Giuseppe Sarti and Giovanni de Gamerra's *Medonte*, the inaugural opera. *Medonte* fulfilled the neoclassicist expectations for edifying entertainment: a seria libretto in the Metastasian tradition that complied with the unities of action, time, and place, with royal characters suitable for the season opening. First performed in Florence in 1777, *Medonte* was already ten years old when it premiered in Madrid. Tenor Giacomo Panati, who had sung the title role in the Florence premiere, was now part of the Los Caños del Peral company.[1] The work had proved a success in Italy and London (1782), a success impresario Juan Bautista Montaldi likely hoped to replicate in Madrid. *Medonte* must have catered to modern tastes since it continued to be staged throughout Europe until the late 1790s. Conspicuously absent from the Madrid premiere was the king, Charles III, as well as any other prominent royal family member.

The few with a libretto could read in it a dedication by the impresario Juan Bautista Montaldi to Princess Maria Luisa of Parma and a prologue of unknown authorship. Montaldi was not a man of letters but a businessman who sought to ingratiate himself with the royal house by being the opera impresario. The Genovese banker was known in Madrid for his high-risk investments, Italian opera being but one of them. Montaldi bankrupted the Banco de San Carlos by selling fraudulent shares later that year. He planned the opening performance for Los Caños del Peral on December 9, 1786, in honor of the birthday of Maria Luisa of Parma (1751–1819), the Princess of Asturias, wife to the king's heir and soon-to-be Charles IV (r. 1788–1808). Maria Luisa of Parma was, unlike the reigning monarch (Charles III), a renowned music lover, born and raised in Parma until age fourteen, when she married the Bourbon Spanish prince Charles. Although the Madrid premiere of *Medonte* was postponed to January 27 and no longer coincided with Princess María Luisa's birthday, Montaldi still dedicated the bilingual printed libretto to her. There is no evidence, however,

---

[1]   Giacomo Panati used the hispanicized forms of his first name: Santiago or Jaime.

134   *Music and Modernity in Enlightenment Spain*

that either the princess or any other royal family member attended the opera's debut or any later performance. In his dedication, Montaldi presents the project of Los Caños del Peral as a "patriotic" effort of "a citizen [Montaldi] to contribute to the greatest relief of the poor and to the recreation of an enlightened people."[2] He made this claim because Los Caños del Peral had been leased to Madrid's Hospital Board and the income from ticket sales was supposed to go to public beneficence.

This chapter explores the clash between government officials and social elites who advanced Italian opera as a tool for civilization and those who lampooned them, distrustful of modern, Europeanized entertainment. Intellectuals, aristocrats, bureaucrats, businessmen, and other men of letters who dominated newspapers and journals saw opera as capable of refining what they viewed as the vulgarities of their national musical theater. Yet others within the same social groups joined less affluent theatergoers in laughing at opera. Between court opera's last breaths in the 1770s and the reopening of Los Caños del Peral in 1787, controversies around Spanish literature, arts, and sciences raged in books, pamphlets, and journals thanks to inflammatory critiques of Spain from French and Italian authors, most notably Nicolas Masson de Morvilliers's "Spain" article in the *Encyclopédie Méthodique*.[3] Foreign authors' attacks and Spanish authors' replies, the latter known as the apologías of Spain, had polarized public opinion. While some saw in the foreign critiques the feedback the Spanish needed to modernize and civilize, following the example of other European nations, others prioritized shielding their nation from any foreign critique or influence. This latter group received Italian opera at Los Caños del Peral with skepticism and hostility. Opera became a topic of contention between two different national projects: one, to modernize and civilize Spain by emulating European nations; the other, to let Spain follow its own cultural path.

The chapter's first section posits that opera's return to the Spanish capital conflicted with audiences' tastes and the prevailing dramatic practices of Madrid's two local theaters. The second section presents the cosmopolitan aspirations for Madrid's civic improvement expressed in the initial project for Los Caños del Peral. I then review editorial efforts to introduce Italian opera as a tool for civilization and Europeanization through three publications meant to educate the public about Los Caños del Peral's first opera. In addition to these editorial efforts, which abided by the precepts of literary neoclassicism, official justification for Italian opera sometimes took the form of policies and rules for the new theater, projecting the Bourbon administration's reform ideals of civic order and *policía*. The last chapter section deals with 1787–1790 press debates comparing Italian opera and performers to Spanish ones. Such debates dovetail

---

[2] *Medonte, drama en música* (Madrid: Imprenta Real, 1787), 5. Emphasis mine.

[3] Nicolas Masson de Morvilliers, "Espagne," in *Géographie Moderne*, Encyclopédie Méthodique (Paris: Chez Panckoucke, 1782).

Cosmopolitan Opera   135

controversies over foreign musical theater with nationalist and public opinion ideas taking form in the late eighteenth century.

The Italian Opera Comeback

Los Caños del Peral's reopening galvanized public life in Madrid, stimulating discussions surrounding music, theater, and social entertainment. While some "enlightened people" in attendance had been eagerly expecting Italian opera's return to Madrid, others remained unconvinced that the Spanish public needed such entertainment. The last attempt to hold an opera cycle at the royal palaces, sponsored by a group of aristocrats two decades earlier, had failed. Long gone were the times of Farinelli, whom Philip V hired in 1737, Ferdinand VI promoted, and Charles III promptly dismissed upon his accession to the throne in 1759: Italian operas organized by Farinelli and performed at the royal palaces came to a halt with the death of Queen Barbara of Portugal (wife to Ferdinand VI) on August 27, 1758. When Charles III ascended the throne and the famous castrato left in 1759, the number of opera performances declined sharply and access to them became even more restricted. Bourbon minister Count of Aranda created the Compañía de los Reales Sitios, which performed some Italian operas, mostly buffas (as opposed to primarily serias under Farinelli) between 1767 and 1776.[4] At this time, opera was performed at court stages but not sponsored by the monarchy as it had been under Ferdinand VI. Instead, it operated commercially, first funded by impresario capital (1767–1769) and then operating through the Compañía de los Reales Sitios, hired by the city, and financed by aristocrats. Financially, Italian opera at the royal palaces ended up burdening impresarios and benefactors alike.[5] It was too hard to sell tickets. In order to get enough spectators to fill the theaters, impresarios often had to give away courtesy tickets—according to Cabarrús, common passersby would not take the tickets even for free. This unsuccessful venture discouraged wealthy sponsors from further attempts, at least for some years.

While Barcelona had a continuous operatic presence throughout the eighteenth century, post-Farinelli Madrid saw a limited number of productions here and there. Consequently, opera did not have roots in the taste of the big Madrid public. It had been a staple of the Bourbon court of Ferdinand VI (r. 1746–1759) and survived for some years after he died, but it could not compete with

[4]   Charles III ordered the end of stage shows at the royal palaces in 1777: Luis Carmena y Millán, *Crónica de la ópera italiana en Madrid desde el año 1738 hasta nuestros dias* (Madrid: Impr. de M. Minuesa de los Rios, 1878), 16–18.

[5]   Francisco Cabarrús, "Memorias sobre medios y arbitrios para los Reales Hospitales de esta Corte y sobre el establecimiento de la Ópera Bufa en beneficio de los mismos: Leídas en la Junta de su Gobierno, los días 19 de febrero y 12 de marzo de 1786," 1786, MSS/13467, Biblioteca Nacional de España, 81.

136   *Music and Modernity in Enlightenment Spain*

the robust tradition of musical theater that animated city life at the coliseos of La Cruz and El Príncipe. There, laborers, professionals, and nobles gathered several times per week to see their favorite performers and plays ranging from Golden Age classics to the newest forays of playwrights and composers, including free adaptations of European hits. Many spoken plays included music, from a brief chorus to a full set of musical numbers. Furthermore, sung-throughout stage tonadillas were routinely performed during intermissions, providing spicy musical amusement in the audience's native language. The public preferred "zarzuelized" adaptations of opera buffa better than the originals. The Madrid public spiritedly acclaimed the "zarzuela" (Spanish) version of Paisiello's *Il Barbiere de Siviglia* performed by the Ribera company at the Coliseo del Príncipe in December of 1787.[6]

Aware of audience preferences, sponsors of Italian opera at Los Caños del Peral deemed it prudent to preface *Medonte* with a prologue advertising opera as an ally of the Spanish dramatic tradition. This prologue was performed at least in the premiere.[7] There is no evidence to confirm whether the prologue was entirely sung, as in opera, or spoken with songs interspersed, as in Spanish theater. The plot features the allegorical characters Comedy, Tragedy, and Opera, in addition to Mars and Jupiter. The libretto includes a two-stanza aria each for Opera, Mars, and Jupiter and a final chorus, but no music survives. The story line is unambiguous: Comedy and Tragedy chase after Opera to kill her, spurred on by Mars's fury. Jupiter intervenes to facilitate peace between the three branches of drama.[8] Given their ubiquity in older genres like autos sacramentales, baroque mythological zarzuela, and in recent short commemorative *loas*, such allegorical characters would have been familiar to Spanish audiences. Through these characters, the prologue invoked Spanish dramatic tradition while subtly referring to early baroque opera prologues such as that of Monteverdi's *L'Orfeo*, where Music justifies why she will tell Orfeo's story. In the case of Madrid's 1787 *Medonte*, Opera literally gets its own voice, and with it, an opportunity to explain its presence on the stage.

The prologue provided a last chance before the actual opera performance to persuade the Madrileño audience of opera's suitability to the Spanish character and its usefulness as a model to improve national theater.[9] Opera first appears on scene as a refugee appealing for clemency. She seeks not to divide, but to join forces with Comedy and Tragedy:

---

[6] "Tarjeta para el Barbero de Sevilla," *Diario curioso, erudito, económico y comercial,* December 24, 1787.

[7] "Coliseo de Los Caños del Peral," *Memorial literario, instructivo y curioso,* February 1787, 265.

[8] *Medonte, drama en música,* 6–17.

[9] Cabarrús, *Memorias,* 75.

Opera:	... ¿En qué cosa os ofendí jamás?	... In what way Have I ever offended you?
	Inocente, extranjera, abandonada,	Innocent, foreign, forlorn,
	a estos puertos la suerte me conduce:	to this harbor luck brings me:
	No perturbé la paz, que os engrandece.	I did not perturb the peace that ennobles you.
	Tu majestad, tu gozo turbar nunca pensé. ¿Qué más queréis?	Your majesty, your joy, I never thought to disturb. What else do you want?
Tragedia:	Tu sangre derramar	To shed your blood
Comedia:	Tu vida caiga expuesta a mi furor	May your life drop down, exposed to my rage

When Opera asks her dramatic counterparts what she had done to deserve death, Comedy accuses her of using music to beguile Madrid audiences away from their own dramatic tradition:

Comedia:	Tu tierno corazón y tus cariños,	(Your gentle heart and your affections,
	tus voces armoniosas, tal vez fueron	Your harmonious voices, may have been
	contrarias a mi honor. El vulgo pide	contrary to my honor. The masses demand
	sólo mis agudezas. Amor halla	my wit only. Love finds
	en mi seno la paz debida; pero	due peace in my bosom; yet
	siempre es falaz un canto lisonjero.	a flattering song is always deceitful.)

Two tropes recur in this short excerpt from *Medonte*'s prologue: the centuries-old stigma that music corrupts people through deceitful pleasure, and the European-wide belief that Spanish theater's strongest suit was wit, the kind of *ingenio* (ingenuity) and *agudeza* (sharpness) of Calderón de la Barca and Lope de Vega's Golden Age comedias that influenced French authors such as Corneille and Molière. The anonymous prologue author assumed that *el vulgo* only cared for Spanish comedias' wit. Fear of the music distorting opera's poetry was more of a concern for intellectuals, committed to the neoclassicist *delectare et docere* (to delight and to teach) principle.

The plot of the prologue deploys the stereotype of the fatherly king to conciliate the differences between Spanish theater and Italian opera. The personification of the monarch through Jupiter compensated for Charles III's absence

138   *Music and Modernity in Enlightenment Spain*

in the Teatro de los Caños del Peral. To Comedy's accusations that Opera was in Madrid to seduce audiences with music, Opera replies that this was a misunderstanding, for singing and drama came from the same father, Apollo. In his fatherly role, Jupiter intervenes to resolve the animosity between Comedy, Tragedy, and Opera. Jupiter commends Spain and the king, proclaiming that the purpose of Opera is to carry, with its voice, the Spanish glory "to the most remote seas." After Jupiter praises Charles III and his subjects, Opera concludes the dispute by compelling everyone to pay homage to the just monarch and "manifest to the world the happy day when Spain, at last, appreciates and honors the Italian muses."[10] If opera was sufficient entertainment for "the world," meaning Europe, it was sufficient for Spain (Hesperia in the passage below). Therefore, it was the obedient subject's duty to make peace with opera, rather than to "spill [opera's] blood:"

Cuando el mundo	When the world
las óperas promueve, ah! No debiera	promotes operas, ah! The always
la siempre excelsa Hesperia	excellent Hesperia should not
tan noble sangre derramar.	such noble blood spill.

If prosperous civilization was the fruit of absolute monarchy, then opera was their herald. The *Medonte* prologue suggested that Charles III's monarchic power was growing and his success merited proclamation through the international language of opera.

To attend the opera at Los Caños del Peral in 1787 Madrid meant to be modern, civilized, European. The oft called *afrancesado* (Frenchified) and revolutionary writer José Marchena wrote in his short-lived journal *El Observador* (June to December 1787): "I am a man who prefers a Metastasio aria to a *tirana* … I have not been to the *comedia* in a long time. … But I do not miss the opera one single day, even if *Medonte, Caio Mario*, or a similar dullness is performed." Although Marchena proclaims a tongue-in-cheek fondness for opera, his other preferences demonstrate a modern attitude open to cosmopolitan exchange. For example, Marchena confesses he cannot listen to the sermons of the University of Salamanca preachers; he ignores logic and metaphysics, the cornerstones of late Spanish Scholasticism, but admires sensists such as Locke and Condillac. He attends the theater "to hear the music," not to engage in partisan disputes between chorizos and polacos, the "fan clubs" of Madrid's city theaters.[11] In other words, he is a modern European ambivalent about defending the nation by protecting Spanish musical theater from competition by foreign genres and performers. The majority of opera supporters in Madrid were far less liberal than Marchena and allied with monarchical rather than revolution-

---

[10]   *Medonte, drama en música*, 13, 15.

[11]   José Marchena, "Discurso II," *El Observador* 2 (1787): 21–22.

Cosmopolitan Opera   139

ary views, but still believed that Spain should improve national theater by emulating more refined models, such as opera.

Opera in the Civilizational Aspirations of Madrid's Aristocracy and the Bourbon Agenda

The Los Caños del Peral project and the debates that took place in the early years of the theater's operation insist on the social benefit of an opera theater. For the Bourbon administration, opera was expected to civilize theater audiences, and civilization facilitated governability. Many in the upper classes of 1780s Madrid showed enthusiasm at the possibility that opera could "civilize" the nation. For Francisco Cabarrús, who crafted the initial Los Caños del Peral project, opera would "mellow and civilize" a "ferocious and rough" idle urban class consisting of foreigners and their servants, artisans, military men, officers, and shop clerks.[12] In the late Spanish Enlightenment, modernity was closely related to the concepts of progress and civilization, as it was in much of eighteenth-century Europe.[13] However, for others, including some intellectuals, writers, and aristocrats, civilization meant otherness and non-Spanishness. "Los modernos," "los civilizados," "los ilustrados" came from outside Spain to change Spanish habits and mentalities according to European models. Disagreements about whether Spain needed to be civilized had been around for about three decades by the time Los Caños del Peral reopened. The 1760s were a critical moment for such polemics, which involved the upper classes' urge to adopt what they perceived as universal norms of social behavior and public interaction.[14]

The first widespread use of the term "civilization" is connected to theater, specifically to Ramón de la Cruz's 1763 sainete *La civilización*.[15] In the plot, a landowner brings a group of urban characters to his estate to civilize the peasants. After many misunderstandings between the urban and the rural characters, the landowner sides with the peasants and decides they are better off without the social refinements of civilization.[16] The sainete compiles and mocks a catalog of "civilized" mores, cast in the court/village, urban/rural, civilized/savage archetypes. De la Cruz's "civilization" is, by definition, modern,

---

[12] Cabarrús, *Memorias*, 71.

[13] Björn Wittrock, "Modernity: One, None, or Many? European Origins and Modernity as a Global Condition," *Daedalus* 129, no. 1 (2000): 31–60.

[14] Joaquín Álvarez Barrientos, *Ilustración y neoclasicismo en las letras españolas*, Historia de la literatura universal. Literatura española. Movimientos y épocas (Madrid: Editorial Síntesis, 2005), 126–27.

[15] "La civilización como modelo de vida en el Madrid del siglo XVIII," *Revista de dialectología y tradiciones populares* 56, no. 1 (2001): 148.

[16] Emilio Cotarelo y Mori, *Don Ramón de la Cruz y sus obras* (Madrid: J. Perales y Martinez, 1899), 43–44.

140   *Music and Modernity in Enlightenment Spain*

in the sense of new and of this century; and it is foreign in the sense of not traditionally Spanish. According to de la Cruz, civilized people read newspapers,
wore satin and silk, engaged in new forms of socialization such as the cortejos, and socialized at the Prado, tertulias, and *botillerías* (refreshment shops).
Los modernos despised tradition, sang in the Italian operatic style, and danced
French and English contradances. *La civilización*'s caricature of civilization
endured through the decades and was repeated in comedias, tonadillas, and
songs. De la Cruz's catalog of "symptoms" of civilization was updated in satires
and stage works of 1770s and 1780s to include owning a lap dog, speaking with
Gallicisms, reading the philosophes, and attending the opera theater when it
became available in 1787. De la Cruz's irreverent attitude toward modernization and the conclusion that Spain was better off without it persisted, clashing
with many elites' cosmopolitan hopes for the Teatro de los Caños del Peral.

Despite widespread misgiving about modern European culture, a group of
Madrid's nobles and government officials, initially under the leadership of Francisco Cabarrús, supported Italian opera as a financial and cultural venture. In
February of 1786, the Junta de Hospitales of Madrid (Hospital Board), which
administered city hospitals and theaters, declared that it intended to reinstate the
Teatro de los Caños del Peral to bring a twofold national benefit: opera revenues
would support city hospitals, and Madrid's audiences would once again enjoy
the musical spectacle that had been sweeping across Europe. The Los Caños del
Peral building was first opened in 1737 and supported by Philip V, who was fond
of opera. It had remained mostly vacant since 1738. Board members had been
studying the viability of rehabilitating the theater for some time. They officially
petitioned for the lease of the dilapidated theater from the reigning king, Charles
III, on March 23, 1786. The initiative of an "opera buffa" at Los Caños del Peral
came from French-Spanish enlightened financier and Hospital Board treasurer
Francisco Cabarrús.[17] Cabarrús justified this initiative in accordance with official
reformism and convinced his fellow board members—and Charles III himself—
that Italian opera could support national modernization.

While previous scholarship has investigated the financial aspects of opera
at Los Caños del Peral, I focus here on the cosmopolitan ideology behind Francisco Cabarrús's 1786 proposal to the Hospital Board.[18] Cabarrús's cosmopolitan point of view was shared among Hospital Board members, including
aristocrats, who supported the opera theater's reopening. I use "cosmopolitan"
in the broad sense of "the ethic and practice of being open to, and respect-

---

[17]   Cabarrús, *Memorias*.

[18]   Michael F. Robinson, "Financial Management at the Teatro de los Caños del Peral,
    1786–99," in *Music in Spain during the Eighteenth Century*, ed. Malcolm Boyd (United
    Kingdom: Cambridge University Press, 1998); José Máximo Leza, "Aspectos pro-
    ductivos de la ópera en los teatros públicos de Madrid (1730–1799)," in *La ópera en
    España e Hispanoamérica: actas del Congreso Internacional La Opera en España e His-
    panoamérica, una Creación Propia*, ed. Emilio Casares Rodicio and Álvaro Torrente
    (Madrid: Ediciones del ICCMU, 2001).

ing, ways of life that may vary significantly from one's own."[19] Opera promoters believed that cultural and economic opening to Europe would stimulate national progress in Spain.

In February 1786, Cabarrús presented a financial document, *Memorias sobre medios y arbitrios*, to the board. In it, he argued for opera to address the hospitals' financial deficit in substitution for bullfights, with the double benefit of ticket sales and popular instruction.[20] The Hospital Board regulated Madrid's state-owned and operated theaters because their revenue was designated to support city hospitals. The board also handled the revenues from other forms of public entertainment, such as bullfights. However, the income from state-operated entertainment was insufficient and the hospitals had been in the red for the previous seven years (1779–1785). The Hospital Board's income further shrank when Charles III and his supporters abolished bullfighting, which represented barbarism and antimodern social mores. Bourbon administrations had attempted to curb bullfighting since the 1750s, but Charles III had issued a stricter sanction on November 9, 1785. The sanction abolished bullfights in all of Spain except in Madrid, where an extension was granted because bullfights provided income to the hospitals.[21] To compensate for soon-to-be-lost bullfighting income, the Hospital Board needed to find a new form of public entertainment agreeable to royal policy.[22] Persuaded by the treasurer's arguments, the Hospital Board approved Cabarrús's opera buffa project and on March 26, 1786, they decided to request the monarch's permission. On June 4, 1786, Charles III granted the privilege. The board would rent the Teatro de los Caños del Peral from the city at a cost of 150,000 reales for the first five years to establish an opera buffa in Madrid.[23]

Cabarrús bet on opera buffa because he admitted that Spanish audiences would not care for opera seria like *Medonte*. In the proposal he recounted how, in the past, Farinelli's and later the Compañía de los Reales Sitios's productions had "the best actors, a truly royal splendor, the greatest [scenic] illusion and propriety, and the sovereign's beneficence and presence," but none of these

---

[19] Susan Mayhew, "Cosmopolitanism," edited by Oxford University Press, *A Dictionary of Geography* (2015), https://www.oxfordreference.com/view/10.1093/acref/9780199680856.001.0001/acref-9780199680856-e-3800.

[20] As Robinson, Leza, and others have noted, Italian opera at Los Caños del Peral was never financially sustainable, therefore failing to contribute to the city hospitals.

[21] Charles III of Spain "[Libro VII. Título XXXIII], Ley VI. El mismo por pragmática sanción de 9 de noviembre de 1785. Prohibición general de las fiestas de toros de muerte. *Novísima recopilación de las Leyes de España*, vol. 3 (Madrid, 1805), 385–86.

[22] Cabarrús was trying to move the hospitals' sources of income from property leases to stock holdings and ticket sales. Public entertainment, he explained, generates income more straightforwardly than renting houses that require maintenance and involve legal disputes with renters. Cabarrús, *Memorias*, 6.

[23] Emilio Cotarelo y Mori, *Orígenes y establecimiento de la opera en España hasta 1800* (Madrid: Tipografía de la "Revista de archivos, bibliotecas, y museos," 1917), 41.

142   *Music and Modernity in Enlightenment Spain*

qualities could "spare" "the admirable works of the immortal Metastasio" the audiences' "tiredness and abandonment." Cabarrús thought Spanish audiences had not engaged with opera seria in past ventures because they were used to the mixture of comedy and tragedy in Spanish theater:

> Used [as we are] to always see on stage plots that, no matter how grave or serious, are always accompanied by comic and joking happenings, we tire quickly of all those plays which excite only terror, fright, and the gelid and costly affection called admiration. Only a creative genius will be able to change the national taste in this respect.[24]

Considering the "national taste" for comedy, Cabarrús continued, opera buffa was "the spectacle that best corresponds to our current dispositions."[25] He was thinking of the opera with a politician's and a marketer's mind.

Rumors of an Italian opera theater in Madrid triggered controversy even before it became a formal project. The prospect of a new theater was fodder for gossip and alarm. Cabarrús recounts in his *Memorias* that plans for the opera had been intentionally spread by word of mouth to sound out the public's reaction, causing "faint-hearted spirits [to] shudder when they hear there is an attempt to open a new school for corruption and libertinage."[26] According to Cabarrús, Italian opera meant social degeneracy for some Madrileños. Cabarrús informed board members who these faint-hearted spirits were: "unenlightened patriots" "disgusted by the introduction of a foreign spectacle." Even those enlightened cosmopolitans who sympathized with the idea of Italian opera in Madrid doubted the theater of Los Caños del Peral's feasibility:

> those who due to their knowledge of the world are free of both concerns [opera being a school of libertinage and a foreign spectacle], at the same time they desire this project's fulfillment, judge it to be reckless and unfeasible, pile up the difficulties and found these difficulties in equivalent examples. Finally, there will always be those who object to the fact that a man invested with public character, and who is a repository of the Nation's confidence in two important establishments, be the one to raise and attempt to clarify this issue, frivolous and indecent in the opinion of many.[27]

---

[24]   Cabarrús, *Memorias*, 75–76.

[25]   Cabarrús, *Memorias*, 77.

[26]   Cabarrús, *Memorias*, 63–64.

[27]   "Por el conocimiento del mundo están libres de ambas preocupaciones[,] al mismo tiempo que desean la realización de este proyecto le gradúan de temerario e impracticable, amontonan dificultades y las fundan en ejemplos de absoluta paridad. Finalmente, no habrá faltado quien repare que un hombre revestido de carácter público, y depositario de la confianza de la Nación en dos establecimientos importantes, suscite y procure ilustrar esta cuestión en la opinión de muchos frívola e indecente." Cabarrús, *Memorias*, 63–64.

Cosmopolitan Opera   143

This excerpt from Cabarrús's report outlines the syllogism undergirding anti-opera pamphlets in the years to come: opera is foreign; what is foreign endangers the nation; therefore, opera endangers the nation.

But why did even those who wanted the Europeanization of Spain deem an impresario-operated Italian opera imprudent? As a Ministro de Hacienda (Secretary of Internal Revenue), Cabarrús refers to himself as a "man invested with public character." The "two important establishments" entrusted to him were the Banco de San Carlos and the Royal Company of the Philippines. For all of his high standing in the Spanish government, Cabarrús was a newcomer, a Spanish-nationalized Frenchman who associated with other foreigners in his financial enterprises. He was the prototype of the up-and-coming bourgeoisie, granted the title of count only in 1789 for his services to the Spanish Crown. As such, he lobbied to end the privileges of hereditary nobility. Cabbarrús's direction of the Banco de San Carlos board, Madrid's first modern bank, was harshly criticized, and he ended up in jail (1790–1792) on charges of fraud under Charles IV's conservative government. Relevant to the matter of Italian opera, the first impresario of Los Caños del Peral was also the former president of the Banco de San Carlos, the Genovese Juan Bautista Montaldi, who was dismissed only a few months later.[28] This tenuous financial history helps us to understand why conservative politicians, landowners, and businessmen in Madrid would reject Cabarrús's opera project as an attempt to infiltrate foreign ideas and capital into Spain.

Opposition notwithstanding, the project of Italian opera in Madrid received support even among the hereditary nobility against whom Cabarrús lobbied. In its capacity as a government organ, the Hospital Board never could have rehabilitated the Teatro de los Caños del Peral without the support of the nobility. The two most powerful groups in the court-city of Madrid were the king's ministers and the grandees (high nobility) of Spain. When the Hospital Board approved the opera project, the board consisted of four grandees of Spain, two politicians with newly acquired nobility titles, and a former Italian prince.[29]

---

[28] By July 24, 1787, the Madrid Hospital Board's president, Pedro de Alcántara Fernández de Híjar y Abarca de Bolea (1758–1808), issued an edict calling for a new impresario for Los Caños del Peral: [Junta de Hospitales de Madrid], "[Edicto]," 1787, PL 954, Fundación Joaquín Díaz.

[29] The other Hospital Board members were Vicente Joaquín Osorio de Moscoso y Guzmán, marquis of Astorga and count of Altamira; Pedro de Alcántara Fernández de Híjar y Abarca de Bolea, duke of Híjar and of Aliaga; Pedro de Alcántara Álvarez de Toledo y Salm-Salm, duke of the Infantado; Gabriel Antonio Beltrán de Santa Cruz y Aranda, former count of San Juan de Jaruco; Jerónimo de Mendinueta y Muzquiz, secretary of the Council of the Inquisition and later count of La Cimera, and Vittorio Filippo, former prince of Masserano in Piemonte: "Adiciones al Reglamento provisional e interino que con fecha de 23 de septiembre de 1793 acordó y firmó la Asociación de Óperas, por todos los señores que se hallaban en Madrid en aquella época," 1793, Mss/14052/3, Biblioteca Nacional de España.

144 *Music and Modernity in Enlightenment Spain*

These two distinct groups had some interests in common and others at odds. Regarding the reopening of Los Caños del Peral, both groups' interests converged. While functionaries like Cabarrús had recently endorsed Italian opera for political and financial motives, the high nobility had a history of investing in the art form. For example, the powerful María Josefa Pimentel y Téllez Girón (1750–1834), countess of Benavente from 1787, was a tireless sponsor of the arts. In January 1787, she provided significant support for Los Caños del Peral when she paid in advance for a box to attend 150 opera performances.[30]

Aristocrats had been involved in Madrid's Italian opera in previous decades and continued to be crucial for Los Caños del Peral during the 1790s. A group of nobles had sponsored opera performances at the royal palaces (Reales Sitios) between 1766 and 1767. The productions were financially unsuccessful and halted in 1777 by Charles III's decree. Even so, some aristocrats like the countess of Benavente remained interested in financing Italian opera. When in 1790 the Hospital Board could not find a suitable impresario for Los Caños del Peral, a few of these aristocrats formed a board of trustees called Asociación para la Representación de Óperas Italianas, headed by the fifteenth marquis of Astorga, Vicente Joaquín Osorio de Moscoso y Guzmán (1756–1816). This board assumed the Los Caños del Peral administration between 1791 and 1795. They supervised finances, decided on production matters, and functioned as an intermediary with the king.[31] They also financed the theater with their own hefty subscriptions, "[imitating] the practice observed in most places in Italy."[32]

Many of Madrid's nobles traveled to other European cities where they attended opera performances. For wealthy Madrileños, nobles or otherwise, opera was a pan-European form of entertainment more attached to the idea of Europe than to the Italian nation. Open letters in newspapers lobbied for placing Madrid among the finest European cities. A letter published in the *Correo de los Ciegos* on April 18, 1787, states that the new theater was rehabilitated "to fill the void that foreigners noticed as soon as they got to know the [Madrid]

---

[30]   The box amounted to 7,500 reales de vellón. She delivered the amount to Juan Bautista Montaldi, the first impresario of Los Caños del Peral. The receipt from January 24, 1787, is in BNE Mss/14016/3-194. Montaldi did not measure up to the role of impresario and Melchor Ronzi, the director, assumed the administration of the theater. Juan Bautista Montaldi, "[Recibí]," 1787, MSS-14016/3 (194), Biblioteca Nacional de España.

[31]   The Society for the Performance of Italian Operas (Asociación para la Representación de Óperas Italianas) operated between 1791 and 1795. It "consisted of a group of opera-loving aristocrats who agreed who take over the assets and liabilities of the company" after two Italian theater directors succeeded Montaldi. Robinson, "Financial Management," 32.

[32]   Petition by Felipe Marescalchi, legal representative of the opera board of trustees, to Charles IV (April 17, 1790). Archivo Histórico Nacional, Consejos 11411/23. Quoted by Josep Martínez Reinoso, "El surgimiento del concierto público en Madrid (1767–1808)" (Universidad de la Rioja, 2017), 97–98.

court."[33] Another example in the *Diario de Madrid* in 1790 extolled the Spanish as the "greatest, most cultured, most beautiful people" who *deserved* an Italian opera theater.[34] For this wealthy class, it followed that if Spain was to belong in modern Europe, Madrid could not lag behind other capitals.

The Bourbon reformist project to make Spain an economically competitive state involved Europeanization, especially under Charles III. Before the French Revolution, many politicians and men of letters of the late Spanish Enlightenment sought to reconcile European and Spanish mentalities. Historian Antonio Calvo Maturana believes that Enlightenment gave Bourbon officials an aura of prestige and allowed them to "recruit members of the intellectual elite and employ them in the service of the state" to endorse the monarchy.[35] This cosmopolitan approach reaffirmed Spain as the metropole of an empire and a bastion for culture and civilization worthy of its place in modern Europe. In their selective cosmopolitanism, government ministers and men of letters working under Charles III privileged French classicist theater and Pietro Metastasio's librettos as the models for edifying dramatic spectacle compatible with the Spanish character. Both genres were in accord with Ignacio de Luzán's *Poetics* and therefore with Spanish neoclassicism because they observed the classical unities and pursued moral edification. But starting in the 1780s, the *apologista* movement headed by Juan Pablo Forner, and later the French Revolution's antimonarchical and anticlerical character, inflamed opposition between supporters of European entertainment and the partisans of the national theater. After the 1789 events in France, Europeanism became antipatriotic rather than a loyalist effort to modernize Spain. The hopes for a productive and peaceable Europeanization plummeted under Charles IV (r. 1788–1808).

As Cabarrús formulates it in his report to the Hospital Board, Italian opera was a top-down tool for national modernization. His report demonstrates Los Caños del Peral's political dimension as encompassing state policing and popular education. He characterizes theater as a "government agent" to convert people prone to "passions and vices" into "the public man" willing to contribute to the "general order." Cabarrús is hinting at the possibility of a public sphere, albeit one dependent on the absolute monarchy to rein in individual passions:

> I am persuaded that none of the cogs that make up the mechanism of society, even the smallest one, is unworthy of examination or investigation by the public man, whose passions, vices, and portion of evil inseparable from any human establishment, those who govern must calculate, to make them contribute to the general order ...

---

[33] Chicharro, "Otra [carta]," *Correo de los Ciegos*, April 18, 1787, 206.

[34] [El Amante del buen gusto], "Carta sobre la necesidad, y utilidad de un teatro de ópera en la Corte," *Diario de Madrid*, January 16, 1790. Emphasis mine.

[35] Antonio Calvo Maturana, "'Is It Useful to Deceive the People?' The Debate on Public Information in Spain at the End of the Ancien Regime (1780–1808)," *Journal of Modern History* 86, no. 1 (March 2014): 7.

146   *Music and Modernity in Enlightenment Spain*

The (second) object [of theater] is to instruct the people through an agreeable means, to incline their ideas toward the end that the government desires, and in one word, form and direct their opinions. Viewed this way, theater could not be more useful, for if *this government agent* completely fulfilled its object, it would ensure public calm, greatly make up for the shortcomings of national education, and finally, decrease the sum of evils, first by decreasing the occasions to commit them, and then battling them with the slow but certain effect of instruction.[36]

Cabarrús saw proof that music had the potential to bolster absolutist monarchy in Frederick the Great, whom he understood to have "handled equally well the scepter and the lyre, the flute and the terrible sword."[37] The idea seemed straightforward: get people in large urban centers to be on the monarchy's side by sating them with an entertainment form that can communicate modern ideas of civility and public order. The practice, however, was complicated by incompatible administrative models (city-operated theaters in Madrid versus the impresario system) and lack of cross-class interest in Italian opera.

Educating the Audience

When the Madrid Hospital Board succeeded in reopening the Teatro de los Caños del Peral in 1787, audiences responded to this new, Europeanized spectacle with curiosity and suspicion. For the first time in decades, the general public of Madrid could access an opera performance by an Italian company. Italian operas' language posed two challenges: first, most in the audience would not understand the words, and second, it was a constant reminder of the genre's foreignness. At the time, aside from Italian parodies, all performances at the city coliseos were in Spanish and all performers were employees of the state. However, the new Teatro de los Caños del Peral imported Italian companies of singers and dancers.

---

[36] "Estoy persuadido a que ninguna de las ruedas que componen el mecanismo de la sociedad por pequeña que sea desmerece el examen o investigación del hombre público a que los que gobiernan deben calcular las pasiones, los vicios, y la porción de mal inseparable de todo establecimiento humano para hacerlos contribuir al orden general…. El (segundo) objeto [del teatro] es instruir a pueblo por un medio agradable, inclinar sus ideas hacia el fin que el gobierno apetece, y en una palabra formar y dirigir sus opiniones. El teatro mirado por este aspecto no puede ser más útil, pues si *este agente del gobierno* llenase completamente su objeto, aseguraría la tranquilidad pública, supliría en gran parte los defectos de la educación nacional, y finalmente disminuiría la suma de los males, primero disminuyendo las ocasiones de cometerlos, y después haciéndoles la guerra con el lento pero infalible efecto de la instrucción." Cabarrús, *Memorias*, 67. Emphasis mine.

[37] Cabarrús, *Memorias*, 78.

Cabarrús, the Hospital Board, and newspaper editors were well aware that many theatergoers would reject the foreign genre, so they counteracted the expected rejection through intensive editorial efforts during January 1787 in preparation for the debut of the first opera at the end of the month. These editorial efforts included a comprehensive summary of the opera genre published in the *Diario curioso, erudito, económico y comercial*, the new prologue to Gamerra-Sarti's *Medonte*, discussed in this chapter's introduction, and the first Spanish translation of Algarotti's *Saggio sopra l'opera in musica* (1755, 1763).[38] All three texts intended to educate Madrid's audiences so that they would embrace the new Italian opera theater and be receptive to an edifying entertainment that was supposed to make Madrid the modern, civilized city Bourbon authorities envisioned. Table 3.1 gives an overview of the preparatory events preceding Los Caños del Peral's reopening in 1787.

In the following sections, I consider the sources presented in this timeline in order to argue that newspaper editors and government entities such as the Madrid Junta de Alcaldes and the Hospital Board saw Italian opera as a means to promote the Bourbon reform project of civilization through Europeanization.

"Instructive Notices" in the Diario curioso, erudito, económico y comercial

In mid-January 1787, the *Diario curioso, erudito, económico y commercial* printed two parts of an article titled "Some Instructive Notices about the Drama Called Opera" ("Algunas noticias instructivas sobre el drama llamado ópera") to dispose Madrid audiences toward the theater's January 27 reopening. As Madrid's only consistent daily, the *Diario* reached many readers. It published daily theater programs, short articles, letters, and classified ads, all within four pages. The *Diario* was privately owned but remained on good terms with the Bourbon administration.

The first part of the *Diario*'s "instructive notices," printed January 17, recounted the past glories of Italian opera performance in Madrid, particularly the ventures at Los Caños del Peral in 1738, sponsored by Philip V, and the Royal Palace of El Buen Retiro from 1747 to 1758, sponsored by Ferdinand VI. Thereafter, according to the author, opera had not been accessible

---

[38] The *Diario de Madrid* was titled *Diario curioso, erudito, económico y comercial* in 1786–1787. "Algunas noticias instructivas sobre el drama llamado ópera," *Diario curioso, erudito, económico y comercial*, January 17, 1787; "Continuación de las noticias sobre la ópera," *Diario curioso, erudito, económico y comercial*, January 18, 1787; Francesco Algarotti, *Ensayo sobre la ópera en musica. Escrito en lengua italiana por el Conde Francisco Algaroti … Traducido al castellano, para instruccion de los que quieran asistir al nuevo teatro italiano, que se ha establecido en esta corte* (Madrid: Miguel Escribano, 1787).

148   *Music and Modernity in Enlightenment Spain*

Table 3.1 January 1787 events prior to Los Caños del Peral opening

January 10	The crown issues the "Reglamento para el mejor orden y policía del Teatro de la Ópera."
January?	Spanish translation of Algarotti's *Saggio sopra l'opera in musica* published.
January 17	First installment of didactic article on opera in the *Diario curioso, erudito, económico y comercial*: "Algunas noticias instructivas sobre el drama llamado ópera."
January 18	Second installment of didactic article on opera in the *Diario curioso, erudito, económico y comercial*: "Continuación de las noticias sobre la ópera."
January 19	"Reglamento para el mejor orden y policía del Teatro de la Ópera" published in the *Diario curioso, erudito, económico y comercial*.
January 22	Royal edict with twenty-three further rules regarding the opera theater approved by the city council.
January 27	Sarti-Gamerra's *Medonte* opens the performances at Los Caños del Peral. Ballets: one based on Metastasio's *Didone abbandonata*, and one called *La Sandrina*, based on *Los villanos en la corte* (*La contadina in corte*).[a]
January 27	One-page summary of Algarotti's *Ensayo sobre la ópera en música* published in *Diario curioso, erudito, económico y comercial*.
January 27	Royal edict with twenty-three further rules regarding the opera theater published in *Diario curioso, erudito, económico y comercial*.
January 27	Los Caños del Peral opens its doors with a performance of *Medonte*.

[a] *Los villanos en la corte* was a famous zarzuela by Ramón de la Cruz (1767) based on the 1765 opera buffa *La contadina in corte*, libretto by Niccolò Tassi and music by Antonio Sacchini.

to the general public. The second part, printed on January 18, provided a history of opera that highlighted the genre's development in Italy and France.[39] The "instructive notices" also tackled the issue of the Italian language, which raised aesthetic as well as practical concerns for the Madrid people. Keeping with the official discourse of civilization and Europeanization, the article pre-

[39] "Continuación," *Diario curioso, erudito, económico y comercial*, 74.

sented Italian opera as an "honest and plausible entertainment," "already well known in Europe's top courts."[40]

The "instructive notices" in the *Diario* appeased both learned and aficionado readers by making opera sound like a friend of Spain rather than a foe. It appealed to the neoclassicists, abiding by Ignacio de Luzán's hierarchy of the arts whereby poetry has primacy. The *Diario* reassured readers that in opera, "music is nothing more than a supporter to highlight poetry and enhance its marvelous effects." To further assert Italian opera's conformity to Spanish neoclassicism and natural reason, the text cautioned that "one cannot do without the rules of art when [writing] opera," as opera buffa composers do, "because they [opera buffa composers] follow rules that are contrary to reason and nature." While the anonymous author admitted that opera buffa broke the rules of dramatic poetry, he proposed Metastasian opera seria as a model for musical drama consistent with that of the ancient Greeks: "Metastasio, as a wise follower of the Greek... never allowed his operas' music to overcome the limits of its good companion [music]." There seemed to be dissension among the neoclassicists about the amount of music in opera insofar as a sung-throughout drama could obscure the text's capacity to communicate an edifying message to the audience. In other words, the fear was that the abundance of music in an opera would thwart the moral purpose of theater.

The author of the brief history of early opera in the second part of the *Diario* "instructive notices" quoted Pietro Napoli Signorelli's *Storia critica de' teatri antichi e moderni* (1777), which adhered to the Spanish neoclassicists' emphasis on verisimilitude and the moral purpose of theater. Signorelli lived in Madrid for nearly two decades (1765–ca. 1783). He frequented the Tertulia de la Fonda de San Sebastián, where he met neoclassicists Nicolás and Leandro Fernández de Moratín, Tomás de Iriarte, José Cadalso, and others involved in the Enlightenment reformation of Spanish theater. Signorelli penned his *Storia critica* during his residence in Madrid. The *Diario* reminded its readers that Signorelli's "narration and origin of melodramas is in agreement with what *our* Luzán says in his rules of poetics" and emphasized the text concordance between Signorelli's *Storia critica* and Luzán's *Poetics*.[41] For the wider reading public, linking a foreign musical genre to a canonical author such as Luzán would assuage the fear of cultural invasion.

Since not all *Diario* readers would be persuaded through neoclassicist arguments, the author turned to several strategies to present a Spanish-friendly opera. For example, he reminded his readers that Italian opera was the preferred spectacle of queens and kings in Madrid throughout the century. He quoted Tomás de Iriarte's still neoclassicist but less orthodox didactic poem *La música* (1779), the authoritative national text in matters of musical aesthetics. To support the value of music in drama, he specifically referred to an oft-cited

---

[40]   "Algunas noticias instructivas," *Diario curioso, erudito, económico y comercial*, 71.

[41]   "Continuación," *Diario curioso, erudito, económico y comercial*, 74. Emphasis mine.

150   *Music and Modernity in Enlightenment Spain*

verse in the fifth canto: "Music and Poetry / in one lyre shall play."[42] Even *Diario* readers who had not read the didactic poem in its entirety had probably seen the famous engraving that Manuel Salvador Carmona created inspired by this verse, included in the 1779 edition of *La música*, printed opposite to the title page of Iriarte's poem (see figure 1.1). By recalling the Spanish court's past interest in opera and citing Iriarte, the *Diario* mitigated readers' potential perception of opera as anti-Spanish.

It was in opera promoters' best interests to promote a welcoming attitude toward Italian music and performers. The new Teatro de los Caños del Peral needed to attract the business of the coliseos' loyal clientele, who would likely reject foreign musical theater at a time when Masson de Morvilliers's *Encyclopédie Méthodique* "Spain" article had wounded national pride and unleashed antiforeign sentiments.[43] The author of the *Diario*'s "instructive notices" flattered his readership by affirming that Spanish and Italian were the only languages appropriate for musical drama. He emphasized the unsuitability of the French language for opera. According to the author, the French had rivaled the Italians in musical theater but never succeeded in "getting the language of the Gaul to become an ally of Apollo's lyre." French language's unsuitability opened an opportunity for Spain to surpass France and the rest of Europe (except Italy) in musical drama, since "all the septentrional [northern] languages" were "equally inimical to the charming Euterpe [the muse of music]."[44] The idea that Spain could profit from emulating and welcoming Italian musical theater and eventually excel in this art through a distinctively Spanish opera was crucial for the Hospital Board's efforts to obtain official support for Los Caños del Peral. Hence, the authors of texts printed in preparation for the theater's opening made an effort to reconcile Italian opera with Spanish dramatic tradition, as the Spanish prologue to *Medonte* did.

The Translation of Algarotti's Saggio sopra l'opera in musica

A Spanish translation of Francesco Algarotti's *Saggio sopra l'opera in musica* (1763) was published in Madrid with the title *Ensayo sobre la ópera en música* almost simultaneously with Los Caños del Peral's reopening. The author of the anonymous Spanish translation of Algarotti's work intended it to be an educational resource in the bigger project of modern Spain. The title page specified that this essay was translated into Spanish "for the instruction of those who

---

[42] "Es, pues, la ópera Italiana entre las representaciones teatrales la más sublime, noble y decorosa, porque con ella se logran a un tiempo los dos encantos más sensibles al hombre, cuales son la poesía y la música." "Continuación," *Diario curioso, erudito, económico y comercial*, 74.

[43] Masson de Morvilliers, "Espagne."

[44] "Continuación," *Diario curioso, erudito, económico y comercial*, 75.

Cosmopolitan Opera 151

wish to attend the new Italian theater."[45] More specifically, the *Ensayo sobre la ópera* addressed the reform of national theater as part of that bigger modernization project. The *Diario curioso, erudito, económico y comercial* announced the *Ensayo*'s publication with a brief summary on January 27, the day *Medonte* opened. The author of the *Diario* summary urged audiences to read the *Ensayo sobre la ópera* in order to "contribute to the reformation of national [Spanish] theater."[46] Several copies of Algarotti's book in Italian survive in Spanish libraries, evincing its pre-1787 availability, but the act of translating the *Ensayo sobre la ópera* into Spanish suggests that those involved in this translation wished for it to get a broader readership.

Because Algarotti's original was reformist in nature, it contained more criticism than praise of opera. While the Spanish translation also sought to reform current musical theater practices, it was mainly intended as a manual for opera lovers and as an effort to try and win over those who disliked the genre. For the Spanish elites who supported the Los Caños del Peral project in the late eighteenth century, opera was the solution to the lack of sophistication in the national theater, not the problem itself. Hence, the translator faced the risk that readers would end up paying too much attention to Algarotti's criticism. The translator wrote a brief disclaimer at the beginning of the *Ensayo sobre la ópera* advising readers to focus not on the genre's defects pointed out by Algarotti but rather on his comprehensive description of the different components of opera, such as drama, music, sets, and theater architecture. In passing, this disclaimer shows contempt for Spanish theater as an inferior dramatic form. The translator's logic is that no matter how defective Italian opera may be, it will always be superior to the current national musical theater, dominated by the taste of the uneducated masses. Opera, the brief introduction concludes, is "one of the best ornaments of society in several European courts," so perhaps the common people of Madrid will follow the example of the educated class and learn to like this genre. The translator lists the shortcomings that make Spanish theater inferior to opera: the sets' slovenliness, the performers' coarseness, and the plays' "irregularity" or lack of observance of the classical unities.[47] It was this kind of cultural elitism that bothered people of all classes who did not support the new theater. Nevertheless, the translator is careful to present Italian opera as an incentive to refine national culture and not as a substitute meant to erase it.

The *Ensayo sobre la ópera en música* abided by neoclassicist aesthetics, like the other pro-opera texts published on the occasion of Los Caños del Peral's rehabilitation. The government often approved of neoclassicist principles, endorsing them in public cultural events and using them as censorship guide-

---

[45] Algarotti, *Ensayo sobre la ópera*, n.p.

[46] "Sobre la ópera italiana," *Diario curioso, erudito, económico y comercial*, January 27, 1787, 116. Algarotti's *Ensayo sobre la ópera* was advertised again in the *Gaceta de Madrid* on February 2, 1787, and April 8, 1788.

[47] "Advertencia," *Ensayo sobre la ópera*, n.p.

152   *Music and Modernity in Enlightenment Spain*

lines. Furthermore, men of letters met government officials in elite cultural tertulias where neoclassicist taste prevailed, fostering a network between intellectuals and reformist Bourbon administrators, with both groups supporting modernization inspired by selective Enlightenment ideas. Even though most neoclassicism advocates welcomed Italian opera, they had concerns about its lack of verisimilitude because it was sung throughout, detracting from the primacy of words over music in public entertainment.

A Review of Medonte and Neoclassicist Aesthetics

Writing in support of the Italian opera theater signaled approval of neoclassicism as the cultural arm of the Bourbon reformist apparatus. Hispanist and eighteenth-century expert Joaquín Álvarez Barrientos posits that the state supported neoclassicist precepts because they were perceived "as part of the measures that tended to civilize Spain, to set it up in the modern trends of the time, and to drive the country to participate in European movements."[48] In his 1737 *Poetics*, Luzán already believed that neoclassicist precepts would improve Spanish literature to the point that Spain would not need to "envy other nations or be wary of their criticisms," instead drawing applause from fellow Europeans.[49] The principles of Luzán's *Poetics* influenced theater regulation and censorship throughout the eighteenth century and were invoked to justify opera's 1787 comeback.

For Luzán, there were two ways of writing theater: the old one, derived from popular tradition and epitomized in baroque Spanish comedias, and the modern or neoclassicist one, based on Aristotle's and Horace's rules.[50] According to Luzán, because Spanish playwrights and theater performers have ignored and transgressed Aristotle's and Horace's precepts, comedias, "the mirror of human life, instead of emending and improving men's mores, have deteriorated them." The indecorous characters and plots of traditional Spanish theater, Luzán continues, have "authorized, with their examples, a thousand principles against morality and good politics."[51] Consequently, reforming theater would lead to better mores and politics, and with these, Spain would gain other nations' admiration. This view would endure in the

---

[48]   "[El apoyo del gobierno al neoclasicismo] se insertaba en las medidas que tendieron a civilizar a España, a instalarla en las corrientes modernas del momento y a contribuir a que el país tuviera parte en los movimientos europeos." Álvarez Barrientos, *Ilustración y neoclasicismo en las letras españolas*, 189.

[49]   Ignacio de Luzán Claramunt de Suelves y Gurrea, *La poetica, ó Reglas de la poesia en general, y de sus principales especies* (Zaragoza: Francisco Revilla, 1737), 9.

[50]   Ignacio de Luzán Claramunt de Suelves y Gurrea, *La poética: O reglas de la poesía en general y de sus principales especies*, Corregida y aumentada, 2 vols. (Madrid: Antonio de Sancha, 1789), 43.

[51]   Luzán, *Poética*, 8.

Cosmopolitan Opera   153

decades to come, to the point that a second, posthumous edition of Luzán's *Poetics* was published with great success in 1789. Luzán's literary precepts of verisimilitude and decorum would coincide with the state-sponsored version of the Enlightenment: religious, scientific, and artistic discourse needed to be cleansed of unrealistic components and made subject to reason if Spain was to modernize.

Luzán's precepts had to be adapted to work in favor of opera. In the *Poetics*, he viewed opera as inferior to poetry and questioned its classical credentials. He refused to connect opera to ancient drama or grant it civic utility. He believed that ancient Greek tragedy was not sung throughout but limited music and dancing to choruses. In his view, choruses had simply disappeared from drama over time, and the musical numbers of modern theater were interlopers unrelated to Greek practices.[52] Luzán was also adamant that only poetry and painting were capable of true mimesis. Even though he thought imitation characterized all the arts, he wanted poetry to stand separate from and above music and dance. For example, he refuted Renaissance literary theorist Antonio Minturno's (1500–1574) definition of poetry because it included harmony and rhythm, "for in fact, what do the moving of the feet or the tone of the voice have to do with poetry? This would be to confound and mistake the boundaries of musician, dancer, and poet; neither can these arts aim to more ... than to be intrusive ornaments of poetry."[53] Luzán even rejected Aristotle's definition of tragedy because it included harmony and dance. He feared music would stir the affections too much and thus overshadow the poet's art. Luzán thought music appealed directly to the senses, bypassing reason and discourse and thus upending the natural order.[54] For the *Poetics*, Luzán drew heavily from Mura-

---

[52] Luzán, *Poética* [corregida y aumentada], 208–9.

[53] "la común opinión ... coloca la esencia de la poesía en la imitación de la naturaleza; tanto, que Aristóteles excluye del catálogo de poetas a los que no imitaran, aunque hayan escrito en verso..." / "Pues de hecho, ¿qué tienen que ver con la poesía el movimiento de los pies o el tono de la voz? Esto sería confundir y equivocar los términos del músico bailarín y poeta; ni estas artes pueden pretender más [...] que ser adornos advenedizos de las poesía." / "se podrá definir la poesía, *imitación de la naturaleza en lo universal o en lo particular, hecha con versos, para utilidad o para deleite de los hombres, o para uno y otro juntamente*." Luzán, *Poética*, 31.

[54] Russell P. Sebold, "Análisis estadístico de las ideas poéticas de Luzán: Sus orígenes y naturaleza," *El rapto de la mente: Poética y poesía dieciochescas* (Alicante: Biblioteca Virtual Miguel de Cervantes, 2001), https://www.cervantesvirtual.com/obra-visor/ anlisis-estadstico-de-las-ideas-poticas-de-luzn---sus-orgenes-y-su-naturaleza-0/ html/ff65b43a-82b1-11df-acc7-002185ce6064_5.html. Luzán adapted some of his ideas from Scipione Maffei's introduction in *Teatro italiano o sia scelta di tragedia per uso della scena* (Verona: Jacopo Vallarsi, 1723). The following paragraph follows Maffei: "Por lo que toca a representarse toda una tragedia o comedia en música, me parece que no es del todo acertado, y que mejor efecto hará, y deleitará más, una buena representación bien ejecutada por actores hábiles y diestros, que todo el

154   *Music and Modernity in Enlightenment Spain*

tori's 1706 *Della perfetta poesia italiana* (among many other works) and agreed with the Italian author's verdict that stage music corrupts the soul. Music and dance offered pleasure to men but could never be of moral use, whereas poetry could both *delectare et docere*, hence its superiority. Given Luzán's strict views on musical drama, intellectuals who supported opera faced a dilemma: how to dignify music and dance as proper entertainment while upholding neoclassicist standards that subordinate music and dance to poetry.[55]

A review of *Medonte* published by the *Memorial literario* (hereafter *Memorial*), a monthly Madrid journal of literary criticism, negotiates Luzán's older neoclassical precepts with newer ideas about the status of music in drama, especially those of Tomás de Iriarte. In spite of their overall neoclassicist perspective, the *Memorial* authors departed from Luzán in two important points: they keep the artistic value of music and dance parallel with poetry and align opera with Greek drama, upholding its mimetic potential and civic usefulness. To clear all doubts about music's mimetic possibilities, the *Memorial* authors affirmed that singing and dancing were natural to the human condition. Furthermore, they agreed with Iriarte that singing heeded to verisimilitude as much as reciting verses, Spanish theater's standard means of vocalization: "Making verses is as natural to the spirit of man as singing, inventing and playing musical instruments, and dancing with concerted harmony and orderly movements, for all these arts are born of the imitation of nature and of actions." The authors also highlighted music's civilizing power by relating the stories of Orpheus and Amphion "subjecting" the "savage," forest-dwelling nomads to "amicable society" with their musical skills.[56]

Iriarte, also a neoclassicist, had defended opera in the fourth canto of his influential didactic poem *La música*, remarking on the contradiction between denouncing opera's lack of verisimilitude because nobody speaks by singing but accepting Spanish theater's verse dialog. Iriarte had made music poetry's equal in the fifth canto's celebrated verse about music and poetry playing the same lyre (see fig. 1.1). Compare Iriarte's conciliatory image to the Spanish prologue of *Medonte* discussed at the beginning of this chapter, where Comedy and Tragedy hunt for Opera to kill her.

---

primor de la música. Porque aunque es verdad que la música mueve también los afectos, nunca puede llegar a igualar la fuerza que tiene una buena representación; demás que el canto, en los teatros, siempre tiene mucha inverisimilitud, a la cual unida la distracción que causa su dulzura, con que enajena los ánimos y la atención, desluce todo el trabajo y esfuerzo del poeta y todo el gusto y la persuasión de la poesía, introduciendo en vez de este deleite (que podemos llamar racional, porque fundado en razón y en discurso) otro deleite de sentido, porque es producido solamente por las impresiones que en el oído hacen las notas harmónicas, sin intervención del entendimiento ni del discurso." Luzán, *Poética*, 101–2.

[55]   For Luzán, "poetry and painting ... have the same value, and music and dance are subject to poetry, only as 'newly arrived ornaments.'" Jacobs, "La función de la música," 54.

[56]   "Teatros. Introducción," *Memorial Literario, Instructivo y Curioso* 38 (1787): 259–60.

Lejos, lejos de aquí todo el que llama	Far, far from here anyone who calls
monstruosa la invención del	the invention of melodrama
melodrama ...	"monstrous" ...
¿Pero qué? ¿Los cantores	So what? Are singers
son acaso los únicos que ofenden	the only ones to upset
la ilusión teatral, cuya	theatrical illusion, the observance of
observancia	which
el cómico y el trágico	the comic and the tragic [actor]
pretenden?	purport?[57]

The *Memorial* review appeared in February 1787, a few days after the opera's January 27 opening at Los Caños del Peral. Specializing in culture, science, art, and literary reviews, the *Memorial* catered to the uppermost classes since its inception in 1784. The review of *Medonte* appeared on a newly created section of the *Memorial* titled "Introducción [a los teatros]," intended to educate readers about the different aspects of drama (plot, conflict and resolution, characters, unities of action, time, and place, affections, gear) by reviewing neoclassicist principles. The *Memorial* routinely included plot summaries and a short commentary on the plays at the Madrid coliseos, but starting in 1787, the editors began prefacing their theater reviews with a didactic "Introducción." The February 1787 issue included for the first time Los Caños del Peral in the theater section of the journal.

The first three pages of the *Memorial*'s February "Introducción [a los teatros]" offered a succinct history of opera to prove that the genre fit into neoclassicist canons because it imitated the Greek and Roman tradition of singing and dancing in choruses—something Luzán had denied, but which Iriarte had maintained.[58] The authors declared modern opera "an imitation, ... a restoration of the tragedies and comedies of antiquity." The article explained that even before the invention of tragedy, music and dance served to express affects in the ancient Greek and Roman ceremonies. According to this history, tragedy started as sung choruses with instrumental accompaniment, to which solo declamation in honor of heroes or gods was added "to take a break in between choruses." These solo declamation episodes were accompanied by background instruments.[59] The *Memorial* authors thus justified opera's choruses, arias, recitative, basso continuo, and orchestra.

After devoting much of the article to tracing opera's ancient origins, the *Memorial* author addressed how music moves the affections, always abiding by the conception of opera as a mimetic, representational expression of passions. The author believed that music is an extension of poetry insofar as it makes language more effective in moving the affections. However, unlike Simplicio

---

[57] Tomás de Iriarte, *La música: Poema* (Madrid, 1779), 75.

[58] See fourth canto of *La música*.

[59] "Teatros. Introducción," 261–62.

Greco y Lira in the 1786 "Discourse 97" of *El Censor* (discussed in chapter 1), this author did not claim that music should remain close to declamation or that only melody holds the power of expression. On the contrary, the *Memorial* acknowledged three musical components of opera, each of which addresses emotions differently. First is *recitado*, where music denotes the subject "without any particular affection." Second is arias and cavatinas, where opera "penetrates the heart." Finally, *sinfonias* serve a mimetic function when they depict storms "and other horrible images of nature," always within the confines of verisimilitude. Like Batteux, the *Memorial* author formulates music's legitimacy as conditional upon mimesis: "The music that knows how to paint and imitate passions, or even any other image of nature, has a strong power over our heart."[60]

The Los Caños del Peral's opening interrupted the *Memorial* editors' planned sequence of "Introduction to the Theaters" articles. The review begins with the authors pointing out that discussing music so early in the series disrupts the traditional neoclassicist dramatic theory established in Luzán's *Poetics*, where music forms part of the theatrical gear and is discussed in the last place, only after more important ground has been covered:

> Debíamos hablar ahora de varias calidades y partes de la fábula dramática; pero por cuanto hemos de dar razón de los dramas llamados óperas, lo interrumpimos. La música y el canto, partes esenciales de las óperas, como también los bailes con que se suelen adornar los fines o intermedios de estos dramas, era asunto igualmente destinado para cuando diésemos razón del aparato teatral.[61]

> (We ought to talk now of the various qualities and parts of the dramatic fable; but since we must now give an account of the dramas called operas, we interrupt it [the plan]. Music and song are essential parts of operas, as are also the dances that customarily adorn the endings or intermissions of these dramas. These were matters destined to when we gave an account of the theatrical gear.)

This interruption was a subtle but meaningful instance of how Italian opera altered the Madrid cultural landscape: while theater debates often dealt with music minimally, now music must be at the forefront. Opera thus challenged the thread of neoclassicist theoretical deliberations, wherein theatrical gear (music, dance, sets, and machinery) was treated as a mere appendage.

While neoclassicists belittled theatrical gear, the public wanted more of it. In the late eighteenth century, Spanish audiences strongly preferred *comedias de teatro* to regular comedias for their use of music, dance, flamboyant sets and costumes, and special effects. In fact, Madrid theatergoers often understood opera to be but one of several high-spectacle dramatic genres available at the

---

[60] "Teatros. Introducción," 262–63.

[61] "Teatros. Introducción," 259.

Cosmopolitan Opera   157

time, such as heroic tragedies or *comedias de magia,* characterized by their higher budget productions. In terms of lavish display, René Andioc likened opera in Madrid to zarzuela and royal festivities.[62] Hispanist John A. Cook wrote that by the 1790s audiences "had developed an inordinate taste for plays with spectacular stage settings," a taste which, in his view, was fed by the 1787 opening of Italian opera.[63] While insisting on the Spanish public's penchant for spectacle as Andioc and Cook do could point to long-held prejudices about Spanish extravagance, the fact is that *comedias de teatro* sold well. Their popularity contradicted governmental policies seeking to restrain excessive luxury.

The authors of the *Memorial* article both recognize and express concern over Italian dominance in opera while remaining hopeful that a Spanish opera could bloom and even parallel Italian opera. For them, no other country had surpassed the beauty of Italian music and the sweetness of the Italian language, but zarzuelas and other musical theater pieces demonstrated that Spain was a worthy contender.[64] Hence, the authors endorse the official view, expressed in Cabarrús's prospect, that Los Caños del Peral's ultimate objective was to facilitate the establishment of national opera in Spanish.

A Space for *Policía* and Civilization

The new Italian opera theater opened a utopian space for the government, men of letters and "personas de distinción" who aspired to Spanish Europeanization. They hoped for a modern European public space far removed from the semi-outdoor seventeenth-century *corrales de* comedias. The elites wanted a theater where audiences would not yell at the performers, whose sets, illumination, and social interaction would remind them of Vienna's and Paris's theaters. Charles III's government was mostly interested in the opera theater as an organ for modeling publicity and *policía*, as demonstrated in officially issued, exhaustive rules for audience behavior in the new theater. Reception of the music and dance performed at Los Caños del Peral is inseparable from how audiences felt in and around the theater building, how they interacted with each other, and

---

[62] René Andioc, *Teatro y sociedad en el Madrid del siglo XVIII,* Pensamiento literario español (Madrid: Fundación Juan March, 1976), 58.

[63] "It seems that the public at this time had developed an inordinate taste for plays with spectacular stage settings. The opening of the Italian opera on January 20, 1787, had introduced to Madrid audiences a type of performance which not only offered an attraction to lovers of music, but also, in the splendor of its settings, stood out in marked contrast to Golden Age comedies and to neo-classic translations of tragedies and comedies from the French and Italian theaters." John A. Cook, *Neo-Classic Drama in Spain, Theory and Practice* (Dallas: Southern Methodist University Press, 1959), 330.

[64] "Teatros. Introducción," 263.

158   *Music and Modernity in Enlightenment Spain*

what the government explicitly told them "going to the theater" should look, sound, and smell like.

From its projection in 1786, Los Caños del Peral became an emblem of sociocultural modernity in contrast to the coliseos of La Cruz and El Príncipe, which political and intellectual elites saw as unsophisticated and shameful in the face of Spain's European neighbors. Policía in the sense of good civic order as prescribed by the law was the prerequisite for civilization and national modernization. The *Diccionario de autoridades* defines "policía" as *disciplina civilis*, "the good order observed and kept in cities and republics, obeying the established laws and ordinances for their better governance."[65] "Cleaning" public entertainment through initiatives such as the new opera theater was tantamount to cleaning and illuminating the city streets to make Madrid a modern European capital. Enlightenment jurist and economist Juan Sempere y Guarinos (1754–1830) compared Spanish theater to the filth that infamously littered Madrid's streets before Charles III's reforms: "Madrid [before Charles III] was without *policía*, full of garbage, without nightlights, without any good promenades or daily entertainment other than stretching out to bask in the sun or a licentious theater corrupted in the morality of its compositions, the performers' acting and behavior, and the excessive liberty of spectators." For his part, Cabarrús thought that opera should serve urban policía by filling winter nights with an honest entertainment that could keep men away from streets and taverns.[66]

Although Charles III hardly ever attended the theater, it was fully within his overall program of political and economic reform to renovate the face of public entertainment, with theater at the top. In a way, his government "delegated" theater reform to intellectuals. According to Calvo Maturana, in the 1780s and 1790s "the government directly supported a neoclassicist intellectual minority" to counteract what they saw as the pernicious morals of Spanish baroque theater, applauded by the public. Furthermore, Calvo Maturana continues, the monarchy "allowed a debate in the form of reviews in print, satires, and polemics between opposing factions, intervening only when the discussion became excessively heated."[67] In other words, government officials facilitated the public circulation of the elite's dramatic tastes, including opera. Presenting the new

---

[65]   Real Academia Española, *Diccionario de la lengua castellana compuesto por la Real Academia Española, reducido a un tomo para su más fácil uso. Segunda edición, en la qual se han colocado en los lugares correspondientes todas las voces del Suplemento, que se puso al fin de la edición del año de 1780, y se ha añadido otro nuevo suplemento de artículos correspondientes a las letras A, B y C* (Madrid: Joaquín Ibarra, 1783), 748, s.v. "policía." This definition matches the English use of the word "police" during the eighteenth century. Historical Thesaurus, Oxford English Dictionary, a1631, s.v. "police."

[66]   Cabarrús, *Memorias*, 70–71.

[67]   Calvo Maturana, "'Is It Useful to Deceive the People?'" 16.

Cosmopolitan Opera 159

opera theater in contrast to the old coliseos bolstered the narrative of reformist modernization that became the trademark of Charles III's government.

Letters from the *Correo de los ciegos* newspaper published in 1787 further illustrate this dichotomy between the new opera theater and the old coliseos. On February 20, roughly one month after Los Caños del Peral had opened, a *Correo* correspondent complained about the tonadilla *El teatro y los actores agraviados*, recently performed at one of the coliseos. The letter demanded that the "corrupted" city theaters be subject to the same rules issued for the renovated Los Caños del Peral, given that dramatic repertory was "an essential branch of *policía*."[68] Another letter from April proposed that coliseo actors and actress-singers emulate Italian opera performers' practice of staying in character and avoiding interaction with the audience.[69] This April letter observed that Los Caños del Peral's neoclassicist architecture, being more spacious and comfortable than that of coliseos and with separate entrances for each section, facilitated the exemplary behavior of both performers and audiences. A third letter, also from April, created a fictional situation where the author attended a tertulia (social gathering akin to a salon) and witnessed a heated argument between chorizos, or fans of the coliseo of La Cruz, and polacos, or fans of the coliseo of El Príncipe. The disputing parties asked a silent attendee who had "visited so many courts [main cities] and attended the best theaters in Europe" for his verdict regarding which of the two coliseos was better. The impartial onlooker replied that both coliseos could use some improvement. He advised that the posters announcing the theater programs be printed like those at Los Caños and other European theaters instead of manuscript. He suggested expedited access into the coliseos buildings and updated toilets to eliminate foul odors. After all, he proceeded, "the perfect way to respond to the foreigners' critics is to amend our flaws."[70] These letters sided with the cosmopolitan belief that openness to European artistic and social practices would lead to national theater's modernization.

Such letters depicted Los Caños del Peral as a utopian microcosm of policía, a modern haven of orderly socialization that turned away from the coliseos' premodern ethos. Another letter to the *Correo de los ciegos* denounced the former practices of whistling and throwing vegetables at the performers when

---

68 "Otra [carta]," *Correo de los Ciegos*, 156.

69 "¿Por qué no se han de observar en estos teatros corrompidos, las sabias reglas ó precauciones que se han establecido para el de la Opera?" (*Correo* no. 39, 156). "Todos guardan bien el carácter que representan, y se nota que se revisten de él. No hay cuchicheos entre ellos, señas ni besamanos á los expectadores, ni se observan entre bastidores mirones, pisan bien las tablas y se señorean del teatro: en fin, en muchos adminículos pueden tomar reglas de ellos nuestros mejores cómicos." Chicharro, "Otra [carta]," *Correo de los Ciegos*.

70 "Yo en ninguna Corte he visto que los carteles que sirven de anuncio á un tan respetable Publico (en el que entran la Grandeza, Ministros, Embajadores) sean manuscritos." [El amigo de los ciegos], "Madrid. Carta.," *Correo de los Ciegos*, April 21, 1787, 214.

160   *Music and Modernity in Enlightenment Spain*

the public did not like the show. According to the letter, "an enlightened policía" had banished these habits which were "once the main entertainment of our public." Now that audience responses at the opera theater and coliseos are more moderate, the author asked, "who will yearn for those times of ignorance and barbarism? No sir, that time is bygone." Like other contemporary texts, this letter considers theaters "an object of policía." The author attributes "the glorious difference" between those years and the modern ones to

> those zealous citizens who ... joining enlightenment to piety, have managed to provide us with a cultured spectacle, so applauded by temperate spirits. Everything in it [opera] is worthy of esteem: everything breathes decency, taste, and comfort. That calm, of which a portion of citizens congregated to enjoy a beautiful leisure time are worthy, [is] never perturbed. That decorum with which a people gathered under the authority of the public magistrate must be regarded is never obliterated [at the opera theater].[71]

Whether the ideal functioning of the new theater corresponded to the public's actual behavior or not, this ideal appealed to the aspirations of upper-class Madrileños—government officials, intellectuals, professionals such as lawyers, bankers, or physicians, military officers, writers, and aristocrats—who wanted to modernize their city in order to match other European capitals.

For their part, the government created sets of rules for the new theater designed to make it operate like a microcosm of the clean, orderly, and rational nation they projected. Many of the rules aimed at managing interactions between audience and performers and controlling their use of the building. These rules, compiled in the "Reglamento para el mejor orden y policía del Teatro de la ópera" (Regulations for the Better Order and Polity of the Opera Theater) were published in the *Diario curioso, erudito, económico y comercial* on January 19, 1787, immediately after the two-part "instructive notes." The initial "Reglamento" was followed on April 16 and 17 with an edict announcing the rules and prices for the food and beverages sold at the Los Caños del Peral *botillería* (cafeteria). The January "Reglamento" and the April botillería rules were issued by city authorities in Charles III's name, making official the government's and the elite's civilizational aspirations.

Italian opera theater rules were devised to establish a new standard for public behavior in Madrid beyond the theater. Both the January and April regulations addressed opera attendees' behavior "to avoid excess and confusion."[72]

---

[71]   [Un Subscriptor], "Carta. Al Señor Editor del Correo de Madrid," *Correo de los Ciegos*, June 27, 1787, 302–3.

[72]   [Sala de Alcaldes de Madrid], "Reglamento para el mejor orden y policía del Teatro de la Opera , cuyo privilegio se ha servido conceder el Rey á los Reales Hospitales, aprobado por S. M., y comunicado á la Sala de Alcaldes para su publicación, en virtud de Real Orden de once de Diciembre de mil setecientos ochenta y seis," *Diario curioso, erudito, económico y comercial*, January 19, 1787.

Cosmopolitan Opera   161

As such, they epitomize the extent to which Bourbon policymakers wished to control the attitudes of city residents. Most likely, audiences barely followed the cumbersome rules, and authorities did not enforce them in practice, but the documents illustrate the ambitions of Bourbon reformism. Furthermore, studying the rules for the new theater shows how the abstract ideal of a civilized, Europeanized Spain took a concrete shape enacted through civic regulations of Madrileños' behavior.

Unlike the coliseos of La Cruz and El Príncipe, the opera theater was a standalone building with access on all four sides. The new rules monitored activity inside and outside the theater building. This standalone location gave authorities ample opportunity to segregate entrances for pedestrians, carriage spectators, men, and women. While the coliseos were built on the site of the outdoor corrales de comedias between private houses, Los Caños del Peral stood in the middle of a plaza and public space belonging to the city.[73]

Even though there had been official rules for the coliseos since 1753, the reopening of Los Caños del Peral reinforced the bond between theater and policy because the upscaled opera theater motivated the king's ministers to increase their surveillance of theater life. Madrid mayor and longtime theater supervisor José Antonio de Armona had recently finished writing two volumes of *Chronological Memories on the Origin of Comedia Performance in Spain* in 1785 (*Memorias cronológicas sobre el origen de la representación de comedias en España*) but saw the need to add an appendix a few years later to include the developments at Los Caños. Tellingly, he titled it *Appendix to the … Chronological Memories, Especially since by Reason of This Entertainment* [of opera] *Having Been Made Public, It merited the Government's Consideration to Establish the Policía in Theaters.*[74] In Armona's view, the type of policía imagined for Los Caños del Peral marked a qualitative leap in the control of public spectacles.

We see concerns regarding public order in Madrid's theaters already in Ferdinand VI's 1753 *Precautions to Be Observed for the Performance of Comedias in the Court* [of Madrid].[75] Several of the items in these *Precautions*, ratified by

---

[73]   Maravillas Astarloa Araluce, "Teatros para la ópera en el Madrid del siglo XVIII" (Universidad Politécnica de Madrid, 2019), 27.

[74]   Armona's two volumes of the *Memorias Cronológicas* have been published in two editions: José Antonio de Armona y Murga, *Memorias cronológicas sobre el teatro en España*, Alaveses en la historia (Vitoria: Diputación Foral de Álava, Servicio de Publicaciones, 1988); *Memorias cronológicas sobre el origen de la representación de comedias en España*, Fuentes para la historia del teatro en España (Woodbridge, Suffolk: Tamesis, 2007). The *Apéndice* exists only in manuscript form. Quoted by Luis Pérez de Guzmán, "Algunas noticias desconocidas sobre el Teatro de los Caños del Peral," *Revista de archivos, bibliotecas y museos* 30, no. 1–6 (1926): 87–88.

[75]   Ferdinand VI (Spain), *Precauciones mandadas observar por S.M. y repetido nuevamente a la Sala de su Real Orden, el cuidado de su puntual cumplimiento para la representacion de comedias, baxo cuya observancia se permite que se executen* ([Spain]1763 [1753]).

162   *Music and Modernity in Enlightenment Spain*

Charles III in 1763, concern the interaction of the sexes and the custom of covering one's face with a cloak or wide-brim hat. "Cloak and cap" (*capa y gorro*) came to represent traditional Spanish attire, a sign of either backwardness or nationalist pride. The 1753/1763 *Precautions* for the Madrid theaters disclose the governmental animosity against cloaks, hats, and shawls that encumbered surveillance and represented antimodern, old-fashioned Spain: covered-up men were not allowed to stand by coliseo entrances and exits, especially those designated for women. Access inside the coliseos was forbidden to "any covered person, with a cap, monstera, or any other disguise that hides their face, for everybody should have them [their faces] uncovered so that they can be recognized."[76] Boxes ought not to have high lattices that obscured what was happening inside them. The intolerance for face coverings reached a peak in 1766 with an ordinance issued by Internal Revenue and War Minister Marquis of Esquilache and signed by Charles III ordering that hats and cloaks should not exceed certain widths or lengths anywhere in the city.[77] Shortly after the attire regulations were issued, the people of Madrid rioted against Esquilache and his policies. The riots remained in the collective memory, so that "cloak and cap" came to symbolize nationalist defiance against Europeanization. Esquilache was Italian and he was always considered a foreigner. Banning face coverings from the opera theater again in the 1787 "Regulations" was but one reminder that the government's civilizing program rubbed against popular sensibilities.

Seven months after the Esquilache riots, Charles III issued a revised regulation for the coliseos on October 31, 1766. These new rules addressed the "composure, tranquility, and good order" of attendees and focused on theaters as public spaces more directly than did the previous rules issued by Ferdinand VI. To the requests that spectators not call out to actress-singers, smoke inside the theater, or wear headgear, subtler ones were added: to maintain a calm demeanor and use polite words. The word "decency" now refers to orderly, polite interaction among middle-class members of the public, rather than exclusively to female modesty. Those seating in the more expensive areas deserved "a distinguished place for those of greater decency in attendance," so only the men in the patio and the women in the *cazuela*, the cheapest seats, were allowed to wear small hats or hair nets, implying that if anyone wanted an upgraded seat, they must dress accordingly. The term "public" is used seven times, compared to two in 1753. The first paragraph refers to the evenings at the city coliseos as "public theater," where decorum is owed to the presiding magistrate and "the spectators' quality."[78] Since the king did not attend the coliseos or the opera, good order and policía had to be justified in terms of public decency.

---

[76]   *Precauciones*, [2].

[77]   Charles III (Spain), "Ley XIII. Prohibición de usar capa larga, sombrero chambergo o redondo, montera calada y embozo en la Corte y Sitios Reales," in *Novísima recopilación de las leyes de España* (Madrid: Galván Librero, 1831 [1766]), 1:503–4.

[78]   "Ley XXXIV," 3:666–68.

Madrid's Sala de Alcaldes de Casa y Corte approved the "Regulations for the better order and polity of the opera theater" on January 10, 1787, two weeks before the Teatro de los Caños del Peral reopened.[79] The Sala de Alcaldes was a government organ composed of twelve high-ranking officials with administrative and judicial powers and functioned as the king's operative hand. The Sala de Alcaldes had jurisdiction over the most diverse aspects of city life, from commerce to jail sentences to urbanization. In other words, the Sala de Alcaldes materialized the king's absolute power, overseeing "[public] safety, decency, and order."[80] Because this government entity had issued them, the opera theater rules had full legal validity. The Sala de Alcaldes delegated the supervision of Los Caños del Peral to a committee headed by the Hermano Mayor of the Hospital Board, at that time the duke of Híjar.[81] Still, the Sala remained actively involved in the policing of theaters. For instance, at least one alcalde had to attend each show in the city to oversee the general compliance of the rules.

The 1787 "Regulations for the Better Order and Polity of the Opera Theater," while based on the earlier regulations for coliseos of 1753 and 1766, expanded policía. City authorities had permanent seats in zones that offered vantage points to survey theater attendees. Mayor Armona and the city council were granted the central box reserved for the monarch in other parts of Europe. The magistrate and his employees were to sit in the lower-level center-right box to quickly access the men sitting or standing in the patio right in front of the stage. From this lower-level box, authorities could also get to the dressing rooms if needed. Dressing rooms were an area of concern for authorities because the actress-singers changed clothes in there. The *alcaldes de sala* and Hospital Board members should be in the center-left box for the same purposes. In previous regulations, if the alcalde on duty perceived anything immoral in the already authorized plays, he must withdraw the piece from repertory after the performance. For Los Caños del Peral, he could interrupt the show. Likewise, the alcalde could "expel from the theater, regardless of class, anybody who would breach the decorum owed to the public and abuse the regular freedom an honest entertainment requires." The regulations threatened performers with jail if they addressed individuals in the audience with gestures or improvised lines. These measures were based on the lively interaction and improvisation between performers and their audience practiced in the coliseos, especially during tonadillas and sainetes, less likely to occur during an opera in a foreign language. Through the "Regulations for the Better Order and Polity of the

---

[79] "Ley XII. D. Carlos III, por real orden de 11 de diciembre de 1786, y bandos publicados en 2 de nov. De 793 y siguientes años," in *Novísima recopilación de las leyes de España* (Madrid: Galván Librero, 1805 [1766]), 3:668–69.

[80] "Reglamento para el mejor orden," *Diario curioso, erudito, económico y comercial*, 79.

[81] Pedro de Alcántara Fernández de Híjar y Abarca de Bolea, ninth duke of Híjar (1758–1808).

opera theater," city authorities tried to correct audience behaviors considered a threat to "the public's safety, decency, and good order."[82]

The opera theater offered the Madrid authorities a clean slate to achieve the idealized public space that failed to materialize in the city coliseos. According to the new theater's regulations, patrons must board their carriages promptly and drive them through specific access streets depending on their assigned entrance door. Orderly access to the theater should continue once inside: all areas of the theater building were to be fully illuminated so that the local authorities that attended each performance could survey them. As in older sets of theater regulations, the opera theater ones paid special attention to the cazuela, the large balcony with banisters designated for women only. The new opera theater should still have a cazuela "in the Spanish fashion," with a separate entrance, to prevent women from mingling with male spectators accessing the common areas of the *lunetas* and the tertulia. All members of the audience sitting in common areas were forbidden to stand up and make noise or to demand that the performers repeat a number, behaviors that were common at the Madrid coliseos. Performers were not to acknowledge praise and applause from the audience or gesture toward them. Hence, under these regulations neither attendees nor performers were to behave as they normally did when they attended the coliseos.

As if the January 1787 "Regulations" were not enough, on April 16–17, 1787, the Sala de Alcaldes issued an additional edict regarding the botillería, the concession shop inside Los Caños del Peral.[83] The cafeteria (botillería) at the opera theater offered a new, sanctioned venue for mingling outside private homes. The rules issued in April were meant to protect the opera theater's botillería from what the government saw as unseemly social habits. While outdoor socialization at Madrid parks and avenues like the Paseo del Prado was common and mostly accepted, few indoor public spaces were considered respectable. Ramón de la Cruz's sainete *La botillería* (1766) confirms that there were refreshment shops in the vicinity of the city coliseos, where people would gather before or after the show to talk briefly (there were only a few chairs) and have beverages. Traditionally, these street botillerías were rudimentary and open to everybody. In de la Cruz's sainete, for example, a gentleman and a lady interact with military offices, poor clergymen, modern bourgeois *petimetres*, and the working-class local types, majos and majas. De la Cruz's sainete demonstrates that botillerías were one of a few of places where men, women, and different classes converged. Indoor social gatherings bothered Bourbon authorities because they were hard to police, so botillerías were regarded with suspicion.

[82] "Ley XII," 668.

[83] "Edicto," *Diario curioso, erudito, económico y comercial*, April 16 and 17, 1787.

The April rules for the opera theater's botillería reflect how the Spanish government imagined civilized social interaction: calm, gender-segregated, restrained, and organized. While non–ticket holders could enter the opera cafeteria before the performance, they would be ushered out once it began. There were three separate "refreshment rooms" for men and women, with bailiffs and policemen overseeing the zone. The botillería regulations also dictated how patrons were to carry themselves while they socialized in the refreshment area: they could not smoke, sing, or whistle, and their gestures and conversation had to manifest decorum. Surveillance was a main preoccupation. For example, patrons could sit at the first available spot on a table, but they could not stand together in groups to talk, presumably because their conversations would be then out of the auditive reach of authorities. This set of rules is even more meticulous than the general "Regulations" previously issued, meant to fashion the theater botillería into a modern, civilized socialization spot.

This trend toward a growing legislative awareness of theaters as public places continued under Charles IV (r. 1789–1807). On November 5, 1793, Charles IV and the Sala de Alcaldes issued a reminder to adhere to the opera theater regulations, "especially those [articles] regarding the observance of decency, good order, and decorum."[84] Some of the articles from 1787 were reprinted and expanded with further insistence on public order. For example, article IX, which stated "it is not allowed to gesture or speak to women from the patio [men only section]," now also read that "because the public is deserving of proper decorum and consideration." Article XII initially prohibited smoking, but a social reason for this prohibition was later appended: "both due to fire risk and because the smoke and the smell offend others in attendance." Likewise, in the 1793 version, caps and shawls are forbidden because both men and women "must be there [at the opera] with decency and decorum." Changing ideas about dramatic spectacle, opera in particular, also appear on the modifications to article XV, prohibiting performers from "making gestures, signals, or curtsying in response to the signals of others," which in 1793 was justified "because in addition to the resulting moral issues ... they combine to destroy the dramatic illusion." The need to constantly reiterate the opera theater regulations suggests that the behavior of audiences changed at a slower pace than authorities desired.

Elite and governmental aspirations toward outward-looking Europeanization coexisted with an incipient inward-looking nationalism under Charles III. The 1787 regulations for Los Caños del Peral evince the ever-lingering suspicions about Italian opera and the corresponding protection of national theater. In the late 1780s, the government expected Italian opera to offer first-class European spectacle to Madrid and fortify national theater. The regulations hoped that "Italian opera will prepare not only another, Spanish opera, but will also contribute to the greater perfection of National Theater." To this end and

---

[84] "Bando," *Diario de Madrid*, November 5, 1793, 1264.

166   *Music and Modernity in Enlightenment Spain*

under rule XVIII the Hospital Board was permitted to substitute Italian operas with Spanish ones and use the theater for other genres when opera was not being performed. Rule XIX instructed the board to favor Spanish over foreign performers. Nonetheless, pieces from the two Madrid companies' repertory were proscribed in the opera theater. Under rule XX, all Spanish theater at Los Caños del Peral had to be "new, whether original or translated, excluding [from the theatrical pieces] anything dissonant with good taste and wholesome morals." The 1787 regulations also ensured that performances at Los Caños did not overlap with the city coliseos' schedule, so as not to "be prejudicial to Spanish *cómicos*" (rule III).[85] These general guidelines issued in 1787 would reach an extreme in 1799 when Charles IV banned all foreign-language theater in Madrid due to the untenable cost of Italian opera companies and the increasingly xenophobic character of Spanish nationalism. Charles IV's drastic measure rounded off the mistrust in cosmopolitan Europeanization brewing for over a decade since Los Caños del Peral had reopened.

Opera, Nationalism, and the Emergent Public Sphere

Not everybody in Madrid was enthusiastic about Italian opera. People from all backgrounds saw in opera a rip-off concocted by government officials such as Cabarrús to refashion civic life according to modern European standards that were discordant with Spanishness. From the beginning, suspicions of anti-Spanishness and excessive public expenditure plagued Los Caños del Peral. The most common arguments deployed against the new theater concerned Italian singers' subpar quality and the elevated costs of financing foreign opera and dance companies in the city. In a fictional adventure at Los Caños del Peral, liberal writer José Marchena put these two objections in the mouth of a working-class man (*chispero*) sitting next to him. Unable to appreciate the opera, the chispero asked Marchena,

> What do you think, Mister, about these *monsieurs* [opera performers] who, with a few scraps of junk come here to take our monies? I claim that if I were king, they would not come to take Spain's money: I would set the first of them to cross the Pyrenees on fire.[86]

Radical nationalists considered anything coming from beyond the Pyrenees invasive, to the point that "transpyrenean" took on pejorative meaning. When Marchena asked what wrong "these poor foreigners" have inflicted upon him, the chispero calls Marchena "rather *franchute*" for defending the Italian singers. Although it may sound strange to conflate Italian opera with Francophilia,

[85]   "Reglamento para el mejor orden," *Diario curioso, erudito, económico y comercial*, 79, 81.

[86]   Marchena, "Discurso II," 21.

Cosmopolitan Opera   167

the terms *franchute* or *afrancesado* basically meant antipatriotic. Marchena's anecdote demonstrates that while some in the elite delighted in opera as cultivated entertainment, others, whom he identifies a working-class, thought it was a foreign scam. In reality, there were opera detractors among the middle and upper classes who wrote letters and articles in magazines and newspapers. In this section, we will take a look at the medium-term repercussions of Los Caños del Peral reopening in Madrid's musical and journalistic life.

Press debates about musical theater in the aftermath of Los Caños del Peral's reopening were loaded with two different approaches to national cultural policy. Those arguing in favor of opera endorsed an open-border policy, whereby Spanish receptiveness to elite European musical practices would enhance national culture. This stance emerges, for example, in a letter by composer Antonio Rosales to the *Diario de Madrid* on July 26, 1789. The missive is titled "In Praise of the Italian Opera Managers, Actresses, Dancers, Ornament, and Orchestra." The cosmopolitan inclinations behind Los Caños del Peral's reopening are evident in Rosales's letter. He encouraged Spaniards to welcome Italian opera singers because "in every educated country, foreigners have an absolute right to hospitality."[87] Rosales carefully delivered his criticism as a commendation, avoiding mentioning the singers' and dancers' shortcomings. He saw Italian opera as a public service provided by the theater's sponsors and royal ministers. Rosales uses the word "public" in the double sense of theater audiences and the greater Madrid public. He thought Italian opera sponsors "served the public" by offering "pleasant and honest" entertainment to Madrileños. Rosales interpreted Los Caños del Peral as one of the multiple governmental efforts to "ornate [Madrid] and to maintain in it the finest and most diligent policía." His letter presented the city of Madrid and the opera theater as parallel, tidy, civilized spaces amenable to the respectful exchange of opinions.

Those arguing against opera in the press of the late 1780s and early 1790s espoused a cautionary approach to cultural imports. They found opera's quality at Los Caños del Peral lacking, unworthy of large-scale expenditure. This standpoint surfaced in the *Diario de Madrid* one month after Rosales's letter was published. A correspondent named Marcelino Torrones refuted Rosales's claim that to welcome foreign cultural practices was a mark of civilized society. Instead, Torrones proposed that civilization is marked by the ability to discern good from bad performers: "In every cultured country, the bad is distinguished from the good, merit is acknowledged, and demerit is not obscured." Torrones characterized the "Madrid people" as the collective subject of opinion that "sees, hears, and knows" to discern when performers merit praise. For Torrones, those who only praised the opera performances at Los Caños del Peral proved that they were not ready to publicly express an opinion because they

---

[87] Antonio Rosales, "Elogio a los autores, actrices, bailarines, ornato y orquesta de la ópera italiana," *Diario de Madrid*, July 26, 1789, 825.

168   *Music and Modernity in Enlightenment Spain*

could not discern between good and bad performers. On the contrary, Torrones proposed that those who criticized opera singers' deficiencies demonstrated that Madrileños were "an enlightened assembly of people" "used to seeing and hearing the greatest delicacies," unwilling to settle for what he saw as average (*sin particularidad*) performers. Torrones claimed that Madrileños were "entitled to the greatest decency, taste, and harmony in all public and private gathering cases. To think otherwise would be to judge the Spanish nation to be ridiculous and brutal in the opinion of the other nations."[88] From Torrones's perspective, Spain becomes a modern nation when its educated people choose which European cultural practices are worth accepting.

New repertories (Italian operas, pantomime dances) forced critics to pay more attention to stage music and dance and reconsider the role of the audience. Was public taste the ultimate judge of opera, and if so, who qualified as part of the public? Or were the educated elites the sole arbiters of musical theater? Because patrons of Los Caños del Peral were also press subscribers, many opera attendees had access to printed communication. Some in this select audience wanted to alter the tone of journalistic criticism from the zealous partisanship of chorizos and polacos (see p. 172) to aesthetic appraisal. As an anonymous letter-writer expressed in the *Correo de los ciegos* (April 21, 1787), the enlightened elite insisted on the qualitative difference between the "monumental absurdities" exchanged in the chorizos' and polacos' conversations and other "well-formed, useful thoughts [about national theater], supported by convincing reasons."[89] The letter implies that whereas chorizos and polacos judged plays and performers based on fanaticism, middle- and upper-class audiences evaluated theater based on rational arguments worthy of public consideration. Thus, Italian opera honed public opinion. It opened a question essential to modernity: Who is the public? Public opinion requires defining who has the right to voice an opinion and under which circumstances.

Press debates about the Madrid opera theater between 1787 and 1792 reveal that their authors differed in their views on whether public opinion should allow for multiple points of view or nurture a single perspective, namely the one endorsed by authorities such as the Crown and the Catholic Church. This debate over who had the right to voice public opinion stemmed from different aesthetic and political receptions of Italian opera at Los Caños del Peral, either accepting the Italian performers or questioning their presence in the Spanish capital. In this sense, Italian opera and the associated ballets and Lenten concerts were factors spurring public opinion in late eighteenth-century Madrid.

---

[88]   Marcelino Torrones, "Carta en respuesta a la des Sr. Rosales de 26 de julio, sobre el mérito de los operistas, bailarines, etc.," *Diario de Madrid*, August 21, 1789, 229. Emphasis mine.

[89]   [El amigo de los ciegos], "Madrid. Carta.," *Correo de los Ciegos*, 214–15.

Lenten Concerts at Los Caños del Peral

Letters to the press defending or attacking Los Caños del Peral often took the form of comparisons between foreigners and nationals, whether singers, dancers, or audiences. Los Caños del Peral provided yet another opportunity to measure Spain's Europeanness with its Lenten concert series from 1787 to 1808. In the decade leading to 1787, concerts and musical *academias* occurred mainly in private residences. Nevertheless, after Los Caños del Peral's reopening, more concerts took place in public spaces and newspapers began consistently advertising them. The "Regulations for the Better Order and Policía of the Opera Theater" specified that the Hospital Board may "give musical academias during the first four weeks of Lent" under the supervision of an alcalde.[90] Given that Lenten concerts were customary during opera's off-season in many European cities, the Hospital Board and the government considered them part of the Italian opera project from the start.

The Los Caños del Peral Lenten concerts emulated public concert formats in London and Paris, giving singers and musicians the opportunity to showcase their individual skill and perform an international repertory. Like at Paris's Concert Spirituel, Italian music prevailed in the programs, especially in the vocal repertory, while Austrian composers commanded the instrumental music repertory.[91] Well-known composers like Domenico Cimarosa, Giovanni Paisiello, Pasquale Anfossi, and Giuseppe Sarti shared the bill with less-known names such Bernardo Mengozzi, whose wife Anna Benini sang at the Los Caños company. The music of composers like Franz Joseph Haydn, Ignaz Pleyel, and Antonio Salieri dominated the symphonic roster. Similar to Paris's Concert Spirituel, virtuoso performers played concerti or sonatas of their own composition. Many of these virtuosos were active in the Los Caños del Peral company or other local orchestras, while a few instrumentalists came from orchestras in European courts, either expressly to perform at the concerts, or as part of a sojourn in Madrid. An example of these touring foreign virtuosos was German violist and violinist Karl Michael Esser, who in 1788 played a violin sonata plucking the strings with a pencil to imitate the psaltery, a very popular instrument in Madrid at the time. Compared to the regular theater season, Lenten concerts presented a more varied bill that mixed members of the Italian opera company with Spanish orchestra musicians who played concertos, sonatas, and symphonies.

The Lenten concerts at Los Caños del Peral both favored and challenged Spanish performers because while some of them had the opportunity to participate in these concerts and expand their repertory performing non-Spanish pieces, the concert series increased market competition among the city theaters. All theater performances in Madrid came to a halt during Lent, including

---

[90] "Reglamento para el mejor orden," *Diario curioso, erudito, económico y comercial*, 81.

[91] Daniel Heartz, *Music in European Capitals: The Galant Style, 1720–1780* (New York: W. W. Norton, 2003), 615.

opera at Los Caños del Peral and Spanish musical theater at the city coliseos. This time of religious observance marked the end of both the theatrical year (*año cómico*) and of the coliseo employees' annual contract. The city issued new contracts for theater staff on Easter, and the line-ups for each of the two local companies were announced in the papers with much anticipation from audiences. Because of this period of unemployment between Lent and Easter, actor-singers supplemented their income by performing shows outside the coliseos (as they also did during the summer when theater programs slowed). The Lenten concerts at Los Caños del Peral occasionally employed local performers, but they also made it possible to keep paying Italian singers during the off-season, perhaps encouraging them to stay for the following year. The Italian newcomers attracted a share of the Madrid audiences during Lent, making it harder for local actress- and actor-singers to generate income during the off-season.

In response to the competition posed by Los Caños del Peral during Lent, the Coliseo del Príncipe company, managed by Eusebio Ribera, programmed its own series of eight concerts during Lent of 1790. The Coliseo del Príncipe titled the series "Spanish Concerts" to demonstrate that Madrid's theater companies could match Italian ones in providing cosmopolitan entertainment with programs that included arias, concertos, and symphonies.[92] The Spanish concerts were an initiative of the enterprising Cristoforo Andreozzi, first violin for the Ribera company. Leading Spanish actor- and actress-singers from Ribera's company performed operatic excerpts just as Italian performers did at Los Caños del Peral. As concert impresario for the Coliseo del Príncipe, Andreozzi encountered resistance from the Hospital Board. By 1790, the Hospital Board had seized control over the administration of Los Caños del Peral due to the lack of a suitable opera impresario. When the government formalized the lease of the theater building to the Hospital Board in 1788, several contractual clauses protected the city coliseos by stipulating that members of the Italian and Spanish companies could not perform at or be poached by the competing companies.[93] These stipulations seem to have relaxed during the off-season, making it possible for the Spanish singers to share the bill with Italian singers. Still, the Hospital Board tried to legally prevent the city-managed Coliseo del Príncipe from giving Lenten concerts, claiming exclusivity over this form of musical entertainment. The coliseo was nonetheless granted permission to hold Lenten concerts provided that the scheduled Spanish concerts alternated days with the Italian concerts at Los Caños del Peral.[94]

---

[92] Paris's Concert Spirituel also had programmed *concerts français* with secular works in French from 1728 to 1733, and then from 1786 to 1790: Eric Blom and Beverly Wilcox, "Concert Spirituel," *Grove Music Online* (Oxford University Press, 2016), http://www.oxfordmusiconline.com/subscriber/article/grove/music/06257.

[93] Martínez Reinoso, "El surgimiento del concierto," 80–81.

[94] Martínez Reinoso, "El surgimiento del concierto," 92.

Like opera, Lenten concerts at Los Caños del Peral sparked contention between supporters of national and foreign entertainment. The two parallel series of Spanish (hosted at the Coliseo del Príncipe) and Italian (hosted at Los Caños) concerts in 1790 offered Madrid a glimpse of the public concert life active in other European cities, where audience members could choose from a number of venues and compare the quality of the entertainment provided by each venue. However, the competition between Los Caños del Peral and the city coliseos during the Lenten season was limited. Unlike in London or Vienna, capitalist competition did not determine concert life in Spain because the government strictly regulated private musical performances to protect the income of the coliseos and the opera, managed by the city. In fact, government intervention in musical events had intensified when Charles IV ascended the throne in 1789 and French revolutionary ideas stoked the crown's fear of large gatherings and cultural imports. In a nationalist move in response to this fear, the secretary of state, the count of Floridablanca, ordered that a symphony composed by conductor Guillermo Ferrer be played at the 1790 "Spanish concerts" at the Coliseo del Príncipe, and that violinist Pablo del Moral provide another symphony.[95] However, neither Ferrer nor del Moral were symphonic composers; rather, they were tonadilla writers. Floridablanca's move was contrived and did not work in practice. After the first concert, the symphonies in the 1790 Lenten season at Coliseo del Príncipe fell back to the hands of the usual suspects: Haydn, Pleyel, Cimarosa, and Paisiello. In 1791 all Lenten concerts, "arranged by the city," Spanish or Italian, took place at the Coliseo del Príncipe, and by 1792 they had returned to Los Caños del Peral.[96] Separate Spanish and Italian Lenten concerts took place again in 1797 and 1798, this time at the Coliseo de la Cruz, the other local theater. Whenever there were two concert series during Lent, letters to the press expressing support for one or the other ensued. The following section looks at a 1790 exchange between two newspaper correspondents and demonstrates the antagonism between the Spanish and Italian concerts was understood in the frame of an older rivalry: the one between chorizos and polacos, the respective devotees of the de La Cruz and El Príncipe coliseos.

The Need to Civilize Public Opinion

The years of separate Spanish and Italian Lenten concert series prompted newspaper readers and theater audiences to compare national and foreign performers and discern whether the Spanish government and audiences should support Italian opera at all. Madrid's middle and upper classes took sides, happy to feed

---

[95]   Felipe Pedrell, *Diccionario biográfico y bibliográfico de músicos y escritores de música españoles* (Barcelona: Tipografía de V. Berdós y Feliu, 1894), s.v. "Ferrer, Guillermo."

[96]   *Diario de Madrid*, March 13, 1791, 295.

172   *Music and Modernity in Enlightenment Spain*

on exciting conversation during Lent. This conversation found its way to letters to the newspapers. Because the concerts were labeled "Spanish" or "Italian," arguments about them quickly led to disagreements over whether to defend national music and performers or to adopt a cosmopolitan openness to performances by Italians, Germans, or other Europeans. Letter writers disagreed over the benefits of an Italian opera theater, but they overall agreed that press reception of opera and nationalism debates should be founded in rational arguments instead of fanatic partisanship. Domestic models for what the elites considered a civilized public opinion were lacking since music and theater criticism were incipient at the time. Nonetheless, the late-eighteenth century periodical press shows constant preoccupation with the notion that exchanges among writers and readers ought to be polite.[97] Press letters reveal fears that the foreign versus national music debate would steep to a vulgar tone unworthy of the Republic of Letters, but similar to the tone of the altercations between chorizos and polacos, the male, working-class followers of actress- and actor-singers performing at the Spanish coliseos.

Dissensions over music at Los Caños del Peral and the city coliseos built upon the long-standing feud between chorizos, or fans of the Manuel Martínez theater company at El Príncipe, and polacos, or fans of the Eusebio Ribera company at La Cruz. Chorizos and polacos were enemies. They wore distinctive color ribbons on their hats to make their affiliation publicly visible. The rivalry between the two fan groups even divided families, and preferences were often passed from father to son.[98] Chorizos and polacos were men from the Madrid barrios, chisperos, smiths, cobblers, plasterers, and other working-class men who filled the coliseos' patios, the standing area in front of the stage where women had no access. The press of the time referred to chorizos and polacos as *apasionados* (enthusiasts) for their ardent yet uncritical support of either Martínez's or Ribera's company. In José Marchena's fictional dialogue with a barrio chispero sitting next to him at los Caños del Peral, the *chispero* explained that he and his friends were apasionados, "which means one likes the actress- and actor-singers, and those who like la Tirana [María del Rosario Fernández] are called chorizos, and those of the other company, polacos."[99] Even though Enlightenment supporters and elites dismissed them as uncivilized and irrational, the behavior of the chorizos and polacos set a precedent for the reception of Italian opera in Madrid's public opinion.

Pitching different opinions against one another, opera reception was often likened to the bickering between chorizos and polacos, although men of letters arguing for and against opera strove to qualitatively differentiate their opin-

---

[97] Mónica Bolufer reports finding similar concerns with politeness in periodicals from Madrid, Málaga, and Cádiz: "Civilizar las costumbres: El papel de la prensa periódica dieciochesca," *Bulletin of Hispanic Studies* 91, no. 9–10 (2014): 108.

[98] D.M.R.F., "[Carta sobre teatros]," *Diario de Madrid*, April 5, 6, and 7, 1790, 378.

[99] Marchena, "Discurso II," 24.

Cosmopolitan Opera   173

ions from those of barrio apasionados. The degree of contention surrounding the Lenten concerts is evident from a three-part letter published in *Diario de Madrid* in April of 1790, the year when the Coliseo del Príncipe first announced a Spanish concerts series.[100] The letter is signed by D.M.R.F., who wrote that the Spanish Lenten concerts at El Príncipe and the Italian ones at Los Caños del Peral were "a matter about which everyone in general believes themselves intelligent, nobody concedes, and the confusion of voices heard in tertulias is such that after one ends up with a dazed head, each one remains with their own opinion, and we are yet left without a point of clarity on this matter." D.M.R.F. was not referring to any specific author, but to the cohort of newspaper correspondents who, like him, engaged in debates through the press: "Some criticize our comedias, others applaud the Spanish actors; here their flaws are exaggerated, and the merit of the Italian ones is extolled, comparing one theater's [Los Caños del Peral] to the others' [Spanish coliseos] dilapidation."[101] To like opera or not, to attend the Italian or Spanish Lenten series, such choices were fraught with national allegiance.

In his letter, D.M.R.F. divided Madrileños debating musical theater and Lenten concerts into three categories: the apasionados of certain performers, the apasionados and antagonists of Spain, and the few who "reason impartially." Among these categories, D.M.R.F. dismissed the chorizos and polacos, who argued about theater based solely on fandom for individual performers, which made them unfit to give an opinion (*voto*) about the good or bad quality of theater shows. Beyond the usual feuds between chorizos and polacos, D.M.R.F. was concerned with the "fans (apasionados) and the antagonists of the national things," or those who used musical theater to either defend or lambaste Spain. The enthusiasts of the nation, which we would now call nationalists, followed a logic similar to that of the apologistas of Spain, whereby the single objective was to put the nation above all other countries, showing an "indiscreet" love for the nation. The antagonists took the opposite stance and insisted on ridiculing "everything that is done in our comedias," accepting Spain's limitations to make room for improvement, taking other European countries as models.[102] D.M.R.F.'s use of the term *apasionados* suggests that he viewed opera detractors and supporters as the upper-class counterpart chorizos and polacos. The simile implied that elites were behaving their like working-class neighbors by vehemently defending either Spanish musical theater or Italian opera. Like the feud between chorizos and polacos, D.M.R.F. saw public opinion concerning foreign and national musical theater (including the Lenten concerts) as two camps in dispute.

D.M.R.F. suggested a less partisan valuation of opera than the one expressed by either apasionados or antagonists of Spanish theater. On the one hand, he

---

[100]   D.M.R.F., "[Carta sobre teatros]," *Diario de Madrid*.

[101]   "[Carta sobre teatros]," *Diario de Madrid*, 377.

[102]   "[Carta sobre teatros]," *Diario de Madrid*, 377–78, 82.

174   *Music and Modernity in Enlightenment Spain*

pondered, Spaniards should love their country; on the other, they should not ignore national shortcomings or automatically resist the modernization of social mores only because they come from abroad. He expresses his cosmopolitan stance when he writes that

> it is a political axiom that all genres of arts, sciences, and manufactures owe their advancement to the mutual communication among nations; that those [nations] which are more advanced provide their discoveries and set the path for those which are not so advanced, and thus, progressively, the ones learn from the others.[103]

From D.M.R.F.'s perspective, there was no harm in imitating European dramatic trends and even building designs, for in the splendor of the arts "the advancement or backwardness of a nation is known."

Despite its cosmopolitan spirit, D.M.R.F.'s three-part letter harbored a concern that would grow throughout the 1790s in Madrid: that an Italian opera house would cost money and attract spectators otherwise destined to the Spanish coliseos, resulting in the "abandonment" of national theater.[104] Controversies about the performance of foreign musical genres had escalated in 1790 because right before the Lenten concert season, members of the opera ballet at Los Caños del Peral had danced a fandango and seguidillas *boleras* as part of Vicente Martín y Soler's opera *Una cosa rara* (1786, libretto by Lorenzo Da Ponte). D.M.R.F. incorporated this event into his letter through an imagined tertulia conversation in which some patrons applauded the Italians who performed Spanish dances but ridiculed the Spanish *cómicos* who sang Italian arias. Many members of the public felt that supporting Italian opera was unfair to local artists. They believed that if Madrileños were to embrace foreign genres, they ought to first support national ones.[105] In D.M.R.F.'s fictional scene, arguments over local theaters escalated to the point of dissolving the tertulia, with the attendees incapable of reaching consensus. Outside this fictional scenario, the struggle for Europeanness to coexist with national pride was also reaching an impasse.

Rejection of Opera and Mercantilist Mentality

Economic concerns over the cost of an Italian opera company underpinned aesthetic ones, so press discussions regarding the merits and demerits of Italian opera weighed whether the City of Madrid should invest in it. According to D.M.R.F., altercations about theater had been escalating in the last four years since Los Caños del Peral's 1787 reopening. To put an end to tertulia squabbles,

---

[103] "[Carta sobre teatros]," *Diario de Madrid*, 378.

[104] "[Carta sobre teatros]," *Diario de Madrid*, 383.

[105] Lorenzo Chamorro, "[Carta]," *Correo de Madrid*, June 21 and 23, 1787.

Cosmopolitan Opera   175

he offered a half-ounce of gold to whomever could provide factual data about the income and expenses of the coliseos of La Cruz and El Príncipe as well as of Los Caños del Peral. With this financial information, he reasoned that middle- and upper-class Madrileños could assess whether Italian opera's purported civilizing benefits were worth its high cost. A response to D.M.R.F. appeared in the *Diario de Madrid* three months later under the initials of D.Q.P.F.[106] The respondent went into budgetary detail, despite lack of access to financial documents. The city administered all three Madrid theaters (Coliseo de la Cruz, Coliseo del Príncipe, Teatro de los Caños del Peral), took a third of their revenue, and paid for the administrative expenses.[107] The remaining two-thirds of the revenue went to the actor-singers' salaries. Additionally, the theaters were supposed to produce dividends destined to the city hospitals, for this had been the justification for their existence since they started as corrales de comedias in the sixteenth century. Los Caños del Peral's more expensive productions and higher performers' salaries meant less revenue and even losses for the city government. Such losses worked against the Hospital Board's and the Enlightenment elites' efforts to convince audiences that Italian opera was what Spain needed to improve national public entertainment.

Cabarrús's 1786 proposal that an Italian opera theater would remedy the Hospital Board's deficit proved inoperable. Emilio Casares Rodicio has proposed that Italian opera failed in Madrid in the 1790s because Los Caños del Peral's administrative infrastructure was always flawed since the impresario system was incompatible with traditional royal patronage of Madrid theaters. The government often subsidized the theaters. Because the theaters' income and expenses were processed through the city administration, theaters did not survive directly from their earnings. Casares Rodicio rejects the conventional theory that Italian opera at Los Caños del Peral did not succeed because Madrid audiences disliked the genre.[108] Instead, according to Casares Rodicio, the public was accustomed to subsidized entertainment, and unlike the press industry, Italian opera in Madrid did not garner enough public subscribers to survive as an institution during the two last decades of the eighteenth century.

---

[106] D.Q.P.F., "Carta de D.Q.P.F. al caballero D.M.R.F. sobre teatros, y dificultades de los aspirantes al premio ofrecido en el Diario de 7 de abril de este año de 1790," *Diario de Madrid*, July 3, 4 1790.

[107] The city took its third after the expenses of off-stage personnel (including musicians) had been covered, and also after the share for the hospitals: [El Cómico retirado], *Carta de un cómico retirado a los diaristas, sobre los teatros* ([Madrid][1788]).

[108] Emilio Casares Rodicio, "La creación operística en España. Premisas para la interpretación de un matrimonio," in *La ópera en España e Hispanoamérica: Actas del Congreso Internacional La Opera en España e Hispanoamérica, una creación propia*, ed. Emilio Casares Rodicio and Álvaro Torrente (Madrid: Ediciones del ICCMU, 2001).

The Italian opera enterprise was never sustainable, and Los Caños del Peral proved insolvent from the start.[109]

Mercantilist ideologies lingering from decades and centuries past permeated into press criticism of Los Caños del Peral's unsustainability, likening support for the expensive Italian opera company to antipatriotic consumption of imported luxury goods. Cabarrús's initial vision for Italian opera at Los Caños del Peral stemmed from a postmercantilist, cosmopolitan approach to economic international relations. Postmercantilist, modern European economic practices called for opening the borders of commerce in order to stay competitive, in accord with Adam Smith's theories. This modern economic attitude paralleled cosmopolitan acceptance of the foreign good that was Italian opera: Cabarrús, like Antonio Rosales in his letter to the Correo de los Ciegos and D.M.R.F. in his letter to the *Diario de Madrid*, believed that Spanish theater should welcome foreign cultural competition to remain up-to-date. The older mercantilist mentality which had long dominated Spain's economy sought to shrink imports and grow exports, prioritizing production over consumption. In this case, Italian opera was a cultural import and a luxury good because it was expensive and primarily consumed by aristocrats and other wealthy sectors. Consuming foreign luxury goods had been considered detrimental to the nation as early as the seventeenth century. The Spanish Crown's fear was that buying imports meant leaking money into other colonial powers instead of reinvesting the income derived from the Spanish colonies in national development.

If opera was considered a luxury import, two centuries of ready-made sumptuary discourse could be readily mobilized against it. Spain had a long history of sumptuary laws destined to curb aristocratic desire for luxury goods that carried over from the seventeenth into the eighteenth century. In his 1788 *Historia del lujo y de las leyes suntuarias de España*, Enlightenment jurist and economist Juan Sempere y Guarinos deemed luxury "one of the chief points [of contention] of morality and politics" and considered the acquisition of luxury goods "a despicable vice." Even though the terms "opera" and "luxury" do not appear together in the press reactions to the reopening of Los Caños del Peral, there were complaints about its foreign origin and high costs. The closed-borders mercantilist mentality came up in Marchena's fictional dialogue with the chispero at the opera, when the chispero asked what Marchena thought of the opera performers "who, with a few scraps of junk come here to take our monies," and then declared that if he were king, "they would not come to take Spain's money."[110] Marchena put this argument in the mouth of a character he saw as backward and ignorant to signal his own progressive view that mercantilism should be left in the past.

---

[109] Robinson, "Financial Management"; Leza, "Aspectos productivos."

[110] Marchena, "Discurso II," 21.

Cosmopolitan Opera   177

Opera supporters like D.M.R.F. advocated for opening Spain's economic and cultural borders to foster international cooperation and improve the quality of national products. Letters and articles arguing for a welcoming attitude toward the Italian and French performers at Los Caños del Peral mirrored liberalist economic trends in favor of open market competition. D.M.R.F. wrote that "any foreign manufacture or invention must be accepted provided that the goal is that the nation's inhabitants improve their own and learn something from their fellow citizens." In contrast with mercantilism's old protectionism, modern approaches to trade and to the circulation of Enlightenment knowledge endorsed international exchange as the path to progress. At the same time, D.M.R.F. believed foreign manufactures could overcome national industry and obtain the gains that would otherwise have gone to national producers. He then applied this economic to opera: "The same can be said about operas. If the Madrid people attends the Italian theater, abandoning the national one, if they spend their wealth in protecting operas' actors with a liberal hand, if they praise it all at the opera and ridiculize it all at the Spanish coliseos," then Italian opera will not be of use to Spain. The solution for D.M.R.F. is to foster cooperation between Italian and Spanish performers, to protect and encourage the least talented ones, and to attend both Italian and Spanish theaters.[111]

The project that Cabarrús and the Hospital Board presented to the king was formulated in cosmopolitan terms, anticipating rejection from more conservative parties: "If only I could prove, as I intend, that our customs shall win and not lose, that this [opera] is the surest means to perfect the national theater." For Cabarrús, importing "honest" theater was a more expeditious solution than fixing national theater, the reform of which "can only result from time, and from the progress of Enlightenment, which authority can accelerate but cannot suddenly produce." The cultural import of opera was not for passive consumption but entailed actively "transplanting and making it establish residency" in national soil. [112] Cabarrús saw other Europeans striving to develop their own national operas, some with more success than others, so he suggested that Spain do the same. Cabarrús's liberalism shows in his belief that Italian opera and Spanish musical theater could coexist without their mutual destruction. Ultimately, royal officials who approved the Hospital Board's project allowed Italian opera to return to Madrid with the main objective of securing the establishment of a Spanish opera in the near future.

---

[111] D.M.R.F., "[Carta sobre teatros]," *Diario de Madrid*, 382–83.

[112] "Si yo lograse probar, como pretendo, que nuestras costumbres ganarán en vez de perder, que este es el medio más seguro de perfeccionar el teatro nacional." "Sólo puede ser un efecto del tiempo y del progreso de las luces que la autoridad misma puede acelerar, pero no producir de repente." "Vemos todos los pueblos de Europa trabajando en transplantarla [opera bufa] y domiciliarla en sus países con igual empeño, aunque con más o menos acierto." Cabarrús, *Memorias*, 38, 72–73, 77.

The cultural debate around Italian opera at Los Caños del Peral must be understood as part of the Bourbon reforms for national modernization. The range of reactions to Italian opera from different sectors of the population attest to a general evaluative attitude that weighed whether cosmopolitan culture and Europeanization would strengthen or weaken Spain's presence internationally.

4

Bourbon Sentimentalities on the Musical Stage

"Your play was splendid in everything,
 celebrated and applauded by the audience,
 for they saw evil censored,
 and watched the praise of virtue.
 The music made it enjoyable,
 The action engaged everyone …"
"The drama, the harmony, the actors,
 among themselves competed fiercely …"[1]

These were some of the words admirers and friends dedicated to the young marchioness of Mortara in 1786 on the occasion of her double role as patroness of and actress in the sentimental play *La Cecilia*. The musical drama was expressly produced to be performed at her Madrid mansion by playwright Luciano Francisco Comella and composer Blas de Laserna. The plot of *La Cecilia*, however, takes place not in Madrid but in a Spanish village, where a Count presides over the peasants, including Cecilia and her husband Lucas. The Count owns the land where the village is located. In addition to the peasants and the Count, *La Cecilia* features a Don Juan-esque character, the Marquis, who arrives from the city and tries to rob Cecilia, a married and impoverished hidalga-turned-peasant, of her virtue. The Marquis's presence disrupts the harmony between master and villagers. With the support of the righteous Count, Cecilia and her husband Lucas enlighten the Marquis through virtuous example. Order is restored as the once corrupt Marquis mends his ways and the villagers return to peace under their master. The action continues in the 1787 sequel, *Cecilia viuda* (*Cecilia, Widow*), also written for performance at the Mortara household. With Lucas and the Count now dead, Cecilia faces renewed threats to her virtue, personified in the crooked administrator Don Nicasio and the ever-unstable Marquis. After intense perils involving attempted suicide and murder, and after much praying, the Marquis steps up to his role as lord of the land, the bad administrator falls off a cliff, and Cecilia retires to a convent. The two-play saga ends with a general admonition: "May all love virtue / may all abhor vice."

---

[1] Luciano Francisco Comella, *La Cecilia*, primera parte (Madrid: Benito Cano, 1786). Opening pages.

180   *Music and Modernity in Enlightenment Spain*

In the two *Cecilias*, Comella and Laserna used pastoral-inspired music and dance to model the ideal rural community of the Bourbon reforms sponsored by Charles III and designed by his ministers: hard-working peasants, full of vim and vigor and obedient to their master. *La Cecilia*'s village represents this New Arcadia in Spain, with its village of happy, productive peasants thriving under the moral authority of their lord the Count and suffering under the tyranny of the bad administrator (the intermediary) in *Cecilia viuda*. Politically speaking, this New Arcadia of burgeoning agricultural communities was meant to stimulate national progress, modernizing Spain to be on par with its European peers. Many contemporary neoclassicist works used the pastoral to represent an idealized version of rural life.[2] However, unlike most of them, *La Cecilia* does not feature high-pastoral characters such as shepherds and nymphs. Instead, the forests and riverbeds of Torquato Tasso and Garcilaso de la Vega have mutated into a small village, and the sanctuary is no longer Diana's temple but the Count's country residence, where the villagers sing praises to their master.

Comella and Laserna adapted the eighteenth-century European trend of portraying aristocrats as enlightened rulers sensitive to their subjects' well-being to fit sociopolitical programs specific to Spain, particularly, agro-economic policy partly inspired by physiocracy (postmercantilism).[3] They used sentimental and pastoral conventions to create a didactic audiovisual text involving music, stage, and recitation to serve up Bourbon reformist policies to their audiences. Bourbon policies were designed to optimize Spain's productivity so that the nation could compete in the modern European economy. Following the theories of the French physiocrats, happy, productive agricultural communities free from abusive intermediaries were a crucial part of Bourbon economic modernization. *La Cecilia* and *Cecilia viuda* wrestle with the contradictions of a model peasant-citizen who is enlightened enough to abide by natural law, respecting nature and social order, while subservient enough to remain loyal to authorities.

The *Cecilias* differ from the Comella-Laserna collaborations that came later in that they were first written for the Mortaras and performed by the marchioness and marquis together with an entourage of friends and protegé(e)s. This is rare in the context of Comella's output from the 1780s and 1790s, mostly produced for the city coliseos. *La Cecilia* and *Cecilia viuda* were the second and third (and last) works the Mortaras commissioned by Comella.[4] The libretti are

---

[2]   For a prime example of the high pastoral topic merged with the Bourbon agricultural agenda, see Pascual Rodríguez de Arellano, *Delicias de Manzanares* (Madrid: Joaquín Ibarra, 1785). See also the study about Montiano y Luyando by Rosalía Fernández Cabezón: "Una égloga inédita de Agustín de Montiano y Luyando," *Anales de Literatura Española* 6 (1988): 217–58.

[3]   Reinhard Strohm, *Dramma per musica: Italian Opera Seria of the Eighteenth Century* (New Haven: Yale University Press, 1997), 273ff.

[4]   The music for the first one, *La Dorinda* (1785), is thus far lost.

Bourbon Sentimentalities on the Musical Stage   181

clearly dedicated to the marchioness, who seems to have been the mind behind the commission and who played the character role. She was Josefa Dominga Catalá de Valeriola y Luján (1764–1814), married to the seventh marquis of Mortara (1762–1801), Benito Osorio y Orozco Lasso de la Vega between 1782 and 1789, when the pope annulled their marriage. Josefa Catalá de Valeriola went on to become the third duchess of Almodóvar, a wealthy and powerful patroness of the arts and education in her native Valencia. Both Laserna and Comella had worked for the Mortara house in the 1770s and remained tied to it because their wives were companion ladies to the marchioness dowager, mother-in-law to the young marchioness who commissioned the *Cecilias*.[5]

Genre and Policy in *La Cecilia*

La Cecilia and *Cecilia viuda* can be studied from many different perspectives, but this chapter focuses on the music and dance numbers and their connections to late Bourbon policy. Whereas the spoken word—especially in monologues—is the vehicle for sentimentality in both *Cecilias*, music and dance give life to the commoners who stand for the lower estate under Bourbon absolutism. *La Cecilia* has two acts, like zarzuela and opera buffa, and *Cecilia viuda* has three, like Spanish Golden Age comedy and opera seria, each act with five scenes. Comella classified both plays as "drama," perhaps in reference to *drame bourgeois*. Although there are no bourgeois characters per se, the title character and her husband, Lucas, in *La Cecilia*, as well as four military men together with the land administrator in *Cecilia viuda*, represent the middle class, between the aristocrats and the peasants (see tables 4.1 and 4.2).

In *La Cecilia* and *Cecilia viuda*, Comella freely mixed traditional Spanish comedia with sentimental aesthetics and *drame bourgeois* to create a multifaceted play that pleased his aristocratic patrons, coliseo audiences, and Bourbon officials. Laserna wrote music that sounded Spanish but was cloaked in galant features, a proto-folklore that sounded national in a refined manner. Influences

---

[5]   They both worked for the sixth marquis of Mortara (Joaquín Antonio de Osorio y Orozco Manrique de Lara, 1734–1782), father-in-law to the young marchioness, who likely commissioned *La Cecilia* and *Cecilia viuda*. Writer and composer collaborated often in musical plays and short theater pieces up until the beginning of the nineteenth century. María Angulo Egea has researched Comella's work in *Luciano Francisco Comella (1751–1812), otra cara del teatro de la Ilustración* (San Vicente del Raspeig: Publicaciones de la Universidad de Alicante, 2006) and has also written about his collaboration with Laserna in *Los melólogos de Comella-Laserna*. On Comella and his works, see also Carlos Cambronero, "Comella, su vida y sus obras," *Revista contemporánea* 102 (1896), Alva Vernon Ebersole, *La obra teatral de Luciano Francisco Comella, 1789–1806* (Valencia: Albatros, 1985), and Rosalía Fernández Cabezón, "El teatro de Luciano Comella a la luz de la prensa periódica," *Dieciocho: Hispanic Enlightenment* 25, no. 1 (2002): 105–20.

182   *Music and Modernity in Enlightenment Spain*

in *La Cecilia* range from Calderón de la Barca's seventeenth-century comedias and mythological zarzuelas, to Ramón de la Cruz's popular zarzuelas from the 1760s and 1770s, to sentimental theater, and to a much lesser degree, Italian opera. Alas, the *Cecilias'* genre hodgepodge, with their secondary plots, comic characters, music, and dance numbers, did not gain the approval of Comella's contemporaries, the neoclassicist critics.

According to official standards derived from neoclassicist literary precepts, all Spanish theater should comply with the Horatian *delectare et docere*: to entertain the public and to instruct it. If any dramatic piece was to make it through censorship, it should communicate a sense of Catholic virtue and regard for reformist policies for civilized behavior. Ignacio de Luzán (1702–1754), the founding figure of Spanish neoclassicism, had praised the sentimental genre because it had a moral-didactic component, at least as Diderot conceived it. Indeed, Diderot's *drame bourgeois* aimed at "inspiring in men the love of virtue, the horror of vice."[6] This elevated purpose, expressed in the sonnets in praise of *La Cecilia* extracted in this chapter's epigraph and the closing lines of *Cecilia viuda* (Let everyone love virtue / Let everyone detest vice), satisfied the moral imperative expected by Spanish authorities. However, neoclassicist standards dictated that tragedy was the dramatic genre par excellence to the exclusion of music, dance, and comic characters. These restrictions put creative authors in a bind because audiences demanded entertainment over moral lessons on stage.

Comella infringed on neoclassicist precepts when he introduced music and dance into sentimental comedies and weaved secondary plots and comic characters into the central drama to make them palatable to late eighteenth-century Spanish audiences. Comella and Laserna lived off their work, and even though they counted on noble patronage from time to time, commercial success was crucial to their careers. Because the *Cecilias* were a private commission before entering the public repertory, adjustments to the librettos and music were made that reveal what made a musical drama a good box-office success. Some authors suggest that Comella and his colleagues added music and dance for comic relief from the tears of sentimentality, but the public's demands for spectacle and the configuration of theater companies probably weighed even more.[7] Most neoclassicist literary critics thought that music did not belong in any genre other than opera and never approved of Comella or his contemporaries. Nonetheless, and as demonstrated by the restagings of the two *Cecilias* between 1787 and 1812, audiences liked sentimental plays with music, dance,

---

[6]   "Quel est l'objet d'une composition dramatique? C'est, je crois, d'inspirer aux hommes l'amour de la vertu, l'horreur du vice." Denis Diderot, "Entretiens sur Le fils naturel," in *Oeuvres de Denis Diderot*, ed. Jacques-André Naigeon (Paris: Desrey & Deterville, 1798), 207.

[7]   Angulo Egea, *Luciano Francisco Comella*, 378.

and comic characters because they mixed traditional Spanish theater with the trend of modern sentimentality.

Even though created for the Mortaras, both *Cecilias* were thereafter adapted for public performance and presented in Madrid, Barcelona (1792, 1794), Valencia, and Seville. *La Cecilia* was performed the Coliseo del Príncipe shortly after the initial performance at the Mortaras's in 1786, while *Cecilia viuda* made its debut with Manuel Martínez's company at the Coliseo de la Cruz on November 16, 1787. The city coliseos programmed *La Cecilia* again in September 1787, December 1792, May 1801, and January 1810. On May 30, 1812, the *Diario de Madrid* announced the play at the Coliseo de la Cruz with the modified title *La honesta Cecilia*, and again in May 1813.[8] When the two *Cecilias* were written in 1786–1787, Laserna worked for the Madrid city theaters, and Comella was a freelance author and playwright. *La Cecilia* was Comella's earliest long-format play to achieve public recognition, catapulting him to household fame. Before 1786, the Madrid coliseos had staged a few of his sainetes and tonadillas, but his heroic-military triumph *Federico II, rey de Prusia* was yet to come (in 1788).[9] In the 1780s, Comella became known for his heroic tragedies and sentimental plays, genres that were crowd-pleasers at the city coliseos. Laserna, in turn, wrote all kinds of music for the theater, standing out as a tonadilla composer.[10] They were active in Madrid's artistic and literary life, although the city's intellectual elites, committed to neoclassicism, did not always acknowledge their works.[11] Given their professional situations, audience demands undoubtedly mattered to the *Cecilias'* creators.

In spite of their unorthodox approach to neoclassicism, Comella and Laserna fully observed the *delectare et docere* espoused by the Bourbon administration, choosing the pastoral topos as a medium. *La Cecilia* depicts a Spanish rural community flourishing under the paternalistic, absolute authority personified in the Count until the Marquis comes from the city and threatens to violate this order. *Cecilia viuda*, in turn, introduces the military as an intermediate estate of the realm whose purpose is to support monarchic projects and safeguard the peasantry. In producing such plays, Comella, Laserna, and the Mortaras

---

[8] The last date annotated in the manuscript prompters' librettos from the coliseos archive is 1810.

[9] Angulo Egea believes that Comella's creative output peaked between 1789–1792. Angulo Egea, *Luciano Francisco Comella*, 79.

[10] For the most detailed biography of Laserna to date, see Julio Gómez, "Don Blas de Laserna. Un capítulo de la historia del teatro lírico español visto en la vida del último tonadillero," in *El músico Blas de Laserna*, ed. José Luis de Arrese, Biblioteca de Corellanos Ilustres (Corella: 1952). For his activity as a tonadilla composer, see Elizabeth Le Guin, *The Tonadilla in Performance: Lyric Comedy in Enlightenment Spain* (Berkeley: University of California Press, 2014), and Subirá, *La tonadilla escénica* (Madrid: Tipografía de Archivos, 1928).

[11] Most notably, Leandro Fernández de Moratín parodied Comella's popularity in the dilettante character of Don Eleuterio in *La comedia nueva* (1792).

nodded to Charles III and his ministers, who at the time were envisioning a prosperous nation that would thrive on government-sponsored agricultural and commercial reforms. In the government's vision, peasants played a crucial (if subordinate) role as the productive force of the economy. Given the resemblance between peasants and shepherds and the topic's ethical implications, the pastoral was a suitable platform for staging late Bourbon ideals of progress.[12] In fact, the pastoral had already been used on stage, in French *pastorales heroïques*, for example, to portray the stratified society characteristic of an absolutist regime, where deities stood for nobles and shepherds stood for commoners.[13] In the case of the *Cecilias*, shepherds and nymphs morphed, with some adjustments, into diligent *labradores* who inhabited nature in productive, instead of contemplative, ways.[14]

More specifically, the play customizes pastoral conventions to fit Bourbon ideals of progress informed by the French economic theory of physiocracy. These ideals dictated that landowners were to deal directly with the peasants harvesting their land, thus eliminating the intermediaries who could take advantage of the rural population, and channeling taxes directly to the crown. To maximize national productivity, peasants needed to be happy. Under Charles III and Charles IV, agricultural philosophy and policy was built partly (but not exclusively) on the physiocratic ideas of French economist and surgeon François Quesnay (1694–1774).[15] For physiocrats, the economic order stemmed from the natural order, and the same universal law dictated both. To ensure the production of wealth, the same laws that govern the physical world must also rule the economy. Colonial functionary Pierre Paul Mercier de la Rivière (1719–1801) elaborated on Quesnay's idea of natural order in *L'Ordre naturel et essentiel des sociétés politiques* (1767). Their conjunct economic theory presupposed enlightened despotism as part of the natural order because the interests of the king were everybody's interests, from landowners and workers to clergy and merchants.[16] French Encyclopédistes like Voltaire

---

[12] In his consideration of the pastoral topic in the eighteenth century, Mantz observes that "from antiquity down, the pastoral was commonly justified on ethical grounds: it was said to be particularly adapted, through a pleasing picture of the life of the most simple people, to offer a salutary example to the harassed denizens of courts and cities." Harold Elmer Mantz, "Non-Dramatic Pastoral in Europe in the Eighteenth Century," *PMLA* 31, no. 3 (1916): 422.

[13] See David Charlton and David Charlton, *Opera in the Age of Rousseau: Music, Confrontation, Realism* (New York: Cambridge University Press, 2012), 166.

[14] *Labrador:* "One who ploughs or cultivates."

[15] François Quesnay developed this theory mostly in *Physiocratie, ou Constitution naturelle du gouvernement le plus avantageux* (Yverdon: Du Pont, 1768).

[16] Pierre-Paul Le Mercier de la Rivière, *L'ordre naturel et essentiel des sociétés politiques* (Paris: chez Jean Nourse, 1767), iii.

criticized physiocracy for its support of absolutism, but Spanish economists embraced it.

According to physiocratic doctrine, God himself designed the laws of society as part of the general order of creation.[17] Theories combining enlightened ideas with religious belief were often popular in Spain, and physiocracy appealed to Spain's Catholic monarchy because it justified absolutism as part of God-given natural law. It also offered a formula for earthly happiness and wealth that agreed with reason. Intellectuals such as Pablo Olavide and Gaspar Melchor de Jovellanos adopted some physiocratic principles and combined them with mercantilist and free-trade ideas to create their own brand of economic and social policy. In *La Cecilia*'s interpretation of a physiocratic order, the Count embodies the benevolent ruler, while the villagers' happiness stems from obeying the natural order and freely subjecting themselves to their master, trusting that he will protect their interests. *Cecilia viuda*'s land administrator Don Nicasio embodies De la Rivière's prototype of the arbitrary despot—not to be confused with the absolute ruler—who ignores natural order and, dominated by the desire for power, threatens the legitimate authority of the monarchy.[18]

Neither the *Cecilias* nor Bourbon projects for progress disrupted the status quo, and they certainly did not question monarchy as a system of governance. Nevertheless, some of the late Bourbon models for agricultural reform, such as those proposed by Olavide and Jovellanos, did grant modest land ownership to peasants to foster national development. The economic structure represented in *La Cecilia* and *Cecilia viuda* avoids this model built on small landowners (*pequeños propietarios*), relying instead on the conservative model where the high aristocracy owned all the land. Comella preferred this latter model probably because it fit with the ruler-and-subjects paradigm of Golden Age Spanish theater. More to the point, the marquises of Mortara owned considerable expanses of land in different regions of Spain. Thus, it is unlikely that Comella and Laserna would want to present their patrons with works supporting the idea of dividing and redistributing their land to small landowners. Instead, both playwright and composer created a flattering representation of aristocrats in their portrayal of the Count, and later of the reformed Marquis, the enlightened lord who runs his estate for the profit of nation and king.

For reference throughout this chapter, tables 4.1, 4.2, 4.3, and 4.4 chart the characters and musical numbers in *La Cecilia* and *Cecilia viuda*.

---

[17] Mercier de la Rivière thought all men have "a portion of happiness" and "an order meant to assure [their] own enjoyment" contemplated "within the general plan of creation." This order is the same underlying the natural world; men can get to know the laws of this order through an inner "divine light," and happily live in society if they follow the rules. Mercier de la Rivière, *L'ordre naturel*, v–vi.

[18] Mercier de la Rivière, *L'ordre natural*, 170–71.

Table 4.1. Characters in *La Cecilia*.

Character	Music	Status
Cecilia	Solo song	Poor *hidalga*, now peasant, married to
Lucas	Solo song	Poor soldier, now peasant
Count	---	Noble, landowner
Marquis	---	Noble, married to the
Marchioness	---	Noble, daughter of the Count
Count's butler	---	Servant
Marquis's lackey	---	Servant
Four village girls	Ensemble singing	Peasants
Four village lads	Ensemble singing	Peasants
Village mayor	---	Peasant, comic
Bailiff	---	Peasant, comic
Deputy	---	Peasant, comic

Table 4.2. Musical numbers in *La Cecilia*.

Act	Scene	Location	Music and dance numbers
1	1	Forest, Cecilia and Lucas's cottage	Song "Lily and Jasmine," eliminated from public performance (Cecilia and Lucas)
	2	Town hall	---
	3	Count's palace	*Bailete** (full ensemble)
	4	Village plaza	Seguidillas** (full ensemble), Canzoneta de payas (female ensemble, see Example 2)
	5	Forest, Cecilia and Lucas's cottage	---
2	1	Forest, Cecilia and Lucas's cottage	---
	2	Town hall	Canzoneta de payos (male ensemble)
	3	Count's palace and village plaza	Bailete repurposed as chorus*, Stick dance (full ensemble)
	4	Street	Seguidillas** repurposed as serenade (full ensemble)
	5	Entry hall of anonymous house	---

* And ** have the same music, different lyrics

Table 4.3. Characters in *Cecilia viuda*.

Character	Music	Status
Cecilia	---	Honest widow
Don Fernando	---	Cavalry lieutenant, platonically loves Cecilia
Don Nicasio	---	Land administrator
Marquis	---	Noble, landowner
Marchioness	---	Noble
Jacinta		Servant to Cecilia
Don Juan	---	Servant to the Marquis
[Marica, Pepa], Paca, Tomasa	[Duet], ensemble singing	Peasants, female ("lasses")
[Luis], Simón, Blas, Benito	[Solo], ensemble singing	Peasants, male ("lads")
Village mayor	---	Peasant, comic
Bailiff	---	Peasant, comic
Deputy	---	Peasant, comic
Two aldermen	---	Peasants, comic
Corporal	Ensemble singing	Military, comic
Soldier	Ensemble singing	Military, comic
Recruit	Ensemble singing	Military, comic

(Characters addressed in this chapter shaded in gray)

Table 4.4. Musical numbers in *Cecilia viuda*.

Act	Scene	Location	Music and dance numbers
Curtain		Outdoors in village	A sweet symphony
1	1	Outdoors in village	Duet (song): "Del olivo el verde ramo," middle of scene (Marica and Pepa)
			Peasant chorus in praise of the sun "Tributen parabienes," song "Del olivo ..." (full ensemble)
			Song reprise: "Del olivo ..." end of scene (full ensemble)
	2	Outdoors in village?	---
	3	Village plaza	Seguidillas (soldiers)
	4	Town hall	---
	5	Cecilia's porch	Hexasílabos: Cecilia, Don Fernando, Nicasio
2	1	Cecilia's living room	---
	2	Chestnut grove	Peasant chorus with two solo stanzas "Del trabajo ...," (full ensemble)
			Storm chorus-prayer "Clemencia ...," middle of the scene (full ensemble)
			Duet "Iris matizado"**, Pastoral* (Marica and Pepa)
			Peasant chorus (full ensemble)
	3	Town hall	---
	4	Village plaza	Seguidillas (soldiers and female ensemble)
	5	Outdoors in village	---
3	1	Village plaza	Duet: "Si al Marqués os escuece ...," Pepa y Marica, middle of scene
			Song "Cuando en los gallineros," Luis, middle of scene
	2	Village plaza	---
	3	Cecilia's porch	---
	4	Palace living room	---

—(*continued*)

Table 4.4—*concluded*

Scene	Location	Music and dance numbers
5	Bigger palace living room	Peasant chorus in praise of Marquis and Marchioness: "Pues hoy ha venido ...," final chorus (full ensemble). Cecilia with her hair down.
	[Contradanza]	

The High Nobility as Landowners

The Count in *La Cecilia* and the Marquis in *Cecilia viuda* stand for the grandees of Spain, nobles of the highest rank, major landowners, and magnanimous authorities emulating the king. Their portrayals follow a template similar to that of the enlightened rulers later found in Comella's heroic tragedies. Comella's heroic plays were inspired by the lives of European monarchs such as Frederic II of Prussia (1788, 1789, 1792) and Catherine the Great (1797).[19] Comella's interest in the role of the enlightened leader, together with the Mortaras's status as landowners, may have motivated his thematic choice for the *Cecilias*.[20]

Spanish grandees like the Mortaras held extensive land property around the country but lived in urban centers such as Madrid, Barcelona, and Cádiz. They managed their estates through administrators such as the character of Don Nicasio in *Cecilia viuda*, seldom venturing into rural areas, and especially not the remote ones. To reshape this pattern and make aristocrats contribute to the central economy, Bourbon authorities insisted that noble landowners supervise their territories in person. To make this direct involvement in their estates palatable to aristocrats, artists and intellectuals looking for official approval

---

[19] About sentimentality in the enlightened despots of heroic tragedies, see Ermanno Caldera, "La figura del déspota ilustrado en el teatro sentimental dieciochesco," *Dieciocho: Hispanic Enlightenment* 25, no. 2 (2002): 19–28.

[20] Little to nothing is known about the personal lives or stances of Benito Palermo Osorio or Josefa Dominga Catalá de Valeriola y Luján (the seventh marquis and marchionness of Mortara) during the time they were married. I have consulted records both at the Arxiu General i Fotogràfic in Valencia and at the Archivo Histórico de la Nobleza in Toledo. There are virtually no primary sources related to *La Cecilia* other than a couple of related expenses. Because Josefa Catalá de Valeriola went on to be a patroness of the arts later in her life, I suggest that she had a personal investment in producing plays at her Madrid abode. Furthermore, Comella dedicated the play specifically to her and gave her the title role, suggesting she paid for the commission. Both the marchioness and the marquis of Mortara owned considerable amounts of land, but she seems to have been wealthier than him. The marriage lasted only seven years, and some financial disputes ensued.

190   *Music and Modernity in Enlightenment Spain*

recreated Spanish villages as Arcadian communities, *loci amoeni*, where the high nobility could escape from the corruption of the cities. Thus, in act 1, scene 2 of *La Cecilia* the Count appears onstage reading newspapers and journals in the comfort of his country palace, where he has retreated to escape city life. In his opening monologue, the Count recalls the pastoral by evoking the Renaissance topic of the *beatus ille* ("happy is the man ...," from Horace's second Epode) and by speaking in the refined *estancia* versification associated with eclogues. He reflects upon the blessings of provincial life in a five-stanza speech (first stanza transcribed here, rhyme scheme and number of syllables per line provided to the right):

Qué placenteros días	a	7
me dispensa el retiro de la aldea!	b	11
Entre sus caserías	a	7
el alma noblemente se recrea	b	11
pues sin la cortesana desventura	c	11
logra, haciendo dichosos, su ventura.[21]	c	11

(What pleasant days
the retreat to the village affords me!
Among its hamlets
the soul finds recreation in noble ways
for, without the courtesan misfortune
it achieves its bliss in making others happy.)

Even though the Count does not sing in the play, the content and form of his monologue harken back to the leisure song of shepherds central to pastoral poetry to indicate that his modern attitude as a landowner spending time at his properties led to a prosperous and harmonious Spain.[22] The specific estancia form of the Count's monologue is the *sexta rima* or *sextina real* stanza (*sesta rima* or *sestina narrativa* in Italian), consisting of six-line stanzas with an ABABCC rhyming pattern.[23] The Count's speech pays heed to the Spanish

---

[21] A similar (much shorter) encomium of the village is found in Goldoni's play *L'incognita* from 1751. In act 1, scene 3, the banker Ottavio enjoys his country home: "Che delizioso soggiorno è la campagna! ... Quanto volentieri spendo la metà dei miei giorni in questa solitudine amena! Non darei un giorno di villa per un mese di abitazione in città."

[22] See Alexander Pope, "A Discourse on Pastoral Poetry," in the *Works of Mr. Alexander Pope* (London: W. Bowyer, for Bernard Lintot, 1717), xxxii. "'Tis natural to imagine, that the leisure of those ancient shepherds requiring some diversion, none was so proper to that solitary life as singing; and that in their songs they took occasion to celebrate their own felicity."

[23] The *sestina narrativa* refers more specifically to a form also called Provenzal *sextina*, which consists of six stanzas of six lines each, plus a *congedo* of three lines. The form is attributed to the twelfth-century Provenzal poet Arnaut Daniel. José Cenizo Jiménez,

Bourbon Sentimentalities on the Musical Stage   191

poets of the Renaissance that neoclassicists revered, because Renaissance poets learned the sextina from Italian poets like Petrarch, who adopted the form from Provençal poetry in the troubadour tradition. The Count's monologue uses a seven-plus-eleven pattern, common in sixteenth-century high-pastoral poems such as Garcilaso's second *Égloga*, or San Juan de la Cruz's (1542–1591) spiritual allegories, *Cántico espiritual* and *Subida al Monte Carmelo*.[24] The alternation of eleven- and seven-syllable lines is sometimes referred to as *versi sciolti* in Italian. *Versi sciolti* are frequently used in recitative, but in *La Cecilia* they function as heightened speech to mark important structural points in the play. Comella only uses this verse meter for three monologues, once for each of the three main characters: the Count, Lucas, and Cecilia.

The Count's monologue casts the *beatus ille* topic in the particular guise of the court (or town) versus village (or country) topic, which Spanish authors had been using recurrently since the Renaissance and which had made a comeback in the second half of the eighteenth century to support the Bourbon policy that aristocrats should embrace country life as part of their duties.[25] In general, the court signified the perils of the modern time, while the village stood for an Arcadian community preserved from corruption. Even though the town versus country topic intersects with the pastoral, there are some differences between the two. First, whereas the pastoral is set during the primal Golden Age, the court versus village dichotomy situates the beatus ille in a more specific histori-cal timeframe, in this case, the Bourbon late Enlightenment. Second, the beatus ille distances itself from idyllic scenes to focus on social values. In other words, the court versus village topic emphasizes ethics over aesthetics, making it all the more suited to advertise the kind of social reform sponsored by Charles III's government. Comella was one of many authors who chose the court versus village topic for their work. Several of his contemporaries, including prominent poets Iriarte and Meléndez Valdés, revisited the court versus village beatus ille to support and promote the Bourbon project of agricultural modernization.[26]

"Recepción de la sextina doble en Italia y en el Renacimiento español," in *"Italia, España, Europa": Literaturas comparadas, tradiciones y traducciones* (Bologna: Arci-bel, 2006), 31–39.

[24]   Garcilaso adopted the Petrarchan style from Naples, where he lived from 1522–23. He personally knew Tasso and Minturno from a second sojourn in Naples between 1530 and 1533.

[25]   The foundational work for the court versus village topic in Spain is Fray Antonio de Guevara's *Menosprecio de corte y alabanza de aldea* (*Disdain for Court and Praise of Village*, 1539). Guevara's sixteenth-century *Menosprecio* continued to be reprinted in the seventeenth (1673) and eighteenth centuries (1735, 1790), and would have been a familiar frame of reference for Comella.

[26]   Tomás de Iriarte, *La felicidad de la vida en el campo* (Madrid: Joaquín Ibarra, 1780); Juan Meléndez Valdés, "El filósofo en el campo," in *Poesías de el Dr. D. Juan Meléndez Valdes* (Madrid: Viuda e hijos de Santander, 1794).

192   *Music and Modernity in Enlightenment Spain*

Despite his connections to the high pastoral, the Count is very much a man of late Bourbon times when it comes to his economic stance.[27] Under Charles III, the high nobility was expected to manage their estates efficiently but yield economic control to the king. At the time *La Cecilia* was written, the Bourbon government was experiencing trouble with intermediary leasers. The grandees would lease their vast lands to local nobility or the rural bourgeoisie, who, in turn, leased them to small farmers. In the eyes of the government, the peasants (*labradores*) were then victims of an economic system in which they paid for the land with the product of their labor, to the detriment of their own sustenance. From this point of view, intermediaries and taxes stood in the way of progress. Politician and political theorist Pablo de Olavide discussed the problem of leasers in his 1768 *Informe sobre la Ley Agraria* (*Report on Agricultural Law*).[28] His solution to the problem of leasers involved convincing the high nobility to negotiate labor and crops directly with peasants, who would then avoid being taxed for their use of the land. This is the model that we see in *La Cecilia*, where the Count goes to the village not only to seek retreat but also to interact personally with the peasants living and working on his land. Thus, the Count embodies the "good father" figure linked to enlightened absolutist leaders who sympathize with the needs and woes of their subjects.[29] Of course, the epitome of the ruler-protector of agriculture was the king, but all aristocrats were encouraged to emulate him.[30] In *La Cecilia,* this paternalistic bond vital to the Spanish economy materialized through music and dance, which frame all the interactions between the Count and the villagers as a group, as will become apparent through a closer look at the musical numbers in the play.

The first choral number of *La Cecilia*, a *bailete*, directly addresses the issues of taxes and the duties of a good aristocrat. In act 1, scene 4, the villagers have

---

[27]   Raymond Monelle, *The Musical Topic: Hunt, Military and Pastoral* (Bloomington: Indiana University Press, 2006). For "high pastoral," see Monelle, 183–270. Monelle defines the high pastoral in connection with the classical topics established in Virgil's and Theocritus's works, and later reworked by Jacopo Sannazaro (*Arcadia*, ca. 1480) and by Torquato Tasso (*Il pastor fido*, 1590). Monelle contends that in the nineteenth century the high pastoral gave way to the rustic or low pastoral "based on the Volkslied and its embodiment of an idealized European peasantry."

[28]   Pablo de Olavide, *Informe de Olavide sobre la Ley Agraria*, edited by Ramón Carande and Joaquín Ruiz del Portal (Madrid: Fundación Ignacio Larramendi, 1956). Meléndez Valdés in *El filósofo en el campo* also refers to seneschals (*mayordomos*) as the cause of the peasants' suffering.

[29]   Caldera, "La figura del déspota," 221–22.

[30]   Tomás de Iriarte ends his 1780 eclogue *La felicidad de la vida en el campo* by praising Charles III as the ultimate protector of agriculture: "Who knows how to love them [*labradores*] more benignly / Who promotes their wellbeing more eagerly / Other than Carlos, the magnanimous?" ("¿Quién más benignamente sabe amarlos / Quién con ansia mayor su bien promueve / que el magnánimo Carlos …?"). Iriarte, *La felicidad*, 20.

assembled to greet the Count's daughter (the Marchioness) and her husband, the Marquis, who have just arrived from the city for a visit. The eight female and male peasants in secondary roles, along with "other lads and lasses" ... "enter [the stage] singing and dancing." The ensuing musical number is titled "Bailete con panderetas" (chorus/dance with tambourines.) The primary purpose of *bailetes* was to create an aura of festivity—often in honor of a king or another ruler—much like ball scenes in opera.[31] Bailetes like this one also signified the pastoral, and on occasion, composers even called them "bailete pastoral."[32] Their music featured traits Raymond Monelle connects to the rustic pastoral: compound meter, drone-like uniform patterns on the bassline (especially the "rocking" Siciliana pattern ♩ ♪), simple melodies with dotted rhythms, nonexpressive harmonies, and major tonality.[33] The music of *La Cecilia*'s bailete (example 4.1) presents all of the rustic pastoral markers listed by Monelle. Through these musical conventions, the chorus/dance evokes the idyllic atmosphere of the pastoral, even though the characters performing it represent rustic villagers. The peasants applaud the Count's progeny in the lyrics because they are grateful for his magnanimity, which manifests itself in a precise way: he does not tax them.

Pues los amos no exigen	For the masters do not demand
tributos de los pobres,	taxes from the poor,
nuestro afecto a sus plantas	may our affection at their feet
tribute corazones,	pay hearts in tribute
coronando de aplausos	crowning with applause
su hermosa prole.	his beautiful progeny

From the point of view of the Bourbon ministers, aristocrats who charged the peasants little to no tax for working their land performed a great service to the nation because it meant more revenue for the king. Moreover, farmers unburdened with taxes felt happier and, under physiocratic logic, worked harder. In fact, Olavide wrote in his *Informe* that taxes should be abolished.[34] Besides Olavide, writers like Pedro Rodríguez de Campomanes (1723–1802) and Juan Sempere y Guarinos (1754–1830) also rejected any tax not paid

---

[31] The term "bailete" derives from the Italian "balletto."

[32] We find "bailetes pastorales" representing peasants and other rustic characters in the musical theater pieces of several Spanish composers. These are but a few examples of pieces with bailetes pastorales (dates and authors correspond to the music, not the text): *La jura del alcalde* (*Sainete*, Antonio Guerrero, 1764), *El alba y el sol* (Comedia, Antonio Guerrero), *Doña Inés de Castro* (Comedia), *Las bodas de Camacho el rico* (Comedia, Pablo Esteve, 1784), *La espigadera* (Comedia, Pablo Esteve, 1785), *La restauración de Madrid* (Comedia, Laserna, 1781), *La fiel pastorcita y tirano del Castillo* (Comedia, Mariano Bustos, 1790).

[33] Monelle, *Musical Topic*, 229ff.

[34] Olavide, *Informe*, 23.

Example 4.1. "Bailete," *La Cecilia*, bars 1–14.

directly to the king.[35] These writers' archetype of a good ruler was influenced not only by physiocracy but also by Ludovico Antonio Muratori's *Della pubblica felicità*, published in 1749 and translated into Spanish in 1790.[36] At the opposite extreme of the good ruler of the Bourbon Enlightenment was the unproductive noble, personified in *La Cecilia* by the Marquis.[37] This type of noble, who lived the city life without any firsthand knowledge of his agricultural territories, distressed Bourbon officials and their intellectual allies endlessly. The Marquis also displays features of what Mercier de la Rivière calls the "arbitrary despot." According to Mercier de la Rivière, once the peasants are at the mercy of the arbitrary despot, their rights become uncertain, and mayhem ensues.[38] This is precisely what happens in *La Cecilia* when the Marquis shows up in the Count's village, altering the equilibrium between lord and peasants. Luckily, Cecilia and Lucas do not fall for his charm and stand up to him, mediating to maintain the precarious social balance.

The issue of noble landowners develops even closer to Bourbon policy in *Cecilia viuda*, where Comella replaces the good-ruler character of the deceased Count with the reformed Marquis and introduces Don Nicasio as the bad administrator. Formerly a threat to the community in his devious ways, the Marquis makes a fresh start and assumes the role of the landowner.[39] However, he makes the mistake of leaving the village's affairs in the hands of administrator Don Nicasio, who wreaks havoc by embezzling Cecilia's stipend and abusing the peasants. In *Cecilia viuda*'s first act, Don Nicasio, now embodying Mercier de la Rivière's arbitrary despot, usurps the Count's speech in a spurious ode. Don Nicasio's ode mimics the Count's court versus village beatus ille elegy but loses its songlike sonority because it is written in romance verse (like the rest of the spoken dialog in the play) instead of the elevated estancia meter. To highlight the dichotomy between landowner/protector and administrator/malefactor, Comella placed Don Nicasio's fake ode in a scene of *Cecilia viuda* parallel to the Count's original speech in *La Cecilia* (act 1, scene 2):

---

[35] The belief that taxes not paid directly to the king impoverish the nation had been around since the seventeenth century.

[36] Muratori accepts the need for taxes (chap. 22) but condemns excessive taxation (chap. 23). Lodovico Antonio Muratori, *Della pubblica felicità: oggetto de' buoni principi, trattato* (Lucca: s. n., 1749; *La publica felicidad objeto de los buenos principes* (Madrid: Imprenta Real, 1790).

[37] In her analysis of *La Cecilia*, Angulo Egea sees the rural environment of *La Cecilia* as an excuse for Comella to contrast old (the Count) and new (the Marquis) noble types. Angulo Egea, *Otra cara*, 106.

[38] Mercier de la Rivière, *L'Ordre*, 173.

[39] According to the laws of *mayorazgo* inheritance, the Count's lands would go to his son-in-law, not to his daughter.

Qué vida tan placentera	How pleasant
es la mía! Todo el pueblo	is my life! The entire village
a mi gusto se sujeta;	submits to my will;
no respeto la justicia,	I disregard justice,
defraudo todas las rentas	I cheat on all the income
y me embolso las limosnas	and I pocket the alms
que los Marqueses me ordenan	that the Marquises instruct me to give

Whereas the good versus bad noble landowner archetypes underpin *La Cecilia*, the push to eliminate intermediaries and deal directly with peasants takes the spotlight in *Cecilia viuda*. Intermediaries such as lesser local nobility and the rural bourgeoisie interfered in the flux of wealth from the rural communities to the landowner and in the paternalistic relations between them.[40] These intermediaries posed a real threat to the old regime and ultimately contributed to its demise. Once Don Nicasio seizes power over the peasants, it is up to Cecilia's virtue to defeat corruption and defend the Bourbon idyll of a happy and productive peasantry.

The Enlightened Peasants

The modest nuclear family unit formed by Cecilia and Lucas, living in the Spanish countryside far from the court in Madrid, was a crucial piece of the physiocratic New Arcadia of late Enlightenment Spain. Their marriage exemplifies the prototype of a farming family content with their subsistence-economy way of life.[41] The social order envisioned by Comella and Laserna in *La Cecilia* required that all peasants accept their fate at the bottom of the economic pyramid. Nevertheless, Cecilia's and Lucas's characters called for a degree of sentimental subjectivity insofar as they derive their happiness and productivity from internal rather than external wealth. This emergent subjectivity separates Cecilia and Lucas from the rest of the villagers in the play, who seem irredeemably bound to comic stereotypes of rural people. To highlight the protagonists' moral agency, the play presents the couple in a mix of pastoral and sentimental terms. The two characters display agency and moral aspirations akin to those

---

[40] Bartolomé Yun Casalilla, "Ingresos, formas de distribución del producto agrario y cambio social en Castilla la Vieja y León en el siglo XVIII," in *Estructuras agrarias y reformismo ilustrado en la España del siglo XVIII*, ed. Seminario sobre Agricultura e ilustración en España (Madrid: Ministerio de Agricultura, Alimentación y Medio Ambiente, 1989), 481–505.

[41] Ideally, peasant families ought to bear children who could contribute to familial economy. However, the Mortaras had no descendants—a potential cause for the marriage annulment in 1789. Comella may have considered this fact when creating the character of Cecilia for the marchioness.

198   *Music and Modernity in Enlightenment Spain*

of the proto-bourgeoisie found in the sentimental genre, though lacking their economic means. The contradiction between Cecilia's and Lucas's moral and politico-economic agency shows the difficulty of reconciling a budding modern subjectivity with the unlimited power of the monarch in the Spanish Bourbon regime.

Cecilia's and Lucas's subjectivity is musically conveyed as solo song in the first scene of *La Cecilia*, where wife and husband sing complementary stanzas of the same song, "Lily and Jasmine."[42] When the curtain opens for the first scene of act 1, the audience sees Cecilia sitting outside her cottage, a *locus amoenus* framed by luscious trees. She spins thread as she sings a memento mori in the mold of the pastoral topic *collige, virgo, rosas*—reap the splendor of youth while you can.[43] After she sings her two verses, she delivers a monologue. Lucas then appears on stage and reprises the song:

Cecilia	Aunque el hombre y la alfalfa	Even though man and alfalfa
Stanza 1	sin contratiempo	enjoy their verdure
Stanza 2	disfruten verdor,	without setbacks,
	cortan su lozanía	time and the farm worker
	al mejor tiempo,	cut their lushness
	tiempo y labrador.	in the best of times.
	Lirio y jazmín	Lily and jasmine,
	rosa y clavel	rose and carnation
	quiero yo coger,	I want to pick
	para hacer guirnaldas	to make garlands
	a mi dulce bien.	for my beloved.
Lucas	Matizados objetos	Embellished objects
Stanza 1	que de este prado	you, who were the delicacies
Stanza 2	fuisteis el primor:	of this meadow:
	Adornad de Cecilia,	Adorn the innocence
	mi dueño amado,	of Cecilia,
	el dulce candor.	my beloved.
	Lirio y jazmín ...	Lily and jasmine ...

---

[42] The song does not have a title either in the libretto or the score. The use of this title is my choice.

[43] Cecilia spinning thread may have recalled the 1765 zarzuela *El amor pastoril*, written for the wedding of Charles IV (then prince of Asturias) to Maria Luisa of Parma. In the opening scene, the shepherdesses are spinning thread. *El amor pastoril* is a translation of Goldoni's (under the pseudonym Polisseno Fegeio) *La Cascina, dramma giocoso per musica* (Venice, 1761). Antonietta Calderone, and Víctor Pagán, "Traducciones de comedias italianas," in *El teatro europeo en la España del siglo XVIII*, ed. Francisco Lafarga (Lleida: Universitat de Lleida, 1997), 365.

Bourbon Sentimentalities on the Musical Stage   199

In the Mortara version, "Lily and Jasmine" established Cecilia (performed by the marchioness of Mortara) as a morally sophisticated *hidalga* turned farm woman—poor on the outside, rich on the inside. "Lily and Jasmine" was eliminated from the public version played at the city theaters. The single press review ever written of *La Cecilia*, published in Madrid's monthly periodical *Memorial Literario*, does not offer any information that could help us understand why the song was discarded. One lone sentence at the end of the review notes that "this play had previously been staged in an illustrious house adorned with some musical songs, omitted from the public performance."[44]

Even though the music for Cecilia and Lucas's song is lost, the poetic meter and lyrical content point to the pastoral and sentimental mood of the first scene.[45] The piece is labeled *"canción."* Comella and other contemporary playwrights often cued solo songs in their librettos as simply *"canción"* or *"canta."* Songs could be in seguidilla meter, which alternated seven- and five- or six-syllable lines. The seguidilla was a genre associated with rural environments and Spanish characters such as peasants or majas. Cecilia's song loosely follows seguidilla meter but is structured in two contrasting stanzas, like an aria da capo (the second stanza functions as a refrain, picked up by Lucas in the reprise). The two-stanza solo song form had been widespread in Spanish theater since the mid-eighteenth century because of the influence of Italian opera. Thus, the opening musical piece of *La Cecilia* is between a traditional song and a pastoral aria.

In terms of sentimental influences, Cecilia and Lucas's opening song and the entire first scene of *La Cecilia* structurally resemble that of Goldoni/Piccinni's *La buona figliuola*, though the characters and the plots differ substantially.[46]

[44] The *Memorial* review found a lack of verisimilitude in Lucas's survival of the Marquis's stabbing at the end of the play. According to this review, the strongest points of the play were Cecilia's displays of sentimentality when Lucas is wounded, the Marquis's repentance, and the town council's comic scenes. "Teatros, La Cecilia," *Memorial Literario, Instructivo y Curioso* 32 (August 1786): 473.

[45] The music for this song has not been found because it did not form part of the version for the public theaters. There is no known score for the Mortara staging of *La Cecilia*.

[46] McClelland suggests that *La Cecilia* is inspired by *La buona figliuola* (161), but a side-by-side reading of both scripts reveals that *La Cecilia* draws just as heavily on other styles, such as sixteenth-century pastoral poetry and seventeenth-century Spanish theater. McClelland herself admits that, like other early Comella scripts, the style of *La Cecilia* is "more traditional than foreign" (162). In his evaluation of Comella's plays, eighteenth-century censor Santos Díez González says, "if I am correct, [*La Cecilia*] is a version of an Italian pastoral ...," but he doesn't mention which one. Based on the research of authors like Angulo Egea, McClelland, and Pataky, and upon comparison of *La Cecilia* with *La buona figliuola*, it is not accurate to say that the former is a version of the latter, because the parallels are too scant. It seems like Comella took the structure of the first scenes of act 1 and act 2 of Goldoni's libretto for the corresponding first scenes of both acts in *La Cecilia*, but the rest of each act is very different, as are the plots and the issues at stake. Beyond that, he may have borrowed other ideas from

200 *Music and Modernity in Enlightenment Spain*

One of the key differences between *La buona figliuola* and *La Cecilia* lies in the latter's emphasis on ethics over romance, making Cecilia a virtuous heroine with sentimental tinges, rather than a fully sentimental character like Cecchina. A side-by-side reading of Cecchina's and Cecilia's opening songs' lyrics illustrates the different emphases in each musical theater work. Even though both texts allude to nature and flowers, Cecchina sings of beauty and pleasure, whereas Cecilia meditates on the fleetingness of life. While Cecchina sings in a garden, Cecilia experiences nature as an agricultural working place, as evidenced by her use of words like "alfalfa" and "farm worker."

Act 1, scene 1

La buona figliuola

What a *pleasure*, what a *delight*
it is to see in this morning
the jasmine competing
in beauty with the rose!
And to be able to say to the herbs,
it is I, with fresh humors,
who is coming to water you.[47]

La Cecilia

Even though man and *alfalfa*
enjoy their verdure
without setbacks,
time and the *farm worker*
cut their lushness
in the best of times.
Lily and jasmine,
rose and carnation
I want to pick
to make garlands
for my beloved.

La buona figliuola had been adapted into a Spanish zarzuela in 1765 and into a spoken comedia in 1784.[48] Attendees at the Mortara performance who

---

French sentimental plays, from other Goldonian librettos, and from baroque Spanish *comedias*. Thus, it is entirely possible that *La Cecilia* reminded audiences, then as now, of other famous operas and plays.

[47] The music for Cecchina's aria could not have been used for Cecilia's song, because the verse meter is different. Cecchina's aria is in octosyllabic verse.

[48] For Spanish versions of *La buona fligliuola*, see Cesáreo Calvo Rigual, "'La buona figliuola' de Carlo Goldoni y sus traducciones españolas." *Quaderns d'Italia* 22 (2017): 241–62. A two-act zarzuela version of *La buena figliuola* in Spanish, by Antonio Furmento Bazo, was performed at the Coliseo de la Cruz in Madrid on November 11, 1765, with the title *La buena fillola* or *La buena muchacha* (date for performance found in René Andioc and Mireille Coulon, *Cartelera teatral madrileña del siglo XVIII 1708–1808* [Toulouse: Presses Universitaires du Mirail, 1997], 643). As in other zarzuela adaptations of operas, the libretto was translated into Spanish and spoken dialogue in verse took the place of recitative. Arias, duets, and other musical numbers were for the most part preserved. Pablo Esteve (a contemporary of Laserna) arranged some of Piccinni's music and added a few new pieces (Juan Pablo Fernández-Cortés, *La música en las Casas de Osuna y Benavente (1733–1882): un estudio sobre el mecenazgo musical de la alta nobleza española* (Madrid: Sociedad Española de Musicología, 2007), 144–45). *La buena figliuola* was staged in Italian at least in Barcelona (1761, 1770), in the court theater of San

Bourbon Sentimentalities on the Musical Stage   201

had seen either the zarzuela or the comedia would recognize Cecilia's song's connection to Cecchina's aria, all the more because the ensuing monologue—recitative, in Cecchina's case—and the reprise of the song by the protagonist's love interest also appear in both works. Following Cecilia's singing, the audience learns that she is spinning out of necessity—although she is of noble birth like Cecchina, she and Lucas lost their land because they offered it as bond to help a friend. Whereas Cecchina laments not knowing her birth origin, Cecilia knows she comes from a wealthier *hidalgo* status. Although Cecchina finds redemption when she is restored to her noble origin, Cecilia finds redemption in turning poverty into virtue.

Cecilia's opening solo song is indebted not only to the arias of sentimental opera heroines but also to traditional Spanish songs in the zarzuelas of the 1760s. In the seventeenth and early eighteenth centuries, zarzuela was a lofty, mythological genre. But in the 1760s, playwright Ramón de la Cruz (1731–1794) and composer Antonio Rodríguez de Hita (1722–1787) reformulated zarzuela focusing on representations of the Spanish popular classes. Much of the libretto text in De la Cruz's zarzuelas is written in simple, even coarse language. Nevertheless, some of the songs he wrote depart from this quotidian register to include metaphors rich in natural elements alluding to simplicity, beauty, and sometimes love. For example, in the opening song for de la Cruz's zarzuela *Las segadoras de Vallecas* (1768), a peasant woman sings: "Fresh little flowers / Embellish my breast / Free, and full / Of simplicity."[49] Akin to operatic arias in their contemplative function, these "nature songs" in de la Cruz/Rodríguez de Hita's zarzuelas evoke the grievances or celebrate the joys of peasant life, introducing tropes of the rustic pastoral into the comic plot.[50] In these zarzuelas, however, the spoken dialogue

---

Ildefonso in Segovia (1767), in the court theater of Aranjuez (1769), and in Valencia (1769). Spanish productions included Cádiz (1762), and probably Sevilla (1764). A *comedia* version in three acts took place at the Coliseo de la Cruz in 1784 with the title *La bella Pamela inglesa* (printed libretto at BNE U/9246). Goldoni's libretto, based on Samuel Richardson's novel, first and most successfully brought the Pamela character to Madrid. Richardson's novel was not translated into Spanish until 1794.

[49]   "Frescas florecillas / adornad mi pecho / libre, y satisfecho / de simplicidad." *Las segadoras* was an original zarzuela with a libretto by de la Cruz and music by Antonio Rodríguez de Hita.

[50]   Many (though not all) of de la Cruz's zarzuelas were adaptations of Italian opera buffa with librettos by Goldoni. Sometimes the original music was preserved, and other times it was arranged or newly composed. Further connections between de la Cruz and Goldoni can be found, among others, in María Angulo Egea: "'Traducido libremente y arreglado al teatro español': De Carlo Goldoni a Ramon de la Cruz y Luciano Comella," *Dieciocho: Hispanic Enlightenment* 32, no. 1 (2009): 75–100; in John Dowling's "Ramón de la Cruz, libretista de zarzuelas," *Bulletin of Hispanic Studies* 68, no. 1 (1991): 173–82; in Elena Marcello's "Il filosofo de campagna goldoniano tradotto da Ramón de la Cruz, Note di lingua e riscrittura," *Quaderns d'Italia* 17, no. 11–26 (2012); and in Juana Inés Rodríguez Gómez's dissertation "Las obras de Carlo Goldoni en Espana (1750–1800)," Universitat de Valencia, 1997. For a comprehensive view of the life and works of Ramón de la Cruz see Emilio Cotarelo y Mori,

202   *Music and Modernity in Enlightenment Spain*

surrounding these "nature songs" is comic, while in the first scene of *La Cecilia* the dialogue is sentimental, preserving the atmosphere set up by the opening song. Neither Cecilia nor Lucas speak with idioms or barbarisms, as do other peasant characters in the play, so one can imagine that their musical language also sets them apart from other commoners.

The first scene of *La Cecilia* points to a few similarities between Cecilia and Lucas and the small landowners (*pequeños propietarios*) imagined—yet never concretized—by Enlightenment writers Pablo de Olavide and Gaspar Melchor de Jovellanos. Olavide and later Jovellanos suggested that farmers could rent a parcel permanently to get a sense of ownership of the land and commit to making it productive. This idea came from physiocratic theory. In physiocracy, land ownership is at the core of the natural and social order. According to François Quesnay, when men do not own the land, they are miserable because they depend on other men, ultimately becoming unproductive.[51] To avoid this situation, Olavide proposed that small landowners lease the same plot of land indefinitely, which would make them feel as rooted in it as if they had owned it. If farmers could live in their own small parcel together with their families and cattle, Olavide assured, they would be contented and contribute to the prosperity of the state.[52] Economist and lawyer Pedro Rodríguez de Campomanes thought that while the farmer worked the land, his wife and daughters could contribute to the familial economy by spinning wool and weaving fabrics.[53] Much like the utopian small landowner, Cecilia and Lucas reside in the same land they farm, as opposed to the day laborers, who lived in villages and hiked long distances to the plots they were hired to farm. However, Cecilia and Lucas are much poorer than the farmers Olavide envisioned: a small proprietary in Olavide's vision ought to possess fifty *fanegas* of land, while Lucas owns only one *fanega* (1.59 acres).

Don Ramón de la Cruz y sus obras (Madrid: J. Perales y Martinez, 1899) and Josep Maria Sala Valldaura, "Los autores y las obras: Ramón de la Cruz," in *Historia del teatro breve en España*, ed. Javier Huerta Calvo (Madrid: Iberoamericanica, 2008), 699–730. For more about his zarzuelas, see John C. Dowling, "Las castañeras picadas de Ramón de la Cruz entonces (1787), después (1898), ahora," in *El siglo que llaman ilustrado*: Homenaje a Francisco Aguilar Piñal ed. José Checa Beltrán, Joaquín Álvarez Barrientos (Madrid: C.S.I.C., 1996), 289–96; and Germán Labrador López de Azcona, "La comedia con música 'Clementina' de Ramón de la Cruz: Un camino inexplorado en la historia de la zarzuela," *Studi Ispanici* 37 (2012): 103–18. Mireille Coulon and Sala Valldaura have studied De la Cruz's costumbrismo, also in his sainetes ("Música y sainetes: Ramón de la Cruz." See *Teatro y música en España: Los géneros breves en la segunda mitad del siglo XVIII* (Madrid: Universidad Autónoma de Madrid, 2008), 289–308.

[51]   Quesnay, *Physiocratie*, xxxi.

[52]   Olavide, *Informe*, 36.

[53]   Pedro Rodríguez de Campomanes, *Discurso sobre el fomento a la industria popular* (Madrid: Antonio de Sancha, 1774). Manufacturing, even of the domestic kind, is not a source of wealth in physiocracy, but it is a fundamental pillar of Bourbon policy (José Luis Fernández Fernández, *Jovellanos: antropología y teoría de la sociedad* [Comillas: Universidad Pontificia de Comillas, 1991], 225).

Bourbon Sentimentalities on the Musical Stage   203

Both *La Cecilia* and the reform attempts by Olavide, Jovellanos, and Campomanes arrive at a similar conundrum: how to foster individual agency to bolster productivity, while restraining access to economic power or upward social mobility to maintain class separation more or less intact. Except for Cecilia and her deceased husband, the rest of the peasants escape the dilemma of agency versus submission, behaving like obedient subjects but not like the moral equals of the higher-status characters.

From Rabble to People

The New Arcadia depicted in the *Cecilias* includes the benevolent ruler (the Count), the utopian farming household (Cecilia and Lucas), and the contented rural community characterized through ensemble numbers where the villagers sing and dance together under the Count's gaze. Collective music and dance *make* the peasant characters emerge as a social group because, in singing and dancing, the villagers perform their roles as healthy and happy people who obey their sovereign out of free will. The connection between productivity and enjoyment of life lies at the core of physiocratic theory. Mercier de la Rivière believed that if men are deprived of the freedom to enjoy life, then they are not motivated to work, the land does not produce goods, and the social order falls apart.[54] Jovellanos conjured up the physiocratic connection between freedom, social order, and happiness in his *Memoria sobre las diversiones públicas* (1790, 1796). In this work, Jovellanos envisaged a lively peasantry akin to the one Comella and Laserna staged in *La Cecilia* and *Cecilia viuda*.

Table 4.5 lists the peasant choral numbers in *La Cecilia* and *Cecilia viuda*. Numbers in gray rows are also performed by peasants but involve solo singing. In this section, I discuss choral numbers only.[55]

Rustic choral numbers like those of *La Cecilia* and *Cecilia viuda* had formed part of Spanish pastoral zarzuelas and comedias since the seventeenth century in the form of choruses called *cuatros* because some of them were written in a four-voice texture. Cuatros in the Spanish musical theater of the seventeenth and eighteenth centuries were often associated with commoners. They expressed popular sentiment, whether rejoicing in a festivity, praising a leader or monarch, enjoying nature, or narrating shared experiences related to work or status. Many cuatros expressed popular sentiment, but only some of them were inspired by popular song.[56] Rustic choruses in the zarzuela and comedia

---

[54] "Désir de jouir et liberté de jouir, voilà l'âme du mouvement social; voilà le germe fécond de l'abondance." Mercier de la Rivière, *L'ordre*, 33.

[55] Blas de Laserna, "Música de la comedia La Cecilia Primera P[a]rte," ([1786], MUS 25–11, Biblioteca Histórica de Madrid); "Música de la comedia en la 2ª. Parte de La Cecilia," ([1787], MUS 36–17, Biblioteca Histórica de Madrid).

[56] Louise K. Stein, *Songs of Mortals, Dialogues of the Gods: Music and Theatre in Seventeenth-Century Spain* (New York: Clarendon Press, 1993), 24ff., 143, 159. Some-

Table 4.5. Peasant musical numbers in *La Cecilia* and *Cecilia viuda*

Act	Scene	Location	Music and dance numbers
1	3	Count's palace	Bailete* (full ensemble)
	4	Village plaza	Seguidillas** (full ensemble),
		Chestnut grove	Canzonetta de payas (female ensemble, see example 2)
2	2	Town hall	Canzonetta de payos (male ensemble)
	3	Count's palace and village plaza	Bailete* repurposed as chorus, Stick dance (full ensemble)
	4	Street	Seguidillas** repurposed as serenade (full ensemble)
Cecilia viuda			
1	1	Village streets	Duet (song): "Del olivo el verde ramo" middle of scene (Marica and Pepa)
			Peasant chorus in praise of the sun "Tributen parabienes," Song "Del olivo ..." (full ensemble)
			Song reprise: "Del olivo ..." end of scene (full ensemble)
	3	Village plaza	Seguidillas (soldiers)
2	2	Chestnut grove	Peasant chorus with two solo stanzas "Del trabajo ...," (full ensemble)
			Storm chorus-prayer "Clemencia ...," middle of the scene (full ensemble)
			Duet "Iris matizado," pastoral (Marica and Pepa)
			Peasant chorus (full ensemble)
	4	Village plaza	Seguidillas (soldiers and female ensemble)
3	1	Village plaza	Duet: "Si al Marqués os escuece ...," Marica and Pepa, middle of scene Song "Cuando en los gallineros ..." Luis, middle of scene
	5	Bigger palace living room	Peasant chorus in praise of Marquis and Marchioness: "Pues hoy ha venido ...", final chorus (full ensemble). Cecilia with her hair down.
		[Contradanza]	

tradition were diegetic: they portrayed working-class people singing a song on stage. These choral numbers represented the commoners and their worldview. There is, for example, a Spanish tradition of harvest songs or *canciones de labradores*, where the peasants sing of the joys and miseries of the laborer to the tune of simple melodies.[57] The "Canzonetta de payos" in the second act of *La Cecilia* and the duet/song in the third act of *Cecilia viuda* are *canciones de labradores* but, unlike the older polyphonic cuatros of zarzuelas, they are written in a two-voice galant texture. Besides their connection to harvest songs and other traditional songs, music and dance numbers in the *Cecilias* were influenced by de la Cruz's zarzuelas from the late 1760s and 1770s, which featured working-class people as the main characters.[58] At the same time, choruses, like dances, provided the audience with entertainment and spectacle.

Comella and Laserna drew from preexisting traditions of rustic songs and choral numbers in Spanish musical theater and gave them a new twist: they used ensembles to choreograph a communal life in line with the Bourbon agricultural project. Peasants were at the foundation of the Bourbon reform edifice. Without a consolidated peasant community, absolutism could not exist, for the old regime thrived on the lord-vassal economic relationship configured during the Middle Ages.[59] Bourbon administrators wanted peasants to be happy so they could be productive. Following the physiocrats, Jovellanos believed that freedom was the condition for happiness, so the role of the state was to guarantee people's freedom so they could enjoy life and love their sovereign.[60] In *La Cecilia*, the Count represents the *res publica*, the guarantor of public order who keeps the Marquis's disruptive threat at bay. In return, the villagers love him, and they manifest their loyalty in their musical numbers.

Comella and Laserna used the middle (third) scene of each of *La Cecilia*'s two acts to stage the villagers as grateful servants. I referred to the bailete in act 1, scene 3, in the section about landowners: the Count does not collect taxes from poor peasants and in return, the peasants offer their hearts to pay moral

---

times the term *"cuatro"* is used even if the chorus has fewer than four parts.

[57] See Margit Frenk, *Nuevo corpus de la antigua lírica popular hispánica, siglos XV a XVIII* (Mexico: Facultad de Filosofía y Letras Universidad Nacional Autónoma de México, El Colegio de México, Fondo de Cultura Económica, 2003).

[58] See, for example, the opening chorus of *Las segadoras de Vallecas* (1768), where peasants implore the sun to treat them mercifully: "Ardent planet / cool down the burning heat / and treat the reapers/ with mercy // Abridge the hours / of slumber and nourishment / may they give us strength / to work." ("Hermoso planeta / templa los ardores / y a los segadores / trata con piedad."). Zarzuelas by Ramón de la Cruz featuring peasants include *Las segadoras de Vallecas*, *Las labradoras de Murcia*, *Las labradoras astutas* (1774, adaptation of *Le contadine bizzare* by Petrosellini/Piccinni). *Las pescadoras* (1765, adaptation of *Le pescatrici* by Goldoni/Bertoni and Galuppi) also features workingwomen.

[59] Yun Casalilla, "Ingresos, formas de distribución," 483.

[60] Fernández Fernández, *Jovellanos*, 150.

206 *Music and Modernity in Enlightenment Spain*

tribute (see example 4.1). In act 2, scene 3, the music of the *bailete* recurs with new lyrics, this time labeled as a chorus. The context for the *bailete* reprise in act 2 is as follows: the Marquis has been seducing the village women, which upsets the men and endangers possible future marriages, hazarding the supply of farming families needed to sustain the rural community. The Marquis is plotting to kidnap Cecilia later that night, yet he falsely promises to put an end to his seductions. The rest of the characters believe his false promises, and thus, the social order is momentarily restored. The reconciliation between landowner and peasants is sealed with music and dance: the villagers sing a chorus honoring the Count, followed by a stick dance interspersed with group recitation.

The stick dance following the *bailete* was Laserna's chance to introduce a traditional show number while portraying *La Cecilia*'s peasants as a modern, orderly social group having healthy fun together. According to the libretto, after the chorus in act 2, scene 3, "Six couples enter the stage to the beat of a march, who form a stick dance, and at the end of each different formation [corresponding to one iteration of the music], the dancers say the following verses [...]; once they are finished, they leave to the beat of the same march."[61] The manuscript score includes a page with two short dances under the title "A march." The first dance is in compound meter and repeats three times—this would be the stick dance, with the peasants changing formations for each repetition and reciting three stanzas in between repetitions. The second dance on the same page of the manuscript score is in duple meter, most likely corresponding to the march for dancers to enter and leave the stage. Dance music in eighteenth-century staged works was frequently used to highlight the dramatic setting and the characters' background.[62] *La Cecilia*'s stick dance is by far the most traditional musical number in both *Cecilias*, drawing attention to the setting of the drama in the Spanish countryside and the peasants' rural character. Stick dances form part of the folklore of nearly every Spanish region, as well as the Spanish Americas; they are highly choreographed, even ritualistic, and are often performed during patron saint festivities. To further emphasize the dance's rustic nature and its relation to popular celebrations, the stanzas

---

[61] Comella, *La Cecilia*, 57.

[62] Reinhard Strohm, *Dramma per musica: Italian Opera Seria of the Eighteenth Century* (New Haven: Yale University Press, 1997), 243. Strohm is talking about dance movements in Metastasian opera sinfonias, yet the same principle applies to this instrumental dance. Strohm goes on to explain that the opera sinfonia (his examples are from Pergolesi, Vinci, and Hasse) expresses "the most important subject matter and characters of the drama, *hierarchically differentiated*." The hierarchy Strohm lays out coincides with that of *La Cecilia*. Thus, "the first movement [of the sinfonia] presents the royal and male subject." This would be *La Cecilia*'s Count, who does not sing but speaks in *arte mayor* declamation akin to that of pastoral eclogues. Cecilia's solo song corresponds to Strohm's second movement of a sinfonia, which presents "a suffering female or conflict with her or within her." Finally, the *bailete pastoral*, chorus, seguidillas, and stick dance, fulfill the function of the third movement, which "catches a glimpse of further characters and their backgrounds" (Strohm, 246).

Bourbon Sentimentalities on the Musical Stage 207

recited in between the dancing include barbarisms (*mosicada* for *musicada*, *beninos* for *benignos*, *endinos* for *indignos*.)

However traditional, *La Cecilia*'s stick dance typifies the collective, public, orderly fun that the Bourbon administration desired and Jovellanos recommended in his *Memoria sobre las diversiones públicas* (*Report on Public Amusements*), which was commissioned by the Spanish Academy of History in 1786, drafted in 1790, and published in 1796. In this report, Jovellanos divided the population into two sectors: those who worked and those who lived a life of leisure. He restated the circulating belief that the government needed to provide entertainment for the latter, but the former must amuse themselves. Jovellanos observed, however, that when the state over-policed public amusements and expressions of happiness such as dances, peasants feared for their safety and stopped gathering to have fun. This prevented peasants from feeling free and motivated enough to do their jobs properly, which led to social unrest and declining productivity. True to physiocratic principles, Jovellanos warned local authorities throughout Spain that

> El estado de libertad es una situación de paz, de comodidad y de alegría: el de sujeción lo es de agitación, de violencia y disgusto: por consiguiente el primero es durable, el segundo expuesto á mudanzas. No basta pues que los pueblos estén quietos: es preciso que estén contentos.... Un pueblo libre y alegre, será precisamente activo y laborioso; y siéndolo, será bien morigerado y obediente á la justicia. Cuanto mas goce, tanto más amará el gobierno en que vive, tanto mejor le obedecerá, tanto mas de buen grado concurrirá á sustentarle y defenderle.[63]

> (Freedom is a state of peace, of comfort and joy, but restriction is a state of agitation, of violence and discontent; therefore, the former endures, but the latter is subject to change. Consequently, it is not enough for people to be at rest; they need to be happy.... Free and happy people will be active and hard-working, and as such, they will be well-behaved and obedient to justice. The more they enjoy life, the more they will love the ruling government; the better they will comply with it, the more enthusiastic and willing they will be to agree to support and defend it.)

In *Memoria sobre las diversiones públicas*, Jovellanos painted a bleak picture of villagers so threatened by police surveillance that they barely ventured out in the public space:

> En los días más solemnes, en vez de la alegría y bullicio que debieran anunciar el contento de sus moradores, reina en las calles y plazas una perezosa inacción, un triste silencio que no se pueden advertir sin admiración ni lástima. Si algunas personas salen de sus casas, no parece sino que el tedio y la ociosidad las echan de ellas, y las arrastran al ejido, al

---

[63] Gaspar Melchor de Jovellanos, *Memoria sobre las diversiones públicas*, Colección Crisol (Madrid: Aguilar 1994), 76–77.

humilladero, a la plaza, o al pórtico de la iglesia, donde, embozados en sus capas, o al arrimo de alguna esquina, o sentados, o vagando acá y acullá sin objeto, ni propósito determinado, pasan tristemente las horas, y las tardes enteras sin espaciarse ni divertirse.[64]

(In the most solemn days [major religious holidays], instead of the joyful hustle and bustle that ought to announce the contentedness of its dwellers, a lazy inactivity reigns on the streets and plazas, a sad silence that cannot go unnoticed without surprise and pity. If anyone leaves their house, it looks like only boredom and idleness prompt them to go out and drag them toward the fields or the small chapels on the village's edges, to the plaza, or to the church's porch, where, covered by their capes, or leaning against a corner, or sitting, or wandering aimlessly, they despondently let the hours go by, and spend entire evenings without any amusements or diversions.)

The working people, Jovellanos argued, must therefore be allowed to pursue fun activities, such as "games of strength, dexterity, or agility; public dances, bonfires, or picnics; strolls, races, parties with costumes or masks; any and all will be good and innocent as long as they are public."[65]

Contrasting sharply with Jovellanos's somber figures, Comella and Laserna's villagers in *La Cecilia* created a convivial public space with their music and dance. Comella packed a bailete, two seguidillas, two peasant songs, a chorus, and the stick dance in a single day in the drama, because he had to comply with the time unity. In having fun and making noise—albeit organized noise—*La Cecilia*'s villagers were the antithesis of the grim reality perceived by Jovellanos. The liveliness of *La Cecilia*'s village is particularly evident in the staging of the bailete and stick dance scene:

Descúbrese la plaza con la fachada del Palacio iluminada, y en el resto del teatro varias luminarias: En el balcón de en medio estarán el Conde, Maldonado, el Marqués, la Marquesa, Beltrán, y demás, y en la plaza Celedonio, Bartolo, y Pascual, mozas y mozos.

(The plaza appears with the palace facade lit up, and around the rest of the theater [stage] are several torches: In the balcony in the middle [of the facade] are the Count, Maldonado and the Marquis, the Marchioness, Beltrán and other servants, and in the plaza Celedonio [the mayor], Bartolo and Pascual, lasses and lads.)

---

[64] Jovellanos, *Memoria*, 72–73.

[65] Jovellanos, *Memoria*, 80–81. Like Jovellanos, Iriarte in *La felicidad de la vida en el campo* (19) praises town dances as a constructive pastime: "In the nearby towns and farmhouses / you can often find / dances and rejoicing / as innocent pastimes." ("No son poco frecuentes / En los cercanos pueblos y cortijos / Los varios pasatiempos de inocentes / bailes y regocijos."

The scene takes place at dusk, but the villagers still have enough energy to assemble to praise their master, thus fulfilling Jovellanos's utopia wherein "men who congregate often to relax and have fun together, will always form a united and affectionate people."[66] The Count, in turn, tolerates their praise as an expression of affection, even though he is not particularly fond of music and dance, as he states immediately after the chorus:

CHORUS:	Esas ardientes teas que al amo se dedican de nuestros corazones el amor simbolizan, deseando a su progenie dichas cumplidas.	These burning torches devoted to the master symbolize the love from our hearts, wishing his progeny fulfilled happiness
Count (spoken):	Todas estas ceremonias, no obstante que las repruebo, me halagan, porque me dicen el afecto de mi Pueblo	Even though I disapprove of all these courtesies, they please me, because they speak of the love of my people.

While the peasants perform the chorus and stick dance down in the village plaza, the Count presides from his palace balcony. Like the good judge Jovellanos describes in his *Memoria sobre las diversiones públicas*, he does not actively participate in village activities but "protects the people during such pastimes, prepares and decorates the venues where they take place, keeps away anything that could disturb them and lets the people fully enjoy the fun and happiness."[67] The music is the same one from the bailete where they cheered the Count for not charging taxes and has the characteristic siciliana rocking pattern indicative of the pastoral ethos of this community.

When Jovellanos in *Memoria sobre las diversiones públicas* asserted that "any and all [small-town leisure activities] will be good and innocent as long as they are public," the key term is "public." By the time *La Cecilia* was written, the Bourbon administration had grown anxious about indoor social activities because women and men could mingle behind the private walls of family homes and mill houses. Local confraternities and associations often organized and sponsored these indoor parties, hosting them beyond the reach of official surveillance and regulation.[68] Jovellanos instead proposed outdoor, communal leisure, which authorities could easily supervise. *La Cecilia*'s music and dance numbers happen

---

[66] Jovellanos, *Memoria*, 77–78.

[67] Jovellanos, *Memoria*, 81.

[68] Pegerto Saavedra, "Ocio y vida cotidiana en la España rural del siglo VIII," in *Trabajo y ocio en la época moderna*, ed. Luis A. Ribot García and Javier Huerta Calvo (Madrid: Actas, 2001), 125, 130–31.

210   *Music and Modernity in Enlightenment Spain*

safely in the public space, reaffirming the peasants' group identity and strengthening community ties while maintaining proper gender separation.

Indeed, the two choral numbers that happen away from the Count's supervision are performed by separate, gender-defined groups. These are the "Canzoneta de payas" in act 1, and "Canzoneta de payos" in act 2, for female and male chorus, respectively. In the female canzonetta of act 1, the peasant girls pick fruit from the village trees, while in the male canzoneta in act 2, the lads return from working in the fields. The term "canzonetta" in Laserna's compositions refers to a simple, cantabile song with rustic pastoral connotations, not meant for dancing.[69] Vocal melodies start on the downbeat, as opposed to those of the dance-based genres of bailete and seguidillas, which start on the upbeat. Neither of the two canzonettas in *La Cecilia* stem from popular tradition directly. Instead, Laserna penned them to emulate traditional songs embellished with orchestral accompaniment, tonal harmonic progressions, and Italianate formal and melodic conventions.[70] These embellishments invoke the pastoral topic. The "Canzoneta de payas," the more Italianate of the two in *La Cecilia* (example 4.2), begins with a siciliana rhythmic pattern (♩♪♩♪) on compound meter, over a pedal simulating a bourdon in the bass, in a moderate allegretto tempo, as befits pastoral music.[71] This female canzonetta presents the folk-inspired trope of a girl confronting her mother in matters of love and marriage matters: "Mother, I earnestly want a fiancé," but Comella writes an original text, and the form is ternary, instead of the more traditional strophic. Likewise, the "Canzoneta de payos" imitates *labrador* songs expressing grief but expands on the melody, phrasing, and harmonic plan of popular tunes. Comella and Laserna's makeover of traditional songs mirrors their revamping of the Spanish rural community. Music and dance in *La Cecilia* shape a proper people, the opposite of the rabble, orderly, but still subservient.

[69]   Both Laserna and his contemporary Pablo Esteve use "canzonetta" in the same way. Most of their canzonettas are in ⁶⁄₈ or ³⁄₈ meter and frequently use siciliana rhythmic patterns in the bass or in the vocal melodies. In contrast, de la Cruz in the 1760s–1770s and Pablo del Moral in the 1790s can use "canzonetta" for a French rustic song. See for example Del Moral's *sainete el tabernero burlado*, where there is a "French" canzonetta in ²⁄₄, followed by a "Spanish" canzonetta in ⁶⁄₈ with a siciliana pattern in the vocal melodies over a bass pedal.

[70]   As Margit Frenk notes, since the second half of the seventeenth century many old traditional songs had become part of the urban repertory, merging with newly composed ones. This makes it difficult to differentiate between anonymous tunes and those traceable to a composer. Frenk, *Nuevo corpus*, 18–19.

[71]   See Monelle, *Musical Topic*, 207ff.

Example 4.2. "Canzoneta de payas," *La Cecilia*, bars 1–7.

212 *Music and Modernity in Enlightenment Spain*

Those Treacherous Seguidillas

In addition to choral numbers and peasant songs, both *La Cecilia* and *Cecilia viuda* feature seguidillas, a popular song and dance genre that hinted at courting because it was danced with a partner. Whereas choruses choreograph an orderly peasantry loyal to their landowner master, seguidillas enact the perils of seduction that jeopardize that orderly community. In *La Cecilia*, the Marquis tries to seduce Cecilia while dancing seguidillas with her. In *Cecilia viuda*, soldiers stationed in the village use the seguidillas to pursue local girls for marriage.

Paradoxically traditional and modern, seguidillas were all the rage in the 1780s and 1790s, whether performed alone or as part of tonadillas or comedias. The genre was traditional because it emulated the music and dance of majas and majos, the prototypical working-class Spaniard of certain Madrid neighborhoods and suburbs whose attire the Madrid aristocrats appropriated in the late eighteenth century. On the flip side, critics attacked seguidillas—especially seguidillas boleras—as a fashionable folly, a useless skill that wealthy young women and men learned to participate in modern socialization The stage seguidilla performer, more often female than male, teased and flirted through their voice and dance. Texts about the licentious consequences of seguidillas abounded during the second half of the eighteenth century. Already in 1767, José Clavijo y Fajardo complained in his periodical *El Pensador* that seguidillas, like contradanzas, were nothing but excuses "to embrace women in public [during private balls], without shame," especially during the ritornello after each sung verse, when the dancers changed positions, brushing against each other as they crossed paths.[72] In 1787, "Discourse 95" of the enlightened periodical *El Censor* ridiculed both the bourgeoisie's conservatism and its penchant for modern fashion under the guise of a mock complaint by a gentleman whose wife refuses to play by the rules of modern sociability. While the wife wants to keep the daughter secluded at home, the husband insists that "his daughter must sing seguidillas [and] dance the fandango as [proficiently as] if she were a theater actress-singer," lest she ends up as a spinster for the lack of flirting skills.[73] Laserna and Comella took the best of both the traditional and the modern worlds for their *Cecilias*, incorporating seguidillas boleras in scenes that involved flirting or mingling of the sexes, while warning of their hazards.

At the same time that critics considered them a modern folly, seguidillas formed a proud part of the national heritage. For example, the 1784 festivities honoring the birth of twin boys to the future Charles IV and the 1783 peace treaty with England over the Florida colonies included a float parade with musicians and dancing troops through the Madrid streets. Several French, English, and American dances were performed aboard the floats, each standing

---

[72] He refers specifically to a contradanza nicknamed *Los Capuchinos*. José Clavijo y Fajardo, "Pensamiento LXXXIV," *El Pensador* 84 (1767).

[73] "Discurso XCV," *El Censor*, 368–69.

Bourbon Sentimentalities on the Musical Stage 213

for the countries involved in the war. The public's favorite numbers were those portraying "joyous Spain:" seguidillas, fandangos, and Galician bagpipes.[74] Seguidillas were included as one of the tokens of Spain for this official event, even though their aura of sensuality clashed with the strict neoclassicist aesthetics of decorum that dictated allegoric float decorations and troupe costumes. The genre would become increasingly valued as a national dance and even the archetypal expression of Spanish creativity and character in the two decades after the *Cecilias* were written.

Unlike choruses or songs, which paint a static tableau to define characters and their environment, seguidillas have a dynamic dramatic function: they develop rather than confirm the course of events. Consisting of a series of sung verses interspersed with ritornellos during which the dancers trade positions, the genre also lent itself to variations within a stable poetic and musical form. For example, in *Cecilia viuda*, the first copla sings the soldiers' viewpoint, while the second states the peasant girls' reprise. When embedded into the structure of a dramatic scene, seguidillas provided continuity and change. The formal characteristics of the seguidillas' music and dance fulfilled this dynamic dramatic purpose.

Danced or sung seguidillas boleras included several stanzas set to the same music. The stanzas could comprise the copla only (four lines), or the copla and estribillo (four plus three lines), as is the case of all the seguidillas in the *Cecilias*. The poetic meter of seguidillas most commonly alternates seven- and five-syllable lines. The uneven verse lengths dynamize the poetic form. In addition, when set to music, each verse line can be fragmented and recombined, generating musical phrases of varying lengths and hence slightly different musical forms. Even though the seguidilla's musical form varies, some traits remain constant: an opening ritornello, a short vocal phrase for the dancers to get in position, and an alternation of sung coplas and short ritornelli. During the coplas, the couple dances a *diferencia*, that is, a particular dance step (see fig. 4.1), and during the short ritornelli, the couple does a *pasar* or *pasacalle*, where the dancers swap positions walking past each other, allowing for a fleeting close-up encounter (see fig 4.2). After two to four *pasacalles* and diferencias, the stanza ends and the music comes to a complete halt, the dancers striking a poised stance known as *bien parado*. Then the next stanza begins and the structure repeats again with new lyrics and new diferencias.

Thus, seguidillas afforded continuously shifting perspectives because the couple changed positions and steps (diferencias) once or twice during each stanza and could switch to a different partner for the new stanza if dancing in a group. After each *pasar*, the dancer who was to the left or to the front moved to the right or the back, and vice versa. Even when the seguidillas were only

---

[74] "Descripción de las fiestas públicas con que la Imperial Villa de Madrid celebró la paz, y el feliz nacimiento de los dos Serenísimos Infantes D. Carlos y D. Felipe en los días 13, 14 y 15 de este mes," *Memorial literario, instructivo y curioso* 2 (July 1784): 75.

Figure 4.1. "Atabalillos en las seguidillas boleras." Atabalillos were one of the diferencias. Marcos Téllez Villar, ca. 1790. Source: Memoria de Madrid. Original from the Museo de Historia de Madrid.

Figure 4.2. "Un pasar en las seguidillas boleras." Dancers walk past each other. Marcos Téllez Villar, ca. 1790. Source: Biblioteca Digital Hispánica. Source: Memoria de Madrid. Original from the Museo de Historia de Madrid.

216 *Music and Modernity in Enlightenment Spain*

sung, the alternation of seven- and five-syllable lines, and the metric adjustment between the four-line copla (7 + 5 + 7 + 5) and the three-line estribillo (5 + 7 + 5) paced the music to fluctuating accents and rhythms. Upper and lower classes alike knew the choreography by heart, because by the second half of the eighteenth century, seguidillas boleras had become part of a repertory of behaviors and attire that Madrid aristocrats appropriated from their co-citizens, the majas and majos. Different forms of the genre were also danced in many regions of Spain beyond Madrid. Because of the widespread familiarity of seguidillas in Spain, the turns and promenades of the dance were inseparable from the listening experience.

Laserna and Comella profited from the asymmetrical nature of the seguidilla form to suggest possible plot complications and to insinuate romantic, even sexual tension. For example, in act 1, scene 4 of *La Cecilia*, the seguidillas are introduced as part of the village festivities honoring the Count, following the praising chorus where the peasants applaud the Count for not taxing them. The seguidillas' narrative function in this scene is to preview the advances of the Marquis toward Cecilia and toward the village women, which will develop in act 2. In the first verse, the peasant ensemble sings an innocent compliment to the fair complexion of the Marchioness (the Count's daughter).

Copla:	Para qué sombrerillo nuestra ama usa, cuando el sol no se atreve con su blancura.	To what end does our mistress wear a hat if the sun does not dare touch her fairness.
Estribillo:	Pues aunque es nieve No es de la que sus rayos derretir pueden.	For even though her complexion is snow it is not of the kind that sunrays can melt.

Despite the lyrics' lack of innuendo, the Marquis says that the music has "tickled" his legs and feet, enticing him to dance. After some spoken dialogue following the first verse, the second verse turns more intimate, sung by a male-female duo while the Marquis and Marchioness dance together. Thereafter, the Marquis seizes the opportunity of the community dance to seek sexual encounters. The third verse of the seguidillas passes off rather uncomfortably, as the Marquis dances with Cecilia "showing restlessness and love in all his moves" according to the libretto, while Cecilia strives to fend him off.[75] In other words, the seguidillas that started as a decent entertainment flattering the Marchioness opened the door to seduction and rape. The Count had cautioned so in his speech at the beginning of the scene:

---

[75] Traditional danced seguidillas have four verses, but there are only three in this scene plus a reprise of the third one.

I loathe these festivities	Yo aborrezco estos festejos
because in milling around	porque a vuelta de las vueltas
carefully, carelessly,	al descuido con cuidado
modesty is trampled on	se atropella la modestia
Thus, even though [it is] inoffensive in itself,	Y así, aunque en sí indiferente,
Bad use taints it	el mal uso lo adultera
though I hope decorum	bien que espero que el decoro
follows from inoffensiveness	seguirá a su indiferencia.

Once advised of the seguidillas' borderline immodesty, the audience would relish the in- vogue dance intertwined with risqué liaisons, while censors would approve of the moral lesson taught by the Count. Seguidillas boleras of the kind performed at theaters, palaces, and balls, were for the most part stylized dance cleaned up of sleazy moves, but the sensual connotations lay latent beneath the surface, threatening to bubble up at any point. This kind of compromise between modern fashion and morality allowed musical plays such as the *Cecilias* to achieve enough success to remain in the city theaters' programs.

Seguidillas also helped portray characters, especially collective ones such as a group of soldiers stationed in *Cecilia viuda*'s village. *Cecilia viuda*'s musical portrayal of commoners differs from that of *La Cecilia* because the sequel introduces military characters in addition to peasants and landowners. While some of *Cecilia viuda*'s musical numbers, like the choruses, incorporate soldiers into the base social group formed by the peasants, others, like two sets of seguidillas in act 1 and act 3, single them out in a class of their own. The seguidillas remark on the dynamics between soldiers and peasants when stationed troops temporarily become part of rural enclaves. More specifically, the seguidillas bring up both the risks and the benefits of marrying a soldier.

In act 1, scene 3 of *Cecilia viuda*, three low-ranking military characters (a corporal, a soldier, and a recruit) appear in uniform and, "with swords under their arms," sing a seguidilla verse applauding their own career choice: soldiers are men of good taste.

Copla:	He who has not served [the army]	El que no ha militado
	in this world	en este mundo,
	is neither a proper man	ni es sujeto de forma,
	nor a man of good taste.	ni de buen gusto.
Estribillo:	For in the military	Que en la milicia
	[even] the coarsest people	las personas más rudas
	get civilized.	se civilizan.

Seguidilla music identifies the soldiers as commoners, but the lyrics, the swords, and the uniforms bestow a certain dignity upon them, rendering

218   *Music and Modernity in Enlightenment Spain*

them desirable yet accessible to the female peasants. The reformist message comes through loud and clear in the estribillo: the military turns a rustic into a civilized citizen. Numerous authors have demonstrated that "to civilize" and "civilization" were double-edged code words for modernization in late eighteenth-century Spain.[76] To become civilized could either mean to renounce one's Spanish essence and go along with modern but questionable behaviors such as cortejos, or to "be educated, to smooth out one's character, condition, rusticity, etc."[77] In *Cecilia viuda*, the soldiers' seguidillas constituted an object of national pride. In the dialogue following the first verse of the seguidilla in act 1, the song is even portrayed as a weapon against English dominance over the American colonies:

> Soldier: Well well well, Mr. Corporal, aren't you always eager to sing.
> Corporal: What else do we have?
> when I was at the Siege of Pensacola
> I scared away bombs this way [singing]
> because they are afraid
> of seguidillas *manchegas*

The Siege of Pensacola took place in 1781 and it was the rare occasion when Spanish troops fended off the British army from West Florida, temporarily asserting domination over this part of the colonies. The image of a Spanish corporal repelling British bombs singing seguidillas was comical but also one of national pride, albeit a resigned pride (what else do we have?).

The second verse of *Cecilia viuda*'s act 1 seguidillas exhorted local girls to marry military men instead of peasants to improve their social standing. Marrying a soldier may not make you rich, sing the soldiers, but it will make you fancier:

Copla:	If the Devil, lass,	Si por querer el Diablo,
	tempts you to love	niña, te tienta,
	seek rosettes instead	busca en vez de polainas
	of spats	escarapelas
Estribillo:	For the rosette's showiness	Que su bambolla,
	will give you honor	si no te da provecho,
	if no other benefit	te dará honra

---

[76]   See, for example, José Escobar, "Civilizar, civilizado y civilización: una polémica de 1763," in *Actas del Séptimo Congreso de la Asociación Internacional de Hispanistas* (Roma: Bulzoni, 1982), 419–27.

[77]   Esteban de Terreros y Pando, *Diccionario castellano con las voces de ciencias y artes y sus correspondientes en las tres lenguas francesa, latina e italiana* (Madrid: Viuda de Ibarra, 1786), 439–40.

Bourbon Sentimentalities on the Musical Stage 219

As in *La Cecilia*, seguidillas were the gateway to romance and sex. However, in this scene of *Cecilia viuda*, the lieutenant Don Fernando, a military officer of higher ranking, thwarts the soldiers' plan to find themselves girlfriends by admonishing the Corporal for singing seguidillas instead of attending Mass. Don Fernando's call for a pious life signaled another Bourbon reformist effort to shed the bad reputation of soldiers to increase recruitment. Ever since the Middle Ages, Spanish soldiers were expected to be devout Catholics because immorality could attract divine wrath leading to defeat in the battlefield. In the eighteenth century, piety was part of the regime's plan to keep military men in good moral shape.[78] Moral instruction books such as the 1788 *Instrucción militar christiana*, which Charles III recommended all Spanish soldiers read, targeted carnal desire, gambling, and drinking among the soldier's worst temptations.[79] Act 1 of *Cecilia viuda* features a seguidilla scene in which the lieutenant Don Fernando and the Corporal enact the archetypes of the virtuous and the dissolute servicemen, respectively, one disapproving of seguidillas, the other finding every opportunity to sing them.

Villagers in rural Spain mistrusted the army not only because soldiers abused the host towns where they were stationed but also because Charles III had recently instituted mandatory military service in 1770, a very unpopular policy.[80] Lieutenant Don Fernando in *Cecilia viuda* keeps a short leash on his soldiers in the hopes that good example will attract worthy voluntary recruits, always in short supply to satisfy the needs of the army. Elsewhere in the play, Don Fernando encourages parents to let their sons enroll.

The soldiers in *Cecilia viuda* temporarily curb their passionate intentions, in order to please their leader after Don Fernando reprimands them in act 1, but they resume the seguidilla game in act 2, scene 4, as they stand in the village plaza watching the lasses walk by. The verses in this scene are set to the same score as those of the first act, perhaps to economize the amount of music Laserna had to write for the play but also threading together the seguidillas in both acts back to the soldiers and their courting of peasant girls. In act 2, the peasant girls fend off the Corporal's unwanted attentions in the seguidilla's second verse:

---

[78] Manuel-Reyes García Hurtado, *El arma de la palabra: Los militares españoles y la cultura escrita en el siglo XVIII (1700–1808)*. (A Coruña: Universidade da Coruña, Servicio de Publicacións, 2002), 434, 441.

[79] *Instruccion militar christiana para el exército y armada de S.M.* (Madrid: Pedro Marín, 1788), 28.

[80] Mandatory military service befell on one out of five men, based on a raffle.

Corporal solo
Copla:

	She who loves a soldier	La que quiere a soldado
	achieves three things:	logra tres cosas:
	high honor, high fame,	mucho honor, mucha fama,
	and plenty of chit-chat	y mucha broma

Estribillo:

	Here's to the good taste	Viva el buen gusto
	of the girl who is not scared	de la que a los soldados
	of soldiers	mira sin susto [score: rinde tributos]

Reprise, female villagers
Copla:

	Three things are achieved	Tres cosas logra aquella
	by the one who loves a soldier:	que ama al soldado:
	plenty of love, plenty of hunger,	mucho amor, mucha hambre,
	and plenty of beatings	y mucho palo

Estribillo:

	Here's to the good taste	Viva el buen gusto
	of the girl who is scared	de la que a los soldados,
	of soldiers	mira con susto [score: rinde tributos]

Near the end of act 2, scene 4, the corporal invites the women to sing again, and they all repeat the estribillo (last three lines) of the seguidilla in amicable camaraderie. In this case, the two seguidilla stanzas present not a developing affair as they do in *La Cecilia* but opposing sides of the same situation: the advantages and disadvantages of marriage to a soldier. The funny but fickle corporal, played at the city theater by the famous comic actor-singer Miguel Garrido, insists that he is a splendid prospective lover, but the local peasant girls reject him so that the benefits of being courted by a soldier remain unclear in the play. The story told by the narrative subthread of the seguidillas in *Cecilia viuda* is outlined in table 4.6.

Comella and Laserna used seguidillas in the two *Cecilias* to make the acts' central scenes enticing and entertaining. They spiced up the play with some romantic intrigue and comedy but kept it at the level of flirtation, except perhaps in the first act of *La Cecilia*, where the erotic moves of the Marquis presaged more serious seduction attempts. Even in those cases when theatrical seguidillas were not danced, body gestures and glances executed the choreography of intergender and interclass dynamics under the surveillance of Bourbon legislators and censors, represented by the Count in *La Cecilia* and by lieutenant Don Fernando in *Cecilia viuda*.

Table 4.6 Narrative thread of seguidillas in Cecilia viuda

Moment		Lyrics	Dance equivalent (my suggestion)
Act 1, scene 3	Stanza 1	Soldiers introduce themselves as civilized, worthy people.	Male partner displays dancing skills
		Spoken dialogue	
Situation moves into romance	Stanza 2	Soldiers present themselves as better romantic material than male peasants.	Male dancer moves closer to female dancer
		Spoken dialogue	
Romantic move truncated by authority	---	No estribillo to close the scene because Don Fernando instructs the corporal to attend Mass instead of singing seguidillas	Stanza cut short
Act 2, scene 4	Stanza 1	Soldiers insist on their advantages as romantic partners.	Male partner takes the lead.
Different opinions	Stanza 2	Peasant girls are not convinced.	Female partner takes the lead.
		Spoken dialogue	
Romantic move neutralized in a friendly manner	estribillo	Soldiers and girls sing together almost at the end of the scene.	Both partners dance around each other.

The Sentimental Musical Tableau

To produce the kind of morally justified entertainment demanded by Bourbon policy and neoclassicist standards, Comella and Laserna created for the two *Cecilias* a series of sentimental tableaux that catered to the spectators' sensibilities. These tableaux happen during musical numbers and passages in heightened speech, for example, the village girls singing while picking chestnuts or the Count reciting estancia verses as he delights in his rural retreat. In these sentimental tableaux, music, poetry, and visuals joined forces to bring in-vogue sentimentality closer to home by conjuring up conventional images and discourses familiar to Madrid spectators. These familiar images and discourses drew from a web of signification that blended foreign and national canons. Whereas *La Cecilia*'s tableaux paint Arcadian scenes of rural Spain with an emphasis on productivity and virtue, *Cecilia viuda*'s tableaux highlight the contemplation of nature.

English and French sentimental plays and novels from the second half of the eighteenth century abound with moments where description prevails over the narrative to elicit an emotional response from the spectator. These descriptive moments, or tableaux, made room for aesthetic contemplation and affective reaction by freezing an instant or by stopping action.[81] Hence, their function can be compared to that of traditional operatic arias, with the difference that tableaux' aural elements often have visual counterparts. Tableaux' visuals could be presented simultaneously with the text or the music, for example, when an onstage song was accompanied by sets and costumes or when a sentimental novel included engravings the reader could look at while reading the book. The visuals could also be produced afterward, inspired by the text of the music. For example, Joseph Highmore's series of twelve *Pamela* paintings from the 1740s, and the ensuing engravings, both posterior to Samuel Richardson's novel, told the Pamela saga at a glance, taking for granted the viewer's acquaintance with the story. The visual component could also precede the written music or text, for example in moral anecdotes in which short tales were written to accompany a preexisting picture.[82] Sentimentality was thus a literary language that coupled action with static pictorial compositions or tableaux.

To elicit an emotional response, sentimental tableaux allowed the spectator to quickly connect the scene at hand to a web of references ranging from other plays and novels to paintings, to nonfictional discourses such as policy or sermons. This web of references shared common signs representing pathos, signs that were familiar enough to late eighteenth century European middle- and upper-class audiences that they could easily interpret them when they saw or heard them, whether alone or combined.[83] As authors resorted to these con-

---

[81] Anne Patricia Williams "Description and Tableau in the Eighteenth-Century British Sentimental Novel," *Eighteenth-Century Fiction* 8, no. 4 (July 1996): 478.

[82] Williams, "Description and Tableau," 466.

[83] Williams, "Description and Tableau," 478.

ventional signifiers of pathos to prompt a reaction, spectators felt a sense of belonging to a group as they were able to grasp that web of references. With respect to sentimental literature and theater, "getting" the tableau implied that you were in tune with modern European ideas about what it meant to be human. Some sentimental signifiers embedded in tableaux held meaning across nations, for example, tilted heads or bodies, closed eyes, tears, or arms reaching out. Yet others varied from place to place, depending on national tastes and social norms. Bedroom scenes ubiquitous in French engravings of the time would be unconceivable in Spain, and the English were more prone to picturesque outdoor settings than the French.

In the case of the *Cecilias*, referents embedded in musical and heightened-speech tableaux cluster around three interpretive axes: pastoralism, sentimentality, and Bourbon policy. The first part of this chapter discussed allusions to agricultural Bourbon policy dressed in pastoral garb. The following section focuses on contemplation of nature and sentimental tableaux. To understand the web of sentimental references within which Laserna and Comella operated, I briefly correlate *La Cecilia*'s musical representation of peasants with a popular engraving series, then analyze two engravings and two musical tableaux from *Cecilia viuda*.

Bucolic Tableaux in La Cecilia

La Cecilia's bucolic songs, which include the two canzonettas of payas and payos, take place in nature, among the trees in orchards or farming fields. The outdoor settings for the payas and payos, in conjunction with the canzonettas' pastoral music, were meant to delight and instruct spectators with a *costumbrismo* snapshot, part pastoral proto-folklore depicting national types, part political propaganda for Bourbon agricultural policy promoting hard-working rural communities. According to stage directions, the payas wore straw hats and held baskets with freshly picked fruit while they sung their canzonetta. For their part, the payos sang theirs "with winnowing rakes on their shoulders." These bucolic tableaux emulated and also inspired the picturesque portraits of the rural and urban working poor widely circulated in late eighteenth- and early nineteenth-century Spain through engraving series depicting women and men from different Spanish regions wearing the local attire, and urban characters such as street vendors or *petimetras*. The earliest of such engraving series is the *Colección de trajes de España* by brothers Manuel (drawings) and Juan (engravings) de la Cruz Cano y Olmedilla (issued 1777–1788). Spanish painters interested in picturesque aesthetics preferred national popular types over landscapes.

Graphic, literary, and performing arts supplied each other with visual and auditive images for creating national types. Tellingly, the brothers' de la Cruz Cano y Olmedilla's *Colección de trajes* includes portraits of Madrid famed actress- and actor-singers such as Miguel Garrido, La Caramba, and Joseph

224 *Music and Modernity in Enlightenment Spain*

Espejo. The popular types found in visual art were also influenced by Spanish *costumbrista* drama, including Ramón de la Cruz's sainetes and zarzuelas—not by coincidence, the playwright was the older brother of painter Manuel and engraver Juan. The brothers' collection includes only a few depictions of peasants (see fig. 4.3, paya holding a basket), but later series abound in them. By the early nineteenth century, the winnowing rakes Comella suggested for the "Canzoneta de payos" became quite standard in drawings of male peasants.[84] Like the peasants of *La Cecilia* and *Cecilia viuda*, painted national characters were idealized stereotypes of real people that writers and painters saw as essentially Spanish. Because popular types represented the nation, picturesque engravings and paintings would "decisively contribute to the formation of Spain's modern image during the romantic age."[85] Over the centuries, Manuel and Juan de la Cruz Cano y Olmedilla's blend of popular types with regional attires would reify into clichés of Spanishness, but in the 1780s Manuel's drawings were a novelty, related to efforts to capture and publicly display the national essence.

There are similar proto-folkloric, bucolic tableaux in *Cecilia viuda*, such as a chorus in the second act where the stage is transformed into a chestnut grove where the peasants shake the trees for nuts while they sing about the "honest tiredness" of the poor who work indefatigably to earn their sustenance.[86]

Contemplation of Nature and the Sublime in the Overture to Cecilia viuda

In addition to bucolic tableaux, *Cecilia viuda* featured a new kind of tableau that highlighted the human experience of and control over nature. Gaspar Melchor de Jovellanos's writings connect the experience of nature to sensibility and the Bourbon project for an enlightened society. He presented the contemplation of nature as part of the process of becoming a civilized Spaniard who respects natural resources. Eighteenth-century agricultural and economic reforms attempted to rectify the unregulated exploitation of the colonies' natural resources that the Bourbons inherited from the Habsburg era, because the unrestrained extractive economy was contributing to the Spanish empire's decline. To recover from the crisis, Charles III's regime deemed it necessary to

---

[84] See *Colección general de los trajes que en la actualidad se usan en España* by Antonio Rodríguez and Joseph Vázquez (1801). Also *Colección de Trajes de España* by José Rivelles and Juan Carrafa (1825). Both are displayed at the Fundación Joaquín Díaz in Urueña, Valladolid, Spain.

[85] Antonio Dorca, "Mesonero Romanos y el cuadro de costumbres ilustrado: 'La posada o España en Madrid,'" in *El costumbrismo, nuevas luces*, ed. Dolores Thion Soriano-Mollá (Pau: Presses de l'Université de Pau et des Pays de l'Adour, 2013), 161–62.

[86] Luciano Francisco Comella, *Cecilia viuda*, 3rd ed. ([Madrid]: Librería de Cerro, 1790 [1787]), 13.

Figure 4.3. "Paya/Paissane." Juan de la Cruz Cano y Olmedilla, 1777–1778.
Source: Biblioteca Nacional de España.

226   *Music and Modernity in Enlightenment Spain*

change economic policy and alter the mentality of the nobility and the clergy, who, as the major landowners, had accumulated vast amounts of wealth that remained stagnant. To counteract older tenets of extractive economy, enlightened thinkers and politicians in the last third of the eighteenth century, like Jovellanos, promoted a reconciliation with the natural world. This new relation to nature demanded the rational use and distribution of plants, animals, and minerals through a streamlined, centralized economy meant to avoid the concentration of riches in any man or family other than the king. Natural science founded on empirical observation should indicate the optimal avenues for this improved exploitation of nature, which was meant to enhance the productivity needed to modernize the nation. This vision of nature as a useful resource fit into the physiocratic economic model and worked well with the Christian notion that God created humankind to dominate the world. In terms of aesthetics, the Spanish neoclassicists valued contemplation of nature in the service of agriculture and economy as an antidote to baroque artificiality and to the speculative presumptions of scholasticism.

Nature-inspired musical tableaux in *Cecilia viuda* merged confidence in the human ability to preside over creation with the interest of 1770s–1780s European artists in the sublime. This approach to natural scenes is manifested from *Cecilia viuda*'s start. In contrast with *La Cecilia*'s overture-less first scene with its intimate, domestic vignette zooming in on Cecilia spinning thread under the trees, *Cecilia viuda* begins with the sun dawning on the village as an overture animates the change from night to day:

> Part of the village; buildings to the left, and forest to the right: a mountain in the background: night with the moon low on the horizon soon to come down, and it will seem as if the day breaks, the theater gradually lightening: a sweet symphony (*sinfonia*) will mimic [first the tranquility of the] night, then dawn, then sunrise, and will end with the cries of the peasants going to the chestnut grove [this symphony will be inside]. Enter Don Fernando, who gazes at the sky, and then says: "already the break / of dawn begins to dispel / the dark of night / with traces of light."[87]

In *Cecilia viuda*'s "dawn" overture, Comella experimented with the expressive power of instrumental music within the limits of mimesis. Mimesis lay at the core of neoclassicist aesthetics, which dominated official artistic discourse in late-Enlightenment Spain. Although Ignacio de Luzán, the father of Spanish neoclassicism, frowned upon the inclusion of music in drama in his 1737 *Poetics* because he considered music inferior to poetry, attitudes toward music's artistic value had started to change in the second half of the eighteenth century. According to Charles Batteux's influential aesthetic treatise of 1746, *Les beaux arts réduits a un même principe*, music could reach the status of fine

---

[87]   Comella, *Cecilia viuda*, 1. Text in brackets is found in the first and second editions of the libretto for *Cecilia viuda* (1787, 1789), but not in the third one (1790).

Bourbon Sentimentalities on the Musical Stage

art, comparable to painting and poetry, when it imitated nature.[88] Batteux's revaloration of music on par with the other arts made its way to Spanish neo-classicist author Tomás de Iriarte's 1779 didactic poem *La música*. Iriarte's poem confirmed that music could imitate nature as powerfully as the other arts.[89] Comella adhered to mimetic principles by having each section of the overture tied to changes in the stage lighting designed to copy a natural event: the day's beginning.

Comella's guidelines for how music should imitate dawn were loose; it was up to Laserna to concretize them into an actual score. The composer interpreted Comella's opening "sweet symphony" as a two-movement Italian overture of about four and a half minutes total. The first and longer movement is a cut-time allegro played by the orchestra, while the second movement is a triple-meter andantino played onstage by a small ensemble of two violas and a flute. Laserna did not invent this layout of a contrasting duple-meter, allegro first movement and a triple-meter, subdued second movement. Similar layouts are found in several of Jommelli's overtures, such as *L'Uccellatrice* (1750), *Didone abbandonata* (1747, 1749, 1763) and *Vologeso* (1766). Piccinni often used a similar template, for example in the overtures for *Cattone in Utica* and, more relevant to the *Cecilias*, for *La buona figliuola* (1760). What *was* Laserna's own idea was to apply this tried-and-true musical design to Comella's visualization of a stage reproduction of the sunrise. The scene is a true tableau, a multimedia experience without words: pure sensation and emotion.

Laserna's first movement depicts the struggle between night and dawn, while the second movement corresponds to sunrise and daylight, the moment when humans appear on the stage and occupy the natural world. Like many other Italian overtures, the one Laserna wrote for *Cecilia viuda* is in D major. The musical style resembles that of Jommelli's overtures, whose first-movement crescendos Stamitz would later rework into the early symphonic sound of Mannheim. Laserna's allegro first movement starts with unison arpeggios and bow strokes over a conspicuous D pedal in the bass, followed by a simple theme with a triplet motive, first in the tonic, then in the dominant A major. The tonic-dominant transition happens over a "Mannheim roller" crescendo from piano to fortissimo (example 4.3, bars 8–17). This first section does not correlate to any specific time of the day, instead grabbing the listener's attention.

Once the dominant is confirmed, there is a full rest (example 4.4, bar 26) before a new section in D minor begins, meant to represent the night's calm. The D minor passage features a lean texture of staccato strings and woodwinds playing piano over a sparse bass. With a sudden forte on bar 49, the

---

[88]   Charles Batteux, *Les beaux arts réduits a un même principe* (Paris: Durand, 1747), 283–84.

[89]   Tomás de Iriarte, *La musica: Poema* (Madrid: Imprenta Real de La Gaceta, 1779), 6.

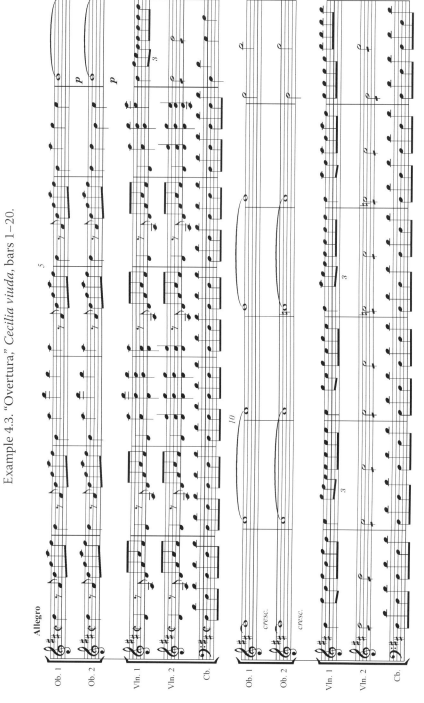

Example 4.3. "Overtura," *Cecilia viuda*, bars 1–20.

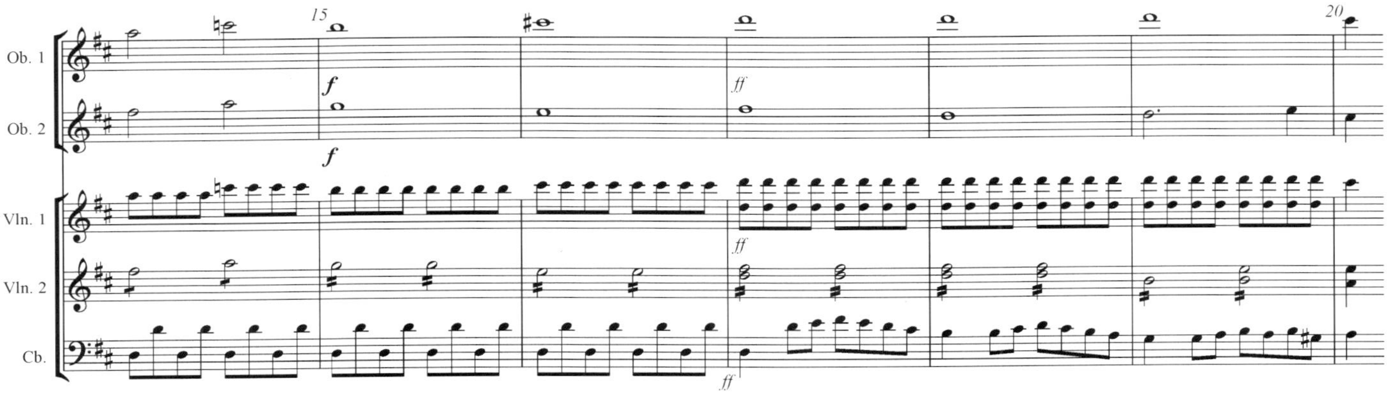
15
20
Ob. 1
Ob. 2
Vln. 1
Vln. 2
Cb.
f
f
ff
ff
ff

Example 4.4. "Overtura," *Cecilia viuda*, bars 26–34.

Bourbon Sentimentalities on the Musical Stage 231

stillness of the night turns into a struggling transition via a ten-bar sequential passage where the violins play relentless sixteenth notes in counterpoint with the bass. The texture thickens considerably. After some chromaticism, including an augmented Italian sixth (example 4.5, bar 57) and a unison scale with a melodic augmented second (example 4.5, bars 59–63), the harmony settles on the dominant A major, signaling the dawn. However, the day has not yet vanquished the night, and after a strong A major cadence on bars 66–72, the forte sixteenth notes in the violins return, veering the music toward B minor (example 4.5, bars 73–76). The first movement ends inconclusively with a unison B minor arpeggio: morning is imminent but not yet there (example 4.6).

Light finally arrives during the triple-meter second movement andantino. The andantino picks up on B minor, where the allegro left off, and progresses back to D major through a sequence and a dominant pivot chord (example 4.7, bars 100–3). It is a short, sweet da capo movement. The "cries of the peasants going to the chestnut grove" described by Comella were probably heard toward the end of the da capo repetition, already firmly on D. As the peasant voices are heard, lieutenant Don Fernando enters the stage alone to start reciting his verses. Whereas night's chaos and dawn's struggle are the empty village's sounds, the calm of sunrise accompanies the human presence.

Cecilia viuda's two-part overture also served to demarcate the public and private spaces, transporting the listening audience from the expected overture style with the orchestra performing in its usual spot to a more intimate second movement, played by a trio located close to the set, yet hidden from view. The implied listeners for the first movement were those sitting (or standing) in the audience, but the second movement addresses the characters onstage. The music's source literally moves onto the stage for the second movement, as the off-stage orchestra remains tacet to be replaced by a backstage ensemble of two violas and a solo flute. According to the score, the ensemble should play "up[stairs], in the dressing rooms," which means that the full orchestra (violins, oboes, flutes, clarinet, bassoon, horns, double bass and continuo) for the first movement was located downstairs on the floor of the theater. The clever combination of an open space (part of the village against the forest and a mountain) with the small chamber ensemble suited Comella and Laserna's pastoral and sentimental fusion in the two *Cecilias*. Laserna led the audience from an overture and symphonic sound characteristic of the public space—bow strokes, theme in the tonic then in the dominant, Mannheim "roller"—to a contemplation of humans in nature as the stage progressively lit up so they could see Don Fernando wander in "gazing at the sky" and hear the villagers' voices in the background. Thus, the second movement aurally matched Don Fernando's gaze, letting the audience partake into his experience of the daybreak and feel the enthusiasm of the peasants merrily starting the new day.

While the overture allegro recreates the sublime force of nature, the solo flute in the andantino recreates the human being dawning on the world.

Example 4.5. "Overtura," *Cecilia viuda*, bars 43–76.

Example 4.6. "Overtura," *Cecilia viuda*, bars 82–86.

Don Fernando and the peasants represented human beings existing in and contemplating nature, not exploring their own internal drama. In Jommelli's and Piccinni's operas, two-movement Italian overtures were often followed by an aria that served as the third movement, but in this case only Don Fernando's monologue confirmed what the music suggested: "Already the break / Of dawn begins to dispel / The dark of night / With traces of light." The experience of daybreak conveyed in the overture andantino supported mimesis because it portrayed a generic rather than an individual reaction to an external reality. As we will see by the end of this chapter, the gap between generic and individual aesthetic experience sets late Spanish Enlightenment apart from other European trends, most notably German Sturm und Drang. Laserna made Comella's indications for a night-to-day transition a struggle back and forth between major and minor tonalities, bringing the overture's imagery a step closer to the narrative of creation: first there was chaos-night, then there was light, and finally, there were humans populating the earth.

Laserna wrote very few overtures for comedias, so there is little context to understand why he used a musical style similar to that of Jommelli and Piccinni for *Cecilia viuda*. By the time he composed the music for the *Cecilias*, Spanish theaters were programming works by Giovanni Paisiello, Domenico Cimarosa, Pasquale Anfossi, Giuseppe Gazzaniga, and their contemporaries.[90] Jommelli's and Piccinni's operas were in Madrid's court opera's repertory during Farinelli's tenure under Ferdinand VI (1746–1759), and for some time after Farinelli left Madrid, before Charles III ceased operatic productions at the royal palaces in 1777. We can only speculate about Laserna's choice of this older Italian overture style. Considering the success of Cimarosa's *L'italiana in Londra* (1785) and Paisiello's *La serva padrona* (1786) and *Il barbiere di Siviglia* (1787), sung by Spanish performers in the Madrid public theaters where Laserna worked, it is hard to imagine he was not familiar with newer models. Laserna may have had in mind Piccinni's overtures for *La buona figliuola* and *La buona figliuola maritata*, prototypes of sentimental opera well known to Spanish composers and audiences. It is also possible that the truncated fast-slow-(fast) plan was better suited to imitate the night-day passage and to highlight the pastoral component, especially because Jommelli wrote several second movements in triple meter, with light instrumentation, using pastoral conventions.

---

[90] For a full list of all court and commercial Italian operas performed in Madrid during the eighteenth and nineteenth centuries, see Luis Carmena y Millán, *Crónica de la ópera italiana en Madrid desde el año 1738 hasta nuestros días* (Madrid: Impr. de M. Minuesa de los Rios, 1878).

Example 4.7. "Overtura," *Cecilia viuda*, measures 86–109.

References to Neoclassicist Aesthetics

Laserna may have had yet another reason to refer to Jommelli's overtures for *Cecilia viuda*'s nature-inspired opening tableaux: Jommelli had Tomás de Iriarte's approval in *La música*. Iriarte had a secure place in the late eighteenth-century neoclassicist circles that dominated Spain's Republic of Letters, to which both Laserna and Comella aspired (in vain) to belong. *La música*'s fourth canto is devoted to theater music. In it, the poetic narrator laments not being able to travel in time to witness firsthand how the ancient Greeks wedded poetry and music. Pondering such a lack of guiding prototypes, the narrator falls asleep, and none other than the recently deceased Jommelli appears in his dreams, surrounded by Greek and Roman musicians in the Elysian Fields. In *La música*, Jommelli's mission in the afterlife is to update the pantheon of illustrious composers and musicians on the current state of music in European theaters (fig. 4.4).[91] To this end, Jommelli describes for them each of the elements of opera—which Iriarte refers to as melodrama—starting with the sinfonia.

The role of the orchestra in the sinfonia, Jommelli instructs in *La música*, is to generate harmony and order out of the chaos of instrumental sounds, and once that harmony is well established, to dispose the listener toward the drama. In Iriarte's words, the overture must "not only quiet the hubbub of the rabble" but also "move to some affection or announce an image" related to the first scene. (However, it should not summarize forthcoming musical themes, for imitation does not work retroactively). Overture for Iriarte meant the three-part (allegro, andante, presto) Italian standard, "long used" (since the seventeenth century) to announce different dramatic situations.[92] According to *La música*, many composers misused the three-part plan so that none of the movements actually prepared the audience for the drama, Jommelli being "one of the few" who had avoided such misuse. The "solid and prudent maestro," Iriarte wrote, "conciliates the listener's attention" (first movement of the overture) and primes their mood (second and third movements) for the action to come. Ideally, Iriarte continues, the overture composer follows Theon of Samos, the ancient Greek painter who had musicians play a blast of trumpets before unveiling his painting of a soldier in the act of running into battle before a large crowd. Once the trumpet blast had inspired Theon's audience "with martial heroism," the painter disclosed the image and thus "the illusion [of the soldier going to war] was greatly increased."[93] Similarly to Theon of Samos's aural and visual experiment, the sinfonia must enhance the mimetic illusion of

---

[91] Iriarte, *La música*, 79.

[92] Iriarte, *La música*, 84.

[93] Ernest Gombrich cited by J. M. Cocking, *Imagination: A Study in the History of Ideas* (London: Routledge, 1991), 31. Iriarte possibly took Theon of Samos's allegory from his teacher, chapel master and composer Antonio Rodríguez de Hita, who included the anecdote in the preface to his theoretical treatise *Diapasón Instructivo* (1757).

Figure 4.4. "Jommelli before the very solemn assembly [of composers and musicians] / thus expounded the character / and progress of musical theater."
Source: Tomás de Iriarte, *La música: Poema* (Madrid, 1779).
Digital image: The British Museum.

240   *Music and Modernity in Enlightenment Spain*

musical theater, making the spectators feel they are inhabiting the space created by the drama.

An engraving opposite the title page of *Cecilia viuda*'s printed libretto for the Mortara performance (1787) evinces how much Comella, and quite possibly Laserna, were in tune with Iriarte's neoclassicist aesthetics (figure 4.5). The engraving, by Madrid printer Rafael Bausac, portrays a laureate Greek or Roman man showing a large painting. The man holds the artwork with his left hand, and a painting brush with his right hand over the painting. He could represent Theon revealing a painting to the audience or simply evoke classical antiquity as the source for mimetic art. The laurel wreath crowning him suggests he is a poet, one who paints with words, the *ut pictura poiesis* of Horace's *Ars poetica*.

The framed painting within the engraving summarizes the aesthetic and moral ideals behind the *Cecilias* in a tripersonal mythological composition. At the center stands a syncretic goddess figure, mainly reminiscent of Athena/ Minerva holding a shield and stake in one hand, a wreath in the other. Her head is crowned with a half-moon and big ivy leaves instead of a helmet, attributes respectively associated with Diana, the hunter (moon), and with Thalia, the muse of comedy (ivy). These attributes balance Minerva's combative side with her wisdom and patronage of the arts and connect her to German painter Anton Raphael Mengs's depiction of Apollo in his fresco *El Parnaso* (1761, see fig. 4.6), an emblem of Spanish neoclassicism that Mengs completed right before Charles III appointed him to work for the Madrid court.

The goddess in *Cecilia viuda*'s engraving stands on a cloud atop a pedestal that reads "*Munero diversioni simplisi* [sic]," "I offer simple entertainment." Several musical instruments emerge from the cloud at the feet of the composite Minerva: guitar, trumpet, and horn to the right, and the more learned bowed instruments and lyre to the left. From the lyre sprouts what looks like a flowering rod, an attribute of Saint Joseph perhaps hinting at the marchioness of Mortara's first name, Josefa. To the left of the goddess stands a female figure in royal garb, offering a large book to Minerva, the spine of which reads "Calderón [de la Barca]." The crowned female figure holding the book represents the City of Madrid. She is positioned in front of a tower denoting Castile and with a dog under her foot to symbolize fidelity to the king.[94] As the birthplace of seventeenth-century luminary playwright Calderón de la Barca, the City of Madrid presents his works to Minerva, taking inspiration from the goddess to provide virtuous entertainment for the court's subjects.[95]

---

[94] See Francisco de Goya, *Alegoría de la Villa de Madrid*, 1808, and Francisco Folch y Carmona, *Retrato alegórico del Conde de Floridablanca*, 1787, with a very similar female figure representing Murcia, his birthplace.

[95] According to Jovellanos, it fell on the government to provide recreational activities for city dwellers: Jovellanos, *Memoria para el arreglo de la policía de los espectáculos y diversiones públicas y sobre su origen en España* (Alicante: Biblioteca Virtual Miguel de Cervantes, 1999), https://www.cervantesvirtual.com/nd/ark:/59851/bmcqv3h2.

Figure 4.5. Engraving opposite of title page of *Cecilia viuda* libretto, 1787.
Source: Biblioteca Nacional de España.

Figure 4.6. *Parnassus* detail. Anton Raphael Mengs, after 1761.
Source: Alamy (Image ID: 2A84M9R).

The male figure at the right of the goddess holds two peculiar items that connect him to the tradition of Spanish pastoral literature of the sixteenth and seventeenth centuries. He has a noose around his neck and a dagger in his right hand, an image taken from a passage in Miguel de Cervantes's pastoral novel *La Galatea* (1585).[96] In Cervantes's passage, the shepherd, kneeling down and dagger in hand, threatens to kill himself while desperately clinging to his beloved shepherdess's shawl as she rejects him (fig. 4.7). Cervantes's episode of the shepherd in love flawlessly matches the sentimental tableaux that Comella and Laserna pursued in the *Cecilias*. In *La Galatea*, the incident is narrated from the perspective of a group of shepherds and shepherdesses observing the scorned lover from behind the bush, at the instance of his sister. Distressed by her brother's lovesickness, the young lass happens upon a bucolic group in the forest and appeals to them, crying—come, look, be moved, and have mercy:

> Si por ventura hay entre vosotros, señores, quien de los extraños efectos y casos de amor tenga alguna noticia, y las lágrimas y suspiros amorosos le suelen enternecer el pecho, acuda quien esto siente a ver si es posible remediar y detener las más amorosas lágrimas y profundos suspiros que jamás de ojos y pechos enamorados salieron. Acudid, pues, pastores, a lo que os digo: veréis cómo, con la experiencia de lo que os muestro, hago verdaderas mis palabras.[97]

> (If there is, by chance, among you sirs, one who has any notion of the strange cases and effects of love, and whose bosom often shivers with amorous tears and sighs, he who thus feels come and see if it is possible to remedy and stop the most amorous tears and deepest sighs to ever come out of eyes and bosoms in love. Come ye, shepherds, to [see] what I say: you shall see how, by experiencing what I show you, I make my words come true.)

Two centuries later, Comella could have used her exact words to appeal to the sensibility of his audience.

Artist and printer José Antonio Ximeno y Carrera captured Cervantes's scorned shepherd scene in a drawing from a series he created for the 1784 Madrid edition of *La Galatea* (fig. 4.9).[98] In the background of Ximeno y Car-

---

[96] "And they saw that a shepherdess was under a green willow tree, dressed as a hunting nymph,.... The shepherd kneeled before her, with a string around his neck and a bare knife in his right hand, and with his left he held the shepherdess from a white sendal she wore on top of her clothes. She was frowning.... with great effort she tried to break loose from the shepherd's hand, who, with abundant tears, loving and tender words, begged her to give him the chance to represent the sorrow he suffered because of her. But the shepherdess, disdainful and angry, moved away from him." Miguel de Cervantes y Saavedra, *La Galatea*, vol. 4 (Madrid: Juan de Zúñiga, 1736), 205.

[97] Cervantes, *La Galatea*, vol. 4, 205.

[98] Miguel de Cervantes y Saavedra, *Los seis libros de Galatea. Dividida en dos tomos. Corregida e ilustrada con láminas finas* (Madrid: Antonio de Sancha, 1784).

Figure 4.7. *El pastor enamorado a los pies de Gelasia*, José Antonio Ximeno y Carrera, ca. 1784. Source: Biblioteca Nacional de España.

rera's drawing we can see the scorned shepherd's sister pointing at him to the onlookers, who peek from among the trees without being seen. "Lacrimous" describes this tableau well: the suicidal lover speaks "with so many tears and sobs" that everybody who listened was "moved to compassion."[99] Bausac's engraving for *Cecilia viuda*'s 1787 printed libretto print interpreted *La Galatea*'s passage as a Spanish foreshadowing of sentimentality, a national pastoral allegory at a time when pastoralism enjoyed the favor of the neoclassicists and could easily be connected with the government's agricultural focus.

Invoking Cervantes's pastoralism in this engraving, like invoking Jommelli's style in the overture, gave *Cecilia viuda* a veneer of respectability for the authorities' and the neoclassicists' judgment while engaging spectators through fashionable sensibility. The scorned shepherd's presence in the engraving on *Cecilia viuda*'s title page strengthened Comella and Laserna's ties to the Spanish pastoral canon, avoiding too much indebtedness to foreign sentimental works, whether English novels, French theater, or Italian opera. This nationalistic veneer camouflaged *Cecilia viuda*'s daring sentimental scenes under the guise of an homage to Spanish cultural production, thus rendering it acceptable for censors. The Real Academia Española had recently published Cervantes's *Quijote* in 1780, bestowing official sanction on this once undervalued novel, and the 1784 edition of *La Galatea* was dedicated to the count of Floridablanca, secretary of state. Other aspects of the engraving also pay respect to neoclassicism and to Spanish identity. For example, of the three books that are included in the composition, Corneille and Racine lay on the ground, while Calderón is upheld by the female figure on the left. The suicidal shepherd is dressed in a classical tunic, rather than in seventeenth-century fashion like Ximeno's (see fig. 4.7) and holds a threshing pole under his foot, coupling pastoral imagery with the agricultural concerns of the Bourbon administration.

Both the overture and the title page engraving prepare *Cecilia viuda*'s audience to feel and judge the events that will take place in the play. Once the play starts, neoclassicist ideals yield at points to decidedly sentimental ones. While pastoralism and sentimentality pervade both *Cecilias*, *Cecilia viuda* ventures further into intense feeling, and Comella experiments more with new literary and dramatic trends. For example, in the last scene of the play Cecilia "storms in, her hair down, beside herself [*fuera de sí*], and throws herself at the Marquis's feet" demanding justice for the crimes of Don Nicasio (the bad administrator). The Marchioness observes that "sorrow has rendered her [Cecilia] a statue," emphasizing the frozen-time quality of the moment.[100] Shortly afterward, Cecilia's body falters as a consequence of what seemed to be poisoning but turns out to be anguish. Throughout the play, men and women alike shiver with emotion and shed tears in reaction to Cecilia's virtue. The Marchioness, for one, "confesses that Cecilia has touched her heart" with her affliction. Don

---

[99]   Cervantes, *La Galatea*, vol. 4, 205.

[100]   Comella, *Cecilia viuda*, 29.

246 *Music and Modernity in Enlightenment Spain*

Fernando weeps when Cecilia, in a magnanimous gesture of forgiveness, burns a letter describing Don Nicasio's crimes.[101] This last event is highlighted in a second engraving found before the first act (fig. 4.8, from left to right: Don Fernando, the Marchioness, the Marquis, Cecilia). These nonmusical tableaux must have struck the audience as boldly modern, comparable to those yet to come in Paisiello's *Nina* or in Goya's feminine drawings from the 1790s—see, for example, *Young Woman Fainting in the Arms of an Officer.*[102]

Jovellanos and the Awe of Nature

Whereas sentimental tableaux, such as the one where Cecilia burned evidence of her abuser's transgressions, happen frequently at climactic points of both *Cecilias*, those highlighting the experience of nature's greatness, such as the overture, are particular to *Cecilia viuda*. In the overture, the second movement's pastoral music restores Arcadian order to the first movement's unbridled nature represented in the night-to-dawn struggle. Comella and Laserna use the same musical strategy to invoke the sublime power of nature at the core of the play, in scene 2 of act 2.

The scene opens with a lush chestnut grove where the peasants sing a chorus extolling the virtues of hard work as they shake the trees to harvest chestnuts. Soon enough, clouds overcast the sky, imperiling the fruitful collaboration between people and nature. In response, the cast sings what is marked in the score as a "storm chorus." The D major chorus pleads to God and the heavens for mercy, because, as the peasants claim, "the fury of thunder, the harshness of lightening, make my vitality faint." Pastoral serenatas, wildly popular in the Madrid court of the 1760s–1770s, often took "nature arias" as an opportunity to introduce flashy instrumental realism, a tradition that Laserna recovered in his music for this storm chorus. The storm's danger rumbles through a chromatic passage leading to the dominant A major (bars 46–56), complete with modal mixture and a root-position Neapolitan chord. Overall, the storm chorus sounds more like a galant version of a Rameau *tempête* than Austro-German Sturm und Drang music. The strings play plenty of sixteenth notes and scalar runs to a brisk duple meter with sudden changes in dynamics, sometimes moving from forte to piano within the same bar. Nonetheless, in other respects *Cecilia viuda*'s storm chorus is very far from those of *tragédie lyrique*. Peasants take the dramatic place of heroes and monsters, and the forces of nature commanded by the Christian God replace mythological deities. The ensemble sings the chorus to placate divine ire because the menacing storm inspires fear of the latter days in the Marquis.

---

[101] Comella, *Cecilia viuda*, 30, 32

[102] Goya's sketches of women are collected in the Sanlúcar album.

Figure 4.8. "Perdonando y a las llamas entregando este testigo." Engraving opposite the first page of act 1, *Cecilia viuda* libretto, 1787. Source: Biblioteca Nacional de España.

248   *Music and Modernity in Enlightenment Spain*

Because both the neoclassicists and Charles III frowned upon and even banned superstition on stage, playwrights and composers had to find new ways to bring the thrill of the spectacular to audiences, and in the case of the storm chorus, substituting supernatural powers with natural ones. Neither furies from hell nor monsters of any kind would have made it through Spanish censors of the second half of the eighteenth century. Accordingly, the visuals during the storm chorus evoke the picturesque instead of the underworld: the Marquis and his lackey hide in a hollow chestnut when they hear thunder roar while the stage darkens. Laserna made sure to amplify the sound of thunder and bring realism to the scene by having the orchestra play on the stage for this scene. Even though there are no signs of percussion in the score, additional violin and double bass manuscript parts suggest supplementary instrumentalists to achieve a louder sound. A singing bass part was later added to the storm chorus, something very rarely found in theater music of the time. These sound effects, together with the thunder-like dimming lights and the hollow tree, convey nature as overwhelming and limitless, standard characteristics of the sublime.

The chorus in act 2, scene 2 effectively dissipates the storm and is followed by a soprano duet sung by peasant girls welcoming the rainbow that appears as the stage slowly brightens up. The soprano duet complements the chorus by bringing the musical calm after the storm, much like the overture andantino "dawns" on the night of the allegro. In both cases, the first section of the music is in duple meter, a fast tempo, and includes chromaticism, whereas the second section is in triple meter, a slower tempo, and uses diatonic harmony. The peasant girls' duet following the storm chorus has two parts, andantino and pastoral. The pastoral part features the standard conventions that late eighteenth century Spanish composers used to create a bucolic atmosphere: compound meter, siciliana rhythmic patterns, simple melodic lines, flutes, and drones in the bass. Visually, the rainbow (*iris*) promised peace between nature and humankind, restoring serenity and beauty to the countryside. A lone shepherd walks across the stage with his flock while the two lasses sing the pastoral, reminiscent of the solo flute at the beginning of the overture's andantino. In both the overture and the storm chorus-soprano duet combo of act 2, scene 2, mollified nature becomes the stage for human presence.

The allegory of calm after the storm, light dispelling darkness, and the rainbow as a peace messenger directed spectators to Bourbon reformist discourse for economic modernization because, in this reformist discourse, modernization was narrativized as an organized reemergence from pre-Enlightenment chaos and darkness. Politician and enlightened writer Jovellanos's *Eulogy to Charles III*, written on the occasion of the monarch's death in 1788, offers a good synthesis of this narrative. Jovellanos situates the dark ages in the feudal economy of medieval times, when Spain "lived consumed by superstition and ignorance," in "anarchy instead of order." Medieval people were, Jovellanos denounces, "like any other herd, victims of their lords' greed," and "public order and well-being [lay] in the abyss of confusion and disorder." After several centuries of chaos, Spain resurged as a nation in the early sixteenth century, when the Catholic monarchs Isabel and Ferdinand centralized sovereignty and the crown rapidly acquired riches through the colonies. The exploitation of natural resources provided a wealth of natural knowledge. Unfortunately, Jovellanos laments, the Habsburg monarchies lacked enlightenment. Hence, all the colonial knowledge of nature was wasted in the conjectural labyrinths of scholasticism, alchemy, and astrology, instead of benefiting the nation. In Jovellanos's narrative, the Bourbon dynasty restored the robustness and splendor of the nation through enlightened education during the eighteenth century. Ferdinand VI (1746–1759) was "determined to let the light into his dominions," an enterprise fulfilled by Charles III, "under whose gaze all darkness would disappear" as the third Bourbon king assessed the final blow to scholasticism.[103]

Jovellanos believed that contemplation of nature was a prerequisite to enlightenment, which he understood as the fruit of systematized empirical observation put to the service of what we now call social sciences. In his *Eulogy to Charles III*, he proposed observing nature and then applying its understanding to social development to cast the shadows of scholasticism aside. Jovellanos thought men are born weak and ignorant but have the potential "to understand the expanse of the land, the depth of the oceans, the height and immensity of the skies, [are] capable of penetrating the most hidden mysteries of nature, available for his [man's] observation: he just needed to study it [nature], to gather, combine and order his ideas in order to subject the universe to his dominion." In his view, the task of "subjecting the universe" required that scientists, who studied nature, work hand in hand with politicians, who studied society.104 Jovellanos ended the *Eulogy to Charles III* with an exhortation to women as materfamilias: "Inspire in men sensibility, that amiable virtue you have received from nature," for sensibility will dispose men to receive enlightenment. Considered through the lens of Jovellanos's narrative of Bourbon reforms, *Cecilia viuda*'s sentimental and nature-contemplative tableaux come close to the kind of enlightened entertainment Bourbon policy supported.

It would be in the 1790s that Jovellanos in his personal diaries fully developed a connection between sensibility, contemplation of nature, and happiness. In a journal entry from 1794, he articulated the same awareness of the world that Comella and Laserna hinted at years earlier with their flute solos for *Cecilia viuda*. Reflecting upon an evening spent on the coast of Palma de Mallorca, Jovellanos wrote the following reflection, where the sentinel's lone

---

[103] Gaspar Melchor de Jovellanos, "Elogio de Carlos III," in *Obras completas*, ed. Vicente Llombart i Rosa and Joaquín Ocampo Suárez (Alicante: Biblioteca Virtual Miguel de Cervantes, 2010), https://www.cervantesvirtual.com/nd/ark:/59851/bmc708k0.

[104] In Jovellanos's words, "while the observant naturalist investigates and discovers the primordial elements of things, penetrates and analyzes their properties and virtues, the politician studies the relations that the Creator's wisdom placed among them [things], in order to ensure the multiplication and happiness of humankind." Jovellanos, *Elogio de Carlos III.*

250   *Music and Modernity in Enlightenment Spain*

voice completes the spectacle of nature, like *Cecilia viuda*'s overture's on-stage solo flute, and like the flute-playing shepherd did in the rainbow scene after the storm chorus:

> The hesitant and sad sky light, the expanse of the ocean revealed from time to time by timid lightnings tearing the faraway horizon, the brute noise of the water ... the solitude, the calm, and the silence of all things living rendered the situation sublime and magnificent beyond any deliberation. In the middle of it, the "who lives?" of a sentinel standing by the chapel porch. Once he heard my reply, he broke into song in the pathetic tune (*tono*) of the country, and this single voice, which I slowly left behind, splendidly contrasted with my silence. Oh man! If you want bliss, contemplate nature and approach it! For it alone is the source of the meager pleasure and happiness available to you.[105]

In this vignette, Jovellanos posits himself as the sentimental spectator par excellence. Similarly, sentimental theater audiences were expected to absorb the sights and sounds in the tableaux before them, to feel the sublime and be moved to virtue. It is the silent spectator's sensibility that connects overpowering nature to human existence in a twofold design in which the sublime yields to the pastoral. In this sense, Comella and Laserna's musical play is rooted in the optimistic vision of humankind characteristic of the Enlightenment.

The musical tableaux in *Cecilia viuda* summon up a modern morality, subject to religion but set in motion by sensitivity to nature. Sensitivity to nature begins with contemplation and culminates in adhesion to natural law. Sentimental tableaux in the *Cecilias* coexist with neo-Calderonian *costumbrismo* captured in "rustic" music and dance and in the many scenes with comic spoken dialogue. Comic characters, music, and rural imagery allowed the *Cecilias* to pass for comedy instead of tragedy, which in turn relaxed the censors' and critics' demands for strict adherence to dramatic unity. For example, censor and neoclassicist critic Santos Díez González wrote that "the two *Cecilias* are less flawed than [Comella's] other pieces, for the action is comic, and the fable as a whole has morality."106

La Cecilia and *Cecilia viuda*'s rustic tableaux started to be repackaged as nationalist proto-folklore by the turn of the nineteenth century, and as nationalist aspects took precedence, sentimental passages faded away. The advertisement for the last of *La Cecilia*'s performances reported in the *Diario de Madrid* in 1812 emphasizes its folkloric aspects, describing the play as "adorned with a great set of an illuminated plaza, and with an entertaining national *bailete.*" Later manuscript copies of both plays' librettos became increasingly shorter, trimming monologues but leaving the comic scenes intact and preserving most of the musical numbers.

---

[105] Jovellanos, *Diarios (memorias íntimas): 1790–1801* (Gijón: Instituto de Jovellanos, 1915), 164.

[106] Carlos Cambronero, "Comella, su vida y sus obras," *Revista contemporánea* 102 (1896): 580.

Bourbon Sentimentalities on the Musical Stage   251

A word must be said about the patroness of the *Cecilias*, Josefa Català de Valeriola y Luján, even though this chapter has not investigated gendered issues in Bourbon reformist discourse because of their enormous breadth and depth. Josefa Català de Valeriola y Luján was for a few years in the 1780s the marchioness of Mortara. Atypically for the time, her marriage to the marquis of Mortara was dissolved on the basis that it was "ratified but not consummated." From the few surviving records dating from her years as the marchioness of Mortara, it seems clear that she was wealthier and more powerful than her husband, and it was definitely her idea to build a theater in her property and to sponsor the *Cecilias*, as well as the 1785 play *La Dorinda*. Her musico-theatrical patronage in Madrid was nipped in the bud when the couple separated around 1788, and she went to stay at the convent of the Order of Calatrava nuns while the economic and legal affairs were settled. The details of the marriage annulment remain buried in the Vatican archives, but we do know that the union produced no children. Neither partner procreated later in life, and Josefa Català de Valeriola remained single thereafter. Cecilia's fate in *La Cecilia* and *Cecilia viuda*'s parallels some of Català de Valeriola's biographical details. The fact that the marquis and marchioness of Mortara did not procreate possibly precluded Comella from portraying Cecilia and Lucas as parents, even though the female protagonists in several of his other sentimental plays have children. By the end of *Cecilia viuda*, Cecilia retired to a convent, like the young marchioness of Mortara did one year after *Cecilia viuda* was written. Josefa Català de Valeriola y Luján became the third duchess of Almodóvar upon her return to her native Valencia after her marriage was annulled. As duchess of Almodóvar, she was a singular and wealthy patroness of the arts and education.

The fruit of the short-lived Mortara patronage, *La Cecilia* (1786) and *Cecilia viuda* (1787) uniquely mix Spanish identity and sentimentality at the tail end of Charles III's reign, representing the cusp of an optimistic disposition toward modernity soon to be shaken by the king's death in 1788 and the French Revolution in 1789. The fusion of sentimentality, pastoralism, agricultural policy, and comedy we see in the *Cecilias* yielded to more decidedly sentimental comedias and melodramas, where pastoral allusions turned toward the idyllic Arcadian prototype in the 1790s. Most sentimental plays Comella and Laserna created after the *Cecilias* take place outside of Spain, in England, France, the Middle East, or indeterminate exotic locations.[107] Sentimental plays acquired an aura of exoticism and cosmopolitanism absent from the *Cecilias* yet quite appealing to upper-class audiences. Pastoral scenes continued to be part of sentimental plays but referred less to Spanish agricultural reality and more to

---

[107] For example, Gaspar de Zavala y Zamora (text) and Pablo Esteve's (music) *Las víctimas del amor, Ana y Sindham* (1788) takes place in London and the English countryside, so that nature-inspired songs do not intend to portray Spanish villages even when the music evokes stylized folk genres. Comella's *El dichoso arrepentimiento* (1790, music by Pablo del Moral) and *La escocesa Lambrún* are similarly set in England.

Arcadian topics. Furthermore, the one-act melodrama, or *melólogo*, became the sentimental genre of choice in the 1790s and the early 1800s.[108] In these melodramas, composers and playwrights experimented extensively with the affective and descriptive powers of instrumental music incipient in Laserna's overture to *Cecilia viuda*.

---

[108] About the late eighteenth-century Spanish *melólogo*, see Joseph R. Jones, "María Rosa de Gálvez, Rousseau, Iriarte y el melólogo en la España del siglo XVIII," *Dieciocho: Hispanic Enlightenment* 19, no. 2 (1996): 165–180, and José Subirá, *El compositor Iriarte (1750–1791) y el cultivo español del melólogo (melodrama)*, 2 vols. (Barcelona: Consejo Superior de Investigaciones Científicas Instituto Español de Musicología, 1949).

Conclusion

I opened this book by invoking Masson de Morvilliers's infamous question, "Mais que doit l'Europe à l'Espagne?"—What does Europe owe to Spain? (Encyclopédie méthodique, 1782)— as one of the cues prompting the late eighteenth-century Spanish public to either embrace or reject modern Europe. Both reactions garnered supporters who participated in an ongoing pro- versus antimodernization *querelle* in which the national project was at stake. Far from being an elite's abstract affair, modernization concerned many an ordinary person, at least in large urban centers like Madrid. Music, specifically musical theater, actualized the ideological quarrel for the Madrid general audience, as the following tonadillas by Blas de Laserna demonstrate.

Let us situate ourselves in one of the (then) two Madrid city theaters, where spectators of all walks of life congregated several times per week. The audience leaned forward with anticipation as the second intermission brought the much-awaited tonadilla on that 1784 evening at Madrid's Coliseo del Príncipe. Actress-singer Joaquina Arteaga came alone on stage, for this was a solo tonadilla. She wore *traje a la española*: a dark-colored two-piece dress with a tight-laced jacket, a long overskirt, and a sheer shawl or mantilla. As Arteaga appeared on stage, the working-class men in the patio, the ground-floor standing area right in front of the stage, cheered loudly. These were the polacos, the diehard fans of Eusebio Ribera's company, one of the two theater companies the city of Madrid managed. Behind and above the polacos, the women sat on benches in a large gallery on the first floor, the cazuela. More affluent patrons, such as military men, nobles, professionals, and wealthy merchants, occupied the boxes. The orchestra, composed of violins, oboes, horns, and bass, sounded the *premier coup d'archet* of a "minuet air" in B flat major.

Although the audience instantly recognized Arteaga's outfit as Spanish, nothing in the music hinted at the upcoming subject matter: the conflict between ancient and modern Spain. Arteaga sang the first phrase, "en este siglo ..." (in this century ...). Those words alone cued that this piece, like many solo tonadillas, was a critique of modern mores. The rest of the opening lyrics confirmed the topic: "In this century, this attire [I am wearing] shall be lost, oh affront!" This century was the eighteenth, the enlightened one, and the attire on the verge of extinction was the *traje a la española*. In only one sentence, Arteaga expressed the collective perception that the demise of traditional Spanish mores on the altar of the modern was imminent, which was a matter of national affront. The audience was accustomed to the kind of rapport Arteaga initiated: I will soon be unfairly forgotten, but you shall miss me. Tonadilla singers customarily pleaded for the audience's sympathy by presenting

254   *Conclusion*

the tonadilla as a flawed tribute designed to please them. Additionally, it was common for female *tonadilleras* to play the coy diva seeking the public's support. Except in this case, Arteaga stood for the traditional version of the nation: Ancient Spain (*La España antigua*, which was the tonadilla's title).

After introducing herself as Ancient Spain time-traveling "from the dark mansion of bleak oblivion" to "this celebrated hemisphere, to see whether its mores and temper have been corrupted," the actress-singer proceeded to sing different musical numbers, narrating in detail how Spain had flipped in modern times from being a grave, virile nation to a frivolous one with a penchant for fashion and flirtatiousness. Composer and lyricist Blas de Laserna provided misogynistic remarks about Spain's feminization as a sign of decay. The matter concluded with a vivacious refrain: "Oh, that seeing these damages, so many still dare call this century, ole! the enlightened century."

Approximately one year later, Laserna revisited the issue with a sequel tonadilla, which Arteaga also performed, this time impersonating Modern Spain (*La España moderna*, 1785). Like her nemesis, Ancient Spain, the modern one felt insulted (*ultrajada*), as she sang in an operatic "rage" refrain. For the sequel, Arteaga was wearing modern fashion; we do not know exactly what, only that the audience would have recognized her looks as foreign and modern. It may well have been the so-called *traje a la francesa*, the eighteenth-century fashion imported from France and consisting of a pleated one-piece light-colored dress with deep cleavage, puffy skirt, pastel colors, and elaborate coiffure and accessories. Unlike her ancient counterpart, Modern Spain seemed unconcerned with the indecency of young women baring their arms and legs in public or wives bossing around their unmanly husbands. Instead, Modern Spain complained that the public did not recognize the full extent of her achievements in science, agriculture, manufacture, and population, the main vectors of Charles III's government's modernizing reforms.

My intention here is not to analyze the tonadillas in detail but to present them as tokens of the cultural turmoil in late Enlightenment Spain. Subtle yet meaningful differences in some of the musical numbers' genre and tonality notwithstanding, most notably the coplas at the tonadilla core, the musical similarities between *La España antigua* and *La España moderna* dominate. Both Ancient and Modern Spain introduce themselves with recitative and finish with pastoral seguidillas. The overall style of the different musical numbers is a mix of galant and regional musics. The balance between the two styles, leaning toward the regional in *La España antigua* and toward the galant in *La España moderna*, hinted at the differences between the ancient and the modern, but the lyrics and the costumes hammered the point home.

The modern polarized the Spanish public sphere of the late eighteenth century. Having an actress-singer embody the nation to perform Madrid's favorite musical spectacle was a brilliant move by Laserna in the tonadillas *La España antigua* and *La España moderna*. The characterization evinced how personal the ancient versus modern debate was for many in Spain. Diverse classes of people attended the Coliseo de La Cruz, where the two tonadillas were performed, from street water vendors and cobblers to the high aristocracy. Laserna would not have brought to the stage an issue concerning only a few in the elite, especially when his job depended partly on his ability to attract patrons.

Laserna's two tonadillas illustrate well the ancient versus modern tensions studied throughout this book. The titles of both tonadillas (*La España antigua* and *La España moderna*) indicate that, in late eighteenth-century Spain, modernization debates were inseparable from the national project. The modern was embedded in the nation's fate and society's collective identity, for better or worse. Late eighteenth-century Spanish modernization involved a confluence of social and epistemological changes. The old entailed the stability and permanency of immutable truths and, consequently, of an unchangeable social order articulated around the estates of the realm; religion; cumulative knowledge; and a clear separation among classes, genders, the public, and the private. To oversimplify, *the old* was traceable to Habsburg Spain, from the Catholic Monarchs (or earlier) to 1700, when the Bourbons gained access to the throne after the Spanish War of Succession. *The new*, by contrast, was tied to the seventeenth-century scientific and philosophical revolutions that materialized into the Enlightenment. In practice, "the modern" took on many faces, some promising and others menacing.

The promising faces of modernization formed a pillar of Charles III's government (1759–1788), which focused on economic, political, and demographic reforms to revitalize the Spanish empire and gain ascendancy in modern Europe. Policymakers adopted various aspects of Enlightenment philosophy and Newtonian science, especially those favorable to industrial and agricultural improvement. For example, Charles III's government wholeheartedly endorsed European economic theories such as French physiocracy, because physiocracy combined modern natural law data-driven economic planning with absolutism. The modernized economy the government aspired to required changes to traditional social roles and even more profound shifts in conceptions about what being a human in the world meant. Thus, physiocracy acknowledged that peasants needed a certain degree of economic capital and personal initiative to function within the natural order in a way that would optimize productivity. At the same time, national progress depended on peasants subordinating their agency to the crown's interests.

Modernization in favor of national progress infused official discourse for decades, finding its way to all kinds of enterprises, including culture and the arts. One could say that Bourbon reformers welcomed modernization as long as it served the crown, under the premise that enlightened absolutism was the ideal mode of government for modern European nations. Any private or public project, such as books, journals, institutions, businesses, or entertainment, had to be justified through the official reformist discourse, which sought to increase efficiency so that Spain could improve its competitiveness in Europe. In the case of arts and entertainment, modernization translated to the neoclassicist ideals of *delectare et docere*. Therefore, every actor-singer, musician, composer, playwright, theatergoer, journalist, or scientist

256   *Conclusion*

was familiar with the hegemonic argument that their artistic and intellectual undertakings should benefit the nation.

However, consensus on what modern Spain looked like or what kind of entertainment would edify the public was tenuous. For the most part, each individual or group interpreted "the national benefit" in various, even contradictory, ways. The elite in government, intellectual, and literary circles concurred that it was the role of the educated class, not the general population, to decide on the course of modernity. Both the elite and common people agreed that Spain must remain religious and Catholic, whether they believed in European modernity or not. Significant differences concerning national betterment often affected how the public received foreign ideas or practices, including musical genres such as Italian opera or behavioral codes within performance spaces, such as keeping quiet during the show.

The perils of modernization were felt well beyond intellectual and political discourse. The modern and its counterparts materialized into a myriad of tokens used and reused in official and popular discourses, Laserna's "Ancient Spain" and "Modern Spain" being two such tokens. Negative modern tokens included using theoretical and philosophical language (often mocked as gibberish), drinking coffee, socializing in public venues, mingling with the opposite gender, or owning a lap dog. Positive modern tokens were clean streets, cordial public behavior, and diligence and industriousness for the working class and culture and moderation for the aristocracy and the bourgeoisie. Once modernity became reified, these tokens could be invoked at all levels of discourse, from state declarations to popular songs and satires. Major Enlightenment ideas and modern science also came to public awareness through tokens of speech, dress, music, and dance on the musical stage. We can see this in Esteve's tonadilla *El atarantulado* (discussed in chapter 2), where disease, contagiousness, and medical treatment come together with a critique of aristocrats. We can also see it in numerous other tonadillas about modern European practices and artifacts such as newspapers, optical lenses, journalistic criticism, coffee shops, opera, or social dancing.

When Manuel Cavaza responded to *El Censor*'s "Discourse 97," Francisco Xavier Cid countered French encyclopedists, Pablo Esteve challenged journalistic critics with a tonadilla, and Laserna created his Ancient Spain and Modern Spain characters, they were reacting to widespread perceptions of Spanish nonmodernity and its consequent non-Europeanness. French, Italian, and other European authors writing in the late eighteenth century revisited the long-standing Black Legend to define Spain as antimodern. This trend is patent in the apologista quarrels of the 1780s and 1790s in Spain, a series of debates that serve as a background for the case studies in this book. Upon facing foreign accusations of anti-modernity, apologistas dismissed "the modern" altogether. Foremost in this group is Juan Pablo Forner, author of the 1786 *Oración apologética por la España*. Other writers joined Forner in his nationalist defense, adopting what became the apologista approach. Forner's extreme stance counted on the support of the count of Floridablanca, de facto leader of the Spanish government under Charles III. Floridablanca's blessing amplified antimodern discourses. Several forms of satire and popular culture, including stage tonadillas, also ridiculed modernity under the pretense of protecting national cultural forms. Most historiographical accounts of eighteenth-century Spain focus on the apologista repudiation of modernity as the only form of reception of modern ideas or musical styles in Spain. Generalizing antimodern stances supports the established narrative of modern Europe that places France, England, and Germany at its center. However, it obliterates the sharp awareness of the modern that Spanish policymakers, authors, performers, and audiences possessed.

There was an extended perception in late eighteenth-century Spain that everything was changing. Few believed change and continuity could coexist, and even for those who did, the modern did not have a neutral status: it was either better or worse than the old. In Laserna's *La España antigua*, the character of Ancient Spain emerges from oblivion to see what is happening in the other "hemisphere," suggesting the ancient and the modern are complementary yet mutually exclusive halves. One year later, Laserna produced *La España moderna* because the "old Spain" and the "new Spain" could not exist without each other. In other words, there was no need to define the old until the modern started taking over. This polarization is evident in popular music and theater, where stereotypes reified the modern into frivolous *petrimetras/es*, *afrancesado* urban types, antipodal to majas/os, the suburban and rural working-class characters chosen as the quintessential Spanish prototypes. Awareness of modernization led to a reification of the "old" Spain.

In reality, there was not one ancient and one modern Spain, but many gradations of both coexisting at any given time. Regarding musical knowledge, two paradigms coexisted uncomfortably in late eighteenth-century Spain, one rooted in Renaissance music theory and the other compatible with Rousseau's linguistic theories. *El Censor*'s "Discourse 97," published in 1786, highlights the crisis between the mathematical and linguistic models of music. This brief essay condemned the practice of counterpoint in pedagogy and music chapels, advocating instead for simple chants, music in the form of heightened language fulfilling the political and philosophical functions it did in ancient Greece. In a way, "Discourse 97" is the journalistic sketch of many ideas that exiled Jesuit Antonio Eximeno fully and systematically developed. However, Eximeno's work did not trigger open controversy (at least in Madrid) until 1796, when his 1774 *Dell'origine e delle regole della musica* was translated into Spanish. *El Censor*'s "Discourse 97" prompted the Royal Chapel's first oboist Manuel Cavaza to recoil and write a lengthy reply. The reply shows evidence of a strong sense that music was a guild craft unreceptive to the input of outsiders, for example, music critics.

A close examination of press debates about musical theater and other musical affairs attests to the conflict between traditional and modern modes of knowledge. Criticism in the sense of public opinion concerning a specific topic that a nonspecialized individual issued disturbed many press readers and theatergoers. Although the government initially welcomed criticism as an agent of

258   *Conclusion*

modernization and progress in the 1780s, deeply rooted ideas about perjury and defamation often prevailed. These ideas, inherited from medieval law, fostered a perception of criticism as personal attacks intended to destroy specific people's reputations. We see this in the character of Modern Spain in Laserna's *La España moderna*, which reacts with anger to Ancient Spain's devaluation of modern mores. We also see it in Pablo Esteve's tonadilla *El teatro y los actores agraviados*, where three actor-singers felt that journalistic theater critics were assailing their profession. The root discrepancy regarding criticism lay in whether remarking on an individual's or the nation's shortcomings stimulated or deterred improvement. For example, Juan Pablo Forner (a staunch opponent of modernity in many of his writings) thought that "criticism, when this term is taken in its legitimate signification, has no relation to virtue."[1] Praise, from this point of view, had better effects.

Musicians, performers, and audiences also distrusted criticism as a form of musical knowledge because criticism was opinion based and admitted multiple points of view instead of a single authoritative one. Critics who commented on Madrid's musical life were disqualified as arrogant because they were not insiders to the musical trade. Disqualification of music and theater criticism had deeper roots in the Spanish rejection of Cartesian rationalism. Cartesianism sourced truth in the individual rational mind and proceeded through methodical doubt. This method undermined cumulative knowledge transmitted since antiquity and reformulated in recent centuries, such as the modal theory underlying the rules of counterpoint. Cartesian rationalism also undermined theology because theology presupposes a transcendent truth independent from opinion and exempt from doubt. Because many in Spain considered theology inseparable from philosophy, the latter became, in popular parlance, an umbrella term for any intellectual endeavor defiant of God and king. Journalistic criticism of musical theater fell under the umbrella of philosophy in its derogatory sense.

Despite suspicion of Cartesianism, by the late eighteenth century, intellectuals, writers, and Bourbon reformers generally agreed that Spanish science needed to be modernized. Enlightened thinkers and other modernizing agents had combatted the remnants of Scholasticism since the early eighteenth century. This fight continued until the last decades of the century, when only a few still supported the stiff learning system based on Thomism and Aristotelianism and emblematized in the University of Salamanca.

Spanish intellectuals favored sensism to explain connections between music and the body. The state-sanctioned need for scientific modernization encouraged Spanish intellectuals to adopt the ideas of moderate empiricists and naturalists such as John Locke, Étienne Bonnot de Condillac, Robert Boyle, and Georges-Luis Leclerc, Comte de Buffon, as tarantism treatises produced in the

---

[1] Juan Pablo Forner, *Demostraciones palmarias de que el censor, su corresponsal, el apologista universal, y los demás papelejos de este jaez, no sirven de nada al Estado, ni á la Literatura de España* (Madrid, 1787), 10.

Conclusion 259

late 1780s show. Jean-Jacques Rousseau was better received than Voltaire and certainly than Montesquieu, the latter two among the most rejected philosophers together with Claude-Adrien Helvétius. Locke and Condillac provided the background for modern conceptions of humanity in Spain, whereas Buffon was the primary reference for natural knowledge. Empiricism offered a way out of the fear that enlightened rationalism would only replace Scholasticism insofar as both philosophical systems relied heavily on logic and intellectual apprehension rather than verifiable evidence.[2] Empiricism thus offered a safe road to proposing new ideas whenever it allowed metaphysics. We see this commendation of empiricism in Francisco Díaz Cid's tarantism treatise, studied in chapter 2. Therapeutic uses of music were the type of science suited for the Spanish mind because they combined empirical observation of symptoms and treatments with an invisible component, namely, how music acted on the mind or soul.

Even though music was not central to public debates in late eighteenth-century Spain, theater was. Hence, musical theater was the subject of printed debates and criticism more than other musical practices. The preeminence of musical theater criticism does not mean other musics were less relevant to the social fabric or less susceptible to modernization's upheaval. It only means we have fewer narratives directly expressing the subjective views of individuals on these musical practices. Changes in music pedagogy, for instance, can be discerned through analyses of treatises and manuals, but these formats did not usually reach the general public or even the educated elite. Musical theater, however, was available in cities like Madrid several times per week to people from nearly all social strata. The king was notoriously absent from either theater or opera between 1776 and the end of the century. During the last decades of the century, Madrid's musical theater was a civic, performative, and ideological event. As such, it is better understood through architecture, laws and regulations, newspaper opinion pieces, literary and musical parodies, and financial records. Composers and the copious manuscript scores available in archives are but one piece of this art form.

Numerous contemporary thinkers and policymakers embraced modernization, often understood as cosmopolitanism or international cooperation conducive to progress, as manifested in the rehabilitation of Madrid's Teatro de los Caños del Peral for Italian opera in 1787. International cooperation included emulation of other European countries in aspects fruitful to the Spanish nation. This was the rationale for Los Caños del Peral: by attending a cosmopolitan musical spectacle, audiences would acquire a taste for civilized entertainment, local performers would feel compelled to improve their skills, and composers and playwrights would learn the operatic language to eventually create a national opera. Reformers, intellectuals, and aristocrats intended, or at least justified, Ital-

---

[2] See *Oración fúnebre dicha en las exequias del Ente de Razón* (Málaga: En la imprenta de los herederos de D. Francisco Martínez de Aguilar, 1787).

260   *Conclusion*

ian opera as a formative example. From this point of view, emulation did not preclude patriotism. The premise was that Spain had things to learn from other Europeans, and Europeans had things to learn from Spain. Pro-modernization thinkers understood international cooperation on a more or less equal footing, even when they admitted that Spain was behind. Italian opera in Madrid was a tool to help Spanish culture regain European prestige.

The ideas and artistic creations of pro-modernization Spanish authors do not fit established narratives of Western modernity, such as Jonathan Israel's "radical Enlightenment" or Jürgen Habermas's theorization of the public sphere. Israel traces Enlightenment back to Baruch Spinoza, Pierre Bayle, Jean Le Clerc, and Denis Diderot, excluding authors of the moderate mainstream Enlightenment such as Locke, David Hume, and Voltaire from the genealogy of philosophical modernity. For Israel, there is no modernity without democracy and secularization of institutions. Habermas makes the modern public sphere depend on the bourgeoisie's ability and willingness to oppose the ruling government. With few exceptions, pro-modernization Spanish thinkers supported the absolutist regime, the Catholic faith, and a stratified society that the enlightened elite directed.

Despite the faith some elites such as wealthy professionals, nobles, and government officials had in international cultural cooperation—concretely through opera—many in the general public and in elite circles viewed emulation of Europe as either *afrancesamiento* or aping, both of which betrayed and ridiculed the nation. The template of *afrancesamiento* was applied to other foreign cultures, for example, Italian opera. *Afrancesamiento* was the equivalent of giving up one's essence to adopt foreign mores. It had a subtext of lacking pride in being Spanish and compensating for a weak moral character with refined, modern mores such as attending the opera. For those who saw emulation of French fashion, language, dance, or enlightened ideas as a betrayal of Spanish essence, emulation could only result in aping. Several newspaper reviews from the late 1780s and early 1790s regarded Los Caños del Peral as a downgraded mimicry of the major European opera theaters. If Spanish performers tried their hand at operatic genres, they risked being called "geese" or "parrots" who made sounds without understanding them. In the end, discrediting the Italian singers at Los Caños del Peral prevailed over applauding them. By the late 1790s, Charles IV's government considered Italian opera a threat to Spanish musical theater and terminated the Los Caños del Peral venture.

Even though Italian opera at the restored Los Caños del Peral 1787 did not fully succeed, the impact of modern European genres on Spanish musical theater is undeniable. Modernization gave Spanish theater's old stereotypes a makeover. Composers and playwrights mixed modern trends with traditional ones to engage the public through familiar codes while presenting and contending new ideas. The pressure to pledge allegiance to the monarchy and Catholic religion fostered creative adoptions of modern beliefs and musical genres. For example, sentimental musical plays, in vogue since the 1780s, could complicate the *petimetre* (urban, modern)majo (suburban, deep-rooted) dichotomy by imbuing characters with redeeming qualities that Bourbon policy propagandized, as in the two *Cecilia* musical plays by Laserna and Luciano Francisco Comella. Upper-class or urban characters appeared less superficial or corrupt, fending off exploitative leaders in their subordinates' favor or fighting to defend their nuclear families. Peasants and other working-class characters were cast as industrious, loyal subjects collaborating for the common good. Thus, sentimentality offered a third avenue that brought modern taste to the Spanish stage while preserving beloved characters and conventions from the seventeenth century.

Musical theater was a decisive medium for generating public ideas that would eventually settle down into realities. Laserna's *La España antigua* and *La España moderna* did more than reflect the dichotomic public opinion: they informed it. Laserna picked up on loose ideas of what the old and the new looked like and wrapped them up neatly in two antagonistic characters. Other artistic and intellectual creations defined the ancient and the modern differently, but Laserna's typification is representative of popular culture at the time. The positive aspects of the modern are grouped around economic progress, whereas the negative aspects are grouped around moral decay. Most modernizers tried to find a way to achieve scientific and economic progress while averting impiety and moral laxity. Thus, Laserna-Comella's Cecilia is both a highly sentimental object of desire and a virtuous wife and, later, a pious widow. Recurrent representations of modern attitudes through song, dance, stage presence, and costumes simplified complex, ambivalent modernization processes.

Gender roles were a vital part of the controversy about the modern, albeit one not discussed in this book. The virilization of ancient Spain and the feminization of modern Spain became even more pronounced during the 1790s and around 1802 when Napoleon invaded Spain and installed his brother José Bonaparte as the ruler. Laserna, one of the composers essential to this book's repertories, was especially fond of sexist stereotypes in his musical theater works. My observation in this regard is that redefinitions of gender roles and family structures were one of the central pathways to Spanish modernization at the time. An entire book could be written about this topic. Nevertheless, one should be aware that a composer (Laserna) who happens to have written a substantial percentage of theater music in the 1780s and 1790s seemed particularly inclined to sexism in his works. This does not necessarily entail that Laserna and possibly other composers were very conservative or anachronistic in their views. Laserna's music is anything but outdated, and his 1791 petition (which was denied) to start a theater and music journal shows he was interested in musical criticism. For excellent discussions of gender in musical theater and Spanish culture in general during the late eighteenth century, the reader may refer to the works of Mónica Bolúfer, Rebecca Haidt, Aurèlia Pessarrodona, Elena Serrano, Theresa Ann Smith, and Marta V. Vicente.

The stories told in this book emerge from multiple manuscript scores, librettos, letters, and mixed documents hosted at Madrid's Biblioteca Histórica Municipal and Spain's Biblioteca Nacional. They also come from

262   *Conclusion*

eighteenth-century periodicals the Biblioteca Nacional's *Hemeroteca Digital* digitized and made available. Further, I surveyed the collections at the Real Conservatorio Superior de Música de Madrid, the Archivo del Real Palacio, the Biblioteca de Catalunya, the Arxiu Històric Municipal de Valencia, and the Archivo Histórico de la Nobleza in Toledo. A different set of sources, for example, cathedral or convent archives, would tell a set of parallel stories spotlighting other aspects of the controversies surrounding modernization.

Whether embraced or rejected, "modernity" in the late Spanish Enlightenment was not one thing but rather a series of tectonic shifts that readjusted the layers of reality through time, shaking the ground in the process. Modernizing shifts occur in specific moments, in concrete parts of the world, provoking chaos and unleashing changes. In the case this book examines, the shifts of modernity shook the core of Spanishness. Internal mistrust of European modernity and external (foreign) pressure to maintain Spain in a premodern role in the project of Europe coalesced into our current historical version of the West. The intellectuals, writers, and policymakers who believed in modernizing the Spanish monarchy did not prevail. The Western eighteenth-century historiography tells us that the ancient regime and modernity or Enlightenment were mutually exclusive projects. However, this history had not yet been written when the people who are the book's subjects were alive. They could pitch different versions of Spanish modernity to the nascent public sphere. They did so time and again in their cultural productions, books, and newspapers. In other words, the fact that later narratives present Spain as premodern or antimodern does not imply that all Spanish intellectuals and dominant classes considered themselves so.

Final Thoughts

The conclusions reached through this investigation apply more directly to the last stage of Charles III's reign and the very first years of Charles IV. The 1790s would prove different from the previous decade. The death of Charles III in 1788 and the French Revolution the following year generated changes in governance and legislation. One such change was the termination of most periodical publications in 1791. Charles IV became king in 1789. Initially, he relied even more than his predecessor on the secretary of state, the count of Floridablanca. Floridablanca had led the public opinion's conservative faction in the previous decades. For example, he twice interrupted *El Censor's* publication temporarily and finally ended it in 1787. He supported Forner's discourses of cultural protectionism. In 1791, panicked over the spread of French Revolutionary ideas, Floridablanca prohibited all periodical publications except the *Diario de Madrid*, the *Mercurio histórico y político*, and the *Gaceta de Madrid*. The government published the latter two. The ban was lifted after less than two years, but many periodicals ceased publication at the time. The 1791 ban effec-

Conclusion   263

tively meant some of the musical debates went unaccounted for, such as the one about Italian opera. Because periodicals constitute one of the main research sources for this book, Floridablanca's interdiction marked a chronological limit in my research.

There are only a handful of music criticism articles in Madrid periodicals from 1791 to 1792. In 1793, critics slowly started to pick up where they had left off. For example, a letter to the *Diario de Madrid*, which someone who had arrived in the capital city two years before submitted, requests more articles on music. Echoing *El Censor*'s "Discourse 97," the letter's author hopes more musical criticism will persuade chapel masters that they need deeper knowledge of poetry. Charles IV issued a 1793 royal mandate confirming some of the rules from the 1787 rules for the Teatro de los Caños del Peral, which was published in the *Diario*. Some articles about tarantism were published in the *Diario* and the *Memorial literario*. Several daily newspapers sprouted across the Spanish peninsula after 1792, including cities like Valencia, Sevilla, Barcelona, Granada, Murcia, Barcelona, Málaga, Zaragoza, and Cádiz. Regional newspapers also participated in musical theater discussions. In 1795, *Semanario de Salamanca* reprinted excerpts from "Discourse 97." That year, journalistic debates revolved around the relationship between music and poetry. In 1796, twenty-two years after the Italian original, Antonio Eximeno's *Dell'origine e delle regole della musica* was translated into Spanish. Eximeno's translation brought his defense of the linguistic paradigm of music to a wider Spanish audience and into public debate.

At this point, a new musical theater genre had come to prominence: the melodrama, also called *melólogo* or *unipersonal* when it was a monologue. A study of musical debates focused on the 1790s and early 1800s would necessarily address the Spanish melodrama, which further delved into the sentimental aesthetics musical theater audiences had favored since the 1780s. Italian opera and Lenten concerts continued at Los Caños del Peral throughout the 1790s, with increasing financial encumbrances. Press debates concerning foreign versus national musical theater carried on from previous decades. Italian opera at Los Caños del Peral came to an end in 1799, when Charles IV banned theater in any language other than Spanish.

In terms of public musical life, censorship's grip under Charles IV grew intermittently tighter. In 1789, the first year of his rule, Charles IV prohibited nightly dances at El paseo del Prado, the popular outdoor corridor that had served as a recreational space and informal music venue in Madrid since the late fifteenth century. Under Charles III, the count of Aranda had mandated extensive renovations of the old Prado, which became a symbol of new urbanism and of a clean, modern Madrid with its fountains, gardens, and statues that neoclassicist architect Ventura Rodríguez designed. From Charles IV's ruling, we learn that city dwellers had used this improved open space to dance to live music until the wee hours. The ruling mandated all music end by midnight, and while allowed, coplas ought not to use any innuendo in their lyrics under the penalty of fines for musicians. Although proscribing dance was not Charles

264   *Conclusion*

IV's idea, for several similar interdictions had tried to regulate El Prado before, the ruling showed renewed anxiety about public gender mingling.

Nevertheless, it would be unfair to evaluate Charles IV's reign as detrimental to musical modernization. Eximeno's work was published in Spain, giving one of the final blows to the older theory and pedagogy retained in musical chapels. Floridablanca's panic in reaction to the French Revolution partially subsided when the count of Aranda and later Manuel Godoy replaced the secretary of state, all in 1791, the same year periodical publications were banned. Anti-European protectionist policies ebbed and flowed throughout the decade. Chamber music at the royal palaces flourished because Charles IV restructured the Real Cámara, where Gaetano Brunetti worked. Although criticism only partially returned to its 1780s buoyancy, lively debates regarding musical theater, dance, and other public musical forms endured.

Bibliography

Primary Sources

"Adiciones al Reglamento provisional e interino que con fecha de 23 de septiembre de 1793 acordó y firmó la Asociación de Óperas, por todos los señores que se hallaban en Madrid en aquella época." 1793. Mss/14052/3, Biblioteca Nacional de España.

Aguilera, Vicente. "Descripción de la tarántula, su picadura y efectos que causa, con las observaciones hechas hasta ahora por D. Vicente Aguilera, Cirujano titular de la Villa de Manzanares." *Memorial Literario, Instructivo y Curioso* 51 (December 1787): 572–78.

Alemán y Aguado [Manuel Casal y Aguado], Lucas. "Otra [carta]." *Correo de los Ciegos*, August 15 1787, 375–76.

Algarotti, Francesco. *Ensayo sobre la ópera en musica. Escrito en lengua italiana por el Conde Francisco Algaroti ... Traducido al castellano, para instruccion de los que quieran asistir al nuevo teatro italiano, que se ha establecido en esta corte.* Madrid: Miguel Escribano, 1787.

———. *Saggio sopra l'opera in musica.* Bologna: F.A.R.A.P. S. Giovanni in Persiceto, 1763 [1755].

"Algunas noticias instructivas sobre el drama llamado ópera." *Diario curioso, erudito, económico y comercial*, January 17, 1787, 70–71.

Andrés, Juan. *Origen, progresos y estado actual de toda la literatura.* Translated by Carlos Andrés. Madrid: Antonio de Sancha, 1784.

Armona y Murga, José Antonio de. *Memorias cronológicas sobre el origen de la representación de comedias en España.* Fuentes para la historia del teatro en España. Woodbridge, Suffolk: Tamesis, 2007.

———. *Memorias cronológicas sobre el teatro en España.* Alaveses en la historia. Vitoria: Diputación Foral de Álava, Servicio de Publicaciones, 1988.

Arteaga, Esteban de. *Le rivoluzioni del teatro musicale italiano dalla sua origine fino al presente.* Bologna: Stamperìa di C. Trenti, 1783.

Baglivi, Giorgio. "Intorno all'anatomia, morso ed effetti della tarantella." Translated by Raimondo Pellegrini. In *Opere complete medico-pratiche ed anatomiche di Giorgio Baglivi*, 679–721. Florence: Sansone Coen, 1841.

"Bando." *Diario de Madrid*, November 5, 1793, 1264–66.

Barbieri, Francisco Asenjo. "Carta de Martínez y Rivera a Don Juan Laví y Zavala." 1787. Biblioteca Nacional de España.

Batteux, Charles. *Les beaux arts [réduits a un même principe].* Paris: Durand, 1747.

266   *Bibliography*

Bea de Navarra, Miguel. "Carta erudita probando los buenos efectos de la música, tomada como medicina." *Diario de Madrid*, December 11, 1789, 1379–80.

Bernal, Antonio. *Segunda carta del sacristán de Berlinches al organista de Móstoles*. [Madrid] 1786.

Boissier de Sauvages, François. *Nosologie méthodique ou distribution des maladies en classes, en genres et en especes suivant l'esprit de Sydenham, & la méthode des botaniste par François Boissier de Sauvages, … traduite sur la dernière édition latine, par M. Gouvion, docteur en médecine. On a joint à cet ouvrage celui du chev. von Linné, intitulé Genera morborum, avec la traduction française à côté*. 10 vols. Vol. 7, 1772.

Bouville, Mademiselle de. *Criticas reflexiones que hace Mademiselle de Bouville … sobre el estado presente de la Literatura Española, en vista de los inumerables papeles que se dán a la luz pública*. Madrid: Hilario Santos Alonso, 1786.

"Boyle." *Correo de Madrid*, February 20, 1790, 2713–14.

Cabarrús, Francisco. "Memorias sobre medios y arbitrios para los Reales Hospitales de esta Corte y sobre el establecimiento de la Ópera Bufa en beneficio de los mismos: Leídas en la Junta de su Gobierno, los días 19 de febrero y 12 de marzo de 1786." 1786. MSS/13467, Biblioteca Nacional de España.

Cavanilles, Antonio José de. *Observations de M. l'abbé Cavanilles sur l'article "Espagne" de la Nouvelle Encyclopédie*. Paris: Chez Alex. Jombert jeune, 1784.

Cavaza, Manuel. "El cantor instruido o Maestro aliviado assi en los difíciles principios de esta nobilísima professión como en todo lo que un cantor debe saber según el moderno y último estilo, dispuesto con exemplos prácticos, que lo declaran para mayor inteligencia del que estudia." ca. 1754. Biblioteca Histórica de la Universidad Complutense.

———. *El músico censor del Censor no músico, ó Sentimientos de Lucio Vero Hispano, contra los de Simplicio Greco, y Lira: Discurso unico*. Madrid: Alfonso López, 1786.

———. "Rudimentos y elementos de la música práctica escrita." 1786. Biblioteca Nacional de España.

Cervantes Saavedra, Miguel de. *La Galatea*. Vol. 4. Madrid: Juan de Zúñiga, 1736.

———. *Los seis libros de Galatea. Dividida en dos tomos. Corregida e ilustrada con láminas finas*. Madrid: Antonio de Sancha, 1784.

Chamorro, Lorenzo. "[Carta]." *Correo de Madrid*, June 21 and 23, 1787, 295–96, 99–300.

Charles III of Spain. "Ley XII. D. Carlos III, por real orden de 11 de diciembre de 1786, y bandos publicados en 2 de nov. De 793 y siguientes años." In *Novísima recopilación de las leyes de España*, 668–69. Madrid: Galván Librero, 1805 [1766].

Bibliography   267

———. "Ley XIII. Prohibición de usar capa larga, sombrero chambergo o redondo, montera calada y embozo en la Corte y Sitios Reales." In *Novísima recopilación de las leyes de España*, 503–4. Madrid: Galván Librero, 1831 [1766].

———. "Ley XXXIV. D. Carlos III, por real resolución de 19 de noviembre de 1785, comunicada al Consejo y Juez de Imprentas, 'El Juez de Imprentas oiga y administre justicia al que se queje del autor de cualquier impreso." In *Novísima recopilación de las leyes de España*, 142. Madrid: Galván Librero, 1805 [1766].

———. "[Libro VII. Título XXXIII], Ley VI. El mismo por pragmática sanción de 9 de noviembre de 1785. Prohibición general de las fiestas de toros de muerte." In *Novísima recopilación de las Leyes de España*, Vol. 3. Madrid: Galván Librero, 1805 [1766].

Chicharro. "Otra [carta]." *Correo de los Ciegos*, April 18, 1787, 206–7.

Cid, Francisco Xavier. "Carta primera, Carta segunda." *Correo de los ciegos*, February 3, 1790, 2674–49.

———. *Tarantismo observado en España ... y memorias para escribir la historia del insecto llamado Tarántula, efectos de su veneno en el cuerpo humano, y curación por la música ...* Madrid: Manuel Gonzalez, 1787.

Clavijo y Fajardo, José. "Pensamiento LXXXIV." *El Pensador* 84 (1767): 189–203.

"Coliseo de Los Caños del Peral." *Memorial literario, instructivo y curioso*, February 1787, 263–66.

Comella, Luciano Francisco. *La Cecilia. Primera parte.* Madrid: Benito Cano, 1786.

———. *Cecilia viuda.* 3rd ed. [Madrid]: Librería de Cerro, 1790 [1787].

Condillac, Étienne Bonnot de. *Essai sur l'origine des connoissances humaines: Ouvrage où l'on réduit à un seul principe tout ce qui concerne l'entendement humain.* 2 vols. Amsterdam: Chez Pierre Mortier, 1746.

"Continuación de la memoria sobre la tarántula." *Diario curioso, erudito, económico y comercial*, October 13 1787, 422–23.

"Continuación de las noticias sobre la ópera." *Diario curioso, erudito, económico y comercial*, January 18, 1787, 74.

Correo de los Ciegos de Madrid. Edited by José Antonio de Manegat. 1786–91.

Correo Literario de la Europa. Edited by [Francisco Antonio Escartín y Carrera?]. 1781–87.

Cruz, Ramón de la, and Emilio Cotarelo y Mori. *Sainetes de Don Ramón de la Cruz en su mayoría inéditos.* Madrid: Bailly Bailliere, 1915.

Cruz Cano y Olmedilla, Manuel de la, and Juan de la Cruz Cano y Olmedilla. "Colección de trajes tanto antiguos como modernos de España." Madrid, 1777–1788.

D.L.A.M. "Advertencias sobre la descripción de la tarántula." *Memorial Literario, Instructivo y Curioso*, 73 (November 1788): 391–401.

D.M.R.F. "[Carta sobre teatros]." *Diario de Madrid*, April 5, 6, and 7, 1790, 377–79, 81–83, 85–87.

Bibliography

D.Q.P.F. "Carta de D.Q.P.F. al caballero D.M.R.F. sobre teatros, y dificultades de los aspirantes al premio ofrecido en el Diario de 7 de abril de este año de 1790." *Diario de Madrid*, July 3 and 4, 1790, 735–36, 39–42.

d'Alembert, Jean le Rond. "Discours préliminaire des éditeurs." In *ARTFL Encyclopédie*, edited by Robert Morrissey and Glenn Roe. 1751. https://encyclopedie.uchicago.edu/node/88.

"Descripción de las fiestas públicas con que la Imperial Villa de Madrid celebró la paz, y el feliz nacimiento de los dos Serenísimos Infantes D. Carlos y D. Felipe en los días 13, 14 y 15 de este mes." *Memorial literario, instructivo y curioso* (July 1784): 48–85.

Diario de Madrid, March 13, 1791, 295.

Diario curioso, erudito, económico y comercial. Edited by Jacques Thevin. 1786–87.

Diderot, Denis. "Entretiens sur Le fils naturel." In *Oeuvres de Denis Diderot*, edited by Jacques-André Naigeon, 109–238. Paris: Desrey & Deterville, 1798.

Diderot, Denis, and Jean le Rond d'Alembert. "Philosophy." In *The Encyclopedia of Diderot & d'Alembert Collaborative Translation Project*. Ann Arbor: University of Michigan Library. http://hdl.handle.net/2027/spo.did2222.0003.145.

"Discurso XCV." *El Censor* 95 (n.d.): 491–509.

"Edicto." *Diario curioso, erudito, económico y comercial*, April 16, and 17, 1787, 434–35, 38–39.

"Efectos admirables, y nuevos de la influencia de la música." *Diario de Madrid*, April 21, 1789, 441–42.

El Amigo de los ciegos [pseud.]. "Madrid. Carta." *Correo de los Ciegos*, April 21, 1787, 214–15.

El Cómico retirado [pseud.]. *Carta de un cómico retirado a los diaristas, sobre los teatros*. [Madrid][1788].

El Amante del buen gusto [pseud.]. "Carta sobre la necesidad, y utilidad de un teatro de ópera en la Corte." *Diario de Madrid*, January 16, 1790, 61–63.

El Apologista Universal. Edited by Pedro Centeno and Joaquín Ezquerra. 1786–88

El Corresponsal del Censor. 1786–88. Manuel Rubín de Celis y Noriega.

"Ensayo sobre la ópera en música, escrito en lengua italiana por el Conde Francisco Algaroti, y traducido al castellano." *Memorial literario, instructivo y curioso*, February 1787, 258.

Espíritu de los Mejores Diarios Literarios que se Publican en Europa. Edited by Cristóbal Cladera. 1787–91.

Esteve, Pablo. "El atarantulado." 1787, Mus 187–4, Biblioteca Histórica de Madrid.

———. "El teatro y los actores agraviados." 1787, Mus 146–3, Biblioteca Histórica de Madrid.

Eximeno, Antonio. *Del origen y reglas de la música, con la historia de su progreso, decadencia y restauración*. 3 vols. Madrid: Imprenta real, 1796.

"Extracto del informe dado a la Real Junta de los Hospitales General y Pasión de esta Corte por el Dr. D. Bartolomé Piñera y Siles, sobre la historia de una nueva especie de corea o baile de San Vito, originada de la picadura de un insecto que por los fenómenos seguidos a ella se ha creído ser la tarántula; curada a beneficio de la música." *Memorial literario instructivo y curioso de la Corte de Madrid*, April 1788, 636–44.

Feijóo, Benito Jerónimo. "Campana, y crucifijo de Lugo / Benito Jerónimo Feijoo / Cartas eruditas y curiosas / tomo 2," 11–23. Madrid: Imprenta Real de la Gazeta, 1773.

Ferdinand VI of Spain. "[Libro VIII. Título XXII], Ley I. D. Fernando VI, en Aranjuez por céd. De 30 de Mayo de 1757. Establecimiento en Madrid de la Real Academia de las tres Nobles Artes con el título de San Fernando; y privilegios de sus individuos y profesores." In *Novísima Recopilación de las leyes de España*, 173–75. Madrid: Galván Librero, 1805 [1766].

———. *Precauciones mandadas observar por S.M. y repetido nuevamente a la Sala de su Real Orden, el cuidado de su puntual cumplimiento para la representacion de comedias, baxo cuya observancia se permite que se executen.* [Spain] 1763 [1753].

Ferdinando, Epifanio. *Centum historiae sev observationes et casus medici.* Venice: Apud Thomas Ballionum, 1621.

Fernández de Híjar y Abarca de Bolea, Pedro de Alcántara. "[Edicto]," 1787, PL 954, Fundación Joaquín Díaz.

Forner, Juan Pablo. *Oración apologética por la España y su mérito literario: para que sira de exornación al discurso leído por el Abate Denina en la Academia de Ciencias de Berlin, respondienco a la qüestion Qué se debe a España?.* Madrid: Imprenta Real, 1786.

———. *Demostraciones palmarias de que el censor, su corresponsal, el apologista universal, y los demás papelejos de este jaez, no sirven de nada al Estado, ni á la Literatura de España.* Madrid, 1787.

Greco y Lira, Simplicio. [Luis María García Cañuelo y Heredia]. "Discurso XCVII." *El Censor* 97 (1786): 525–48.

Guevara, Antonio de. *Menosprecio de corte y alabanza de aldea, en el qual se tocan muchas y muy buenas doctrinas para los hombres que aman el reposo de sus casas, y aborrecen el bullicio de las Cortes.* Madrid: P. Aznar, 1790.

"Historia natural." *Diario curioso, erudito, económico y comercial*, October 12, 1787, 418–19.

Instruccion militar christiana para el exército y armada de S.M. Madrid: Pedro Marín, 1788.

Irañeta y Jáuregui, Manuel. *Tratado del tarantismo, ó enfermedad originada del veneno de la tarántula según las observaciones que hizo en los Reales Hospitales del Quartel General de San Roque ... Se trata de paso de los efectos de otros animales venenosos, y su curacion.* Madrid: Imprenta Real, 1785.

Iriarte, Tomás de. *La felicidad de la vida en el campo.* Madrid: Joaquín Ibarra, 1780.

———. *La música: Poema.* Madrid: Imprenta Real de La Gaceta, 1779.

———. "Los literatos en cuaresma." In *Colección de obras en verso y prosa de D. Tomás de Yriarte.* Madrid: Imprenta Real, 1805.

270   Bibliography

Iza Zamácola, Juan Antonio de [Don Preciso]. *Colección de las mejores coplas de seguidillas, tiranas y polos que se han compuesto para cantar a la guitarra, con un discurso sobre las causas de la corrupción y abatimiento de la música española.* Madrid: Imprenta de Villalpando, 1799.

Jovellanos, Gaspar Melchor de. *Diarios (memorias íintimas).* Gijón: Instituto de Jovellanos, 1915.

———. *Memoria para el arreglo de la policía de los espectáculos y diversiones públicas y sobre su origen en España.* Alicante: Biblioteca Virtual Miguel de Cervantes, 1999.

———. *Memoria sobre las diversiones públicas.* Colección Crisol. Madrid: Aguilar 1994.

———. "Elogio de Carlos III." In *Obras completas*, edited by Vicente Llombart i Rosa and Joaquín Ocampo Suárez. Alicante: Biblioteca Virtual Miguel de Cervantes, 2010. https://www.cervantesvirtual.com/nd/ark:/59851/bmc708k0.

Junta de Hospitales de Madrid. "[Edicto]." 1787. PL 954, Fundación Joaquín Díaz.

Kircher, Athanasius. "De tarantismo, siue Tarantula Apulo Phalangio eiusque Magnetismo, ac mira cum Musica sympathia." Chap. Pars VIII, Cap. 2. In *Magnes siue De arte magnetica opvs tripartitvm, quo praeterqvam qvod vniversa magnetis natvra, eivsqve in omnibvs artibus & scientijs vsus noua methodo explicetur, è viribus quoque & prodigiosis effectibus magneticarum, aliarumq[ue] abditarum naturæ motionum in elementis, lapidibus, plantis & animalibus elucescentium, multa hucusque incognita naturæ arcana per physica, medica, chymica & mathematica omnis generis experimenta recluduntur*, 755–76. Coloniae Agrippinae: Kalcoven Iodocum, 1643.

Lampillas, Saverio. *Ensayo historico-apológetico de la literatura española contra los opiniones preocupadas de algunos escritores modernos italianos.* Translated by Josefa Amar y Borbón. Zaragoza, 1783.

———. *Saggio storico-apologetico della letteratura spagnuola.* Genova: Felice Repetto, 1778.

Laserna, Blas de. "Música de la comedia La Cecilia Primera P[a]rte." [1786], MUS 25–11, Biblioteca Histórica de Madrid.

———. "Música de la comedia en la 2ª. Parte de La Cecilia." [1787], MUS 36–17, Biblioteca Histórica de Madrid.

———. "La España antigua: tonadilla à solo." [1874–94], MC/3054/8, Biblioteca Nacional de España.

———. "La España moderna: tonadilla à solo." [1874–94], MC/3051/10, Biblioteca Nacional de España.

Luzán Claramunt de Suelves y Gurrea, Ignacio de. *La poetica, ó Reglas de la poesia en general, y de sus principales especies.* Zaragoza: Francisco Revilla, 1737. https://archive.org/details/lapoeticaregla00luz/mode/2up?ref=ol&view=theater.

———. *La poética: o Reglas de la poesía en general y de sus principales especies.* Corregida y aumentada ed. 2 vols. Madrid: Antonio de Sancha, 1789.

Bibliography 271

"Madrid. Carta." *Correo de los Ciegos,* August 15, 17, and 19, 1787, 423; 32; 36.

Maffei, Scipione. "Introduction." In *Teatro italiano o sia scelta di tragedia per uso della scena.* Verona: Jacopo Vallarsi, 1723.

———. *Teatro italiano o sia scelta di tragedia per uso della scena,* I–XLIV. Verona: Jacopo Vallarsi, 1723.

Marchena, José. "Discurso II." *El Observador* 2 (1787): 19–31.

Masdeu, Juan Francisco. *Historia critica de España, y de la cultura española: Obra compuesta y publicada en italiano.* Madrid: Antonio de Sancha, 1783.

Masson de Morvilliers, Nicolas. "Espagne." In *Géographie Moderne* [Encyclopédie Méthodique], 554–68. Paris: Chez Panckoucke, 1782.

Mattei, Saverio. *Se i maestri di cappella son compresi fra gli artigiani, probole di Saverio Mattei, in occasione d'una tassa di fatiche domandata dal maestro Cordella.* Naples: G. M. Porcelli, 1785.

Medonte, drama en música. Madrid: Imprenta Real, 1787.

Meléndez Valdés, Juan. "El filósofo en el campo." Chap. 343–57 in *Poesías de el Dr. D. Juan Meléndez Valdes.* Madrid: Viuda e hijos de Santander, 1794.

"Memoria sobre la Tarántula. Por el Conde de B ... Staroste de Polonia e individuo de varias academias." *Espíritu de los mejores diarios que se publican en la Europa,* Nov. 15 1787, 566–68.

Memorial Literario, Instructivo y Curioso de la Corte de Madrid. Edited by Joaquín Ezquerra and Pedro Pablo Trullenc. 1784–90.

Menuret de Chambaud, Jean-Joseph. "Effets de la musique." In *Encyclopédie,* 1765. https://artflsrv03.uchicago.edu/philologic4/encyclopedie0521/navigate/10/3795/?byte=9449483&byte=9449490&byte=9449493&byte=9449513.

Mercier de la Rivière, Pierre-Paul. *L'ordre naturel et essentiel des sociétés politiques.* Paris: chez Jean Nourse, 1767.

Montaldi, Juan Bautista. "[Recibí]." 1787. MSS-14016/3 (194), Biblioteca Nacional de España.

Muratori, Lodovico Antonio. *Della pubblica felicità: oggetto de' buoni principi, trattato.* Lucca: s. n., 1749.

———. *La pública felicidad objeto de los buenos principes.* Madrid: Imprenta Real, 1790.

Olavide, Pablo de. *Informe de Olavide sobre la Ley Agraria.* Madrid: Fundación Ignacio Larramendi, 1956.

Oración fúnebre dicha en las exequias del Ente de Razón. Málaga: En la imprenta de los herederos de D. Francisco Martínez de Aguilar, 1787.

"Otra [carta]." *Correo de los Ciegos,* February 20, 1787, 156.

Piñera y Siles, Bartolomé. *Descripcion histórica de una nueva especie de corea, ó baile de San Vito, originada de la picadura de un insecto, que por los fenómenos seguidos á ella se ha creido ser la tarántula. Enfermedad de la que ha adolecido y curado á beneficio de la música Ambrosio Silvan: narracion de los síntomas con que se ha presentado, y exposicion fiel y circunstanciada del plan curativo que se ha practicado. Informe dado á la Real Junta de Hospitales.* Madrid: Benito Cano, 1787.

272   *Bibliography*

Planelli, Antonio. *Dell'opera in musica*. Naples: Nella stamperia di Donato Campo, 1772.

Pope, Alexander. "A Discourse on Pastoral Poetry." In *The Works of Mr. Alexander Pope*, 1–10. London: W. Bowyer, for Bernard Lintot, 1717.

———. *An Essay on Criticism*. London, 1711.

Quesnay, François. *Physiocratie, ou Constitution naturelle du gouvernement le plus avantageux*. Yverdon: Du Pont, 1768.

"Real Jardín Botánico." *Memorial Literario*, July 1787, 306–8.

"Relación de los Ejercicios públicos de Botánica, tenidos en la Sala de esta enseñanza en el presente mes de diciembre." *Diario de Madrid*, December 20, 1786, 325–26.

"Retrato de la tarántula macho y hembra, de los ovarios y nido que fabrican: su historia natural, y efectos de su veneno, y la relación del tarantado del Hospital Genera." Madrid: Imprenta de González, 1787.

R.J.S.D.S.M. "Otra [carta]." *Correo de los Ciegos*, August 22, 1787, 388.

Rodríguez, Antonio José, O. Cist. "Yatro-Phonia, o Medicina Musica." In *Palestra critico-medica en que se trata introducir la verdadera Medicina, y desalojar la tirana intrusa de el Reyno de la Naturaleza*, 1–51. Madrid: Imprenta Real de la Gaceta, 1744.

Rodríguez de Arellano, Pascual. *Delicias de Manzanares*. Madrid: Joaquín Ibarra, 1785.

Rodríguez de Campomanes, Pedro. *Discurso sobre el fomento a la industria popular*. Madrid: Antonio de Sancha, 1774.

Rodríguez de Hita, Antonio. *Diapasón instructivo consonancias musicas y morales, documentos a los profesores de música, carta a sus discípulos, de don Antonio Rodríguez de Hita … sobre un breve y facil methodo de estudiar la composición, y nuevo modo de contrapunto para el nuevo estilo*. Madrid: Imprenta de la viuda de Juan Muñoz 1757.

Rosales, Antonio. "Elogio a los autores, actrices, bailarines, ornato y orquesta de la ópera italiana." *Diario de Madrid*, July 26 1789, 825–26.

Rousseau, Jean-Jacques, and John T. Scott. "On the Principle of Melody." In *Essay on the Origins of Languages and Writings Related to Music*. The Collected Writings of Rousseau, 260–70. Hanover, NH: University Press of New England, 1998.

Sala de Alcaldes de Madrid. "Reglamento para el mejor orden y policía del Teatro de la Opera , cuyo privilegio se ha servido conceder el Rey á los Reales Hospitales , aprobado por S. M., y comunicado á la Sala de Alcaldes para su publicación , en virtud de Real Orden de once de Diciembre de mil setecientos ochenta y seis." *Diario curioso, erudito, económico y comercial*, January 19, 1787, 79–84.

Sánchez, Patricio. "[Señor Editor del Correo …]." *Correo de Madrid*, December 23, 1789, 2582–84.

Sánchez, Tomás Antonio. *Carta de Paracuellos*. Madrid: Vda. de Ibarra, 1789.

Semanario erudito. Edited by Antonio Valladares de Sotomayor. 1787–91.

Sempere y Guarinos, Juan. *Ensayo de una biblioteca española de los mejores escritores del reinado de Carlos III*. Vol. 4. Madrid: Imprenta Real, 1787.

Serao, Francesco. *Della Tarantola, o sia Falangio di Puglia, lezioni accademiche.* 1742.

"Sobre la ópera italiana." *Diario curioso, erudito, económico y comercial,* January 27, 1787, 115–16.

"Tarantismo." *Diario curioso, erudito, económico y comercial,* August 8, 1787, 159.

"Tarjeta para el Barbero de Sevilla." *Diario curioso, erudito, económico y comercial,* December 24, 1787, 710–11.

"Teatros. Introducción." *Memorial Literario, Instructivo y Curioso* 38 (February 1787): 259–66.

"Teatros, La Cecilia." *Memorial Literario, Instructivo y Curioso* 32 (August 1786): 471–73.

Terreros y Pando, Esteban de. *Diccionario castellano con las voces de ciencias y artes y sus correspondientes en las tres lenguas francesa, latina e italiana.* Madrid: Viuda de Ibarra, 1786.

Tissot, Samuel Auguste. *An Essay on the Disorders of People of Fashion.* Translated by Francis Bacon Lee. London: Richardson and Urquhart, 1771.

Torrones, Marcelino. "Carta en respuesta a la des Sr. Rosales de 26 de julio, sobre el mérito de los operistas, bailarines, etc." *Diario de Madrid,* August 21, 1789, 229.

Un Subscriptor [pseud.]. "Carta. Al Señor Editor del Correo de Madrid." *Correo de los Ciegos,* June 27 1787, 302–3.

Vandermonde, Charles-Augustin. *Dictionnaire portatif de santé, dans lequel tout le monde peut prendre une connoissance suffisante de toutes les maladies, des différents signes qui les caractérisent chacune en particulier, des moyens les plus sûrs pour s'en préserver, ou des remedes les plus efficaces pour se guérir, & enfin de toutes les instructions nécessaires pour être soi-même son propre médecin. Le tout recueilli des ouvrages, tant anciens que modernes, des médecins les plus fameux, & augmenté d'une infinité de recettes particulieres, & de spécifiques pour toutes sortes de maladies. Par Mr. L***, ancien médecin des armées du Roi, & Mr. de B***, médecin des hôpitaux. Nouvelle édition.* 3rd ed. 2 vols. Paris: Philippe Vincent, 1761. 1759.

von der Borch, Michael-Johann. "Mémoire sur la tarentule." *Journal d'Histoire Naturelle* 10 (1787): 57.

Ximeno y Carrera, José Antonio. "El pastor enamorado a los pies de Gelasia." Dibujo preparatorio para la estampa que ilustra Los seis libros de la Galatea, ca. 1784.

Zavala y Zamora, Gaspar. *El amor dichoso.* Madrid: Librería de Cerro, [1793].

Secondary Sources

Aguilar Piñal, Francisco. *Introducción al siglo XVIII.* Historia de la Literatura Española. Edited by Ricardo de la Fuente. Madrid: Júcar, 1991.

Álvarez Barrientos, Joaquín. "El periodista en la España del siglo XVIII y la profesionalización del escritor." *Estudios de Historia Social* 52/53 (1990): 29–39.

274   Bibliography

———. *Ilustración y neoclasicismo en las letras españolas*. Historia de la literatura universal. Literatura española. Movimientos y épocas. Madrid: Editorial Síntesis, 2005.

———. "La civilización como modelo de vida en el Madrid del siglo XVIII." *Revista de dialectología y tradiciones populares* 56, no. 1 (2001): 147–62.

———. "Prólogo." In *La crítica dramática en España (1789–1833)*, edited by María José Rodríguez Sánchez de León. Madrid: Instituto de la Lengua Española, 2000.

Andioc, René. *Teatro y sociedad en el Madrid del siglo XVIII*. Pensamiento literario español. Madrid: Fundación Juan March, 1976.

Andioc, René, and Mireille Coulon. *Cartelera teatral madrileña del siglo XVIII 1708–1808*. Toulouse: Presses Universitaires du Mirail, 1997.

Anguiano, Pedro Martínez de. *Tratado completo de higiene comparada*. Vol. 2. Madrid: José María Magallón, 1871.

Angulo Egea, María. "El gracioso en el teatro del siglo XVIII." In *La construcción de un personaje: el gracioso*, edited by Luciano García Lorenzo, 383–412. Madrid: Editorial Fundamentos, 2005.

———. *Luciano Francisco Comella (1751–1812), otra cara del teatro de la Ilustración*. San Vicente del Raspeig: Publicaciones de la Universidad de Alicante, 2006.

———. "'Traducido libremente y arreglado al teatro espanol': De Carlo Goldoni a Ramon de la Cruz y Luciano Comella." *Dieciocho: Hispanic Enlightenment* 32, no. 1 (2009): 75–100. http://business.highbeam.com/435406/article-1G1-195917915/traducido-libremente-y-arreglado-al-teatro-espanol.

Astarloa Araluce, Maravillas. "Teatros para la ópera en el Madrid del siglo XVIII." Madrid: Universidad Politécnica de Madrid, 2019.

Astigarraga, Jesús. *The Spanish Enlightenment revisited*. Oxford University Studies in the Enlightenment. Oxford: Voltaire Foundation, 2015.

Barbieri, Francisco Asenjo. *Papeles Barbieri*. Las Rozas de Madrid: Discantus, 2020.

Bassiri, Nima. "The Brain and the Unconscious Soul in Eighteenth-Century Nervous Physiology: Robert Whytt's 'Sensorium Commune.'" *Journal of the History of Ideas* 74, no. 3 (2013): 425–48.

Blom, Eric, and Beverly Wilcox. "Concert Spirituel." In *Grove Music Online. Oxford Music Online.* Oxford University Press. http://www.oxfordmusiconline.com/subscriber/article/grove/music/06257.

Bolufer, Mónica. "Civilizar las costumbres: El papel de la prensa periódica dieciochesca." *Bulletin of Hispanic Studies* 91, no. 9–10 (2014): 97–113.

Boyd, Malcolm, and Juan José Carreras López. *La música en España en el siglo XVIII*. Madrid: Cambridge University Press, 2000.

———. *Music in Spain during the Eighteenth Century*. Cambridge: Cambridge University Press, 1998.

Boynton, Susan. *Silent Music: Medieval Song and the Construction of History in Eighteenth-Century Spain*. New York: Oxford University Press, 2011.

Bibliography   275

Broberg, Gunnar. "The Broken Circle." In *The Quantifying Spirit in the 18th Century*, edited by Tore Frängsmyr, H. L. Heilborn, and Robin E. Rider, 45–71. Berkeley: University of California Press, 1990.

Brown, Theodore M. "The College of Physicians and the Acceptance of Iatromechanism in England." *Bulletin of the History of Medicine* 44, no. 1 (1970): 12–30.

———. "From Mechanism to Vitalism in Eighteenth-Century Physiology." *Journal of the History of Biology* 7, no. 2 (1974): 179–216.

Browne, Janet. "Classification in Science." In *The Oxford Companion to the History of Modern Science.* https://www.oxfordreference.com/view/10.1093/acref/9780195112290.001.0001/acref-9780195112290-e-0136.

Caldera, Ermanno. "La figura del déspota ilustrado en el teatro sentimental dieciochesco." *Dieciocho: Hispanic Enlightenment* 25, no. 2 (2002): 219–28.

Calderone, Antonietta, and Víctor Pagán. "Traducciones de comedias italianas." In *El teatro europeo en la España del siglo XVIII*, edited by Francisco Lafarga, 364–402. Lleida: Universitat de Lleida, 1997.

Calvo Maturana, Antonio. "'Is It Useful to Deceive the People? The Debate on Public Information in Spain at the End of the Ancien Reegime (1780–1808)." *Journal of Modern History* 86, no. 1 (March 2014): 1–46.

Calvo Rigual, Cesáreo. "'La buona figliuola' de Carlo Goldoni y sus traducciones españolas." *Quaderns d'Italia* 22 (2017): 241–62.

Cambronero, Carlos. "Comella, su vida y sus obras." *Revista contemporánea* 102 (1896): 567–82.

Carmena y Millán, Luis. *Crónica de la ópera italiana en Madrid desde el año 1738 hasta nuestros dias.* Madrid: Impr. de M. Minuesa de los Rios, 1878.

Carreras, Juan José. "Hijos de Pedrell: La historiografía musical española y sus orígenes nacionalistas (1780–1980)." *Il saggiatore musicale: Rivista semestrale di musicologia* 8, no. 1 (2001): 121–69.

Casares Rodicio, Emilio. "La creación operística en España. Premisas para la interpretación de un matrimonio." In *La ópera en España e Hispanoamérica: Actas del Congreso Internacional La Opera en España e Hispanoamérica, una creación propia*, edited by Emilio Casares Rodicio and Álvaro Torrente, 21–57. Madrid: Ediciones del ICCMU, 2001.

Cenizo Jiménez, José. "Recepción de la sextina doble en Italia y en el Renacimiento español." In *"Italia, España, Europa": literaturas comparadas, tradiciones y traducciones*, 31–39. Bologna: Arcibel, 2006.

Chakrabarty, Dipesh. "The Muddle of Modernity." *American Historical Review* 116, no. 3 (June 2011): 663–75.

Charlton, David. "Genre and Form in French Opera." In *The Cambridge Companion to Eighteenth-Century Opera*, edited by Anthony R. DellDonna and Pierpaolo Polzonetti, 153–83. Cambridge: Cambridge University Press, 2012.

———. *Opera in the Age of Rousseau: Music, Confrontation, Realism.* New York: Cambridge University Press, 2012.

276   *Bibliography*

Cocking, J. M. *Imagination: A Study in the History of Ideas*. London: Routledge, 1991.

Cook, John A. *Neo-classic Drama in Spain, Theory and Practice*. Dallas: Southern Methodist University Press, 1959.

Corral, Íñigo, and C. Corral. "Neurological Considerations in the History of Tarantism in Spain." *Neurosciences and History* 4, no. 3 (2016): 99–108.

Cotarelo y Mori, Emilio. *Don Ramón de la Cruz y sus obras*. Madrid: J. Perales y Martinez, 1899.

———. *María del Rosario Fernández, La Tirana, primera dama de los teatros de la corte*. Madrid: Sucesores de Rivadeneyra, 1897.

———. *Orígenes y establecimiento de la opera en España hasta 1800*. Madrid: Tipografía de la "Revista de archivos, bibliotecas, y museos," 1917.

Coulon, Mireille. "Música y sainetes. Ramón de la Cruz." In *Teatro y música en España: los géneros breves en la segunda mitad del siglo XVIII*, 289–308. Madrid: Universidad Autónoma de Madrid, 2008.

Darnton, Robert. *The Business of Enlightenment: A Publishing History of the Encyclopédie, 1775–1800*. Cambridge: Belknap Press, 1979.

De Martino, Ernesto. *La terra del rimorso*. Milan: EST, 1996.

De Martino, Ernesto, and Dorothy Louise Zinn. *The Land of Remorse: A Study of Southern Italian Tarantism*. London: Free Association, 2005.

Delgado, Elena L., Jordana Mendelson, and Oscar Vázquez. "Introduction: Recalcitrant Modernities–Spain, Cultural Difference and the Location of Modernism." *Journal of Iberian and Latin American Studies* 13, no. 2–3 (2007): 105–19.

Diz, Alejandro. *Idea de Europa en la España del siglo XVIII*. Madrid: Centro de Estudios Políticos y Constitucionales, 2000.

Dorca, Antonio. "Mesonero Romanos y el cuadro de costumbres ilustrado: 'La posada o España en Madrid.'" In *El costumbrismo, nuevas luces, edited by Dolores Thion Soriano-Mollá*, 161–76. Pau: Presses de l'Université de Pau et des Pays de l'Adour, 2013.

———. "Ramón de la Cruz en el teatro lírico del XVIII: el poema y la música." In *El teatro español del siglo XVIII*, edited by Josep Maria Sala Valldaura, 487–524. Lleida: Universitat de Lleida, 1996.

Dowling, John. "Ramón de la Cruz, libretista de zarzuelas." *Bulletin of Hispanic Studies* 68, no. 1 (1991): 173–82.

Ebersole, Alva Vernon. *La obra teatral de Luciano Francisco Comella, 1789–1806*. Valencia: Albatros, 1985.

Escobar, José. "Civilizar, civilizado y civilización: una polémica de 1763." In *Actas del Séptimo Congreso de la Asociación Internacional de Hispanistas*, 419–27. Roma: Bulzoni, 1982.

Etzion, Judith. "Spanish Music as Perceived in Western Music Historiography: A Case of the Black Legend?" *International Review of the Aesthetics and Sociology of Music* 29, no. 2 (1998): 93–120.

Ewalt, Margaret R. "How Eighteenth-Century Spain and Spanish America Challenge Scholarly Models of Modernity and Postmodern Enlightenment Paradigms." *Eighteenth-Century Studies* 43, no. 2 (2010): 267–74.

Feldman, Martha. "Denaturing the Castrato." *Opera Quarterly* 24, no. 3–4 (2008): 178–99.

Fernández Cabezón, Rosalía. "Una égloga inédita de Agustín de Montiano y Luyando." *Anales de Literatura Española* 6 (1988): 217–58.

———. "El teatro de Luciano Comella a la luz de la prensa periódica." *Dieciocho: Hispanic Enlightenment* 25, no. 1 (2002).

Fernández Fernández, José Luis. *Jovellanos: antropología y teoría de la sociedad.* Comillas: U Pontificia de Comillas, 1991.

Fernández-Cortés, Juan Pablo. *La música en las Casas de Osuna y Benavente (1733–1882): un estudio sobre el mecenazgo musical de la alta nobleza española.* Madrid: Sociedad Española de Musicología, 2007.

Frenk, Margit. *Nuevo corpus de la antigua lírica popular hispánica, siglos XV a XVIII.* Mexico: Facultad de Filosofía y Letras Universidad Nacional Autónoma de México, El Colegio de México, Fondo de Cultura Económica, 2003.

Garcia Càrcel, Ricard. *La leyenda negra: Historia y opinión.* Madrid: Alianza Editorial, 1992.

García Garrosa, María Jesús. "Algunas observaciones sobre la evolución de la comedia sentimental en España." In *El Teatro español del siglo XVIII*, edited by Josep María Sala Valldaura, 427–46. Lleida: Universitat de Lleida, 1996.

García Hurtado, Manuel-Reyes. *El arma de la palabra : los militares españoles y la cultura escrita en el siglo XVIII (1700–1808).* A Coruña: Universidade da Coruña, Servicio de Publicacións, 2002.

Goldman, Peter B. "Dramatic Works and Their Readership in 18th-Century Spain—Social Stratification and the Middle Classes." *Bulletin of Hispanic Studies* 66, no. 2 (April 1989): 129–40.

Gómez, Julio. "Don Blas de Laserna. Un capítulo de la historia del teatro lírico español visto en la vida del último tonadillero." In *El músico Blas de Laserna*, edited by José Luis de Arrese, 119–208. Biblioteca de Corellanos Ilustres. Corella, 1952.

Gozza, Paolo. "Number to Sound. Introduction." In *Music and the Renaissance. Renaissance, Reformation, and Counter-Reformation*, edited by Philippe Vendrix. London: Taylor and Francis, 2001.

Graham, Helen, and Jo Labanyi. *Spanish Cultural Studies: An Introduction. The Struggle for Modernity.* Oxford: Oxford University Press, 1995.

Grout, Donald Jay, J. Peter Burkholder, and Claude V. Palisca. *A History of Western Music.* Tenth edition. New York: W. W. Norton, 2019.

Gruszczynska Ziolkowska, Anna. "La danza de la araña: En torno a los problemas del tarantismo español (1)." *Revista de Folklore* 317 (2007): 147–65.

Guinard, Paul-J. *La presse espagnole de 1737 à 1791, formation et signification d'un genre.* Thèses, mémoires et travaux, 22. Paris: Centre de recherches hispaniques, Institut d'études hispaniques, 1973.

278   *Bibliography*

Hall, Stuart. "Introduction to Formations of Modernity." In *Modernity: An Introduction to Modern Societies*. Cambridge: Polity Press, 1995.

Heartz, Daniel. *Music in European Capitals: The Galant Style, 1720–1780*. New York: W.W. Norton, 2003.

Heartz, Daniel, and Thomas Bauman. *Mozart's Operas*. Berkeley: University of California Press, 1990.

Hernández Mateos, Alberto. *El pensamiento musical de Antonio Eximeno*. Salamanca: Ediciones Universidad de Salamanca, 2013.

Herr, Richard. *The Eighteenth-Century Revolution in Spain*. Princeton, NJ: Princeton University Press, 1958.

Hontanilla, Ana. *El gusto de la razón: Debates de arte y moral en el siglo XVIII español*. La cuestión palpitante. Los siglos XVIII y XIX en España. Madrid: Iberoamericana, 2010.

Hunter, Mary Kathleen. *The Culture of Opera Buffa in Mozart's Vienna: A Poetics of Entertainment*. Princeton Studies in Opera. Princeton, NJ: Princeton University Press, 1999.

Izbicki, Thomas, and Matthias Kaufmann. "School of Salamanca." In *The Stanford Encyclopedia of Philosophy*, edited by Edward N. Zalta. https://plato.stanford.edu/archives/sum2019/entries/school-salamanca/.

Jacobs, Helmut C. "La función de la música en la discusión estética de la Ilustración española." *Dieciocho: Hispanic Enlightenment* 32, no. 1 (2009): 49–74.

Jones, Joseph R. "María Rosa de Gálvez, Rousseau, Iriarte y el melólogo en la España del siglo XVIII." *Dieciocho: Hispanic Enlightenment* 19, no. 2 (1996): 165–80.

Kerr, Heather, and Claire Walker. *Fama and Her Sisters: Gossip and Rumour in Early Modern Europe*. Beligum: Brepols, 2015.

Kriesel, Karl Marcus. "Montesquieu: Possibilistic Political Geographer." *Annals of the Association of American Geographers* 58, no. 3 (1968): 557–74.

Kristeller, Paul Oskar. "The Modern System of the Arts: A Study in the History of Aesthetics (I)." *Journal of the History of Ideas* 12, no. 4 (1951): 496–527.

Labrador López de Azcona, Germán. *Gaetano Brunetti (1744–1798): Catálogo crítico, temático y cronológico*. Madrid: AEDOM, 2005.

———. "La comedia con música 'Clementina', de Ramón de la Cruz: un camino inexplorado en la historia de la zarzuela." *Studi Ispanici* 37 (2012): 103–18.

Labrador López de Azcona, Germán, Begoña Lolo, and Albert Recasens Barberà. *La música en los teatros de Madrid*. Madrid: Editorial Alpuerto, 2009.

Larriba, Elisabel. *El público de la prensa en España a finales del siglo XVIII (1781–1808)*. Translated by Daniel Gascón. Ciencias sociales. Zaragoza: Prensas de la Universidad de Zaragoza, 2013.

———. *Le public de la presse en Espagne à la fin du XVIIIe siècle (1781–1808)*. Bibliothèque de littérature générale et comparée. Paris: Honoré Champion, 1998.

Le Guin, Elisabeth. *Boccherini's Body: An Essay in Carnal Musicology*. Berkeley: University of California Press, 2006.

———. *The Tonadilla in Performance: Lyric Comedy in Enlightenment Spain*. Berkeley: University of California Press, 2014.

Lehner, Ulrich L., and Michael O'Neill Printy. *A Companion to the Catholic Enlightenment in Europe*. Leiden: Brill 2010.

León Tello, Francisco José. *La teoría española de la música en los siglos XVII Y XVIII*. Madrid: Consejo Superior de Investigaciones Científicas, Instituto Español de Musicología, 1974.

León-Sanz, Pilar. "Music Therapy in Eighteenth-Century Spain: Perspectives and Critiques." In *Music and the Nerves, 1700–1900*, edited by James Kennaway, 98–117. New York: Palgrave MacMillan, 2014.

Lesch, John E. "Systematics and the Geometrical Spirit." In *The Quantifying Spirit in the 18th Century*, edited by Tore Frängsmyr, H. L. Heilborn and Robin E. Rider, 73–111. Berkeley: University of California Press, 1990.

Leza, José Máximo. "Aspectos productivos de la ópera en los teatros públicos de Madrid (1730–1799)." In Rodicio and Torrente, *La ópera en España e Hispanoamérica*, 231–62.

———. *El teatro musical*. [Madrid]: Gredos, 2003.

———. *Historia de la música en España e Hispanoamérica: La música en el siglo XVIII*. Madrid: FCE, 2014.

———. "Ispirazioni per la riforma: Trasformazioni operistiche nella Spagna di fine Settecento." In *D'une scène à l'autre, l'opéra italien en Europe: Les pérégrinations d'un genre*, edited by Damien Colas and Alessandro di Profio, 189–214. Wavre: Mardaga, 2009.

———. "Metastasio on the Spanish Stage: Operatic Adaptations in the Public Theatres of Madrid in the 1730s." *Early Music* 26, no. 4 (1998): 623–31.

Lolo Herranz, Begoña. "Itinerarios musicales en la tonadilla escénica." In *Paisajes sonoros en el Madrid del S. XVIII: La tonadilla escénica*, edited by Museo de San Isidro, 14–31. Madrid: Museo de San Isidro, 2003.

Lombardía, Ana. "From Lavapiés to Stockholm: Eighteenth-Century Violin Fandangos and the Shaping of Musical 'Spanishness.'" *Eighteenth-Century Music* 17, no. 2 (September 2020): 177–99.

Madero, Marta. "El duellum entre la honra y la prueba según las Siete partidas de Alfonso X y el comentario de Gregorio López." *Cahiers d'Études Hispaniques Médiévales* 24 (2001): 343–52.

Mantz, Harold Elmer. "Non-Dramatic Pastoral in Europe in the Eighteenth Century." *PMLA* 31, no. 3 (1916): 421–47.

Maravall, José Antonio. "La palabra 'civilización' y su sentido en el siglo XVIII." Paper presented at the Actas del Quinto Congreso Internacional de Hispanistas, Bordeaux, 1977.

Marcello, Elena E. "Il filosofo de campagna goldoniano tradotto da Ramón de la Cruz. Note di lingua e riscrittura." *Quaderns d'Italia* 17, no. 11–26 (2012).

Marías, Julián. *España inteligible: Razón histórica de las Españas*. Madrid: Alianza, 1985.

280 Bibliography

———. "La España posible en tiempos de Carlos III." In *Obras*. Madrid: Revista de Occidente, 1966.

Marín, Miguel Angel, and Màrius Bernadó. *Instrumental Music in Late Eighteenth-Century Spain*. Kassel: Edition Reichenberger, 2014.

Martínez Reinoso, Josep. "El surgimiento del concierto público en Madrid (1767–1808)." Universidad de la Rioja, 2017.

Mayhew, Susan. "Cosmopolitanism." In *A Dictionary of Geography*. Oxford University Press. https://www.oxfordreference.com/view/10.1093/acref/9780199680856.001.0001/acref-9780199680856-e-3800.

McClelland, Ivy Lilian. *"Pathos" dramático en el teatro español de 1750 a 1808: La alta tragedia*. Liverpool: Liverpool University Press, 1998.

McInerny, Ralph, and John O'Callaghan. "Saint Thomas Aquinas." In *Stanford Encyclopedia of Philosophy*, edited by Edward N. Zalta. https://plato.stanford.edu/archives/sum2018/entries/aquinas/.

Medina, Ángel. *Los atributos del capón: Imagen histórica de los cantores castrados en España*. Música Hispana Textos. Estudios. Madrid: ICCMU, 2001.

Menéndez y Pelayo, Marcelino. *Historia de las ideas estéticas en España por el doctor D. Marcelino Menéndez y Pelayo*. Madrid: Impr. de A. Pérez Dubrull, 1890.

Monelle, Raymond. *The Musical Topic: Hunt, Military and Pastoral*. Bloomington: Indiana University Press, 2006.

Monk, Samuel Holt. *The Sublime; A Study of Critical Theories in XVIII-Century England*. Ann Arbor: University of Michigan Press, 1960.

Myers Brown, Sandra. "'Cartas de España'. Noticias musicales en la correspondencia diplomática. Madrid-Londres, 1783–1788." *Revista de Musicología* 32, no. 1 (2009): 411–28.

Neville, Don. "Rondò." In *Grove Music Online. Oxford Music Online*. Oxford University Press. https://doi.org/10.1093/gmo/9781561592630.article.23788.

Núñez Olarte, Juan Manuel. *El hospital general de Madrid en el Siglo 18: Actividad médico-quirúrgica*. Madrid: Editorial CSIC, 1999.

Ortega, Judith. "El mecenazgo musical de la casa de Osuna durante la segunda mitad dell siglo XVIII: el entorno musical de Luigi Boccherini en Madrid." *Revista de Musicología* 27, no. 2 (2004): 643–98.

———. "La música en la Corte de Carlos III y Carlos IV (1759–1808): De la Real Capilla a la Real Cámara." Universidad Complutense de Madrid, 2010.

Outram, Dorinda. *The Enlightenment*. New Approaches to European History. Cambridge: Cambridge University Press, 2019.

Paquette, Gabriel. "The Reform of the Spanish Empire in the Age of Enlightenment." In *The Spanish Enlightenment Revisited*, edited by Jesús Astigarraga, 149–67. Oxford: Voltaire Foundation, 2015.

Parsons, Nicola. *Reading Gossip in Early Eighteenth-Century England*. London: Palgrave Macmillan, 2009.

Pataky Kosove, Joan Lynne. *The "Comedia Lacrimosa" and Spanish Romantic Drama (1773–1865)*. London: Tamesis, 1977.

Pedrell, Felipe. *Diccionario biográfico y bibliográfico de músicos y escritores de música españoles*. Barcelona: Tipografía de V. Berdós y Feliu, 1894.

Pérez de Guzmán, Luis. "Algunas noticias desconocidas sobre el Teatro de los Caños del Peral." *Revista de archivos, bibliotecas y museos* 30, no. 1–6 (January–June 1926): 87–92.

Pessarrodona, Aurèlia. *Jacinto Valledor y la tonadilla: Un músico de teatro en la España ilustrada (1744–1809)*. Sant Cugat (Barcelona): Editorial Arpegio, 2018.

———. "Viva, viva la Tirana: Clarifying an Elusive Spanish Dance Song." *Journal of Musicology* 39, no. 4 (Fall 2022): 469–539.

Pessarrodona i Pérez, Aurèlia. "El estilo musical de la tonadilla escénica dieciochesca y su relación con la ópera italiana a través de la obra de Jacinto Valledor (1744–1809)." *Revista de musicología* 30, no. 1 (2007): 9–48.

———. "La tonadilla a la Barcelona del darrer terç del Set-cents més enllà de la Casa de Comèdies." *Scripta: Revista internacional de literatura i cultura medieval i moderna* (Ejemplar dedicado a: Erotisme i obscenitat en la literatura catalana antiga) 3 (2014): 122–42.

Petrobelli, Pierluigi. "Tartini, Giuseppe." In *Grove Music Online. Oxford Music Online*. Oxford University Press. https://www.oxfordmusiconline. com/grovemusic/view/10.1093/gmo/9781561592630.001.0001/omo-9781561592630-e-0000027529.

Powers, Harold S., Frans Wiering, James Porter, James Cowdery, Richard Widdess, Ruth Davis, Marc Perlman, Stephen Jones, and Allan Marett. "Mode." In *Grove Music Online. Oxford Music Online*. Oxford University Press. http://www.oxfordmusiconline.com/subscriber/article/grove/music/43718.

Robertson, Ritchie. "The Catholic Enlightenment: Some Reflections on Recent Research." *German History* 34, no. 4 (December 2016): 630–45.

Robinson, Michael F. "Financial Management at the Teatro de los Caños del Peral, 1786–99." In *Music in Spain during the Eighteenth Century*, edited by Malcolm Boyd, 29–52. United Kingdom: Cambridge University Press, 1998.

Rodríguez Gómez, Juana Inés. "Las obras de Carlo Goldoni en España (1750–1800)." Universitat de València, 1997.

Rodríguez Perez, Yolanda. "Being Eurocentric within Europe: Nineteenth-Century English and Dutch Literary Historiography and Oriental Spain." In *Eurocentrism in European History and Memory*, edited by Marjet Brolsma, Robin de Bruin and Matthijs Lok, 157–78. Amsterdam: Amsterdam University Press, 2019.

Rodríguez Sánchez de León, María José. *La crítica dramática en España (1789–1833)*. Madrid: Instituto de la Lengua Española; Consejo Superior de Investigaciones Científicas CSIC, 2000.

———. "Tres intentos fracasados de publicar una revista de teatros (1795, 1802 y 1804)." In *El siglo que llaman ilustrado: Homenaje a Francisco Aguilar*

Piñal, edited by José Checa Beltrán, 745–54. Madrid: Consejo Superior de Investigaciones Científicas, 1996.

Rodríguez-Millán, Roberto. "Noah's Grandson and St. James: Rewriting the Past in Eighteenth-Century Spain." *European Legacy* 25, no. 7–8 (2020): 733–42.

Román Gutiérrez, Isabel. "De polémicas y apologías: el debate sobre el progreso de la España en las respuestas a Masson de Morvilliers y la historiografía ilustrada." *Dieciocho: Hispanic Enlightenment* (2021): 125–62.

Rubio, Samuel. *Forma del villancico polifónico desde el siglo XV hasta el XVIII*. Cuenca: Instituto de Música Religiosa de la Ecxma. Diputación Provincial, 1979.

Saavedra, Pegerto. "Ocio y vida cotidiana en la España rural del siglo VIII." In *Trabajo y ocio en la época moderna*, edited by Luis A. Ribot García and Javier Huerta Calvo, 111–38. Madrid: Actas, 2001.

Sala Valldaura, Josep Maria. "Los autores y las obras. Ramón de la Cruz." In *Historia del teatro breve en España*, edited by Javier Huerta Calvo, 699–730. Madrid: Iberoamericana Vervuert, 2008.

Sánchez-Blanco, Francisco. *El absolutismo y las Luces en el reinado de Carlos III*. Madrid: M. Pons, 2002.

———. *La mentalidad ilustrada*. Madrid: Taurus, 1999.

Sarrailh, Jean. *L'Espagne éclairée de la seconde moitié du XVIIIe siècle*. Paris: Impr. nationale, 1954.

Schneider, Marius. *La danza de las espadas y la tarantela. Ensayo musicológico, etnográfico y arqueológico sobre los ritos medicinales*. Madrid: Institución Fernando el Católico, 2016.

Sebold, Russell P. "Análisis estadístico de las ideas poéticas de Luzán: sus orígenes y naturaleza." In *El rapto de la mente: Poética y poesía dieciochescas* Alicante: Biblioteca Virtual Miguel de Cervantes, 2001. https://www.cervantesvirtual.com/obra-visor/anlisis-estadstico-de-las-ideas-poticas-de-luzn---sus-orgenes-y-su-naturaleza-0/html/ff65b43a-82b1-11df-acc7-002185ce6064_5.html.

Shuttleton, David E. "The Fashioning of Fashionable Diseases in the Eighteenth Century." *Literature and Medicine* 35, no. 2 (Fall 2017): 270–91.

Singy, Patrick. "The Popularization of Medicine in the Eighteenth Century: Writing, Reading, and Rewriting Samuel Auguste Tissot's Avis au peuple sur sa sante." *Journal of Modern History* 82, no. 4 (December 2010): 769–800.

Soler, Antonio, and Samuel Rubio. *Siete villancicos de navidad*. Cuenca: Instituto de Música Religiosa de la Excma. Diputación Provincial, 1979.

Soriano Fuertes, Mariano. *Historia de la música española desde la venida de los Fenicios hasta el ano de 1850*. Madrid: D. Bernabé Carrafa, 1855.

Soto Carrasco, David. "Contra la *tibetanización* de España. Una mirada sobre las lecturas del s. XVIII de Marías, Maravall y Díez del Corral." *Res Publica* 22 (2009): 399–412.

Stein, Louise K. *Songs of Mortals, Dialogues of the Gods: Music and Theatre in Seventeenth-Century Spain*. New York: Clarendon Press, 1993.

Sterne, Jonathan. *The Audible Past: Cultural Origins of Sound Reproduction.* Durham: Duke University Press, 2003.

Stevenson, Robert. *Christmas Music from Baroque Mexico.* Berkeley: University of California Press, 1974.

———. *Latin American Colonial Music Anthology.* Washington, DC: Organization of American States, 1975.

Strohm, Reinhard. *Dramma per musica: Italian Opera Seria of the Eighteenth Century.* New Haven: Yale University Press, 1997.

Subirá, José. *El compositor Iriarte (1750–1791) y el cultivo español del melólogo (melodrama).* Barcelona: Consejo Superior de Investigaciones Científicas. Instituto Español de Musicología. Monografías, 1949.

———. *La tonadilla escénica.* Madrid: Tipografía de Archivos, 1928.

Taruskin, Richard, and Christopher Howard Gibbs. *The Oxford History of Western Music.* 2nd ed. New York: Oxford University Press, 2019.

Thomas, Downing A. *Music and the Origins of Language: Theories from the French Enlightenment.* New Perspectives in Music History and Criticism. Cambridge: Cambridge University Press, 1995.

Torres Mulas, Jacinto. "Music Periodicals in Spain: Beginnings and Historical Development." *Fontes Artis Musicae* 44, no. 4 (October–December 1997): 331–42.

Valladares Reguero, Aurelio. "El médico ubetense Bartolomé Piñera y Siles y la polémica sobre los efectos curativos de la música: El tarantismo en el siglo XVIII." *Códice* 12 (1997): 39–48.

Vartija, Devin J. "Introduction to the Special Issue 'Enlightenment and Modernity." *International Journal for History, Culture and Modernity* 8, no. 3–4 (December 2020): 235–45.

Venn, Couze. *Occidentalism: Modernity and Subjectivity.* London: SAGE Publications, 2000.

Voskuhl, Adelheid. *Androids in the Enlightenment: Mechanics, Artisans, and Cultures of the Self.* Chicago: University of Chicago Press, 2013.

Wald, Priscilla. *Contagious: Cultures, Carriers, and the Outbreak Narrative.* Durham, NC: Duke University Press, 2008.

Williams, Anne Patricia. "Description and Tableau in the Eighteenth-Century British Sentimental Novel." *Eighteenth-Century Fiction* 8, no. 4 (July 1996): 465–84.

Wittrock, Björn. "Modernity: One, None, or Many? European Origins and Modernity as a Global Condition." *Daedalus* 129, no. 1 (2000): 31–60.

Yun Casalilla, Bartolomé. "Ingresos, formas de distribución del producto agrario y cambio social en Castilla la Vieja y León en el siglo XVIII." In *Estructuras agrarias y reformismo ilustrado en la España del siglo XVIII,* edited by Seminario sobre Agricultura e ilustración en España, 481–505. Madrid: Ministerio de Agricultura, Alimentación y Medio Ambiente, 1989.

Index

Page numbers in bold type indicate figures, examples, and tables. Initial Spanish articles are ignored in alphabetical sorting.

actor-singers   53–5, 67, 72, 114,
  169–70, 253–4
  see also Garrido, Miguel;
    tonadillas
affective language   46
afrancesamiento   166–7, 257, 260
agriculture policy   27, 180, 184,
  191–2, 193, 196, 205, 223
  see also peasants
Aguilera, Vicente   128, 129
Algarotti, Francesco   36, 46, 147,
  150–2
Ambrosio   *see* Silván, Ambrosio
ancient Greece   *see* Greek antiquity
ancient-modern debates   19, 41–2,
  48–9, 52, 253–7
  see also Greek antiquity;
    modernity
Andreozzi, Cristoforo   32 n.5, 170
anti-Cartesianism   96, 97–8, 107
  see also empiricism
apologistas   4–5, 20, 21–3, 24–5,
  49, 134, 145, 256–7
  see also Forner, Juan Pablo
Aranda, count of   135, 263, 264
aristocrats
  Bourbon policy on   189–90,
    191–2, 193, 196
  critiqued in *El atarantulado*   114,
    115–8, 123, 126, 256
  depicted in *La Cecilia* and *Cecilia
    viuda*   183, 185, 189–93,
    196–7, 261
  see also elites
Aristotle   20, 104, 152, 153, 258

Armona, José Antonio de   62, 161,
  163
Arroyal, León de   48
Arteaga, Esteban de   25, 33, 39,
  40–1, 51–2
Arteaga, Joaquina   253–4
artificiality   39, 46–8, 97
Asociación para la Representación
  de Óperas Italianas   144
El atarantulado (Esteve)
  cast and characters of   74–5, **83**
  as critique of aristocrats   114,
    115–8, 123, 126, 256
  "fashionable" diseases depicted
    in   26, 74–5, 114, 115–8, 123,
    126
  musical numbers in   75, **78–82**,
    84, 85–6, **87**, 88–9, 115–8,
    119–22, 123, **124–5**
  public depicted in   73, 76–7, 90,
    93–4, 112
  public opinion shaped by   26, 83,
    94
  tarantism depicted in   75–7, 83,
    85–6, 88–9, 93–4, 112
audiences
  attitudes toward opera   130, 134,
    136, 139–42, 156–7, 166–8,
    175–6
  behavior rules for   157–65
  efforts to educate   146–52, 154–7
  preference for sentimentality   27,
    182–3, 222–3, 250, 263
  preference for spectacle   70,
    156–7, 182, 205, 248

286   *Index*

audiences (*cont'd*)
  for tarantism treatment   112–5
  for tonadillas   25–6, 60–2, 63, 67,
    83, 136, 163, 253–4
  see also chorizos and polacos (fan
    clubs); public opinion
autos sacramentales   9, 47 n.26, 54,
  136

Baglivi, Giorgio   74, 92, 94–6, 97–8,
  100–1, 110–1, 112
bailetes   192–3, **194–5, 204**, 205–6,
  208
Banco de San Carlos   133, 143
Batteux, Charles   25, 34, 35–8, 156,
  226–7
battle trope   65, **66**, 67
Bausac, Rafael   240, **241**
Bea de Navarra, Miguel   90, 130
beatus ille topic   190–1
Black Legend   4, 21, 256
  see also Spain: presumed
    backwardness of
Boissier de Sauvages, François   92,
  95, 96, 97–8, 99–100, 109, 132
Borch, Count of   127–8, 131
La botillería (de la Cruz)   164
botillerías   140, 160, 164–5
Bourbon period   7, 10, 27, 249, 255
  see also Bourbon policies and
    reforms; Charles III; Charles IV
Bourbon policies and reforms
  on agriculture   27, 180, 184,
    191–2, 193, 196, 205, 223
  on class   27, 181, 183–4, 189–90,
    191–2, 193, 196, 207–10, 261
  on the economy   27, 176, 184–5,
    193, 196, 248–9, 255. *see also*
    physiocracy; postmercantilism
  on Europeanization   19, 145, 147,
    165–6, 178, 259–60
  on the military   219
  on nature   224, 226
  on neoclassicism   31, 35, 151–2,
    182, 255–6

on the press   3–4, 64–5, 258
on religion   9
on theater   134, 135, 139, 157–66,
  176–8, 182, 222, 259–60
see also Charles III; Charles IV;
  neoclassicism; physiocracy
Boyd, Malcolm   16
Boyle, Robert   102, 258
Boynton, Susan   16
Buffon, Comte de (George-Louis
  Leclerc)   97, 258–9
bullfighting   141
La buona figliuola (Goldoni/
  Piccinni)   118, 199–201

Cabarrús, Francisco   135, 139,
  140–4, 145–7, 158, 166, 175–6,
  177
Cadalso, José   11, 21, 149
Calderón de la Barca, Pedro   15, 69,
  137, 182, 240
Calvo Maturana, Antonio   145,
  158
canciones de labradores   205, 210
Los Caños del Peral   *see* Teatro de
  los Caños del Peral
Cañuelo Heredia, Luis María
  García   33, 34
  see also Simplicio Greco y Lira
canzonettas   210, **211**, 223
capones   47–8
  see also castrati
Carmena y Millán, Luis   17
Carmona, Manuel Salvador   **45**,
  150
Carreras, Juan José   12, 16, 17
Cartesianism   96, 97–8, 107, 258
Casal y Aguado, Manuel   92–3
Casares Rodicio, Emilio   175–6
castrati   34, 47–8
  see also Farinelli
Catalá de Valeriola y Luján, Josefa
  Dominga   *see* Mortara,
  marchioness of (Josefa Dominga
  Catalá de Valeriola y Luján)

Catholicism
  authority disrupted by the
    press   29–30, 168
  and the Enlightenment   8–9, 19,
    28, 74, 109
  in the Habsburg period   7, 8, 249,
    255
  and modernity   9, 19, 256, 260
  and physiocracy   185
  and tarantism   74, 99, 109
Cavanilles, Antonio José   21–2
Cavaza, Manuel
  "The Instructed Singer"   49–50
  as musician-theorist   32–3, 39,
    42, 49–50, 52–3, 64, 257
  El músico censor   25, 30–1, 33,
    42–4, 46, 49, 53, 256, 257
  "Rudimentos y elementos de la
    música práctica"   49–50
  and Thomist realism   43–4
La Cecilia (Comella/Laserna)
  "Bailete con panderetas" (act 1,
    scene 4)   192–3, **194–5**, 205
  bailete reprise (act 2, scene
    3)   205–6
  "Canzonetta de payas" (act 1, scene
    3)   210, **211**, 223
  "Canzonetta de payos" (act 2, scene
    2)   205, 210, 223, 224
  characters in   **186**
  commissioning of   179, 180–1,
    182, 251
  compared to *La buona
    figliuola*   199–201
  Count's monologue (act 1, scene
    2)   190–2
  depiction of aristocrats in   183,
    185, 189–93, 261
  depiction of peasants in   183–5,
    192–3, 197–203, **204**, 205–10,
    223–4, 261
  and genre   27–8, 181–3
  "Lily and Jasmine" (act 1, scene
    1)   198–9
  musical numbers in   **186, 204**

pastoral conventions in   183–4,
    223–4
performances of   182–3
plot and setting of   179–80
references to neoclassicist
    aesthetics in   190–1, 240, 243,
    245
seguidillas in   212, 216–7, 220
sentimental tableaux in   222,
    223–4, 246, 250
stick dance (act 2, scene 3)   206–
    7, 208–9
Cecilia viuda (Comella/Laserna)
  characters in   **187**
  commissioning of   180–1, 182,
    251
  depiction of aristocrats in   183,
    185, 196–7, 261
  depiction of peasants in   183–5,
    196–7, 203, **204**, 205, 224, 246,
    248, 261
  depiction of soldiers in   217–20
  Don Nicasio's ode (act 1)   196–7
  final scene   245–6
  and genre   27–8, 181–3
  musical numbers in   **188–9, 204,
    221**
  overture   226–7, **228–30**, 231,
    232–4, 235, **236–7**, 246
  pastoral conventions in   183–4,
    246, 248
  performances of   182–3
  plot and setting of   179–80
  printed libretto for   240, **241**, 246,
    247
  references to neoclassicist
    aesthetics in   238, 240, 243,
    245–6
  seguidillas in   212, 213, 217–20,
    221
  sentimental tableaux in   222–3,
    224, 226–7, 231, 235, 245–6,
    247, 248, 249, 250
  storm chorus (act 2, scene
    2)   246, 248

288   *Index*

El Censor   22, 24, 25, 30–1, 33, 59,
    212, 262
  see also "Discourse 97" (*El Censor*)
censorship   25, 33, 151–2, 153, 182,
    262–4
Cerone, Pietro   30, 50
Cervantes, Miguel de   15, 68, 243,
    245
Chakrabarty, Dipesh   10
chapel system   31–3, 38, 39, 44,
    47–9, 52–3, 72
Charles III
  agricultural policy under   180,
    184, 191–2, 224, 226
  and Europeanization   145
  Jovellanos's eulogy to   248–9
  and opera   133, 135, 140–1, 144,
    157–9, 235, 259
  opposition to superstition   9, 47
    n.46, 248
  praised in *Medonte*
    prologue   137–8
  and the press   64–5
  reign of   3–4, 262
  theater rules issued under   157–9,
    160, 161–2
Charles IV   3–4, 145, 165, 166, 171,
    184, 260, 262–4
Cheyne, George   106
chorizos and polacos (fan
    clubs)   67, 138, 159, 168, 171,
    172–4, 253
Cid, Francisco Xavier
  Baglivi's influence on   73–4, 94–8,
    100–1
  influence of   89–90, 92, 93,
    111–2, 128
  responses to criticism   115,
    130–2
  scientific ideas of   26, 73–4, 92,
    94–102, 132, 259
  on the soul   26, 103–9, 259
  on the tarantella   86, 88, 102–3

*Tarantismo observado en
    España*   77, 89–90, 94–100,
    102–9, **104**, **105**, 111–3
La civilización (de la Cruz)   139–40
civilization
  Italian opera as tool for   23, 26–7,
    130, 134, 137–40, 145–51,
    157–66
  and modernity   139–40, 145–6,
    218
  and Spain   139–40, 145–6
Cladera, Cristóbal   127
classification of music   34–8, 44, 46
  see also paradigms of music
Clavijo y Fajardo, José   55, 212
Colección de trajes de España (de la
    Cruz Cano y Olmedilla)   223–4,
    225
Coliseo de la Cruz and Coliseo del
    Príncipe
  audience at   136, 172–4
  La Cecilia at   183
  La España antigua and *La España
    moderna* at   253–5
  fans of (chorizos and polacos)   67,
    138, 159, 168, 171, 172–4, 253
  Lenten concerts at   170–1, 172
  location of   161
  management of   62, 170–1, 175
  repertoire of   136
  reputation of   158, 159, 170
coliseos   158, 159, 161, 162, 163–4,
    169–71, 172–4, 177
  see also Coliseo de la Cruz and
    Coliseo del Príncipe
colonialism   6, 15, 21, 176, 224, 249
  see also Spanish empire
comedias   61, 116–7, 137, 152,
    156–7, 161, 203, 205
Comella, Luciano Francisco
  and Bourbon ideals   27–8,
    179–82, 183–5, 191, 196,
    205–6, 251

career of   180–1, 183, 251
neoclassicist criticism of   181–2, 183, 238
style and influences of   27–8, 181–3, 189, 208, 210, 220, 226–7
see also *La Cecilia* (Comella/ Laserna); *Cecilia viuda* (Comella/Laserna)
common sensorium   104
Compañía de los Reales Sitios   135, 141–2
Condillac, Étienne Bonnot de   24, 34, 38, 40, 110, 138, 258–9
coplas   67, 83, 85, 213
Correo de Cádiz   60–1
Correo de los Ciegos
  goal of   60
  tarantism discussed in   92–3, 130–2
  theater discussed in   62, 70–2, 144–5, 159–60, 168, 176
cosmopolitanism   26–7, 138–41, 144–5, 159, 167, 173–4, 176, 177–8, 259–60
Cotarelo y Mori, Emilio   17
counterpoint   34, 40–1, 43–4, 50, 53
criticism
  association with philosophy   67–9
  as defamation   63–5, 67, 131, 258
  defense of   70–2
  versus empiricism   96–100
  as modern form of knowledge   25, 29–30, 31, 60, 63–4, 67–9, 257–8
  perceived arrogance of   43–4, 258
  and the rise of the periodical press   33, 55, 59–63, 72
critics
  versus artists   25–6, 30–1, 34, 39, 53–5, 60–5, 67–72, 258

figure of   29, 63–5, 67–70
versus the public   30, 53
rebuked in *El teatro y los actores agraviados*   29, 31, 54–5, 63–5, 67–70, 258
as "sayers"   25, 31, 55, 67–72, 99, 258
La Cruz   *see* Coliseo de la Cruz and Coliseo del Príncipe
cuatros   204, 205

d'Alembert, Jean le Rond   36, 50, 110
de la Cruz Cano y Olmedilla, Juan   223–4, **225**
de la Cruz Cano y Olmedilla, Manuel   223–4
de la Cruz, Ramón   54, 116–7, 139–40, 201, 205, 224
defamation   63–5, 67, 131, 258
del Moral, Pablo   171
Delgado, Elena   2
Dell'origine (Eximeno)   51, 52–3, 257, 263, 264
Denina, Carlo   21
Descripción histórica de una nueva especie de corea (Piñera)   77, 86, 88, 112, 128
Diario curioso, erudito, económico y comercial   147–52, **148**, 160
Diario de Madrid
  music criticism discussed in   263
  opera and theater discussed in   145, 167–8, 173–4, 175, 176–7, 250
  tarantism discussed in   90–3, 126–8, 129–32, 263
Díaz Rengifo, Juan (Diego García)   41
Diccionario de autoridades   68, 158
Diderot, Denis   182
Díez González, Santos   250
"Discourse 95" (*El Censor*)   212

290   *Index*

"Discourse 97" (*El Censor*)
  Cavaza's criticism of   25, 39,
    42–4, 46, 52–3, 64, 256
  on the chapel system   25, 47–9,
    50–1, 72, 257, 263
  on music and nature   33–5, 36,
    38, 39–43
  on music as a fine art   33–5,
    36–8, 44, 46
  on the musician-philosopher
    figure   40–1, 51, 71
  publication of   33
  on singing   44, 46–9, 52–3
  on the verbal paradigm of
    music   34, 37, 39–43, 51,
    155–6, 257
  see also Simplicio Greco y Lira
D.M.R.F.   173–4, 175, 176, 177
Don Lazarillo Vizcardi
  (Eximeno)   51
D.Q.R.F.   175

elites   5, 23, 70–2, 133–4, 139–41,
  143–5, 151–2, 157, 172–3
  see also aristocrats
empiricism   26, 96–100, 105–10,
  132, 226, 249, 258–9
Encyclopédie   102, 127, 132
Encyclopédie Méthodique   1, 4–5,
  20–1, 36, 134, 253
  see also Masson de Morvilliers,
  Nicolas
encyclopedism   7, 19, 73, 94, 99,
  110, 184–5
engravings   **45**, 150, 222–4, 240,
  241, 246, **247**
Enlightenment
  and Catholicism   8–9, 19, 28, 74,
    109
  and criticism   67–9
  modernity as broader than   3, 9
  narratives of   8–9, 13, 15, 28, 260
  and nationalism   11, 19
  and nature   249–50
  as reemergence from chaos   248–9

versus scholasticism   42–3
and the state   25, 145, 152–3
and tarantism   26, 73–4, 109, 256
terminology for   1–2
see also "Discourse 97" (*El
  Censor*); modernity
La España antigua (Laserna)   253–
  5, 256, 257, 261
La España moderna (Laserna)   254–
  5, 256, 257, 258, 261
Espíritu de los mejores diarios   92–
  3, 126–7, 132
Esquilache, Marquis of   162
Esquilache Riots   3 n.3, 162
Esser, Karl Michael   169
Esteve, Pablo   69, 70, 113, 114, 123,
  126, 256
  see also *El atarantulado* (Esteve);
    *El teatro y los actores
    agraviados* (Esteve)
Etzion, Judith   14–5
Europe, relationship with Spain   1,
  4–8, 12, 13–5, 18, 19–21,
  139–40, 145
Europeanization   19, 145, 147,
  157–8, 161, 165–6, 178, 259–60
  see also cosmopolitanism
Eximeno, Antonio   25, 42–3, 51,
  52–3, 257, 263, 264

fandango   86
Farinelli   15–6, 32, 135, 141–2, 235
"fashionable" diseases   *see*
  psychosomatic diseases
Federico II, rey de Prusia
  (Comella)   183
Fenómeno raro y singular
  (anon.)   111–2
Ferdinand VI   135, 161–2, 235
Ferdinando, Epifanio   108
Ferrer, Guillermo   171
fibro-centrism   101
fine arts   36–7, 39, 44, 46–7, 51, 72
Floridablanca, count of   24, 171,
  245, 256–7, 262–3, 264

Forner, Juan Pablo   11, 21, 22–3,
    145, 256, 258, 262
fourth wall   67
French Revolution   4, 24, 145, 171,
    251, 262, 264

galant style   50, 116, 181, 205, 246,
    254
La Galatea (Cervantes)   235, 245
Gamerra, Giovanni de   133
    see also *Medonte* (Sarti and
        Gamerra)
García, Rosa   **83**
Garcilaso de la Vega   15, 180, 191
Garrido, Miguel
    in *El atarantulado*   75–6, **83**, 112
        n.97, 113, 116–7
    career of   63 n.82
    in *Cecilia viuda*   220
    in *El teatro y los actores
        agraviados*   63–5, 67, 70
gender roles   210, 251, 261
Ginger, Andrew   12
Golden Age of Spanish literature   7,
    14–5, 27, 61, 65, 69, 137, 191
Goldoni, Carlo   190 n.21, 198 n.44,
    199–200, 201 n.50
Graham, Helen   12, 24
Greek antiquity   30, 34–5, 40, 41–2,
    51–2, 149, 153–5, 238, 240
guild system   31–3, 67, 72
    see also chapel system

Habermas, Jürgen   260
Habsburg period   7, 224, 249, 255
Hall, Stuart   10
Hernández Mateos, Alberto   17
Herr, Richard   8
Highmore, Joseph   222
Híjar, Ninth Duke of (Pedro de
    Alcántara Fernández de Híjar y
    Abarca de Bolea)   115, 163
historiography, Spanish   7–12,
    13–9, 257, 262
Horace   152, 182, 190, 240

Hospital Board (Madrid)   140–3,
    146–7, 163, 166, 169, 170, 175,
    177–8

iatro-mechanism   101–6
iatro-phonics   101–6
"The Instructed Singer"
    (Cavaza)   49–50
intermezzo   14, 116
Irañeta y Jáuregui, Manuel   113
Iranzo y Herrero, Agustín   53
Iriarte, Tomás de
    and the court versus village
        topic   191, 192 n.30
    on the critic's role   70
    on opera and theater   149–50,
        154–5, 238
    on oratory   44, 46
    as philosopher-artist   33, 41
    on Spain   4, 22
    see also *La música* (Iriarte)
Israel, Jonathan   260
Italian opera
    banning of   4, 166, 260, 263
    comeback in Madrid   3–4, 132–9
    costs of   130, 174, 175–8, 263
    educating audiences about   146–
        52, 154–7
    elite support for   23, 133–4,
        140–1, 143–5, 151–2, 157
    influence on Laserna   227, 235
    in Madrid before 1787   32, 135–6,
        141–2, 235
    mocking of   134, 166
    as model for Spanish theater   151,
        173–4, 259–60
    opera buffa   116, 135, 136, 140–2,
        149
    press debates on   26–7, 134–5,
        144–5, 167–8, 169, 172–4,
        175–8
    quality of   166–8
    seen as degenerate   142–3
    and Spanish nationalism   165–7,
        260

292   *Index*

Italian opera (*cont'd*)
  and theater policies   134, 157–66
  as tool for civilization   23, 26–7,
     130, 134, 137–40, 145–51,
     157–66
  see also opera; Teatro de los Caños
     del Peral

Johnston, John   100
Jommelli, Niccolò
  as character in *La música*   238,
    239
  works of   227, 235, 238
Jovellanos, Gaspar Melchor de   11,
    33 n.7, 185, 202–3, 205, 207–9,
    224, 248–50
Juan de la Cruz, San   15, 191
Junta de Alcaldes   *see* Sala de
    Alcaldes
Junta de Hospitales   *see* Hospital
    Board (Madrid)

Kircher, Athanasius   74, 94–5, 100,
    109

La Mettrie, Julien Offray de   105–6
Labanyi, Jo   12, 24
Labrador López de Azcona,
    Germán   17
Laserna, Blas de
  and Bourbon ideals   27–8,
    179–82, 183–5, 205–10
  career of   180–1, 183, 251
  La España antigua and *La España
    moderna*   253–5, 256, 257,
    258, 261
  and music education   32
  style and influences of   27–8,
    181–3, 210, 220, 227, 231, 235,
    246, 248
  on tonadillas' impermanence   62
  see also *La Cecilia* (Comella/
    Laserna); *Cecilia viuda*
    (Comella/Laserna)

Le Guin, Elisabeth   16, 17, 116
Leclerc, Georges-Louis (Comte de
    Buffon)   97, 258–9
Lenten concerts   169–74, 263
Leza, José Máximo   17, 18
linguistic paradigm of music   *see*
    verbal paradigm of music
Linnaeus, Carl   96–7, 109
Los literatos en cuaresma
    (Iriarte)   70, 71
Locke, John   28, 38, 138, 258–9
Lombardía, Ana   16
Lope de Vega   15, 69, 137
Lucio Vero Hispano   *see* Cavaza,
    Manuel
Luzán, Ignacio de   37, 38, 41, 149,
    152–6, 182, 226

majas(os)   2, 164, 199, 212, 216,
    257, 260
El mal de la niña (de la Cruz)   116–
    7
Marchena, José   138, 166–7, 172,
    176–7
Maria Luisa of Parma,
    Princess   133–4
Marías, Julián   11
Marín, Miguel Ángel   16, 17
Martínez, Manuel   62–3, 172
  see also Coliseo de la Cruz and
    Coliseo del Príncipe
Martínez, Martín   96
Masson de Morvilliers, Nicolas   1,
    4–5, 6, 18, 20–2, 134, 150, 253
mathematical paradigm of music   2,
    30–1, 33–4, 36–7, 39, 40–4, 51,
    72, 257
Mattei, Saverio   40–1, 52
mechanicism   74, 94, 100–1, 106,
    107, 109
  see also iatro-mechanism
Medonte (Sarti and Gamera)   133–
    4, 136–8, 141, **148**, 154–7
Meléndez Valdés, Juan   191

melodrama 251, 252, 263
Memoria sobre las diversiones públicas (Jovellanos) 203, 207–9
Memorial literario 128–9, 154–7, 199
Mendelson, Jordana 2
Menéndez y Pelayo, Marcelino 7
Mengs, Anton Raphael 240, **242**
Menuret de Chambaud, Jean-Joseph 102, 106
mercantilism 176–7, 185
Mercier de la Rivière, Pierre Paul 184, 185, 196, 203
Merlo, Bernardo 111
Metastasio, Pietro 145, **148**, 149
mimesis 33–4, 36–9, 42, 153–6, 226–7, 240
Minturno, Antonio 153
modernity
  ancient-modern debates and 19, 41–2, 48–9, 52, 253–7
  as anti-Spanish 21–3, 256–7
  associated with Europe 1, 19–21, 23–4, 253, 259–60, 262
  and Catholicism 9, 19, 256, 260
  and "civilization" 139–40, 145–6, 218
  and criticism 25, 29–30, 31, 60, 63–4, 67–9, 257–8
  definitions of 2–3, 19
  as epistemological change 2–3, 31, 255
  in *La España antigua* and *La España moderna* (Laserna) 228, 253–5, 256, 257
  and gender roles 261
  and illness 115–6, 123, 126, 129–30, 132, 258–9
  musicological perspectives on 6–7, 13–9
  and nature 249–50
  and opera 134, 139–40, 145–6, 157–66
  as polysemic 3, 19, 68, 255, 262

as reemergence from pre-Enlightenment chaos 248–9
rejection of. *see* apologistas
and religion 3, 8–9, 19, 28, 256, 260
as self-reflexive 9–12
and Spanish historiography 7–12
terminology for 1–2
two faces of 19–20, 23–4
see also civilization; empiricism; Enlightenment; neoclassicism; physiocracy
Molière 116
Monelle, Raymond 193
Montaldi, Juan Bautista 133–4, 143, 144 n.30
Montesquieu 21, 127–8, 259
Mortara, marchioness of (Josefa Dominga Catalá de Valeriola y Luján) 179, 180–1, 184, 185, 189, 199, 251
Mortara, seventh marquis of (Benito Osorio y Orozco Lasso de la Vega) 180–1, 184, 185, 189, 251
Mortara, sixth marquis of (Joaquín Antonio de Osorio y Orozco Manrique de Lara) 181 n.5
Morvilliers, Nicolas Masson de *see* Masson de Morvilliers, Nicolas
Muratori, Lodovico Antonio 38, 153–4, 196
music education 41, 49–51
music treatises 32–3, 40–1, 49–51
La música (Iriarte)
  engraving of music and poetry in 44, **45**, 46, 149–50
  Jommelli as character in 238, **239**
  and neoclassicism 25, 154, 227, 238, 240
  ubiquity of 4, 25, 51, 149
  used by other writers 4, 25, 41, 44, 149–50, 154

294   *Index*

musical theater   10–1, 19, 23–4, 25–6, 53–5, 135–6, 151, 156–7, 260–1
 see also *La Cecilia* (Comella/Laserna); *Cecilia viuda* (Comella/Laserna); Coliseo de la Cruz and Coliseo del Príncipe; coliseos; comedias; tonadillas
musician-philosopher figure   40–1, 51–2, 71
El músico censor (Cavaza)   25, 30–1, 33, 42–4, 46, 49, 53, 256, 257
 see also Cavaza, Manuel
musicology, views of Spanish modernity in   6–7, 13–9

Nassarre, Pablo   32, 41, 49, 50
nationalism   11, 19, 22, 162, 165–7, 173–4, 250
nature, contemplation of   224, 226–7, 231, 235, 246, 248–50
Navarro, Alfonso   65, 67, 74, **83**, 112 n.97, 117
neoclassicism
 in *La Cecilia*   190–1, 240, 243, 245
 in *Cecilia viuda*   238, 240, 243, 245–6
 and criticism of Comella   181–2, 183, 238
 Iriarte and   25, 154, 227, 238, 240
 and national improvement efforts   35–7, 72, 255–6
 and opera   133, 134, 137, 151–7, 158–9
 and theater reform   47 n.46, 54, 69–70, 72, 133, 145, 151–7, 158–9, 182–3
 view of the fine arts in   35–7, 46, 149, 226–7
neo-Hippocratism   105–6, 113
New Arcadia   180, 189–90, 191, 197, 203
New World, music from   6
Nipho, Francisco Mariano   54, 55

Nollet, Jean Antoine   91, 126, 127

Olavide, Pablo de   185, 192, 193, 202–3
opera
 audience attitudes toward   130, 134, 136, 139–42, 156–7, 166–8, 175–6
 as character in *Medonte* prologue   136–8
 neoclassicist views of   133, 134, 137, 151–7, 158–9
 policies for   134, 157–66
 public opinion on   27, 134, 142–3, 166–8, 172–4
 see also Italian opera
opera buffa   see under Italian opera
oratory   44, 46
Ortega, Judith   17
Ortega y Gasset, José   8
Osorio de Moscoso y Guzmán, Vicente Joaquín   144
Osorio y Orozco Lasso de la Vega, Benito   see Mortara, seventh marquis of (Benito Osorio y Orozco Lasso de la Vega)
overtures   226–7, 231, 235, 238

Pamela (Richardson)   222
Panati, Giacomo   133
Paquette, Gabriel   6
paradigms of music
 mathematical   2, 30–1, 33–4, 36–7, 39, 40–4, 51, 72, 257
 verbal   2, 30–1, 33–8, 39–42, 44, 46–8, 51–2, 72, 257
El paseo del Prado   263–4
pastoralism   180, 183–4, 190–3, 243, 245, 246, 248, 251–2
pathos   46, 52, 85, 222–3
payos(as)   2, 205, 210, 223–4
 see also peasants
peasants
 Bourbon policy on   184–5, 192, 193, 196, 205, 207–9, 255

depicted in *La Cecilia* (Comella/
  Laserna)   183–5, 192–3, 197–
  203, **204**, 205–10, 223–4, 261
depicted in *Cecilia viuda*
  (Comella/Laserna)   183–5,
  196–7, 203, **204**, 205, 224, 246,
  248, 261
see also agriculture policy
Pedrell, Felipe   7–8
periodical press
  accessibility of   60
  development of   3–4, 55, 59–60,
    89
  opera debated in   26–7, 134–5,
    144–5, 167–8, 169, 172–4,
    175–8
  regulation of   64–5, 262–4
  and the rise of criticism   33, 55,
    59–63, 72
  as rival and complement of the
    theater   60–4, 259
  seguidillas criticized in   212
  subscription model for   59
  tarantism in   73–4, 89–93,
    126–32
  see also *El Censor*; *Correo de los
    Ciegos*; *Diario de Madrid*
Pessarrodona, Aurèlia   16–7
petimetres(as)   2, 164, 223, 257, 260
Petrarch   191
Philip V   135, 140, 146
philosophy   22, 34, 40–1, 43–4,
  51–2, 67–9, 258
physiocracy   2, 27, 180, 184–5, 193,
  197–8, 202–3, 255
  see also postmercantilism
Piccinni, Niccolò   118, 227, 235
Pimentel y Téllez Girón, María
  Josefa (countess-duchess of
  Benavente and duchess of
  Osuna)   144
Piñera y Siles, Bartolomé   26, 73–4,
  75, 76–7, 83, 85–6, 88–9, 109–15
Planelli, Antonio   35–6
Pluche, Noël-Antoine   94–5, 100

Poetics (Luzán)   41, 145, 149,
  152–4, 156, 226
polacos   *see* chorizos and polacos
  (fan clubs)
policía   157–66, 167
postmercantilism   176–7, 180
  see also physiocracy
*Precautions to Be Observed for the
  Performance of Comedias in the
  Court*   161–2
presentational acting   67
El Príncipe   *see* Coliseo de la Cruz
  and Coliseo del Príncipe
psychosomatic diseases   74, 91–2,
  113, 115–8, 126–30, 132
public opinion
  formation of   26, 55, 59–63, 74,
    132, 172–4, 261
  on opera   27, 134, 142–3, 166–8,
    172–4
  on tarantism   26, 73–4, 77, 83, 89,
    91–3
  see also criticism
Pythagorean approach to
  music   36–7
  see also mathematical paradigm of
    music

Quesnay, François   184, 202

Rameau, Jean Philippe   41, 50
rationalism   91, 96, 97–8, 258, 259
"Reglamento para el mejor orden y
  policía del Teatro de la ópera"
  (1787)   160–1, 162, 163–4, 169,
  263
representational acting   67
reputation, legal history of   64–5
Retrato de la tarántula (anon.)   77,
  89–90, 92–3
rhetoric (fine art)   44, 46
Ribera, Eusebio   62–3, 170, 172
  see also Coliseo de la Cruz and
    Coliseo del Príncipe
Richardson, Samuel   222

296   *Index*

Robertson, Ritchie   9
Robinson, Michael F.   16
Rodrigo, Francisca   74, **83**, 112 n.97, 117
Rodríguez, Antonio   101–2, 109
Rodríguez de Campomanes, Pedro   3 n.3, 193, 196, 202–3
Rodríguez de Hita, Antonio   32, 44 n.39, 50, 201
Roger, Joseph-Louis   101–2
Rojo, Fermín   **83**
rondò (vocal)   117–8, **119–22**, 123
Rosales, Antonio   167, 176
Rousseau, Jean-Jacques   25, 34, 38, 39, 46, 97, 259
Royal Academy of San Fernando   36–7
"Rudimentos y elementos de la música práctica" (Cavaza)   49–50

Saggio sopra l'opera in musica (Algarotti)   **148**, 150–2
sainetes   54, 116–7, 139–40, 164
Saint Vitus's dance   109, 111
Sala de Alcaldes   147, 163, 164–5
Sánchez, Patricio   130–1
Sánchez Blanco, Francisco   8–9
Sarrailh, Jean   8
Sarti, Giuseppe   133
   see also *Medonte* (Sarti and Gamerra)
satire   23, 33, 54–5, 115–8, 123, 126, 140, 257
   see also *El Censor*
scholasticism   42–4, 110, 138, 249, 258–9
Se i maestri di capella (Mattei)   52
secularization   3, 28, 260
seguidillas   199, **204**, 208, 212–3, **214–5**, 216–20, **221**
self-reflexivity   9–12
Sempere y Guarinos, Juan   33, 158, 176, 193, 196
sensism   26, 28, 38, 74, 109, 258–9

sentimental tableaux   222–4, 226–7, 231, 235, 245–6, **247**, 248–50
Serao, Francesco   95–6, 100, 126, 131
Signorelli, Pietro Napoli   149
Silván, Ambrosio   73, 75, 76–7, 83, 85–6, 88–90, 109–13, 132
Simplicio Greco y Lira   33, 34–5, 36–42, 44, 46–8, 51, 155–6
   see also "Discourse 97" (*El Censor*)
sochantres (chant leaders)   47–8
Soler, Antonio   32
Soriano Fuertes, Mariano   8
Spain
   and "civilization"   139–40, 145–6
   historiography of   7–12, 13–9
   Iriarte on   4, 22
   marginalized in musicology   13–4
   presumed backwardness of   4, 6–8, 12, 18, 20–1
   relationship with Europe   1, 4–8, 12, 13–5, 18, 19–21, 139–40, 145
Spanish empire   5–6, 15, 218, 224, 255
   see also colonialism
Spanish music, historiography of   7–8, 12, 13–9
stage tonadillas   *see* tonadillas
Stein, Louise   15
Sterne, Jonathan   2
stick dances   **204**, 206–7, 208–9
stock characters   2–3, 116, 223
Subirá Puig, José   17
Sydenham, Thomas   105, 109

tarantella   85–6, 90, 102–3, **104**, **105**, 111, 112, 128–9
tarantism
   cases of   73, 108, 109–13
   and Catholicism   74, 99, 109
   and Enlightenment   26, 73–4, 109, 256

and invisible phenomena 26,
100–9
medical treatises on 26, 73,
94–100
music-and-dance treatment
for 73–4, 75, 77, 83, 85–6,
88–9, 100–9, 111–3, 127–30,
132
narrative components of 112
in the press 73–4, 89–93,
126–32, 263
public opinion on 26, 73–4, 77,
84, 89, 91–3, 112–3
as social phenomenon 74, 75–7,
85, 89–91, 115
as spectacle 112–5
understood as legitimate
disease 89, 90, 94–100,
109–13, 126, 128–9, 132
understood as psychosomatic 74,
91–2, 126–30, 132
understood as social panic 89,
91–2, 95–6
see also *El atarantulado* (Esteve);
Cid, Francisco Xavier; Piñera
y Siles, Bartolomé; Silván,
Ambrosio
Tarantismo observado en España
(Cid) 77, 89–90, 94–100,
102–9, **104**, **105**, 111–3
Tartini, Giuseppe 41, 43
Teatro de los Caños del Peral
costs of 174, 175–8, 263
Lenten concerts at 169–74, 263
press debates about 23, 26–7,
157–60, 166–8, 172–4, 175–8
reopening of 3, 133–9, 140–7,
148, 150, 155, 156, 177–8,
259–60
rules for 160–1, 163–6, 263
El teatro y los actores agraviados
(Esteve)
critics rebuked in 29, 31, 54–5,
63–5, 67–70, 258
reception of 26, 70–2, 159

style of 55, **56–8**, 65, **66**, 67
Téllez Villar, Marcos **214–5**
Tertulia de la Fonda de San
Sebastián 149
theater
guidelines and regulations
for 70–2, 152–3, 157–66,
170–1
as media channel 60–1, 63, 77,
83
periodical press as rival and
complement of 60–4, 259
relationship with audiences 63,
67, 70, 72
see also coliseos; musical theater;
opera; Teatro de los Caños del
Peral; *El teatro y los actores
agraviados* (Esteve); tonadillas
theater composers 2, 53–4, 61
see also Esteve, Pablo
Thevin, Santiago (Jacques) 126–7
Thomism 43–4, 258
Tissot, Samuel 26, 101–2, 123, 126,
129
tonadillas
audiences for 25–6, 60–2, 63, 67,
83, 136, 163, 253–4
as communication media 23,
60–3, 77, 83, 132
ephemerality of 61–2
genre traits of 23, 54, 67, 76, 85,
116, 136
modernity satirized in 23, 61,
253–6
and the press 26, 31, 53–5, 60–5,
67–72
in scholarship 14
see also *El atarantulado* (Esteve);
La España antigua (Laserna);
La España moderna (Laserna);
*El teatro y los actores
agraviados* (Esteve); theater
Torrente, Álvaro 17
Torres, José de 32, 41
Torres, Josefa 65, 67, **83**

Torrones, Marcelino   167–8

University of Salamanca   42–3

Valmont de Bonare, Jacques-
  Christophe   91
Vandermonde, Charles-
  Augustin   95, 96, 97–8, 99–100,
  109
Vartija, Devin J.   10
Vázquez, Oscar   2
verbal paradigm of music   2, 30–1,
  33–8, 39–42, 44, 46–8, 51–2, 72,
  257

villancicos   15
virtuosity   46–7, 116, 169
vitalism   101, 106
Voltaire   97, 184–5, 259, 260

Waisman, Leonardo   17
Whytt, Robert   104–5 n.74, 106

Ximeno y Carrera, José
  Antonio   243, **244**, 245

zarzuelas   7–8, 15, 136, 157, 182,
  200–2, 203, 205

Music in Society and Culture
Volumes already published

History in Mighty Sounds:
Musical Constructions of German National Identity, 1848–1914
Barbara Eichner

Music and Ultra-Modernism in France: A Fragile Consensus, 1913–1939
Barbara L. Kelly

The Idea of Art Music in a Commercial World, 1800–1930
Edited by Christina Bashford and Roberta Montemorra Marvin

Nation and Classical Music: From Handel to Copland
Matthew Riley and Anthony D. Smith

Musical Debate and Political Culture in France, 1700–1830
R. J. Arnold

Performing Propaganda:
Musical Life and Culture in Paris during the First World War
Rachel Moore

Musical Journeys: Performing Migration in Twentieth-Century Music
Florian Scheding

Béla Bartók in Italy: The Politics of Myth-Making
Nicolò Palazzetti

The Creative Labor of Music Patronage in Interwar France
Louis K. Epstein

America in the French Imaginary, 1789–1914: Music, Revolution and Race
Edited by Diana R. Hallman and César A. Leal

Music, Nature and Divine Knowledge in England, 1650–1750:
Between the Rational and the Mystical
Tom Dixon

Music, Medicine and Religion at the Ospedale di Santo Spirito in Rome:
1550–1750
Naomi J. Barker

Printed in the United States
by Baker & Taylor Publisher Services